# Create Rapid Low-Code Web Applications In Oracle APEX 21.2

A platform to develop stunning, scalable data-centric web apps fast

*Riaz Ahmed*

*Saad Muavia*

# Create Rapid Low-Code Web Applications in Oracle APEX 21.2

This is my twelfth book on Oracle Application Express (APEX) co-authored with my son Saad Muavia. Just like my previous books that exposed the technology to thousands around the globe, this book is also aimed at beginners who wish to learn from self-paced professional guidance and need a solid foundation in Oracle APEX.

Oracle APEX is an amazing low-code development platform in which you can build robust web applications. Not only it provides an environment where you can rapidly develop data-centric web applications, it also allows end-users to interact with their data via tools like interactive report, interactive grid, faceted search, different types of charts and more.

The most convincing way to explore a technology is to apply it to a real world problem. Without involving the audience too much into the boring bits, the book adopts an inspiring approach that helps beginners practically evaluate almost every feature of Oracle APEX. In this book, you'll develop an application that demonstrates the use of those features to get hands-on exposure to Oracle APEX anatomy. The sticky inspirational approach adopted in this book not only exposes the technology, but also draws you in and keeps your interest up till the last exercise.

The ultimate objective of this book is to introduce you to the art of building web applications by iteratively developing the sample database application (provided with Oracle APEX) from scratch. The application demonstrates how to display summary information, use reports and forms for viewing, updating, and adding information, include charts to visualize information, and create dedicated mobile pages. This application has been chosen as an example because you can learn most of the techniques from it for your own future work. The primary purpose of this book is to teach you how to use Oracle APEX to realize your own development goals. Each chapter in this book explores a basic area of functionality and delivers the development techniques to achieve that functionality. By the time you reach the end of the examples in this book, you will have a clear understanding of Oracle APEX and will be able to extend the application in almost any direction.

The short list below presents some main topics of Oracle APEX covered in this book:

- Browser-based online application development
- Rapid web application development for desktops, laptops, tablets, and latest smartphones
- Create comprehensive applications declaratively without writing tons of code
- Tweak application pages using Page Designer
- Create applications with the help of wizards
- Create custom application pages by adding components manually
- Use same interface and code to develop applications for a wide array of devices
- Present data using a variety of eye-catching charts
- Produce highly formatted PDF reports, including invoices, grouped reports, and pivot tables
- Implement APEX's built-in security module

If you are looking for a concise and concrete Oracle APEX book written for beginners, then I must say that this is the book that will return more than what you have paid for it.

**Special offer!** For those who are new to SQL and PL/SQL or those who want to refresh their knowledge in these areas, we are providing a SQL/PLSQL eBook for FREE! Please send the purchase proof of this book to oratech@cyber.net.pk to get the free e-book.

## URL to Download Book Code

https://tinyurl.com/code21

- Riaz Ahmed & Saad Muavia
Authors
oratech@cyber.net.pk

> **NOTE:**
> If you are not able to download the book code from this URL, please let me know via my email to get the code.

## ABOUT THE AUTHORS

Riaz Ahmed is an IT professional with more than 30 years of experience. Saad Muavia is a passionate web application developer and he has developed some very useful web applications in Oracle APEX.

## BOOKS AUTHORED BY RIAZ AHMED

### Oracle APEX – for Absolute Beginners
No-Code Oracle APEX For Thirteen To Ninety
ISBN – 9798633930535

### Oracle APEX – Beginners Guides
Version 20 – ISBN: 979-8633931839
Version 19 – ISBN: 9781094779096
Version 18.1 – ISBN: 9781723335372
Version 5.1 – ISBN: 9781542452540
Version 5.0 – ISBN: 9781512003307
Version 4.2 – ISBN: 9781492314189
Version 4.0 – ISBN: 9781466350656

### Oracle APEX – Pro Version
Oracle Application Express – Pro Hacks (First Edition)
ISBN-9781698624761

Oracle Application Express – Pro Hacks (Second Edition)
ISBN-9798663034210

### Cloud Computing Using Oracle APEX
Rapidly develop internet facing business applications accessible anywhere and anytime
ISBN-13: 9781484242421

### Business Intelligence in Oracle APEX
Transition of BI from IT to End Users
ISBN-13: 9781720582489

### Implement Oracle Business Intelligence
Analyze the Past
Streamline the Present
Control the Future
ISBN-13: 9781475122015

### SQL – The Shortest Route For Beginners
A hands-on book that covers all top DBMS and teaches SQL in record time
ISBN-13: 9781514130971

### Beginning Windows 10 With Anniversary Update
A compact guide to explore the latest operating system
ISBN-13: 9781532831065

### Learning SAP Analytics Cloud
SAP all-in-one BI solution in the cloud
ISBN-13: 9781788290883

### Full Stack Web Development For Beginners
Learn Ecommerce Web Development Using HTML5, CSS3, Bootstrap, JavaScript, MySQL, and PHP
ISBN: 979-8738951268

### Find latest editions of my books on Amazon
https://www.amazon.com/Riaz-Ahmed/e/B006V7K0Y2

# CONTENTS

# 1

# THE LEARNING

# APPROACH

## 1.1 How are you going to learn Oracle APEX?

Oracle Application Express (APEX) is a browser-based rapid application development (RAD) tool that helps you create rich interactive Oracle-based web applications very quickly and with relatively little programming effort. A web application is an application that is accessed by users over a network such as the Internet or an intranet. It is software coded in a browser-supported programming language (such as JavaScript, combined with a browser-rendered markup language like HTML) and dependent on a common web browser to render the application. The popularity of web applications is due to the ubiquity of web browsers, which is the only requirement to access such applications. Another major reason behind the popularity of web applications is the ability to update and maintain these applications without distributing and installing software on potentially thousands of client devices.

Developing web applications can be a real challenge because it's a multidisciplinary process. You have to be proficient in all the core technologies involved such as HTML, CSS, JavaScript (on the client side) and PHP or any other scripting language to interact with the database on the server side. Also, you've to take into account the type-less nature of the web environment and above all, the need to put it all together in a manner that will allow the end users to execute their jobs efficiently and in a simplified manner.

Oracle APEX is a hosted declarative development environment for developing and deploying database-centric web applications. Oracle APEX accelerates the application development process. Thanks to its built-in features such as user interface themes, navigational controls, form handlers, and flexible reports that off-loads the extra burden of proficiency acquisition in the core technologies.

Declarative development is the most significant feature, which makes Oracle APEX a good choice for rapid application development. Most of the tasks are performed with the help of built-in wizards that help you create different types of application pages. Each wizard walks you through the process of defining what you are expecting to achieve. After getting the input, the wizard data is stored as metadata in Oracle database tables. Later on, you can call page definition to modify or enhance the metadata to give your page the desired look. You can even add more functionality by putting your own custom SQL and PL/SQL code. Once you're comfortable with Oracle APEX, you can ignore the wizards and generate your applications directly. The Application Express engine renders applications in real time using the metadata. When you create or extend an application, Oracle APEX creates or modifies metadata stored in database tables. When the application is run, the Application Express engine reads the metadata and then displays the application.

When you create a new application in Oracle APEX, the *Create Application Wizard* uses Universal Theme. It is an application user interface, which enables developers to build modern web applications without requiring extensive knowledge of HTML, CSS, or JavaScript. Universal Theme is an example of a responsive user interface theme. Responsive design enables you to design web pages so that the layout fits the available space regardless of the device on which page displays (for example, a desktop computer, laptop computer, tablet, or smartphone). By implementing a responsive design, the user gets the same full experience as they would on larger screens. On smart phones and tablets, the layout can adjust to the size of the specific device. During this resizing process, elements shift position, resize, or become hidden. The goal of responsive design is to present all essential content in a user friendly way for all possible screen sizes.

## 1.2 Understanding the Application

The format of this book is to introduce you to the art of building web applications by iteratively developing the sample sales application (provided with Oracle APEX) from scratch. This application has been chosen as an example because you can learn most of the techniques from it for your own future work. The primary purpose of this book is to teach you how to use Oracle APEX to realize your own development goals. Each chapter in this book explores a basic area of functionality and delivers the development techniques to achieve that functionality. By the time you reach the end of the examples in this book, you will have a clear understanding of Oracle APEX and will be able to extend the application in almost any direction. There are a number of features that provide Oracle APEX a clear edge over other available RAD development tools. Oracle APEX uses SQL and PL/SQL as core languages for development and because of this ability people who have been working with Oracle database can easily tread the path.

The application you will be creating in this book features an easy-to-use interface for adding, updating, deleting and viewing order and related products and customers' information. Users can navigate among the pages using a navigation menu. The same application will be accessible from a variety of mobile devices including latest smartphones and tablets. Before we dig into details of the application, let's first have a quick look at some of the major areas of our sample Sales Web Application to know what we're going to create.

## 1.2.1 Chapter 4 - Prepare Application Dashboard

**Figure 1-1** Application Home Page (Dashboard)

In Chapter 4, you'll create the home page of the application. It is a dashboard that users see when they successfully access the application after providing valid credentials. Let's first take a look at the tagged areas to acquaint ourselves with different sections of this page:

    A. Application name and logo
    B. Navigation Bar
    C. Main Navigation Menu icon
    D. Buttons
    E. Regions
    F. Text Links
    G. Developers Toolbar
    H. Install App
    I. Application Banner

The Home page contains six regions to display different summarized information. It uses a 12 columns layout to place these regions accordingly. Besides application name and logo (A), the page carries a main navigation menu (C), which is used to move to other application segments. The navigation bar (B) on the top right side allows you to log out from the application. By default, it displays the id of the currently logged-in user, along with a Sign Out link. The Feedback option on the Navigation bar provides a mechanism for end users to post general comments for application administrators and developers. You can add more options to this bar. The body of a page can have multiple regions (E) that act as containers to display information from database tables. You can place buttons (D) in regions that allow you to drill into further details. In addition to buttons, the page also contains text links (F) to dig details of the summarized information. Using the options provided in the Developers Toolbar (G), you can switch to the Page Designer instantly and perform various other development tasks. The Install App option (H) appears when you choose Progressive Web App (PWA) option while creating a new application. When users tap the Install App option, the application is opened in a standalone window, which is free of the browser's UI. You can also add a banner (I) to your application.

## What You'll Learn

- How to create dashboards in web applications
- Adding multiple regions to a page to segregate content
- Use of 12 columns grid layout to arrange multiple regions on a page
- Create links to drill-down into details
- Badge List, Pie Chart, and Bar Chart to display data in different graphical formats
- Summarized text information
- Using buttons to navigate to other application pages

## 1.2.2 Chapter 5 – Customers Profiling

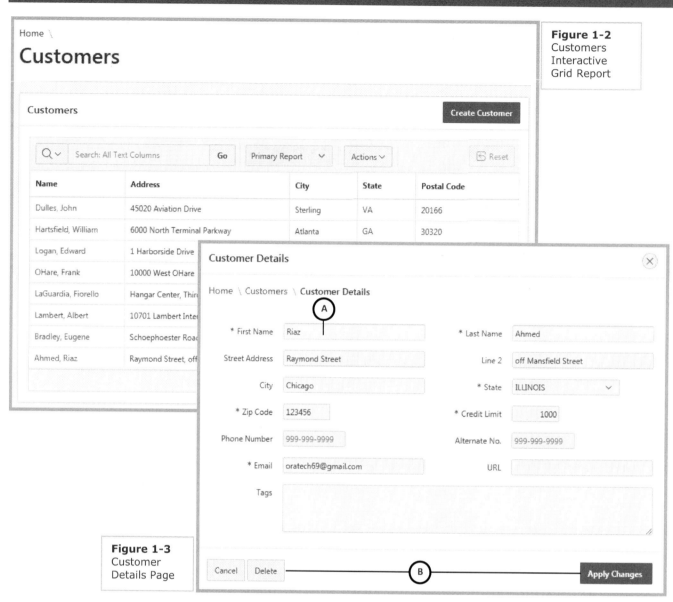

**Figure 1-2**
Customers
Interactive
Grid Report

**Figure 1-3**
Customer
Details Page

The sales application to be created in this book comprises some setups, including this one. Using this module you will create customers profiles. Each customer will be provided a unique ID that will be generated automatically through a database object called a Sequence. After creating customers' profiles, you will use this information in Chapter 7 (Taking Orders), where you will select these customers to process orders. The setup consists of two pages. The first page (Figure 1-2) is a report (based on an Interactive Grid) that lists all customers. The first column in the interactive grid (Name) acts as a link to call the details page (Figure 1-3), which is a form where you can create, modify, or delete customer's records individually. The form page is a modal page that pops up on top of the report page to display and receive information of customers in page items (A). The page also contains a bunch of auto-generated buttons (B) to perform DML actions.

## What You'll Learn

- Create application pages using wizards

- Using Interactive Grid to display information in tabular format

- Web input form to insert, update, and delete data

- Use of Modal Page

- Change type of page items

- Customizing wizard-generated pages to make them more professional

- Creating custom links to switch between the two module pages

- Positioning form input elements using 12 columns  layout

- Marking mandatory fields

- Enforce data validation

- Understand how APEX transparently manages DML operations (Insert, Update, and Delete) without writing a single line of code

## 1.2.3 Chapter 6 – Set Up Products Catalog

**Figure 1-4**
Products
Interactive
Report Page

**Figure 1-5**
Product Details
Page

Since sales applications are developed to handle sales of products, a properly designed product setup is an integral part of such applications. To fulfill this requirement, you will create a comprehensive products setup for the sales application to manage products information along with respective images. The products you set up here will be selected in customers' orders. Just like the Customers setup, this segment also comprises two pages. The initial page (Figure 1-4) is an interactive report that will be customized to create three different views to browse product information. The second page (Figure 1-5) of this module is an input form where you can add, modify, or delete a product.

## What You'll Learn

- Interactive Report
- Image handling (upload, download, save, retrieve, and delete from database)
- Customize interactive report to get different views of data
- Use of Cascading Style Sheet (CSS) to add custom styles to a page
- Change item type and associate List of Values (LOVs)
- Hiding report columns
- Replacing wizard-generated links with customized links
- Displaying data in an HTML table element
- Styling HTML table element
- Saving an Interactive Report as primary report
- Set dimensions of a modal page
- Making and marking page items as mandatory

## 1.2.4 Chapter 7 – Taking Orders

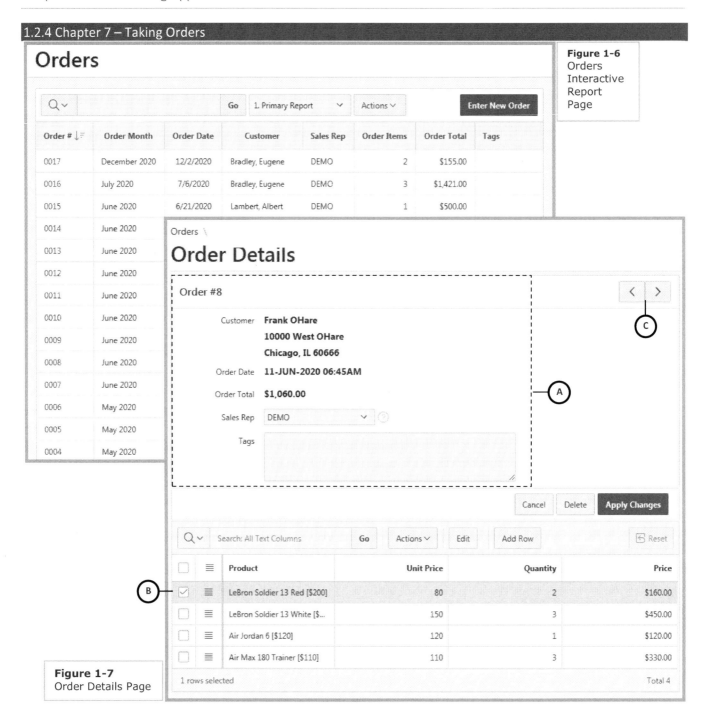

**Figure 1-6**
Orders Interactive Report Page

**Figure 1-7**
Order Details Page

This is the most comprehensive chapter of the book. It will teach you lots of techniques. In this chapter, you will create a module to take orders from customers. Initially, you'll create this segment with the help of wizards and later you will customize it to record orders through a sequence of wizard steps. The module will use two database tables (Order Master and Order Details) to view, add, update, and delete customer orders. The initial page of this module, as illustrated in Figure 1-6, is an interactive report that lists all orders. The first order number column acts as a link. When you click an order number, you see another page of this module, as illustrated in Figure 1-4. This page will show details of the selected order. The upper pane (A) of this page retrieves data from the master table, while the lower pane shows order details in an interactive grid (B). The page also contains a couple of auto-generated buttons (C) for record navigation. You can use these buttons to move from one customer order to another.

## What You'll Learn

- Implement master/detail forms
- Sorting Interactive Report
- Add Control Breaks to interactive report to group related data
- Apply highlight rules to mark specific records
- Using Aggregate functions
- Using Chart and Group By views in an interactive report
- Creating Primary, Public, and Alternative versions of an interactive report
- Utilizing Copy Page utility
- APEX Collection
- Adding custom processes and dynamic actions
- Using HTML in PL/SQL code
- Using CSS in APEX pages

## 1.2.5 Chapter 8 – Graphical Reports & Mobile Integration

**Figure 1-8** – Graphical Report & Mobile Integration in Oracle APEX

After getting thorough knowledge of data manipulation techniques, you move on to present graphical output of the sales data. In this chapter, you will be taught the use of different types of charts, tree, and calendar to present data from different perspectives.

Oracle APEX's Universal Theme is designed to work just as well on small screen devices (such as smartphones and tablets) as it does on larger screen devices (including laptops and desktops). The UI components in Universal Theme work across varying screen resolutions while maintaining the same or similar functionality. Although the Universal Theme is optimized to work well on mobile devices, not all components are mobile friendly. When creating reports for mobile devices, Oracle recommends use of List View, Column Toggle Report, and Reflow Report that provide an optimal user experience for small screens. You will also go through these mobile report types in this chapter.

## What You'll Learn

- How to display summarized information through Stacked Bar, Donut, Range, Line with Area, Gantt, Box Plot, and Pyramid charts
- Display customer orders in a calendar
- Hierarchical presentation of data using a tree component
- Drill-down to details from charts
- List View, Column Toggle Report, and Reflow Report for mobile integration

## 1.2.6 Chapter 9 – Produce Advance Reports

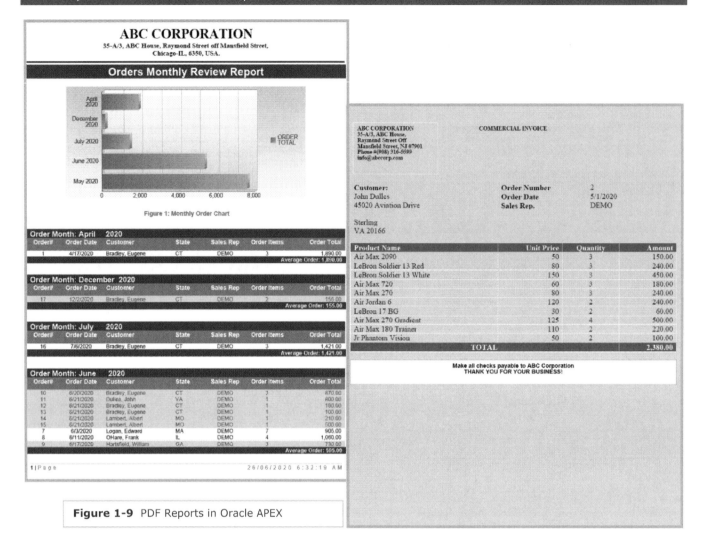

**Figure 1-9**  PDF Reports in Oracle APEX

By default, APEX has the ability to produce simple generic matrix reports comprising rows and columns. This chapter will show you how to produce advance report in APEX. Here, you will be provided with step-by-step instructions to generate:

- A highly formatted MIS report
- Commercial Invoice
- Pivot Table

## What You'll Learn

- Create Report Query

- Design report layout in Microsoft Word using XML data

- Data grouping and sorting

- Formatting reports using standard Microsoft Word tools

- Add conditional formatting to display data differently in the same report

- Add calculations

- Create parameterized report

- Upload RTF layout to APEX

- Attach custom report layout to the default report query

- Add link in the application to run advance reports

## 1.2.7 Chapter 10 – Managing Users and Access Control

After creating all segments of an application, you apply security to these segments. In this chapter you will utilize Oracle APEX's built-in access control feature. You will also be guided in this chapter to create users for your application with different roles. The built-in access control feature auto-generates some authorization schemes as well that are used to control access to an application, individual pages, or page components.

### What You'll Learn

- Make your application secure from unauthorized access
- How to add users to an APEX application
- Implement built-in roles and rights

## 1.2.9 Chapter 11 – More Features

This chapter will provide hands-on exposure to some miscellaneous but significant features provided in Oracle APEX to help improve your application development experience. You will learn about Faceted Search that provides additional search capabilities and is useful to narrow down search results. You will learn about Theme Roller which enables you to give a new look to your application. Button styling is also covered in this chapter. In the final section you will use Calendar component to manage events.

## 1.2.10 Chapter 12 – Deploy APEX Application

In this chapter, you will be guided to export an application from your development PC to a production environment. For this purpose, you will utilize APEX's Export and Import utilities. To keep things simple, you will deploy the application in the same workspace to understand the deployment concept. First, you will export the application to a script file and then, using the Import utility, the same script file will be imported to create the application in the same workspace with a new ID. The same technique is applicable to the production environment.

### Summary

This chapter provided an overview about the essence of the book: a web-based data-centric application. You'll create this application using the browser-based declarative development environment to get hands-on exposure to the features provided by Oracle APEX. The next chapter is aimed at providing some core concepts about Oracle APEX. Read the chapter thoroughly because the terms used in that chapter are referenced throughout the book.

# 2

# ORACLE APEX
# CONCEPTS

## 2.1 Introduction to Oracle Application Express (APEX)

If you are interested in developing professional web applications rapidly, then you have chosen the right track. Oracle APEX is a low-code rapid application development (RAD) tool that runs inside an Oracle database instance and comes as a free option with Oracle database. Using this unique tool you can develop and deploy fast and secure professional web applications. The only requirements are a web browser and a little SQL and PL/SQL experience.

Oracle APEX provides a declarative programming environment, which means that no code is generated nor compiled during development. You just interact through wizards and property editor to build web applications on existing database schemas. Reports and charts are defined with simple SQL queries, so some knowledge of SQL is very helpful. If you want to create more robust applications, then you can add procedural logic by writing PL/SQL code. Oracle APEX is a declarative tool and has a vast collection of pre-defined wizards, HTML objects, database handling utilities, page rendering and submission processes, navigation and branching options, and more. You can use all these options to build your database-centric web applications comprising web pages carrying forms, reports, charts, and so on with their layouts and business logic. The APEX engine translates it all into an HTML code for the client side and SQL and PL/SQL code for the server side. If you do not get a solution from built-in options, Oracle APEX allows you to create your own SQL and PL/SQL code for the server side and HTML, CSS, and JavaScript code for the client side.

## 2.2 Why Use Oracle APEX?

Velocity in the demand for new applications and functionality rises as businesses grow. As a developer, you are expected to rapidly respond to these needs. Over the years, desktop database and spreadsheet tools have enormously contributed to data management due to the ease and user friendliness these applications extend to their users. Besides benefits, these applications have scalability and functionality limitations that not only results in dozens of different applications and data sources but also adds extra overhead in their maintenance. Because of these issues, organizations are unable to continue their standard practices, leaving mission-critical data at risk. These fragmented systems may also cause loss of business opportunities. Last but by no means least, significant amount of time and resource is required to put these data blocks together to get the desired information. Keeping in view these constraints, the following list provides some advantages of using Oracle APEX.

## Oracle APEX Advantages

**Low-Code:** A low-code platform in which enterprise apps are built 20x faster with 100x less code.

**Robust and Proven:** Oracle APEX is capable to produce a wide variety of apps for any industry – from the simplest app that is created from a spreadsheet file, to mission-critical apps which are used daily by tens of thousands of users. The elegant architecture of Oracle APEX has been used to power thousands of applications around the globe for years. Oracle APEX has a much lower barrier to entry for creating responsive and powerful business applications.

**Installation:** No installation of software is required on client machines – the only requirement is a supported browser.

**Central Management:** Being central, data and applications become a part of regular backup procedure.

**Secure:** Data and application access control, empowered by audit trail. Oracle APEX is designed to build web apps which are highly secure out of the box. In a world of ever-changing web standards, evolving security standards, and resourceful hackers, the focus on security means that your applications stay protected and remain state-of-the-art.

**Portable:** You can run Oracle APEX everywhere – on the Oracle Cloud, on-premises, or anywhere else there is an Oracle Database. And you can deploy your Oracle APEX applications across any environment with ease.

**Reporting:** Oracle APEX includes powerful self-service reporting features. You can easily add custom filters, sort, aggregate, pivot and chart your data, and even create reports which get emailed to you on a periodic basis.

**Apps for Enterprises:** In an enterprise setting, Oracle APEX provides a scalable and proven platform for applications which can scale across the enterprise. Oracle APEX includes native functionality to integrate with REST and SOAP Services in your organization and in the cloud.

## 2.3 Anatomy of Oracle APEX

I know you are curious to start the proceedings, but first you need to understand some basic concepts before you dive into Oracle APEX's pool. This chapter will introduce some basic structures of Oracle APEX you must be aware of prior to executing the exercises. As depicted in Figure 2-1, Oracle APEX (B) is an integral part of an *Oracle database* (A). It is a free low-code rapid application development tool that runs inside an Oracle database instance. In Oracle APEX, you can create multiple *workspaces* (C) to host different types of *applications* (D). Each workspace can hold multiple applications. Database applications created in Oracle APEX comprise two or more *pages* (E). Each page can carry multiple *Regions, Dynamic Actions, Validations, and Processes. Regions* (F) are containers that are used to display and receive information. With *dynamic actions* (G) you can define complex client-side behavior declaratively without the need for JavaScript. *Processes* (H) are logic controls that are used to execute Data Manipulation Language (DML) or PL/SQL. The data is fed and displayed using *page items* (I) such as Text field, Select List, Radio Group, and so on. Just like desktop applications, you use *buttons* (J) in Oracle APEX to submit requests. The sub-sections listed next provide further details on these structural elements.

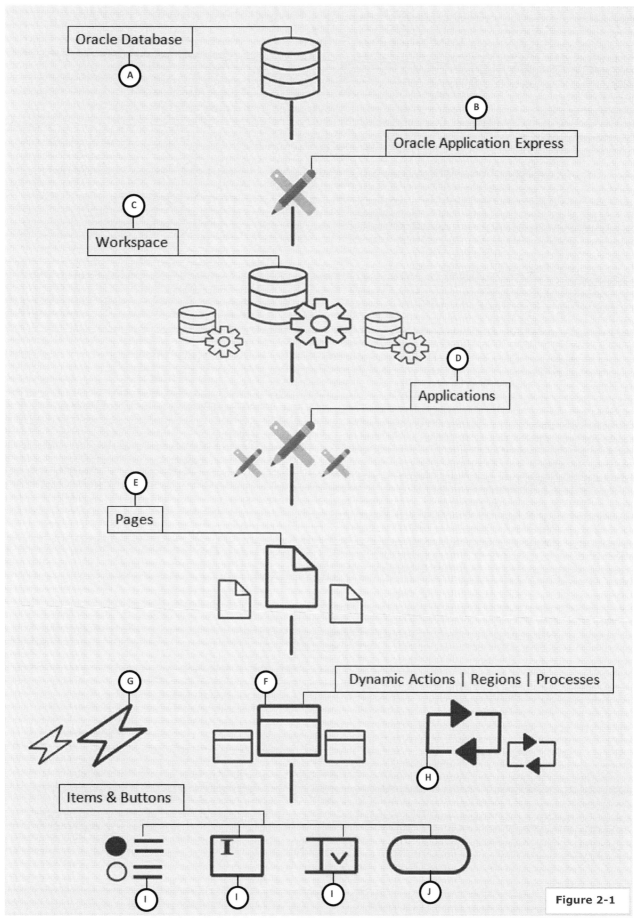

Oracle Database (A)

Oracle Application Express (B)

Workspace (C)

Applications (D)

Pages (E)

Dynamic Actions | Regions | Processes

(G)

(F)

(H)

Items & Buttons

(I) (I) (I) (J)

Figure 2-1

## 2.3.1 Workspace

To access Oracle APEX development environment, users sign in to a shared work area called a *Workspace*. A workspace is a virtual private container allowing multiple users to work within the same Oracle APEX installation while keeping their objects, data and applications private. You have to create a workspace before you create an application. It is necessary because you have to specify which workspace you want to connect to when you log in. Without this piece of information, you are not allowed to enter Oracle APEX.

To use the exercises presented in this book, you have to select a development option from the following:

- Download and install Oracle APEX on your own PC or within your private cloud.

- Get your own free workspace from Oracle to execute the exercises online on their servers. This is the most convenient way for beginners. So, execute the following steps to request a free workspace that will be provided to you in minutes.

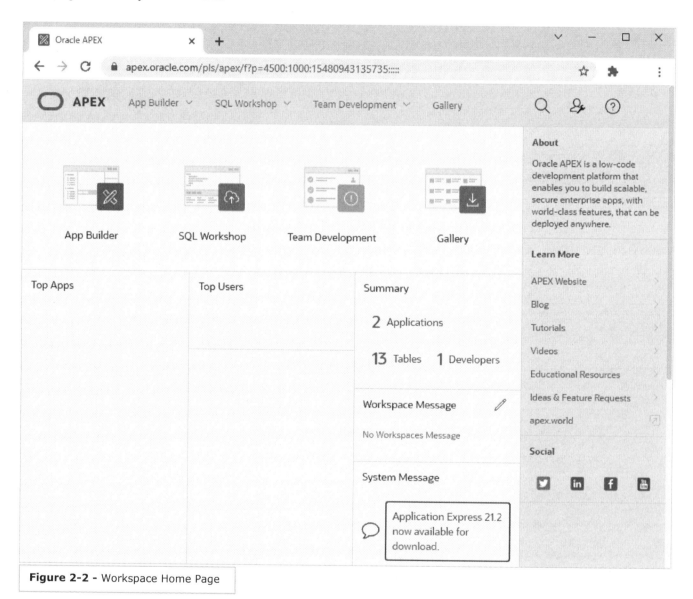

**Figure 2-2 -** Workspace Home Page

## Requesting a Free Workspace

Follow the instructions mentioned below to get your free workspace:

1. Open your internet browser and type **https://apex.oracle.com/en/** in the address bar to access Oracle APEX site. On the home page, click the **Get Started for Free** button.

2. On the Get Started page, click the **Request a Free Workspace** button.

3. On the Identification wizard screen, enter your first and last names, e-mail address, and the name of the workspace you intend to create – for example, MYWS. If the workspace name already exists, try a different one. After providing this information, click the **Next** button to proceed to the next wizard step.

4. On Survey screen, select **Yes** for 'Are you new to Oracle Application Express?' and select appropriate option for the second query. Click **Next** to proceed.

5. On Justification screen provide a justification like, "**I want to evaluate Oracle APEX**" and click **Next**.

6. On the next wizard screen read and accept the agreement terms.

7. Click the **Submit Request** button on the final Confirmation screen. A confirmation box will pop up with the message "You will receive an email to activate your workspace once this request has been approved."

8. Soon after submitting the request, you'll get an e-mail from Oracle carrying your workspace credentials and a button labeled Create Workspace. Take a note of your credentials because you need this information whenever you attempt to access your online Oracle APEX workspace. Click the **Create Workspace** button to complete the approval process. You will be taken to Oracle APEX's website, and after a little while, your request will be approved with the message "Workspace Successfully Created."

9. Click the **Continue to Sign In Screen** button.

10. A screen appears requesting to change password. Enter and confirm your password and click the **Apply Changes** button. Write down the password along with the workspace credentials.

11. Here you go! Your Workspace Home Page comes up resembling Figure 2-2.

12. To leave the Oracle APEX environment, click your name (appearing at top-right) and select **Sign Out**.

## 2.3.2 Applications

Applications in Oracle APEX are created using App Builder and each application consists of one or more pages that are linked together via navigation menu, buttons, or hypertext links. Usually, each page carries items, buttons, and application logic. You can show forms, reports, charts, and calendars on these pages and can perform different types of calculations and validations. You can also control movement within an application using conditional navigation. You do all this declaratively using built-in wizards or through custom PL/SQL code.

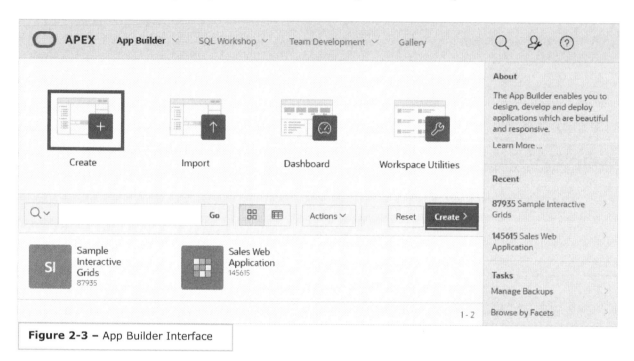

**Figure 2-3 –** App Builder Interface

Developers use App Builder to create and manage applications and application pages. The App Builder home page displays all installed applications in the current Oracle APEX instance. When a developer selects an application to edit, the Application home page appears. Using the Application home page you can create, modify, delete, run, import, or copy applications.

The *Create* button and icon on the App Builder page launches the Create Application wizard comprising the following options:

- **New Application**

  Create a fully functional database application based on tables you select or by providing a valid SQL. You can add pages that include various components including calendars, cards, charts, dashboards, simple input forms, master detail forms, interactive grids, reports, and more. Add application-level features such as an about page, role-based user authentication, end user activity reports, configuration options to enable or disable specific functionality, a feedback mechanism to gather end users comment, and a Customize button to enable end users to choose their own theme style. These applications interact with a backend database to store and retrieve data. It is a collection of pages linked together using menus, buttons, or hypertext links. Pages are created declaratively through wizards. Each page can have multiple containers called regions. Each region can contain text, reports, charts, web service content, calendars, or forms. Web forms hold items such as text fields, radio groups, checkboxes, date pickers, list of values, and more. In addition to these built-in types, you can create your own item types using plug-ins. When you build a database application, you can include different types of navigation controls, such as navigation menu, navigation bar entries, lists, breadcrumbs, and trees. Most of these navigation controls are shared components, which mean you create them at the application level and use them in any page within your database application. All pages in a database application share a common session state that is transparently managed by Oracle APEX.

- **From a File**

  As the name suggests, this option lets you create an application by uploading data from a CSV, XLSX, XML, or JSON file. When you run the Create Application Wizard and select this option, the Load Data Wizard appears where you load a CSV, XLSX, XML, or JSON file. Oracle APEX creates a new table based on the definitions of the selected file and loads the data into it. You also have the option to Copy and Paste column delimited data. After loading the data into the database table, the wizard creates some application pages based on the new table.

- **Starter App**

  Starter Apps include a set of business productivity and sample applications which can be installed with just a few clicks. These apps are fully developed point-solutions designed to provide real functionality. Starter apps can be installed, run, and removed. Applications in *Sample Apps* category highlight specific functionality and are intended to serve as a developer guide on how to make use of a particular feature. *Plug-ins* enables you to extend your APEX applications with custom functionality that is not available natively in the platform.

## 2.3.3 Page

A page is the basic unit of an application – see figures in chapter 1. When you build an application using App Builder, you create pages containing user interface elements, such as regions, items, navigation menu, lists, buttons, and more. Each page is identified by a unique number. By default, page creation wizards automatically add controls to a page based on your selections. You can add more controls to a page after its creation by using the Page Designer interface. Usually, the Create Page wizard is used to add components such as report, chart, form, calendar, or tree to a page. In addition to creating application pages through wizards, you have the option to create a blank page and add components to it according to your own specific needs. The Application Express engine dynamically renders and processes pages based on data stored in Oracle database tables. To view a rendered version of your application, you request it from the Application Express engine with a URL. When you run an application, the Application Express engine relies on two processes:

**Show Page** is the page rendering process. It assembles all the page attributes (including regions, items, and buttons) into a viewable HTML page. When you request a page using a URL, the engine is running Show Page.

**Accept Page** performs page processing. It performs any computations, validations, processes, and branching. When you submit a page, the Application Express engine is running Accept Page or performing page processing during which it saves the submitted values in the session cache and then performs any computations, validations, or processes.

You can create the following types of pages for your application:

- **Blank Page** Creates a page without any built-in functionality.

- **Report** Used to present a SQL query in a formatted style, a report has the following options:

*Interactive Report.* Creates an interactive report based on a custom SQL SELECT statement you provide. Users can alter the layout of report data by selecting specific columns, applying filters, highlighting, and sorting. They can also contain breaks, aggregations, different charts, and their own computations.

*Interactive Grid.* An interactive grid presents users a set of data in a searchable, customizable report. Functionally, an interactive grid includes most customization capabilities available in interactive reports plus the ability to rearrange the report interactively using the mouse. Users can lock, hide, filter, freeze, highlight, and sort individual columns using the Actions menu. Users can also define breaks, aggregations, and computations against columns. They can also directly customize the appearance of an interactive grid and can use the mouse to resize the width of a column and drag and drop columns into different places in the grid.

*Classic Report.* Creates a report based on a custom SQL SELECT statement or a PL/SQL function.

- **Form** The following list provides different types of form pages you can create in Oracle APEX.

  *Editable Interactive Grid.* An interactive grid presents users a set of data in a searchable, customizable report. In an editable interactive grid, users can also add, modify, and refresh the data set directly on the page. Functionally, an interactive grid includes most customization capabilities available in interactive reports plus the ability to rearrange the report interactively using the mouse. You choose a table on which to build the interactive grid.

  *Report with Form.* This option creates two pages – Report and Form. The developer selects the report type (that is, interactive grid, interactive report, or classic report). Each row in the report includes a link to the form page to enable users to update each record. You can select the table on which to build the report and form.

- **Master Detail** A master detail is a type of page, which reflects a one-to-many relationship between two tables in a database. Master detail pages enable users to insert, update, and delete values from two tables or views. Typically, a master detail page type displays a master row and multiple detail rows within a single HTML form. Developers can create a single page or two page master detail.

  You choose the tables on which to build the master and detail regions. Master Detail page options include:

  - **Stacked** - Creates a single page master detail with editable interactive grids.

  - **Side by Side** - Creates a single page (or Side by Side) master detail with a master table and detail table. The left side contains a master list to navigate to the master record. The right side contains the selected master record and the associated detail report.

  - **Drill Down** - Creates a two page (or Drill Down) master detail. The first page contains an interactive report for the master table. The second page features a standard form for the master and an interactive grid for the detail.

- **Plug-ins** Creates a new page based on a region type plug-in. Plug-ins enable developers to declaratively extend, share, and reuse the built-in types available with Oracle APEX.

- **Chart** Enables you to create graphical charts. Chart support in Oracle Application Express is based on the Oracle JET data visualization components. Oracle JET empowers developers by providing a modular open source toolkit based on modern JavaScript, CSS3, and HTML5 design and development principles. The Oracle JET data visualization components include customizable charts, gauges, and other components that you can use to present flat or hierarchical data in a graphical display for data analysis. Each Oracle JET visualization supports animation, accessibility, responsive layout, internationalization, test automation, and a range of interactivity features. The charts provide dozens of different ways to visualize a data set, including bar, line, area, range, combination, scatter, bubble, polar, radar, pie, donut, funnel, and stock charts.

- **Tree** Creates a tree to graphically communicate hierarchical or multiple level data.

- **Calendar** Generates a calendar with monthly, weekly, and daily views.

- **Data Loading** Invokes a data loading wizard allowing the end user to manage the loading of data into a table to all schemas for which the user has privileges.

## 2.3.4 Region

You can add one or more regions to a single page in an Oracle APEX application – see Figure 1-1 in chapter 1. It is an area on a page that serves as a container for content. You control the appearance of a region through a specific region template. The region template controls the look of the region, its size, determines whether there is a border or a background color, and what type of fonts to display. A region template also determines the standard placement for any buttons placed in region positions. You can use regions to group page elements (such as items or buttons). Oracle APEX supports many different region types including Static Content, Classic Report, Interactive Report, Interactive Grid, Chart, and more.

## 2.3.5 Items

After creating a region on a page, you add items to it – see Figure 1-3 in chapter 1. An item can be a Text Field, Textarea, Password, Select List, Checkbox, and so on. Each item has its own specific properties that affect the display of items on a page. For example, these properties can impact where a label displays, how large an item is, and if the item displays next to or below the previous item. The name of a page item is preceded by the letter P followed by the page number. For example, P7_CUSTOMER_ID represents customer ID item on page 7.

## 2.3.6 Buttons

Just like desktop applications where you place buttons on your forms to perform some actions, in web applications too, you can create buttons to *submit* a page or to take users to another page (*redirect*) within the same site or to a different site. In the former case where a user *submits* a page, the Oracle APEX engine executes some processes associated with a particular button and uploads the page's item values to the server – see Figure 1-3 in chapter 1. In case of a *redirect*, nothing is uploaded to the server. If you change some items' values on a page and press a button created with a redirect action, those changes will be lost. You have three button options that you can add to a web page, these are: Icon, Text, and Text with Icon. You can place buttons either in predefined region positions or with other items in a form – see Figures 1-1, 1-3, and 1-7 in chapter 1.

Being an important component to control the flow of database applications, buttons are created by right-clicking a region in which you want to place the button and selecting *Create Button* from the context menu. By placing buttons (such as Create, Delete, Cancel, Next, Previous, and more) on your web page, you can post or process the provided information or you can direct user to another page in the application or to another URL.

Buttons are used to:

- Submit a page. For example, to save user input in a database table. When a button on a page is clicked, the page is submitted with a REQUEST value that carries the button name. You can reference the value of REQUEST from within PL/SQL using the bind variable :REQUEST. By using this bind variable, you can conditionally process, validate, or branch based on which button the user clicks. You can create processes that execute when the user clicks a button. And you can use a more complex condition as demonstrated in the following examples:

  ```
  If :REQUEST in ('EDIT','DELETE') then ...
  If :REQUEST != 'DELETE' then ...
  ```

  These examples assume the existence of buttons named EDIT and DELETE. You can also use this syntax in PL/SQL Expression conditions. Be aware, however, that the button name capitalization (case) is preserved. In other words, if you name a button *LOGIN*, then a request looking for the name *Login* fails.

- Take user to another page within the same application with optional additional properties for resetting pagination, setting the request value, clearing cache, and setting item values on the target page.

- Redirect to another URL.

- Do nothing–for example, if the button's behavior is defined in a Dynamic Action.

## 2.4 Oracle APEX Development Environment

Oracle APEX has the web-based application development environment to build web applications. You are not required to install any client software to develop, deploy, or run Oracle APEX applications. Following are the primary tools provided by Oracle APEX:

**App Builder** – to create dynamic database driven web applications. This is the place where you create and modify your applications and pages. It comprises the following:

**Create:** This is the option in the App Builder that is used to create new applications. See section 2.3.2 for further details.

**Import:** Used to import an entire Oracle APEX application developed somewhere else, along with related objects.

**Dashboard:** Presents different metrics about applications in your workspace including: Developer Activity, Page Events, Page Count by Application, and Most Active Pages.

**Workspace Utilities:** It contains various workspace utilities. The most significant one is Export. Using this utility, you can export application and component metadata to SQL script file format that you can import on the same or another compatible instance of Application Express.

 **SQL Workshop** – to browse your database objects and to run ad-hoc SQL queries, SQL Workshop is designed to allow Application Developers to maintain database objects such as tables, packages, functions, views, and so on. It is beneficial in hosted environments like apex.oracle.com where direct access to underlying schemas is not provided. It has five basic components:

**Object Browser:** to review and maintain database objects (tables, views, functions, triggers, and so on).

**SQL Commands:** to run SQL queries.

**SQL Scripts:** to upload and execute script files.

**Utilities:** includes Query Builder, Data Workshop, Generate DDL, Schema Comparison, and more.

**RESTful Services:** to define Web Services using SQL and PL/SQL against the database.

 **Team Development** – Team Development allows development teams to better manage their Oracle APEX projects by defining milestones, features, to-dos, and bugs. Features, to-dos, and bugs can be associated with specific applications and pages as necessary. Developers can readily configure feedback to allow their end-users to provide comments on applications. The feedback also captures relevant session state details and can be readily converted to a feature, to-do or bug.

 **Gallery** – Starter Apps are a suite of business productivity applications, easily installed with only a few clicks. These solutions can be readily used as production applications to improve business processes.

The Oracle APEX environment has two broad categories:

- **Development Environment:** Here you have complete control to build and test your applications, as mentioned in this book.

- **Runtime Environment:** After completing the development and testing phase, you implement your applications in a production environment where users can only run these applications and do not have the right to modify them.

## 2.5 About Browser Requirements

Because Oracle APEX relies upon standards-compliant HTML5, CSS3, and JavaScript, Oracle recommends that you use the latest web browser software available for the best experience.

## 2.6 The Page Designer

The Page Designer is the main development interface where you manipulate page components. You use the Page Designer to view, create, and edit the controls and application logic that define a page. It was a feature incorporated in Oracle APEX 5, which greatly improves developer's productivity and quickly enhances and maintains pages within Oracle APEX. It allows you to undo and redo changes as necessary before saving the page. In the Layout tab (F), it visually presents how your regions and items appear on the page. Moreover, you can drag new components from component Gallery and move or copy existing components within a page. Similarly, you can drag to move multiple components at once in the Tree pane. It also has a new code editor with new functionalities, such as: SQL and PL/SQL validation with inline errors, auto completion, syntax highlighting, search and replace, and undo/redo support.

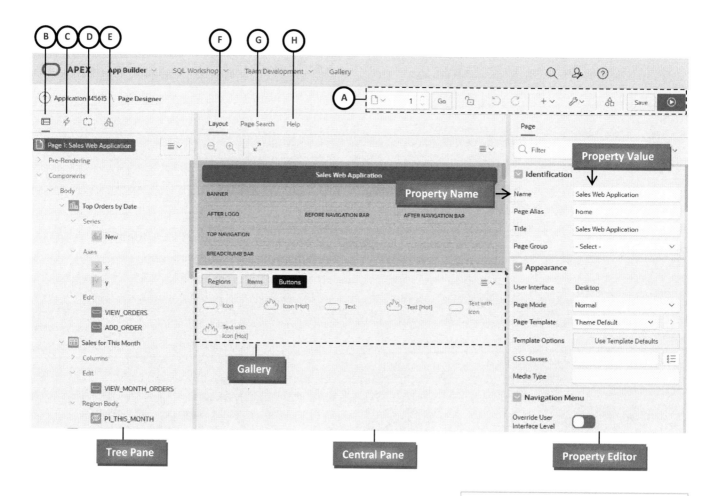

**Figure 2-4 –** Page Designer Interface

### 2.6.1 Toolbar

The Page Designer toolbar (A) appears at the top of the page. It comprises various tools to find a page, lock/unlock a page, undo/redo actions, save and run page, and so on. When you pass your cursor over an active option, a tooltip indicates what that particular toolbar option does. The *Utilities* menu has an option that lets you delete the page being displayed in your browser. A lock icon indicates whether a page is currently locked. If a page is unlocked, the icon appears as an open padlock. If the page is locked, the icon appears as a locked padlock. An indication (a locked padlock) for a locked page is displayed in Page Designer as well as on the Application home page – as illustrated in Figure 2-5. This feature enables you to prevent conflicts during application development. By locking a page you prevent other developers from editing it.

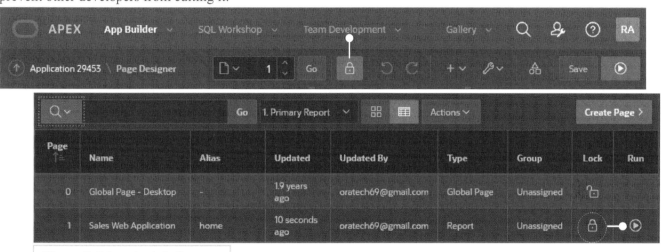

**Figure 2-5** Page Lock Indicator

### 2.6.2 Tree Pane

The Tree pane is displayed on the left side in the Page Designer. It contains regions, items, buttons, application logic (such as computations and processes), dynamic actions, branches, and shared components as nodes on a tree. It comprises four tabs:

**Rendering (B)** - Displays regions, page items, page buttons, and application logic as nodes in a tree. The components defined in this section appear when a page is rendered. These components can be viewed as a tree, organized by processing order. Rendering is divided in three stages. In the *Pre-Rendering* stage preliminary computations are performed. The Components rendering stage comprises regions and its components, while the *Post-Rendering* stage also carries computations that occur after rendering a page.

**Dynamic Actions (C)** - Displays dynamic actions defined on this page. By creating a dynamic action, you can define complex client-side behavior declaratively without the need for JavaScript. Refer to Dynamic Actions entry in the book's index to see its varied utilization in the project application.

**Processing (D)** - Use this tab to specify application logic such as computations, validations, processes, and branches. *Computations* are Oracle APEX's declarative way of setting an item's values on the page. These are units of logic used to assign session state to items and are executed at the time the page is processed. *Validation* is a server-side mechanism designed to check and validate the quality, accuracy, and consistency of the page submitted data, prior to saving it into the database. If a validation fails, further processing is aborted by the server and the existing page is redisplayed with all inline validation errors. *Processes* are logic controls used to execute Data Manipulation Language (DML) or PL/SQL. Processes are executed after the page is submitted. A page is typically submitted when a user clicks a button. *Branches* enable you to create logic controls that determine how the user navigates through the application.

**Page Shared Components (E)** - Displays shared components associated with this page. The list on this tab gets populated automatically when you use shared components on a page.

## 2.6.3 Central Pane

The central pane in the Page Designer has two sections. The upper section contains three tabs: Layout, Page Search, and Help. The lower pane is called Gallery and it is associated with the Layout tab.

**Layout (F)** - Layout is a visual representation of the regions, items, and buttons that define a page. You can add new regions, items and buttons to a page by selecting them from the Gallery at the bottom of the page.

**Page Search (G)** - Use Page Search to search all page metadata including regions, items, buttons, dynamic actions, columns, and so on.

**Help (H)** – The Help displays help text for properties available in the Property Editor. Click a property in the Property Editor and then click the Help tab (in the Central pane) to see the purpose of the selected property. As you move from one property to the next in the property editor, the Help tab displays the help text for the currently selected property.

## 2.6.4 Property Editor

The Property Editor appears in the right pane and displays all the properties and values for the current component. As you select different components in either Tree View or Layout tab, the Property Editor automatically updates to reflect the current selection. Properties are organized into functional groups (Identification, Source, Layout, Appearance, and more) that describe their purpose. When you modify or add a value to a property, a colored vertical bar appears as a visual modification indicator before the property name.

## 2.7 Understanding Oracle APEX URL Syntax

Oracle APEX applications support two types of URL syntax: Friendly URL Syntax and f?p Syntax. Each application has its own unique ID and is referenced by this ID in URL. Similarly, you create pages in an application with respective numbers that uniquely identify each page. The Application Express engine assigns a session ID, which is used as a key to the user's session state when an application is run. The f?p URL Syntax is a legacy syntax that creates a unique URL structure that identifies the address of Oracle Application Express, the application ID, page number, and session ID.

Here is the URL syntax example for the f?p type:

http://apex.abc.com/pls/apex/f?p=101:1:440323506685863558

This example indicates:

- *apex.abc.com* is the URL of the server
- *pls* is the indicator to use the mod_plsql cartridge
- *apex* is the database access descriptor (DAD) name. The DAD describes how HTTP server connects to the database server so that it can fulfill an HTTP request. The default value is *apex*.
- *f?p=* is a prefix used by Oracle APEX to route the request to the correct engine process.
- *101* is the application being called. The application ID is a unique number that identifies each application.
- *1* is the page within the application to be displayed
- *440323506685863558* is the auto-generated session id that keeps track of user's session state

It is important to understand how f?p syntax works. App Builder includes many wizards that automatically create these references for you. However, you may have to create the syntax yourself in some situations. For instance, in section 6.3.1 (Chapter 6) you will create a manual link in a SQL statement using this syntax, and in section 4.3.2, a link will be created on a column using the *Target* property of that column.

## 2.7.1 Using f?p Syntax to Link Pages

Here is the syntax you can use to create links between pages in your application.

**f?p=App:Page:Session:Request:Debug:ClearCache:itemNames:itemValues:PrinterFriendly**

The following are the arguments you can pass when using f?p syntax:

**App:** Indicates an application ID or alphanumeric alias.

**Page:** Indicates a page number or alphanumeric alias.

**Session:** Identifies a session ID. Web applications use HTTP by which browsers talk to Web servers. Since HTTP doesn't maintain state, it is known as a stateless protocol. Here, your Web server reacts independently to each individual request it receives and has no way to link requests together even if it is logging requests. For example, a client browser requests a page from a web server. After rendering the page, the server closes the connection. When a subsequent request is forwarded from the same client, the web server doesn't know how to associate the current request with the previous one. To access values entered on one page on a subsequent page, the values must be stored as session state. It is very crucial to access and manage session state while designing an interactive, data-driven web application. Fortunately, Oracle APEX transparently manages session state behind the scenes for every page and provides developers with the ability to get and set session state values from any page in the application. When a user requests a page, the Application Express engine uses session ID to get session state information from the database. You can reference the session ID either using *&SESSION.* substitution string or by using *:APP_SESSION* bind variable. See substitution string and bind variables in section 2.8. Whenever you run an Oracle APEX application page during development phase, you see a horizontal bar at the bottom of the page. This is a *Developer Toolbar*. Among other tools for developers it contains a *Session* option, which shows you the current session state. Clicking it opens a window (called *Session Page, shown in Figure 2-6*) carrying all items and their current session values. It is useful for developers to debug pages. When you change some item value on a page and submit it, the value in the session window for that item changes to reflect the current state. Use the *Page*, *Find*, and *View* parameters to view session state for the page. The drop-down *View* menu comprises *Page Items*, *Application Items*, *Session State*, *Collections*, and *All* options. Select an option from this list and click the *Set* button to refresh the Session State report.

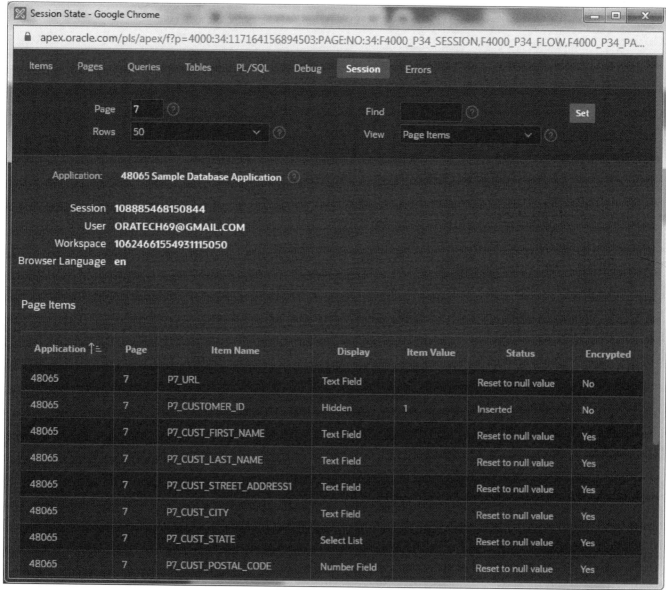

| Application ↑≡ | Page | Item Name | Display | Item Value | Status | Encrypted |
|---|---|---|---|---|---|---|
| 48065 | 7 | P7_URL | Text Field | | Reset to null value | No |
| 48065 | 7 | P7_CUSTOMER_ID | Hidden | 1 | Inserted | No |
| 48065 | 7 | P7_CUST_FIRST_NAME | Text Field | | Reset to null value | Yes |
| 48065 | 7 | P7_CUST_LAST_NAME | Text Field | | Reset to null value | Yes |
| 48065 | 7 | P7_CUST_STREET_ADDRESS1 | Text Field | | Reset to null value | Yes |
| 48065 | 7 | P7_CUST_CITY | Text Field | | Reset to null value | Yes |
| 48065 | 7 | P7_CUST_STATE | Select List | | Reset to null value | Yes |
| 48065 | 7 | P7_CUST_POSTAL_CODE | Number Field | | Reset to null value | Yes |

**Figure 2-6** Session Page

**Request:** Here you place an HTML request. Each application button sets the value of REQUEST to the name of the button, which enables the called process to reference the name of the button when a user clicks it. You can assess requests using the *:REQUEST* bind variable.

**Debug:** Displays application processing details. Valid values for the DEBUG flag include: Yes or No. Setting this flag to YES you get details about application processing. You can reference the Debug flag using *&DEBUG.* substitution string.

**ClearCache:** You use Clear Cache to make item values null. To do so, you provide a page number to clear items on that page. You can also clear cached items on multiple pages by adding a list of page numbers separated by comma. For example, typing 4,5,8 in the Clear Cache position in the URL will clear the session state for all items on pages 4, 5, and 8.

**itemNames:** Comma-delimited list of *item names* used to set session state with a URL.

**itemValues:** List of *item values* used to set session state within a URL. See Chapter 4 Section 4.3.2 for the utilization of itemNames and itemValues syntax parameters.

**PrinterFriendly:** Determines if the page is being rendered in printer friendly mode. If PrinterFriendly is set to Yes, then the page is rendered in printer friendly mode. The value of PrinterFriendly can be used in rendering conditions to remove elements such as regions from the page to optimize printed output.

## 2.7.2 Friendly URL Syntax

Friendly URL Syntax creates a URL structure that identifies the address of Oracle Application Express, the application, the page, and uses a standard URL hierarchy and passes parameters in a similar fashion. Applications created using Oracle Application Express release 20 or later use Friendly URL Syntax. You can change existing applications to use Friendly URLs by editing the Friendly URLs attribute in the application definition – *Shared Components | Application Definition Attributes | Properties*.

Friendly URL Syntax creates a URL with the following directory hierarchy and syntax:

```
https://apex.oracle.com/pls/apex/myws/r/my-app/my-home-page?session=16167973992554
```

Where:

- myws is the path_prefix which is URI path prefix used to access RESTful Services. When you create a workspace, this value defaults to workspace name. You can customize the URI path prefix by editing the Path Prefix attribute in *Administration | Manage Service | Set Workspace Preferences | SQL Workshop*.
- r is the router shortcut. This value is a constant and should never be changed.
- my-app is the app_alias. In a new application, the Application Alias defaults to the application Name. You can edit the Application Alias in the application Definition. The Application Alias must be unique within the workspace.
- my-home-page is the alias of the page being displayed. You can edit the Page Alias in Page Designer. Page aliases must be unique within the application. When creating a new page, if a Page Name is already used as a Page Alias, then a numeric value is appended to the new Page Alias to make it unique.
- ?session=16167973992554 identifies the session ID.

## 2.8 Substitution Strings and Bind Variables

To make your application more portable, Application Express provides many features. On top of the list are the Substitution Strings that help you avoid hard-coded references in your application. As mentioned earlier, every application in Oracle APEX has its own unique ID and which is used to identify the application and the corresponding metadata within the Application Express repository. When you move these applications from your development environment to the production environment, and if you've hard-coded application references, you might be placed in an awkward situation. For example, you hard-coded the application ID (101) like this: f?p=101:1:&APP_SESSION.. If you take this application to the production environment that already has an application with the same ID, you'll be forced to use a different ID, which will point all your links within the application to the wrong ID.

To avoid such situations, you should always use substitution strings. You can avoid hard-coded application IDs by using the &APP_ID. substitution string, which identifies the ID of the currently executing application. With the substitution string, the URL looks like this: f?p=&APP_ID.:1:&APP_SESSION.. This approach makes your application more portable.

The following table describes the supported syntax for referencing APP_ID.

| Reference Type | Syntax | Example |
|---|---|---|
| Bind variable | :APP_ID | :P7_CUSTOMER_ID |
| Substitution string | &APP_ID. | &P7_CUSTOMER_ID. |

You need to know how to get a page to access the value of a session state variable. There are two ways. If you want to reference the variable from within SQL or PL/SQL code, use bind variable, in other words, precede the item name with a colon. If you want to reference an item from within an HTML expression, then make use of substitution string. In substitution string you prefix an ampersand to the item name and append a period at its end. For example, consider an item named P7_CUSTOMER_ID on a page. To refer to it as a substitution string, write "&P7_CUSTOMER_ID.". To refer to it as a bind variable, write ":P7_CUSTOMER_ID".

### About Using Substitution Strings

You can use substitution strings in the following ways:

- Include a substitution string within a template to reference component values
- Reference page or application items using &ITEM. syntax
- Use built-in substitution strings

### Substitution Strings within Templates

Special substitution strings available within a template are denoted by the number symbol (#). For example: #PRODUCT_ID# - see Chapter 4 Section 4.3.2, 4.3.5, and 4.3.6.

**Substitution Strings for Page or Application Items**

To reference page or application items using substitution variables:

1. Reference the page or application item in all capital letters.
2. Precede the item name with an ampersand (&).
3. Append a period (.) to the item name.

For example, you would refer to a page item named P7_CUSTOMER_ID in a region, a region title, an item label, or in any of numerous other contexts in which static text is used, like this: &CUSTOMER_ID.

Notice the required trailing period. When the page is rendered, Application Express engine replaces the value of the substitution string with the value of item P7_CUSTOMER_ID.

**Using Built-in Substitution Strings**

Oracle APEX supports many built-in substitution strings. You can reference these substitution strings to achieve specific types of functionality. APP_ID, APP_FILES, APP_PAGE_ID, APP_SESSION, APP_USER, LOGIN_URL, and LOGOUT_URL are some of the built-in substitution strings you will use in this book.

## 2.9 Start Building the Application

Now that you have gone through the necessary basic concepts about Oracle APEX, let's start the thrill! Follow the instructions mentioned in this section to create the barebones of your application.

1.  If you have logged out, sign back in to Oracle APEX development environment by typing the URL **https://apex.oracle.com/pls/apex/f?p=4550** in your browser's address bar.

2.  Enter the credential comprising your Workspace, Username (your e-mail address) and Password (you provided in Section 2.3.1) in the Sign In form and hit the Sign In button.

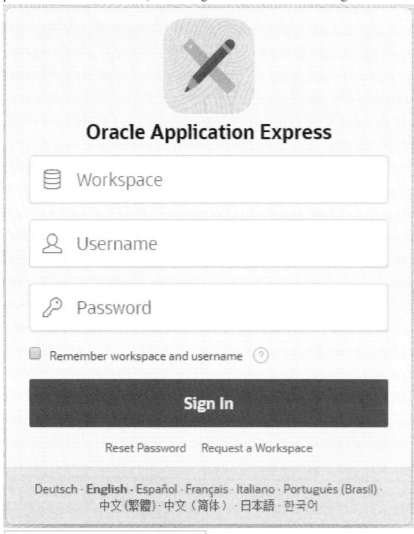

**Figure 2-7** Workspace Login Page

3. Click the **App Builder** icon. You as a developer will use App Builder to create and manage applications and application pages. The App Builder home page displays all applications in the current Oracle Application Express workspace. When you select an application to edit, the Application home page appears. Use the Application home page to run, edit, import, export, copy, or delete applications.

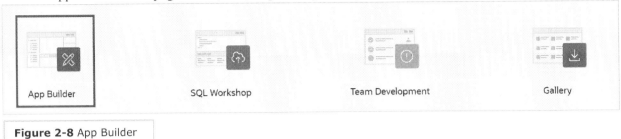

**Figure 2-8** App Builder

4. On the App Builder page, click the **Create** icon (or click the *Create* button - A) to create a new application.

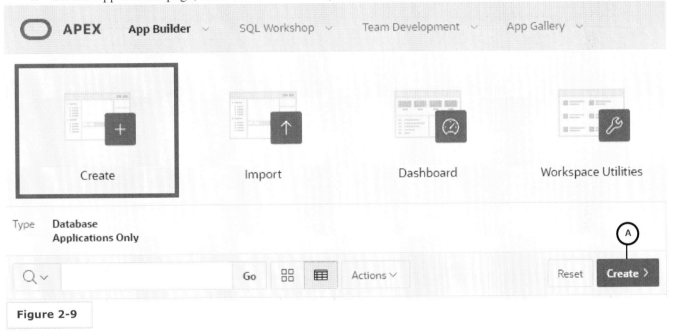

**Figure 2-9**

5.  Select the first **New Application** option. This option will create a new database application containing multiple pages based on database tables. A database application is a collection of pages linked together using navigation menus, tabs, buttons, or hypertext links. Application pages share a common session state and authentication. To create a database application, you run wizards to declaratively assemble pages and navigation. Once created, you can modify an application by editing application attributes and add new pages using the Create Page Wizard. When you click the *New Application* option, the *Create an Application* page is displayed.

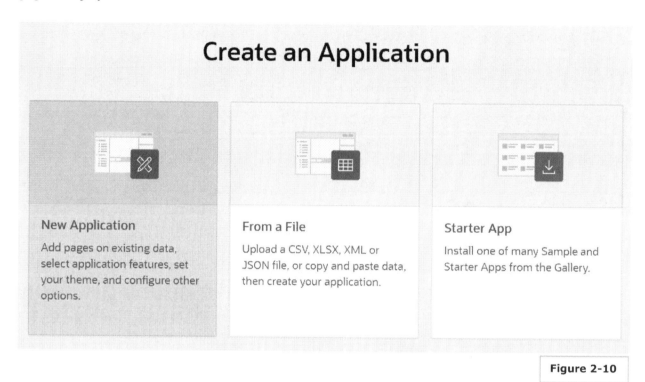

Figure 2-10

6.  On the next screen, as illustrated in the following figure, enter **Sales Web Application** in the *Name* box (A). In the *Name* attribute you provide a short descriptive name for the application to distinguish it from other applications in your development environment. In the *Appearance* section, click the **Set Appearance** icon (B).

Figure 2-11a

7. On the *Appearance* page, select a *Theme Style*, or accept the default Vita option (C). In Oracle APEX, you can alter a database application's user interface and page layout through themes and theme styles. Themes are collections of templates that enable developers to define the layout and style of an entire application. In the *Navigation* section, select the **Mega Menu** option (D). The Mega Menu renders application navigation as a collapsible floating panel that displays all navigation items at once. Users can expand or collapse a Mega Menu by clicking on the menu icon from the header. Mega menus are especially useful when you want to display all navigation items at once to your user. You can switch to the two options any time through *Shared Components | Edit Application Definition | User Interface | Navigation Menu*. Click the **Choose New Icon** button (E), and select an icon (F) and its color (G) for your application from the *Choose Application Icon* page. After making your selection, click the **Set Application Icon** button (H) to move back. Click **Save Changes** (I) on the *Appearance* page to switch back to the *Create an Application* page.

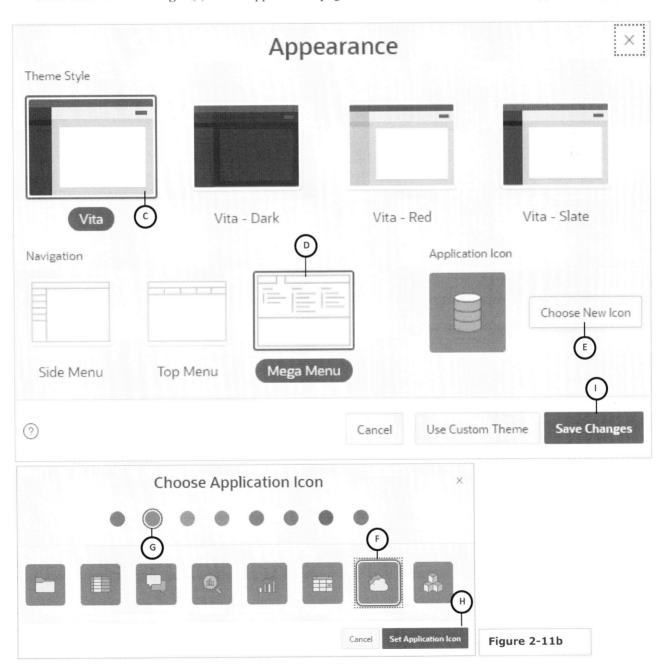

Figure 2-11b

41

The *Pages* section in the *Create an Application* interface lets you add pages to include in your initial application. By default, the App Builder process creates a Home page (J) for your application along with a couple of pages (Login and Global – note visible in this list). The *Add Page* option on this screen allows you to create more pages. Since you will create other pages for your application in subsequent chapters, you do not need to add any page at the moment.

Figure 2-11c

8.  In the *Features* section, click the **Check All** link (K) to select all listed features for this application. The *Features* section provides application-level functionality and can only be added once per application. Available features include Progressive Web App, an application About page, role-based user authentication, end user activity reports, configuration options to enable or disable specific functionality, a feedback mechanism to gather end users comment, and a Customize button to enable end users to choose their own theme style. The most significant among these features is Access Control that you will use in Chapter 10. Adding the Access Control feature to an application creates multiple pages (including an Administration page and a corresponding menu entry), access roles, and authorization schemes. Details of these features are provided on a subsequent page.

Figure 2-11d

In the *Settings* section, accept all the default values. Here, the *Application ID* (K) is a unique, numeric identifier, which is generated automatically to identify your application. If required, you can provide another non-existent number for your application. The *Schema* drop-down list (L) contains the name of the schema you are connected to. Your schema is where the database objects (tables, sequences, triggers etc.) of your application are stored. Oracle APEX provides a number of predefined authentication mechanisms, including a built-in authentication framework and an extensible custom framework. In the default *Application Express Accounts* authentication scheme (M) users are managed and maintained in the Oracle APEX repository.

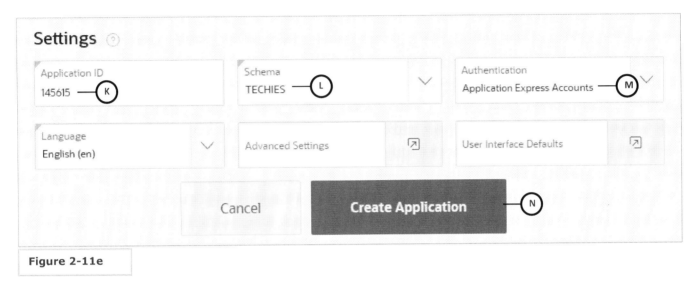

**Figure 2-11e**

9. Click the **Create Application** button (N) to complete the process. A progress bar will appear on your screen and the application will be created within seconds.

The application will be created with some default pages, including Page 1 Home, Page 9999 Login Page and Page 0 Global Page (A). Using the two buttons (*View Icons* and *View Report* – B) you can get different views of this interface. The following screen shot presents the iconic view. You can see the ID and the name of your application (C) in this interface. At this stage, if you want to modify properties of your application (for example, application name or menu position), then click the *Edit Application Properties* button (D). In the *Edit Application Definition* interface you will see a small question mark icon next to each property. Click this icon when a property is unfamiliar and you want to learn about it. To delete an application click the *Delete this Application* link (E), or make a copy of your current application using the *Copy this Application* link (F). The link makes an exact copy of the application under a different ID. You will use the *Create Page* button (G) in subsequent chapters to create new application pages. The *Run Application* icon (H), as the name implies, will run the application.

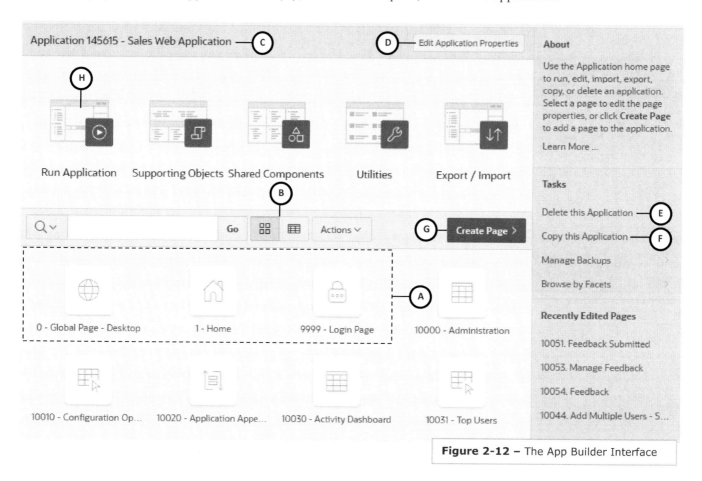

**Figure 2-12** – The App Builder Interface

 To access the *Create Page* button form anywhere in the APEX interface, click App Builder in the main Oracle APEX menu followed by Database Applications. On the Database Applications page, click the Edit icon for the Sales Web Application, as shown in the following figure. The application's main page (as illustrated in Figure 2-12) will be rendered carrying the Create Page button. The Run icon (I) can also be used to invoke an application.

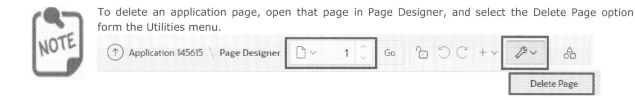

To delete an application page, open that page in Page Designer, and select the Delete Page option form the Utilities menu.

10. Click **Run Application** (H in Figure 2-12). The application login page (A), created by the App Builder, will come up. Type the same username (your e-mail ID) and the password you entered earlier to access the development environment and click the **Sign In** button. The new browser window will show the Home page (B) of your application. This page is also created by the App Builder. At the bottom of this page, you will see a horizontal strip (C) displaying different options. This strip is called the *Developer Toolbar* and it appears whenever you run a page during the development phase. The *App* option (D) takes you to the App Builder page, where you can select a different page to work on. The *Page* option (E) in this toolbar takes you to the *Page Designer* to edit the current page. The *Session* option brings up a page (see Figure 2-6) that displays the current state of the application so that you can verify its behavior. The **Sign Out** option (F) under your id helps you exit the application.

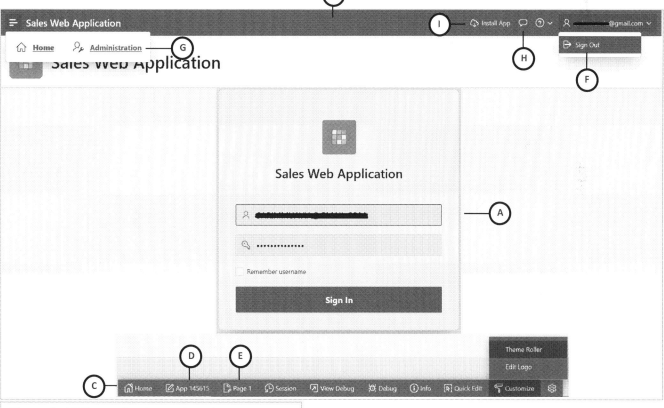

**Figure 2-13** The Application Login and Home Pages

Recall that while creating the application you selected all admin features in step 8. When you click the Administration menu option (G) in your application, you see an Administration page that lists all the features you selected in step 8. The following table provides some details of these features.

| Feature | Description |
|---|---|
| Install Progressive Web App | The Progressive Web App (PWA) technology transforms your APEX application that looks and feels like a native desktop application. You usually choose this feature while creating a new application – see Figure 2-11d. When you choose this feature, a new navigation bar entry labeled *Install App* (I) is displayed. When users tap the *Install App* option, the application is opened in a standalone window, which is free of the browser's UI – see Chapter 11 for further details on PWA. |
| Configuration Options | Enables application administrators to enable or disable specific functionality within the application. This feature is useful if you select features that need additional development effort before they can be used by end users. This feature can also be expanded to application-specific features. If developers define additional build options and associate them with specific functionality throughout the application, then they can be added to the configuration settings for administrators. |
| Theme Style Selection | The Theme Style Selection in the Features section enables administrators to select a default color scheme (theme style) for the application. Administrators determine whether end users can choose their own theme style by enabling and disabling *Enable End Users to choose Theme Style* attribute in *Shared Components | User Interface Attributes*. If enabled, end users simply click on the Customize link that is provided at the bottom of the home page at runtime and select from the available theme styles. For example, users with visual impairment may prefer to utilize the Vista theme style which has a much higher color contrast |
| Activity Reports | Include numerous reports on end user activity for your application. Determine the most active users, the most used pages, the performance of pages, and errors raised, to better understand how your application is being utilized and areas for improvement.<br>– Top Users report<br>– Application Error Log report<br>– Page Performance, activity and performance by page<br>– Application activity by page report<br>– Page Views detail report |
| Access Control | Incorporate role based user authentication within your application. Users can be defined as Administrators, Contributors, or Readers. You can then readily define different access to different roles for various components throughout your application, such as pages, menu entries, regions, columns, items, buttons and so forth. For further details, see Chapter 10. |
| User Feedback | Feedback provides a mechanism for end users to post general comments for application administrators and developers. The posts include useful session state information to help developers determine where the end user sent the feedback from.<br>– Creates a Navigation bar icon which users can click to leave feedback (see H in Figure2-13).<br>– Creates a report for viewing and updating feedback.<br>– Captures the application and page ID, feedback comments, date and time, and user information. |

## 2.10 Create Database Objects

We interact with many databases in our daily lives to get some information. For example, a phone book is a database of names and phone numbers, and an email list is a database of customer names and email addresses. A database can simply be defined as a collection of individual named objects (such as tables) to organize data. In APEX you create data-centric web applications that are powered by Oracle database. In this section, I will walk you through to create database objects interactively for the sales application you just created. The application will use five tables to store information: DEMO_STATES, DEMO_CUSTOMERS, DEMO_PRODUCT_INFO, DEMO_ORDER, and DEMO_ORDER_ITEMS. These tables will be generated interactively (that is, without writing any SQL code) with the help of built-in wizard. In addition to these tables, some other database objects, such as sequences and triggers, will be generated automatically to handle data in these tables.

 If you are new to database or want to strengthen you knowledge about database and its objects, then drop me a line (along with the purchase proof of this book) at my email address (oratech@cyber.net.pk) to get my free SQL/PLSQL eBook.

Execute the following steps to create the first table named DEMO_CUSTOMERS for the sales web application. This table will be used to store profiles of customers.

1. Click the **SQL Workshop** menu (A).

2. Select the **Object Browser** option (B) from the menu, which is used to review and maintain database objects (such as, tables, sequences, views, functions, triggers, and so on).

3. In the Object Browser page, select the **Tables** option (C) from the select list. This action will show a list of existing tables in the left pane, if there are any.

4. Click the **Create** menu (D), and select **Table** (E) from the menu list to create a new table. This will invoke a wizard named Create Table, discussed next.

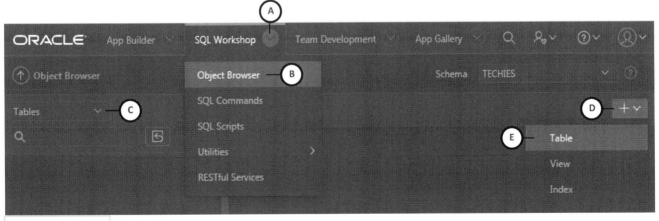

**Figure 2-14**

5. On the first wizard page you provide a name for the new table and information about its columns – name, type, precision, scale, and not null. Enter **DEMO_CUSTOMERS** for the table name (A). Enter **CUSTOMER_ID** in the first Column Name (B). Select **NUMBER** (C) for the Type of this column. Place a check mark for **Not Null** (D). This information specifies that the first column in the table named CUSTOMER_ID is a numeric column that will hold ids of customers. By placing a check mark in the Not Null option, we specified that it is a mandatory column and must have some value. Input information of other table columns as indicated in the screenshot below. The values in the Scale column specify the number of characters each column will hold. Use the Add Column button (E) to add more rows to the form. After providing the column information, click Next (F) to proceed to the next wizard step.

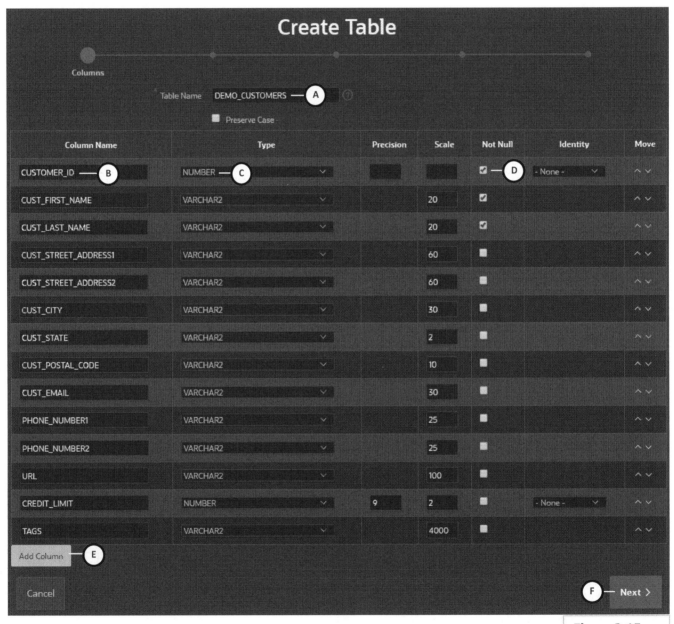

Figure 2-15

6. The next wizard screen titled Primary Key collects information about the primary key of this table, which is a column in a table that uniquely identifies each record and prevents duplicates. The primary key (CUSTOMER_ID) in the customers table will be populated automatically with the help of a database object named Sequence. From the Primary Key options, select **Populated from a new sequence** (A). As you click this option, three additional fields pop up on your screen. Accept **DEMO_CUSTOMERS_PK** (B) for the *Primary Key Constraint Name*. You can specify any other name if you wish to. This is the name of your primary key constraint to uniquely identify each row/record in the customers table. For Primary Key, select **CUSTOMER_ID** (C) from the adjacent list. This is the column that will act as the primary key to uniquely identify each record in the table. Accept the name of the default Sequence Name or enter any other name. A Sequence is a database object which generates unique integer values automatically in the background. Here, it will generate unique primary keys for each customer's record, and these values will be stored in the CUSTOMER_ID column. Press the Next button thrice skipping *Foreign Key* and *Constraints* wizard screens. On the final *Confirm* screen, click the **Create Table** button. The table will be created and its definitions will appear on your screen. Click the *SQL* tab to see the auto-generated SQL statements for this table. The trigger (BI_DEMO_CUSTOMERS) created for this table will be responsible to auto-generate ids of customers with the help of DEMO_CUSTOMERS_SEQ sequence object. You can view both these objects using the drop down list in the left pane (under the *Object Browser* label).

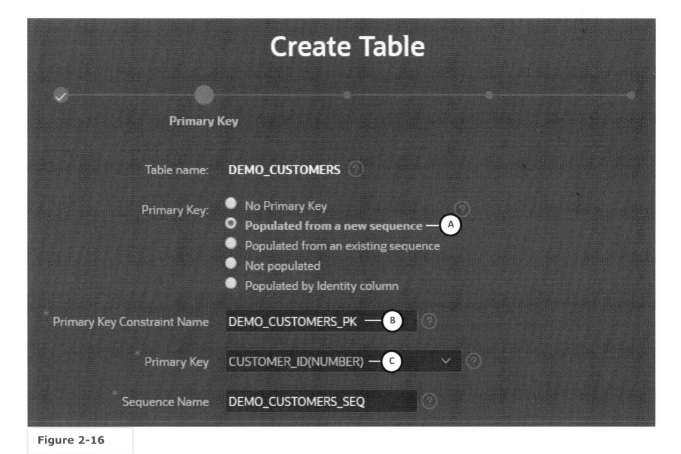

Figure 2-16

7. Repeat **steps 4** to create another table named **DEMO_PRODUCT_INFO** (A). As the name suggests, this table will store information about products that will be sold to customers. Enter columns definitions for this table as depicted in the following screenshot. Besides number and varchar2 column types, this table is using the BLOB (Binary Large Objects) type (B), which is an Oracle data type that can hold up to 4 GB of data. BLOBs are handy for storing digitized information, such as images, audio, and video. This type can also be used to store document files like PDF, MS Word, MS Excel, MS PowerPoint and CSV to name a few. We are also using a TIMESTAMP type (C) to store the date when a product image is updated. Click **Next** to proceed.

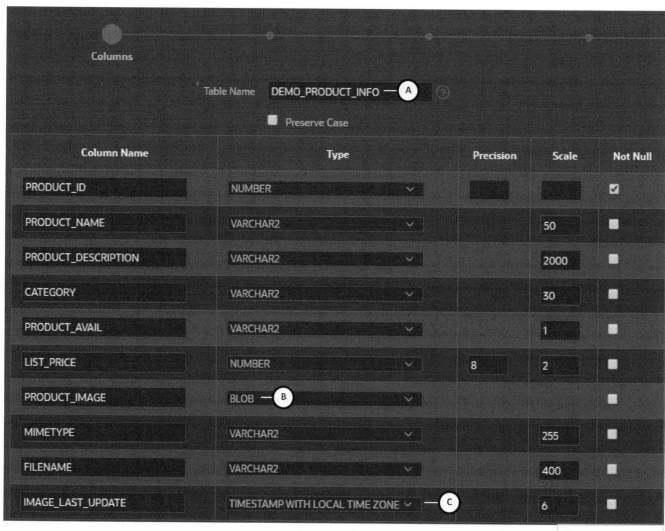

Figure 2-17

8. Once again select **Populated from a new sequence** (A) on the *Primary Key* screen. Accept the default values for *Primary Key Constraint Name* and *Sequence Name*. Select the **PRODUCT_ID** column (B) for Primary Key. This is the column that will uniquely identify each product in the table. Click **Next**. Skip the *Foreign Key* and *Constraints* wizard screens by clicking the Next button. On the final screen, click the **Create Table** button.

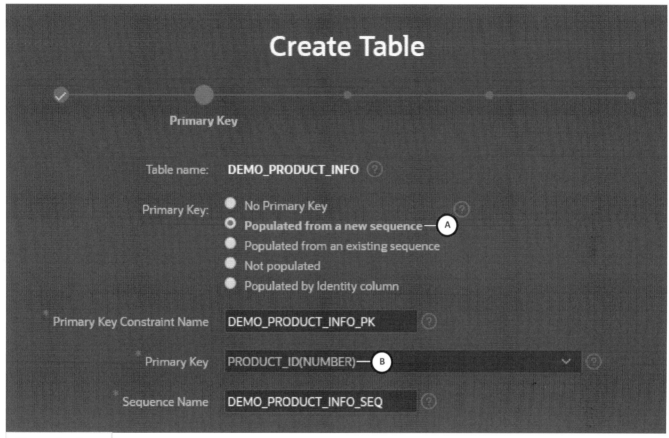

**Figure 2-18**

9. After creating the parent tables, let's create two more tables (DEMO_ORDERS and DEMO_ORDER_ITEMS) to store customers' order information. These two tables will have a master/detail relationship. The DEMO_ORDERS table will act as the master table to store master information, like order id, customer id, order date and more. The DEMO_ORDER_ITEMS will be the child table for the DEMO_ORDERS table and it will store line item information, such as product id, unit price, and quantity. So, let's first create the master table. Again, execute **steps 1** to initiate the Create Table wizard. Fill in the information for this table as indicated in the following screenshot, and click Next.

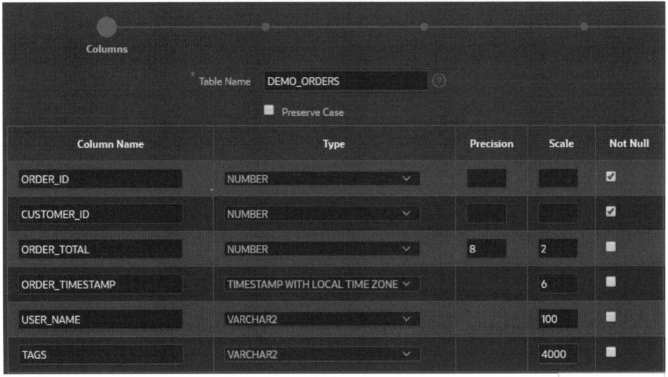

| Column Name | Type | Precision | Scale | Not Null |
|---|---|---|---|---|
| ORDER_ID | NUMBER | | | ☑ |
| CUSTOMER_ID | NUMBER | | | ☑ |
| ORDER_TOTAL | NUMBER | 8 | 2 | ☐ |
| ORDER_TIMESTAMP | TIMESTAMP WITH LOCAL TIME ZONE | | 6 | ☐ |
| USER_NAME | VARCHAR2 | | 100 | ☐ |
| TAGS | VARCHAR2 | | 4000 | ☐ |

**Figure 2-19**

10. As usual, select the **Populated from a new sequence** option to automatically populate the primary keys for this table as well. Accept the default values for *Primary Key Constraint Name* and *Sequence Name*. Select the **ORDER_ID** column (A) for *Primary Key*. Click **Next** to proceed to the *Foreign Key* screen, where you will create a relationship between DEMO_CUSTOMERS and DEMO_ORDERS table.

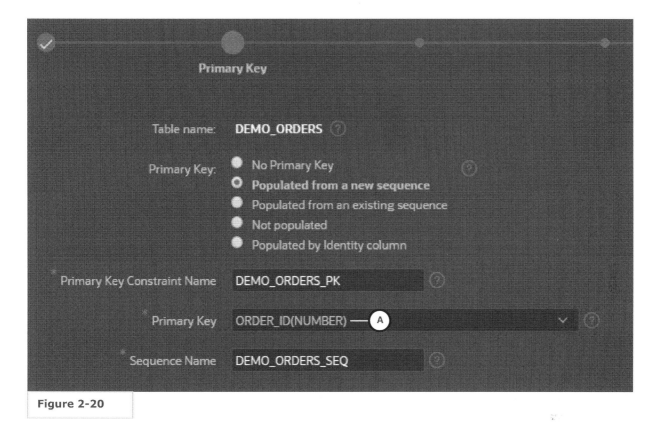

**Figure 2-20**

11. The following wizard screen collects information about Foreign Key. A foreign key establishes a relationship between a column or columns in one table and a primary or unique key in another table. Here, you are establishing a relationship between the DEMO_ORDERS and DEMO_CUSTOMERS tables. Accept the default name (**DEMO_ORDERS_FK** - A) for the foreign key constraint name. The default **Disallow Delete** option (B) will block deletion of rows from the customers table when they are utilized in the orders master table. From the left pane in the *Select Key Column(s)* section, move the **CUSTOMER_ID** column to the right pane (C) using the single right-arrow icon (>). This action specifies that the CUSTOMER_ID column in this table is a foreign key and has a reference in some other table. Click the icon next to the *References Table* (D), and pick the **DEMO_CUSTOMERS** table. All columns from this table will appear in the *Referenced Column(s)* left pane. In the *Referenced Column(s)* section, move the **CUSTOMER_ID** column to the right pane (E). Here you are telling APEX that this is the column in the customers table that will be referenced by the CUSTOMER_ID column in the orders master table. Now the two tables have a relationship based on the CUSTOMER_ID column. Click the **Add** button (F). The details of the FK constraint (G) will appear on the page. Press the **Next** button twice, and then click the **Create Table** button on the *Confirm* screen to create the orders master table.

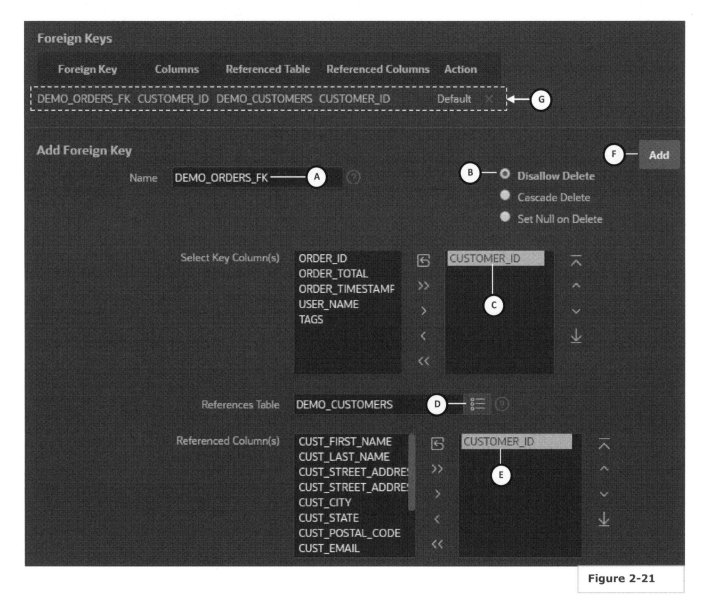

Figure 2-21

54

12. Create the orders child table (DEMO_ORDER_ITEMS) of your application, as illustrated in the following figure. This table will be used to store line item information of each order placed by customers. Click the Next button, after providing the column information.

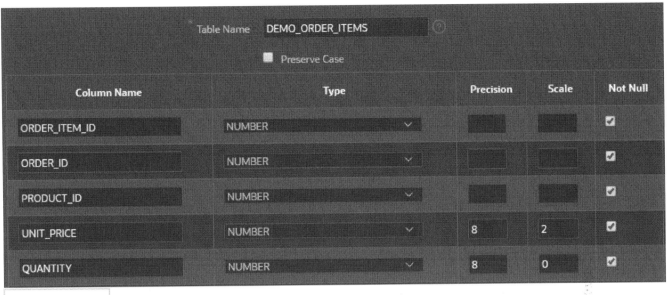

| Column Name | Type | Precision | Scale | Not Null |
|---|---|---|---|---|
| ORDER_ITEM_ID | NUMBER | | | ☑ |
| ORDER_ID | NUMBER | | | ☑ |
| PRODUCT_ID | NUMBER | | | ☑ |
| UNIT_PRICE | NUMBER | 8 | 2 | ☑ |
| QUANTITY | NUMBER | 8 | 0 | ☑ |

**Figure 2-22**

13. Select the **ORDER_ITEM_ID** column as the *Primary Key* column for this table, and click **Next**.

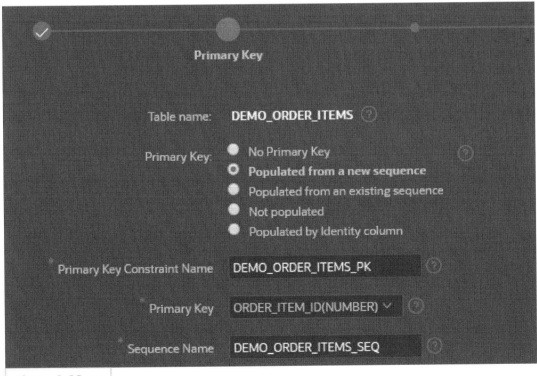

**Figure 2-23**

14. The DEMO_ORDER_ITEMS has two foreign key references: ORDER_ID and PRODUCT_ID. So, you will create two foreign key constraints on the *Foreign Keys* page. The first one is illustrated in the following figure in which you relate this table to its parent (DEMO_ORDERS). For this relationship, you selected the **Cascade Delete** option (A), which simultaneously removes both parent and child records from the two tables when you delete an order. After selecting the ORDER_ID columns from the two tables, click the **Add** button (B) to create the foreign key constraint. The next step will be executed on the same page to create another foreign key reference.

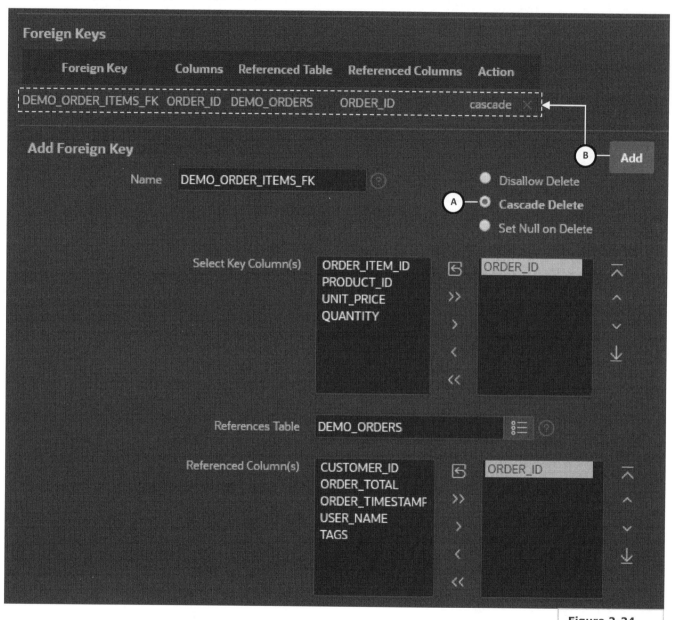

**Figure 2-24**

15. In this foreign key constraint you are creating a relationship between DEMO_ORDER_ITEMS table and DEMO_PRODUCT_INFO table using the PRODUCT_ID column, which exists in both tables. Enter **DEMO_ORDER_ITEMS_PRODUCT_ID_FK** (A) for the name of this foreign key. Select **Disallow Delete** for delete option, and select tables and columns as depicted in the following figure. After that, click the **Add** button (B). A new foreign key constraint (C) will be added just under the previous one. This constraint will prevent deletion of those products that are utilized in customers' orders. Click **Next** twice to skip the *Constraint* wizard screen. Click the **Create Table** button on the final screen.

**Figure 2-25**

16. Create the final table (DEMO_STATES), as illustrated in the following figure. This table will store states information and it will be associated to the Customers module to store each customer's state. Click the Next button, after providing the column information.

Figure 2-26

17. On the *Primary Key* screen, select the default **No Primary Key** option, because this table is not going to have any primary key. Click **Next**.

18. Skip the remaining two wizard screens by clicking **Next** twice and create the table.

Here is the summary of the whole exercise you just carried out.

The **Table** tab displays structure of the selected table. You can use the underneath buttons to add, modify, rename, and drop columns. Use Copy and Drop buttons to make a copy of the selected table or drop it.

The triggers defined for the selected table can be accessed from the **Triggers** tab.

The **SQL** tab holds a script which was used to create the tables, triggers, and constraints.

Select **Tables** from the objects list to see a list of all tables.

The **Data** tab will display data once you add some records to a table.

The **Constraints** tab contains all constraints defined for the selected table.

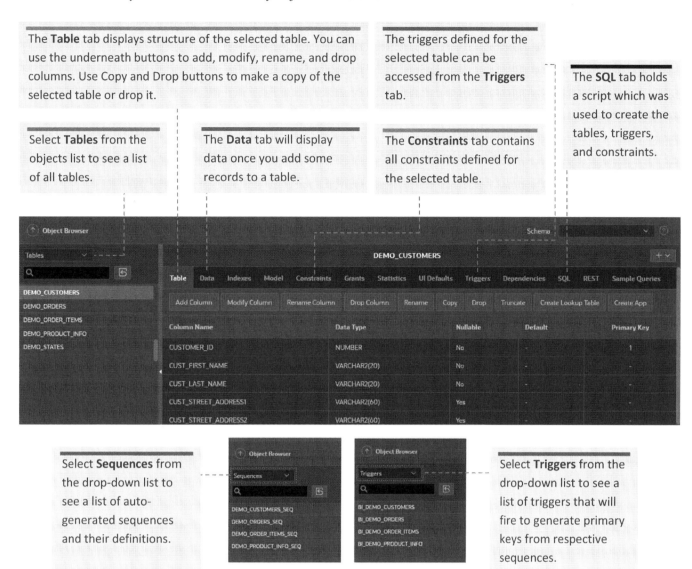

Select **Sequences** from the drop-down list to see a list of auto-generated sequences and their definitions.

Select **Triggers** from the drop-down list to see a list of triggers that will fire to generate primary keys from respective sequences.

**Figure 2-27**

## 2.11 Add Data to Database Tables

After creating the database tables our next move is to interactively add some seed data to these tables. This task will also be performed via wizards and built-in features of Oracle APEX.

Execute the following steps to first upload data to the DEMO_CUSTOMERS table.

1. From the main Oracle APEX menu, select **SQL Workshop | Utilities | Data Workshop**.

2. On the *Get Started* page, click the **Load Data** button.

**Figure 2-28**

3. On the next screen, click the **Choose File** button. In the Open dialog box, select **DEMO_CUSTOMERS** csv file and open it. The csv file is available in BookCode\Chapter2 folder.

**Figure 2-29**

4. The *Load Data* page will appear on your screen. Select options on this screen as illustrated in the following figure. By selecting the **Existing Table** option you are informing that you want to upload the csv file data to the existing DEMO_CUSTOMERS table that you need to select from the provided Table list. Once you select the database table, Oracle APEX will automatically map the columns. Click the **Load Data** button on this page. A message "Data in table DEMO_CUSTOMERS appended with 7 new rows!" should appear on your screen. Click the **View Table** button to browse the data.

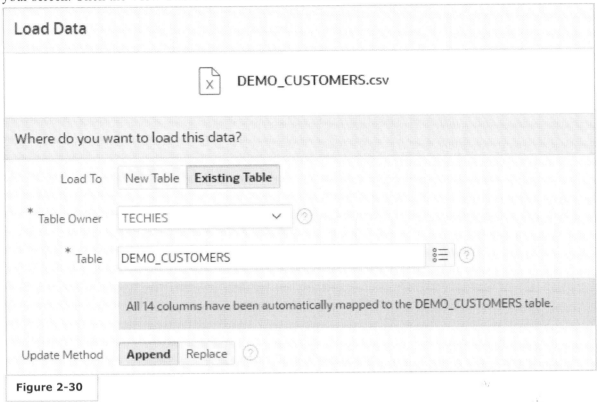

**Figure 2-30**

5. Repeat steps 1 through 4 to upload data to the remaining tables in the following sequence using their appropriate csv files: DEMO_STATES, DEMO_PRODUCT_INFO, DEMO_ORDERS, and DEMO_ORDER_ITEMS.

## Summary

This chapter introduced some of the important basic concepts of Oracle APEX. Besides the theoretical stuff, you were guided on how to request a free workspace. You also created the basic structure of your application with some default pages (you will work in detail on the Home page in Chapter 4 to convert it into a dashboard). You also learned how to interactively create backend database objects and populate tables with some seed data.

In the next chapter, you will create the building blocks (shared components) of your application. The Shared Components wizards allow us to define a variety of components we can use and re-use throughout our application. In the coming chapters, our main focus will be on the practical aspect of this robust technology. Once you get familiar with Oracle APEX, you can explore other areas on your own to become a master. The rest of the book will guide you to build professional looking web-based data-centric application that will provide you the techniques in building your own.

# 3

# CREATE APPLICATION COMPONENTS

## 3.1 The Shared Components

Shared components are application structures used in application pages. These structures are called shared components because you create them once and utilize them across all the pages in the application. For example, in this chapter you will create a list comprising application menu options that will appear on every application page. The *Page Shared Components* tab in the Page Designer displays a list of common elements applied to that particular page. Note that shared components are only displayed in this section after you add them to a page.

**Figure 3-1**

The following sub-sections provide details about shared component elements. The Shared Components page in Oracle APEX can be accessed through the Shared Components icon (A).

### 3.1.1 Application Definition Attributes

This link (which appears under *Application Logic* section on the Shared Components page) will take you to the *Edit Application Definition* page where you can modify your application attributes, including its name, version, and availability options. Application attributes control the behavior of an entire application and are divided into the categories: Definition, Security, Globalization, and User Interface.

### 3.1.2 Application Processes

*Application Processes* run PL/SQL logic at a specific point from multiple pages of an application. You can apply conditions to control when the process executes. Currently there are eight different types of process that you can include in your application. A significant one among these processes is *On Demand Application Process*. It is a special type of application process which executes when called from a page-level On Demand process or from an Ajax call from the browser. On Demand processes are useful when you have PL/SQL logic that you would like to run from different execution points across multiple pages. For example, assessing a customer's outstanding balance and using that value on customer invoice, age analysis report, customer balances report and so on.

### 3.1.3 Authentication Schemes

The significance of security cannot be ignored when building web applications, as it enables us to prevent unauthorized access and activity in our applications. Not all applications require security; a public website doesn't, for example. However, for many applications, we need to be able to control who can run and gain access to them. Once users are logged into our application, we also need to further control what functionality they have permission to access. In Application Express, these security features are implemented through the use of *Authentication* and *Authorization Schemes*. These schemes enable us to declaratively define the security for our applications quickly and easily. Authentication is the process of establishing the identity of every user of your application. The most common type of authentication process requires a user to provide some type of credentials such as a username and password. These credentials are then evaluated either through the built-in *Application Express Authentication* scheme or using a custom scheme with more control. Authentication could involve the use of digital certificates or a secure key, too. If the credentials pass, the user is allowed to access the application. Otherwise, access is denied. Once a user has been identified, the Application Express engine keeps track of each user by setting the value of the built-in substitution string APP_USER.

As you create your application, you must determine whether to include authentication. You can:

- **Choose to not require authentication.** Oracle APEX does not check any user credentials. All pages of your application are accessible to all users. A public informational application website is a good candidate, which doesn't require authentication.

- **Select a built-in authentication scheme**. Create an authentication method based on available preconfigured authentication schemes. Here are the preconfigured authentication schemes available in Oracle APEX. Each scheme follows a standard behavior for authentication and session management.

  - *Application Express Accounts.* These are user accounts created within and managed in Oracle APEX user repository. When you use this method, your application is authenticated against these accounts.

  - *Database Account Credentials.* It utilizes database schema accounts. This authentication scheme requires that a database user (schema) exist in the local database. When using this method, the username and password of the database account is used to authenticate the user.

  - *HTTP Header Variable.* It supports the use of header variables to identify a user and to create an Application Express user session. Use this authentication scheme if your company employs a centralized web authentication solution like Oracle Access Manager, which provides single sign-on across applications and technologies.

  - *LDAP Directory Verification.* You can configure any authentication scheme that uses a login page to use Lightweight Directory Access Protocol (LDAP) to verify the username and password submitted on the login page. App Builder includes wizards and pages that explain how to configure this option. These wizards assume that an LDAP directory accessible to your application for this purpose already exists and that it can respond to a SIMPLE_BIND_S call for credentials verification.

  - *Application Server Single Sign-On Server.* This one delegates authentication to the Oracle AS Single Sign-On (SSO) Server. To use this authentication scheme, your site must have been registered as a partner application with the SSO server.

- **Create custom authentication scheme**. Using this method you can have complete control over the authentication interface. To implement this approach you must provide a PL/SQL function the Application Express engine executes before processing each page request. The Boolean return value of this function determines whether the Application Express engine processes the page normally or displays a failure page. This is the best approach for applications when any of the following is true:

  - Database authentication or other methods are not adequate
  - You want to develop your own login form and associated methods
  - You want to control security aspects of session management
  - You want to record or audit activity at the user or session level
  - You want to enforce session activity or expiry limits
  - Your application consists of multiple applications that operate seamlessly (for example, more than one application ID)

### 3.1.4 Authorization Schemes

By defining authorization schemes, you control users' access to specific components of your application. It is an important security measure implemented to augment the application's authentication scheme. An authorization scheme can be specified for an entire application, page, or specific page components such as a region, button, or item. For instance, you can apply an authorization scheme to determine which menu options a user can see, or whether he is allowed to create a new order (using the Create button).

### 3.1.5 List of Values

List of values (abbreviated as LOVs) are defined by running the LOV wizard. Once created, LOVs are stored in the List of Values repository and are utilized by page items. You can create two types of LOVs: static and dynamic. A static LOV displays and returns predefined values such as Yes and No, while a dynamic list is populated using a SQL query that fetches values from database tables. After creating an LOV you associate it to page items such as select list, radio group, checkbox, and so on. By creating a list of values at the application-level, you have the advantage to add it to any page within an application, and since all LOV definitions are stored in one location, it makes them easy to locate and update.

### 3.1.6 Plug-Ins

With the increase in Application Express usage the demand for specific features also surfaced. To meet these demands, the plug-ins framework was introduced in Oracle APEX 4.0, which allows developers to create their own plug-ins to add additional functionality in a supported and declarative way.

Usually, a tool like Ajax is used to add custom functionality. The con of this approach is to place the code in different locations such as within the database, in external JavaScript files, and so on. On the other hand, turning that code into a plug-in is more convenient to use and manage because the code resides in one object. With the help of open source jQuery components you can create plug-ins without generating huge amount of code manually.

Plug-ins are shared component objects that allow you to extend the functionality of item types, region types, dynamic actions, and process types. The plug-in architecture includes a declarative development environment that lets you create custom versions of these built-in objects. For example, you can create your own star rating item that allows your user to provide feedback using a one-to-five star graphic. This new item type can then be used across all your applications. The main part of a plug-in consists of PL/SQL code and can be supplemented with JavaScript and CSS code. A plug-in consists of one or more PL/SQL functions. These functions can either reside in the database (in a package or a set of functions) or be included within the plug-in.

The Plug-in OTN page (*https://www.oracle.com/tools/technologies/apex-plug-ins.html*) has several different plug-ins developed by the APEX community.

## 3.1.7 Shortcuts

By using shortcuts you can avoid repetitive coding of HTML or PL/SQL functions. You can use a shortcut to define a page control such as a button, HTML text, or a PL/SQL procedure. Once defined, you can invoke a shortcut using specific syntax unique to the location in which the shortcut is used. Shortcuts can be referenced many times, thus reducing code redundancy.

When you create a shortcut, you must specify the type of shortcut you want to create. Oracle APEX supports the following shortcut types:

- PL/SQL Function Body
- HTML Text
- HTML Text with Escaped Special Characters
- Image
- Text with JavaScript Escaped Single Quotes
- Message
- Message with JavaScript Escaped Special Quotes

## 3.1.8 Lists

A list is a collection of links. For each list entry, you specify display text, a target URL, and other attributes to control when and how the list entry displays. Once created, you can add a list to any number of pages within an application by creating a region and specifying the region type as *List*. You control the display of the list and the appearance of all list entries by linking the list to a template. Lists are of two types:

- **Static Lists** – When you create a static list you define a list entry label and a target (either a page or a URL). You can add list entries when you create the list (from scratch), by copying existing entries or by adding the list entries. You can control when list entries display by defining display conditions.

- **Dynamic Lists** – Dynamic lists are based on a SQL query or a PL/SQL function executed at runtime.

## 3.1.9 Navigation Menu

You might have seen a horizontal bar at the top of a website. The options provided on this bar help you navigate to different pages within that site. Application Express provides you with a similar component called Navigation Menu. It is an effective way to navigate users between pages of an application. A navigation menu is basically a list with hierarchical entries. When you create an application, the Create Application Wizard automatically creates a navigation menu for you and populates it with one or more list entries. Types of navigation menus include *Side Menu*, *Top Menu*, or *Mega Menu*. By default, the navigation menu is displayed as a left sidebar. Users can expand or collapse the *Side Navigation Menu* by clicking on the menu icon from the header. This navigation menu renders the navigation items using a tree component that enables users to expand or collapse sub items. A *Top Navigation Menu* displays at the top of the application. You can change how and where a navigation menu displays by editing the application User Interface Details. The *Top Navigation Mega Menu* template renders your application navigation in a pop-up panel that can be opened or closed from the header menu button. Users can expand or collapse a Mega Menu by clicking on the menu icon from the header. Mega menus are especially useful when you want to display all navigation items at once to your user.

### 3.1.10 Breadcrumb

A breadcrumb (A) is a hierarchical list of links rendered using a template. For example, you can display breadcrumbs as a list of links or as a breadcrumb path. A breadcrumb trail indicates where you are within the application from a hierarchical perspective. In addition, you can click a specific breadcrumb link to instantly view the page. For example, in the screen shot below you can access the application home page by clicking its breadcrumb entry (B). You use breadcrumbs as a second level of navigation at the top of each page, complementing other navigation options such as Navigation Menu and Navigation Bar.

Figure 3-2

### 3.1.11 Navigation Bar List

Just like menus, lists, and breadcrumb, a navigation bar is also created to link users to various pages within an application. Typically, a navigation bar carries links such as user id, logout, feedback, help, and so on. It appears on top-right of every application page. While creating a navigation bar, you can specify an image name, label, display sequence, and target location.

### 3.1.12 User Interface Attributes

The application user interface determines default characteristics of the application and optimizes the display for the target environment. This is the place where you define your application logo and set other useful attributes.

### 3.1.13 Themes and Templates

Instead of telling the App Builder how to design and style your pages using HTML, CSS, and JavaScript code that you may not be familiar with, you only apply theme and templates you want to use and the Oracle APEX engine does the rest of the job for you.

A theme is a named collection of templates that defines the look and feel of application user interface. Each theme contains templates for every type of application component and page control, including individual pages, regions, reports, lists, labels, menus, buttons, and list of values.

The Application Express engine constructs the appearance of each page in an application using Templates. Templates define how pages, page controls, and page components display. Templates control the look and feel of the pages in your application using snippets of HTML, CSS, JavaScript and image icons. As you create your application, you specify templates for pages, regions, reports, lists, labels, menus, buttons, and pop-up lists of values. Groups of templates are organized into named collections called themes.

The App Builder also allows you to access the themes and template mechanism so you can create new ones according to your own requirements or amend existing ones. Oracle APEX ships with an extensive theme repository. Administrators can add themes to the theme repository, as follows:

- Workspace administrators can create themes that are available to all developers within the workspace. Such themes are called *workspace themes*.

- Instance administrators can create *public themes* by adding them to the Oracle APEX Administration Services. Once added, these public themes are available to all developers across all workspaces in an instance.

- Applications you create with the Create Application Wizard use the Universal Theme. Universal Theme - 42 features a responsive design, versatile UI components and enables developers to create web applications without extensive knowledge of HTML, CSS, or JavaScript. Responsive design enables you to design web pages so that the layout fits the available space regardless of the device on which page displays (for example, a desktop computer, laptop computer, tablet, or smartphone).

## 3.1.14 Static Application/Workspace Files

Use these two links to upload, edit, and delete static files including images, custom style sheets and JavaScript files. An application file can be referenced from a specific application only, whereas a workspace file can be accessed by any application in the workspace. In this book, you will use the *Static Application Files* option to upload your application logo and CSS files.

## 3.1.15 Report Queries

A report query is a printable document, which can be integrated with an application using buttons, list items, branches, or any other navigational components that allow for using URLs as targets. A report query is based on a standard SQL query. It can be downloaded as a PDF document, a Word document (RTF based), an Excel Spreadsheet (HTML based), or as an HTML file. The layout of a report query is customizable using RTF templates.

## 3.1.16 Report Layouts

Use Report Layouts in conjunction with a report region or report query to render data in a printer-friendly format, such as PDF, Word, or Excel. A report layout can be designed using the Template Builder Word plug-in and uploaded as a file of type RTF or XSL-FO. Report regions use a generic XSL-FO layout, which is customizable.

## 3.1.17 Globalization Attributes

If you want to develop applications that can run concurrently in different languages, then Application Express is the right platform for this. In the Globalization interface, you can specify options such as the application Primary Language, Date/Time format, and some other options related to application globalization.

## 3.1.18 Translate Application

A single Oracle database and Oracle APEX instance can support an application in multiple languages. Translating an application involves multiple steps. To translate an application developed in App Builder, you must map the primary and target language, seed and export text to a translation file, translate the text, apply the translation file, and publish the translated application.

Having gone through the conceptual sections, the following are some of the Shared Components you will create for the Sales Web Application:

- Lists
- List of Values (LOV)
- Application Logo
- Cascading Style Sheet (CSS)

If you are logged off, log back in to the application development environment to create some shared components. Execute the following three steps to access the Shared Components page.

1. Select **Database Applications** from the App Builder menu.

2. Click the **Edit** icon (A) under Sales Web Application.

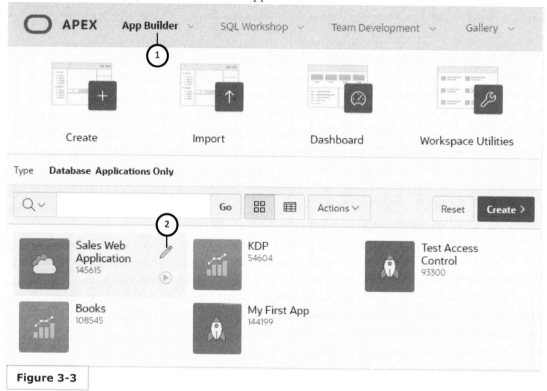

**Figure 3-3**

3. On the next screen, use either of the two **Shared Components** icons.

**Figure 3-4**

## 3.2 Create Lists

First, we are going to play with the *Lists* shared component. A list is a collection of links rendered using a template. For each list entry, you specify display text, a target URL, and other properties to control when and how the list entry displays. You control the display of the list and the appearance of all list entries by linking the list to a template.

### 3.2.1 Modify Navigation Menu List

Oracle APEX creates a default navigation list named *Navigation Menu* (under *Navigation | Navigation Menu*) as a shared component for each new application. It is a hierarchical list of navigation, which appears either as a responsive side bar or at the top of the window. Based on the available space, the navigation bar either displays a full menu or collapses to a narrow icon bar. The default menu list (*Navigation Menu*) carries two item labeled: Home & Administration. In this exercise, you'll modify this list to add more application menu entries, as illustrated in the following figure.

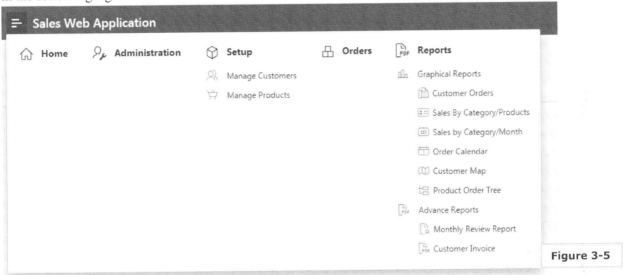

Figure 3-5

1. In Shared Components, click the **Navigation Menu** option in the *Navigation* section.

2. On the Lists page, click the **Navigation Menu** option, which carries two entries (Home and Administration, as illustrated in Figure 3-6) created by the App Builder wizard to access the application Home & Administration pages.

3. On the *List Details* page, click the **Create Entry** button (A) to create a new menu item named Setup. This menu entry will have sub-entries that will allow you to access Products and Customers modules. Fill in the values for this menu entry as highlighted in Figure 3-7. Do not select anything in the first attribute (*Parent List Entry*), because initially you will create level-one entries that do not have parent entries. Click the pop-up LOV icon representing *Image/Class* attribute. From the *Show* list, select **Font APEX**, and from *Category*, select **Web Application**. Click the **Go** button to refresh the view. Scroll down to the middle of the icons list and select **fa-database** icon. This image will be displayed for the Setup menu at run time. Note that you can select any image from the list or input its name directly in the *Image/Class* attribute if you do not want to bother selecting it from the image list. Type **Setup** in the *List Entry Label* field. This label will appear in the application menu. In the Target Type attribute you specify a page in the current application or any valid URL. Since the *Setup* menu entry itself is not associated to any application page, its *Target Type* is set to *No Target*.

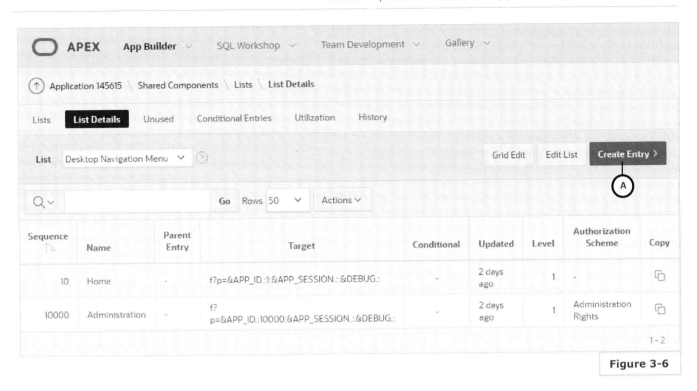

Figure 3-6

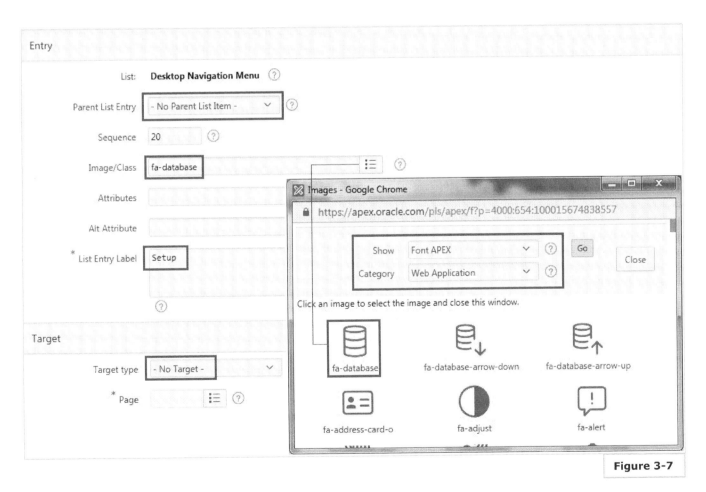

Figure 3-7

73

4.  Using the button labeled **Create and Create Another**, create two more level-1 entries as follows. After adding the last entry (Reports), click the *Create List Entry* button. The *Target Type* and *Page* properties inform Oracle APEX where to land when a menu item is clicked – for example, the *Orders* entry will take you to page 4.

| Parent List Entry | Image/Class | List Entry Label | Target Type | Page |
|---|---|---|---|---|
| No Parent List Item | Choose any image | Orders | Page in this Application | 4 |
| No Parent List Item | Choose any image | Reports | Page in this Application | 26 |

These entries along with the Setup entry (created in step 3) will form the main menu of our application and because of this reason we set *No Parent List Item* for all three entries. Note that the *Setup* entry has no target because it is not directly linked to any application page. In the next step, you will create submenus under this main entry to call respective pages.

5.  Using the same process you executed in the previous step, create the following level-2 menu entries:

| Parent List Entry | Image/Class | List Entry Label | Target Type | Page |
|---|---|---|---|---|
| Setup | Select an image | Manage Customers | Page in this Application | 2 |
| Setup | Select an image | Manage Products | Page in this Application | 3 |
| Reports | Select an image | Graphical Reports | Page in this Application | 26 |
| Reports | Select an image | Advance Reports | Page in this Application | 26 |

The first two entries will come under the main *Setup* menu item, while the *Reports* menu will contain two child entries (Graphical Reports and Advance Reports).

If you make a mistake while creating these menu entries, you can easily rectify it. After creating the last entry, click the *Create List Entry* button on *Create/Edit* page to move back to the *List Details* page. On this page, click the menu entry you want to modify (under the *Name* column) to call its definition in *Create/Edit* page. Rectify the error and click the *Apply Changes* button.

6. Now create level-3 entries as follows. Note that the *Page* attribute for *Monthly Review Report* entry is set to zero, because it will be invoked through a print request that will be configured in Chapter 9.

| Parent List Entry | List Entry Label | Target Type | Page |
|---|---|---|---|
| Graphical Reports | Customer Orders | Page in this Application | 17 |
| Graphical Reports | Sales By Category/Products | Page in this Application | 16 |
| Graphical Reports | Sales by Category/Month | Page in this Application | 5 |
| Graphical Reports | Order Calendar | Page in this Application | 10 |
| Graphical Reports | Product Order Tree | Page in this Application | 19 |
| Advance Reports | Monthly Review Report | Page in this Application | 0 |
| Advance Reports | Customer Invoice | Page in this Application | 50 |

The first six entries will appear as submenu choices under *Graphical Reports* menu. Similarly, *Monthly Review Report* and *Customer Invoice* will be placed under *Advance Reports*. All the previous settings will set up a hierarchical navigation for your application, as shown previously in Figure 3-5.

After making any modification in your application you can test it immediately. For example, after creating the navigation menu, hit the Run Page button (at top-right) to see the application menu.

## 3.2.2 Reports List

In this section you will create a list named *Reports List*. The list will have several links that will lead to different reports in your application. Note that you created the same links in the navigation menu in the previous section to call some of these reports from the application menu. The *Reports List* being created here will be used on a dedicated report page to call respective reports – see Chapter 8 section 8.2.

1. Go to *Shared Components | Navigation | Lists*. Click the **Create** button to create a new list.

2. Select **From Scratch** on the *Source* wizard screen and click **Next**. On the next screen, enter **Reports List** for *Name*, select **Static** as the list *Type*, and click **Next**. When you create a static list you define a list entry label and a target (either a page or URL).

3. Enter the following values in *Query or Static Values* screen. Initially, the wizard allows you to create five entries. The remaining entries and *Image/Class* properties are created and set after saving the first five.

| List Entry Label | Target Page ID | Image/Class |
|---|---|---|
| Customer Orders | 17 | Choose any image |
| Sales by Category and Product | 16 | Choose any image |
| Sales by Category / Month | 5 | Choose any image |
| Order Calendar | 10 | Choose any image |
| Product Order Tree | 19 | Choose any image |
| Gantt Chart | 20 | Choose any image |
| Box Plot | 21 | Choose any image |
| Pyramid Chart | 22 | Choose any image |
| List View (Mobile) | 23 | Choose any image |
| Column Toggle Report (Mobile) | 24 | Choose any image |
| Reflow Report (Mobile) | 25 | Choose any image |

4. After entering the first five list entries click **Next**, accept the default values in the next screen, and click the **Create List** button. You will be taken back to the Lists page, where you will see this new list.

5. Modify the list by clicking the **Reports List** link in the *Name* column.

6. Click the **Create Entry** button to add the sixth entry. Enter **Product Order Tree** in *List Entry Label*. Set *Target Type* to **Page in this Application** and enter **19** in the *Page* attribute. Click the **Create and Create Another** button to add the remaining entries, as shown in the table.

7. Modify each entry by clicking its name in the *List Details* interface and add image references. Click the **Apply Changes** button after adding the image reference.

### 3.2.3 Order Wizard List

This is another utilization of lists. Rather than associating list items to pages in the application, you'll use it for visual representation. It will be used while creating orders in Chapter 7. In our application, we will create an order using a set of wizard steps in the following sequence:

a) Identify Customer
b) Select Items
c) Order Summary

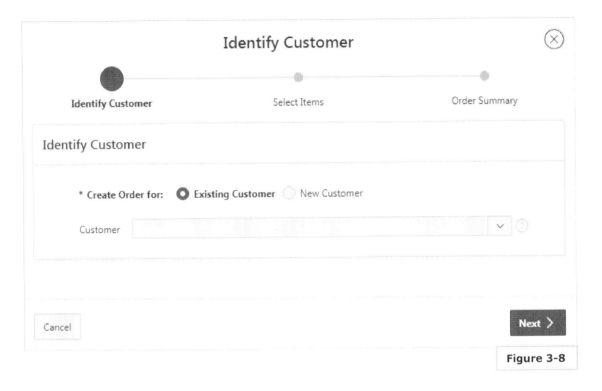

**Figure 3-8**

1. Go to *Shared Components | Navigation | Lists* and click the **Create** button.

2. Select the first **From Scratch** option and click **Next**.

3. Type **Order Wizard** in the *Name* box, set *Type* to **Static**, and click **Next**.

4. On the *Query or Static Values* screen, enter the following values and click **Next**.

**Figure 3-9**

5.  Click the **Create List** button on the *Confirm* screen.

6.  Modify the newly created **Order Wizard** list.

7.  Edit each list item and set *Target Type* attribute to **No Target** for all three list items. The *No Target* value is set because this list is intended to display the current order wizard step where the user is within the order processing module, and not to call a page in the application. In the *Current List Entry* section, set *List Entry Current for Pages Type* to **Comma Delimited Page List** for the three list items, and set the *List Entry Current for Condition* attribute individually, as shown in the following table and screenshot. Click the **Apply Changes** button to save the modifications.

| Property | Identify Customer | Select Items | Order Summary |
|---|---|---|---|
| List Entry Current for Condition | 11 | 12 | 14 |

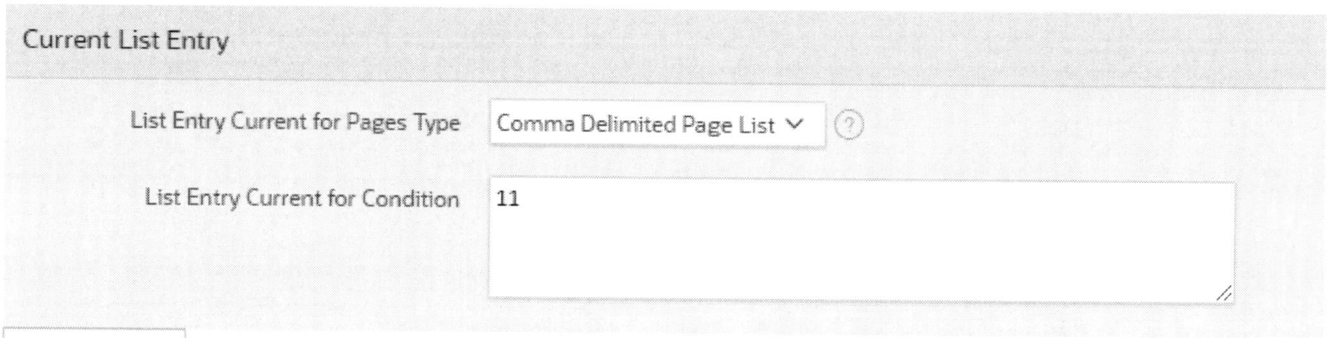

### Current List Entry

| | |
|---|---|
| List Entry Current for Pages Type | Comma Delimited Page List ⌄  ⑦ |
| List Entry Current for Condition | 11 |

**Figure 3-10**

The *List Entry Current for Pages Type* attribute specifies when this list entry should be current. Based on the value of this attribute, you define a condition to evaluate. When this condition is true, the list item becomes current. The template associated with list item gives users a visual indication about the active list item. The following figure illustrates the use of Order Wizard list. Being the first step in the order wizard, the *Identify Customer* list item is marked as current (when Page 11 is called to enter a new order), while the remaining two are displayed as non-current. After selecting a customer, when you move on to the next step to select ordered items, the *Select Items* entry becomes current and the first and last entries become inactive.

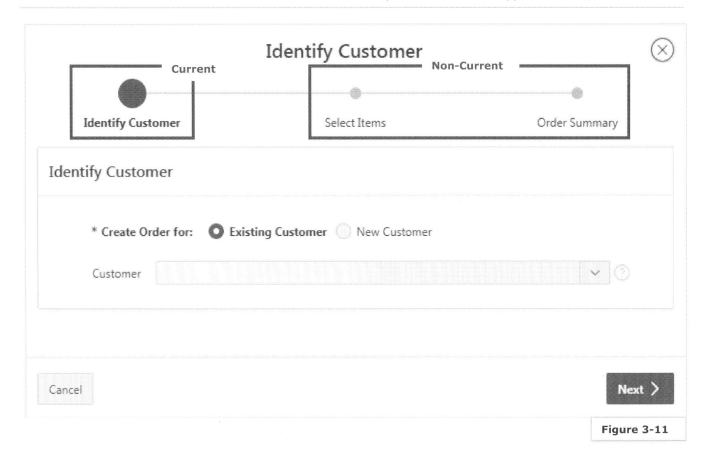

Figure 3-11

## 3.3 Navigation Bar

As discussed earlier, a navigation bar is also used to link various pages within an application. Typically, a navigation bar is used to access Help pages and also carries a Sign Out link. The location of a navigation bar depends upon the associated page template. When you create a navigation bar, you specify an image name, label, display sequence, and target location (a URL or a page). The navigation bar used in our application will show feedback page icon, Page Help entry, About Page entry, the id of the currently logged in user and a Sign Out link. All these entries are created automatically when you create a new application.

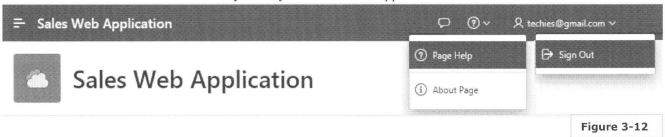

Figure 3-12

## 3.4 List of Values (LOV)

List of values is used to control input values and limits the user's selection. You can define two types of lists: Static and Dynamic. A static list of values is based on predefined display and return values. A dynamic list of values is based on a SQL query, and it is executed at runtime. In the following exercise, you will create both types of LOVs.

### 3.4.1 CATEGORIES LOV

In our application we have a Products setup module. The module will make use of three product categories. Each product in the application will fall under one of these categories. This LOV is created with the intention to present the three categories to the user (while creating a product record) to associate each product with one of these categories. The LOV will be utilized in Chapter 6 section 6.4.2.

1.  In Shared Components, click **Lists of Values** under the *Other Components* section.

2.  Click the **Create** button.

3.  Select the **From Scratch** option and click **Next**.

4.  Enter **Categories** for the LOV *Name*, select **Static** as the LOV type, and click **Next**.

5.  Fill in the values as shown in the following figure and click the **Create List of Values** button.

| Sequence | Display Value | Return Value |
| --- | --- | --- |
| 1 | Men | Men |
| 2 | Women | Women |
| 3 | Kids | Kids |

**Figure 3-13**

In the last step you entered a pair of static *Display* and *Return* values. At runtime these entries will display in the order they are entered. *Return Value* does not display, but is the value that is returned as a user selection to the Application Express engine.

## 3.4.2 PRODUCTS WITH PRICE LOV

Similar to the categories list of value, this one also limits user's selection by displaying product names with prices during order creation. Here you'll generate the list dynamically with the help of a SQL statement. The first column in the query, which concatenates product name and price, is used to display product information to the user, while the second column (product id) is returned for backend processing. You will utilize this LOV in Chapter 7 section 7.4.2.

1. Once again, click the **Create** button in *Lists of Values*.

2. Select **From Scratch** and click **Next**.

3. Enter **Products with Price** in the *Name* box. This time, select the **Dynamic** *Type* and click **Next**.

4. On the *List of Values Source* screen, select **SQL Query** for the *Source Type*, and enter the following query in the *Enter a SQL SELECT statement* box. The SQL query is available in BookCode\Chapter3 folder. If you are new to SQL, read Chapter 3 - *Fetch Data From Database* in my free SQL eBook.

```
SELECT apex_escape.html(product_name) || ' [$' || list_price || ']' d, product_id r
FROM demo_product_info
WHERE product_avail = 'Y'
ORDER BY 1
```

5. On the final *Column Mappings* screen, select **R** for *Return Column*, **D** for *Display Column* and click the **Create** button to finish the wizard.

### APEX_ESCAPE.HTML

The function APEX_ESCAPE.HTML is used to protect against XSS (Cross Site Scripting) attacks. It replaces characters that have special meaning in HTML with their escape sequence.

It converts occurrence of & to &amp
It converts occurrence of " to &quot
It converts occurrence of < to &lt
It converts occurrence of > to &gt

### 3.4.3 STATES LOV

This is a dynamic LOV and is based on a SQL SELECT query to fetch State names from the DEMO_STATES table. The query fetches both columns from the table. The LOV will be used in Chapter 5 section 5.4.2, where it will be attached to an input form page item.

1.  In *Lists of Values*, click the **Create** button.

2.  Select the **From Scratch** option and click **Next**.

3.  Enter **States** in the *Name* box, select **Dynamic** for its type, and click **Next**.

4.  On the *List of Values Source* screen, select **SQL Query** for the *Source Type*, and enter the following query in the *Enter a SQL SELECT statement* box. Click **Next**.
    ```
    select state_name display_value, state_id return_value
    from demo_states order by 1
    ```

5.  On the final *Column Mappings* screen, select **RETURN_VALUE** for *Return Column*, **DISPLAY_VALUE** for *Display Column* and click the **Create** button to create the LOV.

### 3.4.4 NEW OR EXISTING CUSTOMER LOV

This static list will be incorporated in the initial Order Wizard step (Chapter 7 Section 7.5.4) to select an existing customer for a new order or to create a new one.

1.  In *Lists of Values*, click **Create**.

2.  Select **From Scratch** and click **Next**.

3.  Enter **NEW OR EXISTING CUSTOMER** in the *Name* box, select **Static** as its *Type* and click **Next**.

4.  Fill in the display and return values as shown in the following figure and click the **Create List of Values** button.

| Sequence | Display Value | Return Value |
|---|---|---|
| 1 | Existing Customer | EXISTING |
| 2 | New Customer | NEW |

**Figure 3-14**

## 3.5 Images

You can reference images within your application by uploading them to the Images Repository. When you upload an image, you can specify whether it is available to all applications or a specific application. Images uploaded as shared components can be referenced throughout an application. They may include images for application menus or buttons or may represent icons that, when clicked, allow users to modify or delete data. One important point to remember here is that the images uploaded to the images repository should not be directly related to the application's data such as images of products and employees. Such images must be stored in the application's schema alongside the data to which the image is related. You'll follow this approach in Chapter 6 to save each product's image along with other information in a database table.

Application Express images are divided into two categories:

- **Workspace images** are available to all applications for a given workspace

- **Application images** are available for only one application

In the following set of steps, you'll add your application's logo to the images repository. The logo appears at the top of every page in the application.

1. In Shared Components, click **Static Application Files** under the *Files* section.

2. Click the **Create File** button.

3. Click the **Drag and Drop Files** button and select *logo.ico* file, which is available in the book code.

Figure 3-15

4. Click the **Create** button. After uploading the image, you need to tell Oracle APEX to use this file as your application logo. To pass this information, execute the following steps.

5. In Shared Components click **User Interface Attributes** under *User Interface* section.

6. In the Logo section, select **Image and Text** for *Logo* property.

7. Enter **#APP_FILES#logo.ico** in *Image URL* box, and enter **Sales Web Application** in the *Text* box. An application logo can be an image, text, image and text, or based on custom markup. When you select a type for your application logo, additional attributes appear depending upon your selection. With this selection, your application logo and application name both will be displayed on each application page. The APP_FILES built-in template substitution string is used to reference uploaded images, JavaScript, and cascading style sheets that are specific to a given application and are not shared over many applications. You must use this substitution string if you upload a file and make it specific to an application. Note that you must use the correct case for the image file name and extension, else the logo will not be displayed at runtime. Click the **Apply Changes** button.

Run the application. The application logo and text should resemble the following figure.

**Figure 3-16**

## Summary

In this chapter, you created all the components with relevant references required by the application. These shared components were created declaratively with the help of Oracle APEX wizards to demonstrate the log-code nature of this technology and tackling redundancy. From the next chapter, you will create pages of your web application (starting with the Home page) and will see all these shared components in action. After creating an application page, you can see a list of all Shared Components utilized on that page by accessing its Shared Components tab ⚙ in the Page Designer.

# 4

# PREPARE APPLICATION

# DASHBOARD

## 4.1 About the Home Page

Every website on the Internet has a home page. Technically referred to as the default page, it is the page that comes up when you call a website without mentioning a specific page. For example, if you call Oracle's official website using the URL www.oracle.com, the first page you see is the default or home page of the website. It is the page that represents the objective of a website. Similar to a website, a web application also carries this page. In Oracle APEX this page is created by default when you create a new application. The login page, which you used to access the application in previous chapters, doesn't require any modification or enhancement. It comes with out-of-the-box functionalities and utilizes current authentication scheme to process login requests. The Home page, on the other hand, is created as a blank slate and needs to be populated with content relevant to your application's theme. For instance, the Home page of your Sales Web Application, as illustrated in the following figure, will show charts and other summarized information related to sales.

**Figure 4-1 –** The Application Home Page

Let's experience the Oracle APEX declarative development environment by completing this page of our web application, which is a dashboard and holds six regions to present different views of sales data.

## 4.2 Modify the Home Page

Before you start the proceedings, I'd recommend to first take a look at Chapter 2 section 2.6 and 2.9 to acquaint yourself with the Page Designer interface and how to access your workspace. Once you're comfortable with that, execute the following steps to modify properties of the Home page.

1.  Sign in to your workspace. Click the **App Builder** option in the main menu and then click the **Edit** icon under the *Sales Web Application* - see Figure 3-3 in chapter 3.

2.  Click the **Home** page icon (if you're browsing the page in Icon view). This action will open the definitions of the Home page in the Page Designer interface.

## 4.2.1 Modify Page Attributes

Modify *Name* and *Title* properties of the Home page with meaningful labels. The *Name* property gives the page a meaningful name for recognition, while the Application Express engine uses the title you specify here in place of the #TITLE# substitution string used in the page template. This title is inserted between <TITLE> and </TITLE> HTML tags.

On the *Rendering* tab to your left, click the root node to refresh the Property Editor (on the right side) with the Home page properties. Set the properties mentioned in the following table and click the **Save** button (at the top-right corner). These are the properties that are usually enough to set for the main page. However, there are some more you must be curious to know about. Click a property in the *Property Editor* and then click the *Help* tab (in the Central pane) to see the purpose of that attribute. Each page in an application is recognized by a unique number, which is used for internal processing – for example, in a URL. By providing a unique name, you *visually* differentiate it from other application pages. The value you provide for the *Title* property is displayed in your browser's tab.

| Property | Value |
|---|---|
| Name | Sales Web Application |
| Title | Sales Web Application |

## 4.3 Create Regions

You put items (Text Field, Select List, Radio Group, and so on) on a page under a specific region. A region is an area on a page that serves as a container for content. You can create multiple regions to visually segregate different sections on a page and to group page elements. A region may carry a report, chart, static HTML content, items, buttons, and some other types of page items. Each region can have its own template applied, which controls its appearance. The following sub-sections demonstrate how you can create multiple regions to present different information on a single page. Some of these regions will use Oracle JET Charts. Charts in Oracle APEX have been completely revamped. Now Oracle APEX has integrated charting based on Oracle JavaScript Extension Toolkit (JET) charting library. Oracle JET Charts is a component of the Oracle JavaScript Extension Toolkit (JET), an open source toolkit based on modern JavaScript, CSS3, and HTML5 design and development principles. These charts are fully HTML5 capable and work on any modern browser regardless of platform, screen size, or features.

87

To remove a component (such as a region or an item) from a page, right-click the desired component in the Rendering section, and select Delete (A) from the context menu. If you just created the component, simply click Undo (B) on the Toolbar to remove it from the page.

## 4.3.1 Top Orders by Date

Let's create the first region on the Home page. This region will display top five orders by date from the database using a bar chart. The chart is populated using a SQL SELECT statement, which fetches summarized sales figures for each date from the Orders table.

On the *Rendering* tab (A), right-click **Components** (B), and select **Create Region** (C) from the context menu to create a new region. This action will place a new region </> **New** under the *Body* node.

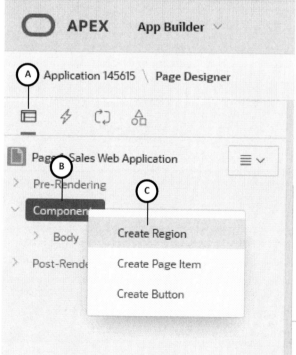

**Figure 4-2**
Create a New Region

Besides the region properties in the Property Editor, there is an *Attributes* tab, which contains region-specific properties. For example, the properties of a *Static Content* type region are different from a Chart region. Click the </> **New** node and set the following properties under the Region tab in the Property Editor on the right side. After setting the second attribute (*Type*), you will be informed through the Messages tab that there are some errors on the page. These messages relate to some mandatory properties you will set accordingly in subsequent sections.

| | Property | Value |
|---|---|---|
| 1 | Title | Top Orders by Date |
| 2 | Type (*under Identification*) | Chart |
| 3 | Location | Local Database |
| | Type (*under Source*) | SQL Query |
| | SQL Query | select to_char(o.order_timestamp,'Mon DD, YYYY') order_day,<br>　　　　SUM(o.order_total) sales<br>from  demo_orders o<br>group by to_char(o.order_timestamp,'Mon DD, YYYY'), order_timestamp<br>order by 2 desc nulls last<br>fetch first 5 rows only |
| 4 | Start New Row | On (*default*) |
| 5 | Column | Automatic (*default*) |
| 6 | Column Span | 4 |
| 7 | Show Region Icon (*under Template Options*) | Place a check mark to select this option |
| | Body Height (*under Template Options*) | 240px   (*Click OK to close the dialog screen*) |
| | Icon | fa-lg fa-apex |
| Click the **Attributes** tab in the Property Editor pane and set the following properties: | | |
| 8 | Type | Bar |
| 9 | Orientation | Horizontal |
| Click the **New** sub-node under *Series* and set the following properties: | | |
| 10 | Location (*under Source*) | Region Source |
| 11 | Label | ORDER_DAY |
| 12 | Value | SALES |
| 13 | Type (*under Link*) | Redirect to Page in this application |
| Click **No Link Defined** under *Target* and set the following properties in the Link Builder dialog box: | | |
| 14 | Type | Page in this application |
| 15 | Page | 4   (*Click OK to close the dialog screen*) |

The first property provides a meaningful title to the region – see Figure 4-1. It is a good practice to always provide a unique title to every region on a page. The title not only describes the purpose of a region, but also distinguishes it from others in Page Designer. If you are familiar with HTML and CSS, then you can also style this property by adding some HTML & CSS elements, like this:

```
<span style="color:blue"><i><b>Top Orders by Date</b></i></span>
```

In the second attribute, we set the *Type* of this region to *Chart*, because we want to display sales data graphically. By default, a new region is assigned the type *Static Content* with an empty source text, which is often used to explain the purpose of a page or a page component. For example, the *About* section on the right side of the App Builder interface is a static content region whose source is the displayed text. In the third attribute, we specified the location of the data, which is sourced from the local database in the current scenario. The two other available sources are *REST Enabled SQL* and *REST Source*. In *REST Enabled SQL* data is sourced from a remote database, while in *REST Source,* data is sourced from a RESTful web service defined using REST Data Sources. The *Type* attribute specifies how the data is queried. We set it to *SQL Query* to retrieve the data using a SQL Query, which fetches summarized sales data from the DEMO_ORDERS table.

The database applications created in Oracle APEX use a layout (comprising 12 columns) to position page elements. The fourth attribute (*Start New Row*) used in this region is set to *Yes* (which is the default) to put the region on a new row. Compare this value with the next region (*Sales for This Month*), where it is set to *No* to place that region adjacent to this one. The value *Automatic* in the *Column* attribute (5) automatically finds a column position for the region. Since there exists no elements on the current row, column number 1 will be used as the starting place to position this region. As you can see in Figure 4-3, there are three regions on a single row. Equally divided in a 12 columns layout, each region spans 4 columns and this is the value we will set for all the six regions on the Home page. The first region will span from column number 1 to 4, the second one from 5 to 8, and the third one from 9 to 12 – see Figure 4-3.

We also defined the height of this region in attribute 7, which you can set by clicking the *Template Options*. If the *Template* property is set to the default *Standard* value for a region, you can place an icon in the region header. First, select the *Show Region Icon* option (under the *Template Options*) to display the region icon in the region header beside the region title. Then, click the LOV for the *Icon* property (under *Appearance*), select a *Style* (for example, *Large*), and choose and icon from the provided list.

On the *Attributes* tab (8 and 9) you set the *Type* of this chart to horizontal bar.

When you set the region type to *Chart* (2), a *Series* node is placed under *Attributes* with a *New* sub-node under it. In this node you specify *Location* (10) for the *Series*. Since an SQL Query has already been defined, we set it to *Region Source*, which points to the region's SQL Query defined in the third attribute. By default, a chart is created with one series (named *New*), but you can add more (see Chapter 8 section 8.3 steps 5 and 6). The chart's *Label* attribute (11) is set to *ORDER_DAY* column to display values from this column as labels. The *Value* property (12) is set to *SALES* to show sales figures.

You can also define links on charts (as done in properties 13-15) that let you call another application page for browsing details. When you click *No Link Defined* under *Target*, a small window titled *Link Builder* comes up, where you specify details of the target page. Once you set the link type to "*Redirect to Page in this Application*", a property named *Target* appears where you provide the ID of the target application page you want to link with the chart (properties 14 and 15). The *Template* property (not indicated in the previous table) is set to *Standard* by default, which forms a border around the region and displays the region's title across the top.

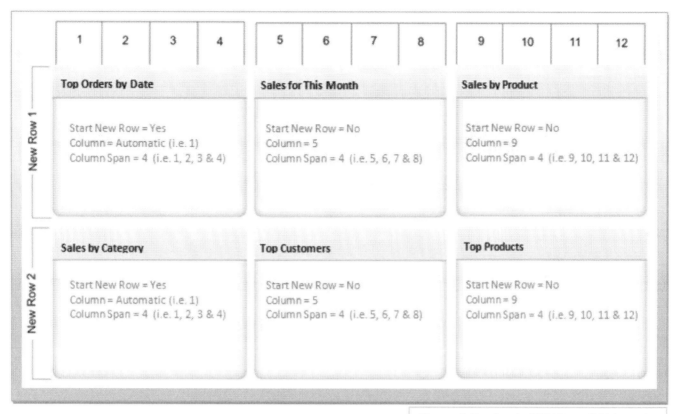

**Figure 4-3** – Oracle APEX Page Grid Layout

Oracle APEX enables you to test your work from time to time. For example, after completing this region you can save and run the page (by clicking the *Save and Run Page* button  appearing at the top-right corner) to check how the region appears on it. At this stage, your Home page will show just one region (*Top Orders by Date*) containing a bar chart. If you click any bar in the chart, the application tries to open Page 4 and throws an error, because the page doesn't exist. After completing Page 4 (Orders) in Chapter 7, when you run the Home page and click any of these links, Page 4 will be rendered carrying a list of orders.

## 4.3.2 Sales For This Month

As the name implies, this region will present sales figures in graphical format (using a Badge List) along with number of orders placed for the current month. The list is dynamically rendered based on a SQL Statement each time the page is viewed.

On the *Rendering* tab to your left, right-click **Components**, and select **Create Region** from the context menu. Again, a new region will be created just under the previous one. Set the following properties for this region in the *Property Editor*.

| | Property | Value |
|---|---|---|
| 1 | Title | Sales for This Month |
| 2 | Type | Classic Report |
| 3 | Location | Local Database |
| | Type | SQL Query |
| | SQL Query | SELECT sum(o.order_total) total_sales,<br>    count(distinct o.order_id) total_orders,<br>    count(distinct o.customer_id) total_customers<br>FROM demo_orders o<br>WHERE order_timestamp >=<br>    to_date(to_char(sysdate,'YYYYMM')\|\|'01','YYYYMMDD') |
| 4 | Start New Row | Off |
| 5 | Column | 5 |
| 6 | Column Span | 4 |
| 7 | Body Height *(under Template Options)* | 240px |

If a region is not created in the desired location, drag and drop it to the appropriate location in the rendering tree.

A *Classic Report* is a simple Oracle APEX report, which is based on a custom SQL SELECT statement or a PL/SQL function. In this exercise, we used it to fetch the desired data set. Later on, we will transform it to present the fetched data in graphical format. When you specify a SQL Query for a region, all columns you define in the query appear in a separate node (*Columns*) under that region.

Next, create a hidden page item by right-clicking the *Sales for this Month* region and selecting **Create Page Item** from the context menu. A new node named *Region Body* will be created with a new item ▣ P1_NEW. Click the new item and set the following properties:

| Property | Value |
|---|---|
| Name | P1_THIS_MONTH |
| Type | Hidden |
| Value Protected | On *(default)* |
| Type *(under Source)* | PL/SQL Expression |
| PL/SQL Expression | to_char(sysdate ,'MM')\|\|'01'\|\|to_char(sysdate ,'YYYY') |

The page item *P1_THIS_MONTH* is a hidden item and is used in the next section. It is added to store first day of the current month. You create hidden items on a page to store some values for behind-the-scene processing. This one evaluates current month using the *sysdate* function. Hidden items can be seen in the Page Designer, but they do not appear on the page at run time. Note that whenever you refer to a page item in links, you present it as a substitution string, which is preceded with an & and terminated with a period – see the *Value* property in serial 6 in the following table.

The *Value Protected* property specifies whether the item is protected. The *Yes* value prevents the value stored in the item from being manipulated when the page is posted. Note that if the Order Date column on Page 4 is rendered as 09-JAN-2017, then you will have to change the PL/SQL Expression like this:

'01-'||to_char(sysdate ,'MON')||'-'||to_char(sysdate ,'YYYY')

In the *Rendering* section, expand the **Columns** node under the *Sales for This Month* region, and click the **TOTAL_SALES** column.

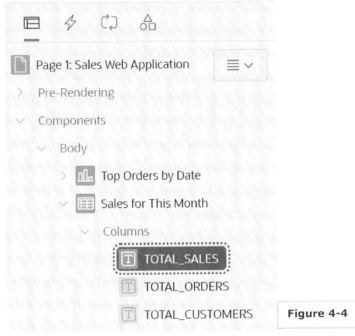

Figure 4-4

This will refresh the *Properties* pane to show properties of the currently selected column. Set the following properties for TOTAL_SALES to transform it into a link.

| | Property | Value |
|---|---|---|
| 1 | Type | Link |
| 2 | Format Mask | 5,234 |
| **Click No Link Defined** under *Target* and set the following properties: | | |
| 3 | Type | Page in this application |
| 4 | Page | 4 |
| 5 | Name *(under Set Items)* | IRGTE_ORDER_DATE |
| 6 | Value *(under Set Items)* | &P1_THIS_MONTH. *(do not forget to add the trailing period)* |
| 7 | Clear Cache | RIR,4 |
| 8 | Action | Reset Pagination |
| **Click OK to close the Link Builder - Target** dialog box | | |
| 9 | Link Text | #TOTAL_SALES# |

In the first attribute (*Type*), you specify that the column is to be displayed as a link. The *Format Mask* property (2) is actually a list of values that shows some common currency and date/time formats when you click the up-arrow. When you select a format from this list, its mask appears in the property's text box. In the current scenario, you selected 5,234.10 as the format mask for TOTAL_SALES column, which produces the mask

999G999G999G999G990D00. In this mask, 9 denotes an optional digit, 0 a required digit, G stands for thousand separator, and D is for decimal point. Here, the sales value will be displayed with thousand separators and two decimal places.

The remaining properties actually define the link. First, you specify that the link should call a page in the current application (property 3) followed by the target page number (property 4). To call another application page, it is suffice to transform a column into a link by setting these three values (*Link*, *Page in this application*, and *Page Number*). Recall that in the previous region you formed a similar kind of link. In the *Set Items* section in the *Link Builder* dialog, you select a *Name* and *Value* to specify session state for an item. Using this section you configure the values to be passed from the current page to the target page. In the current scenario, the *Name* (5) and *Value* (6) properties form a filter argument to display current month's order on the target page (Page 4 – Orders, to be created in Chapter 7). The values for these properties are usually picked from the adjacent LOVs using the Page attribute, but due to absence of Page 4 of our application, we entered them manually.

In the current scenario, we used just one name/value pair to filter the interactive report on the target page. However, this section allows you to set as many filters as you want. Each time you provide a value, another row is appended, thus allowing you to enter another pair of name/value. You can use this section to also specify target page's items in the *Name* column and can set their values using the *Value* box. For example, to set a customer's credit limit item's value on the target page, enter the name of that item (P7_CREDIT_LIMIT) in the *Name* box and type the corresponding value (5000) in the *Value* box. This way, when you call the target page, the value (5000) appears in the credit limit item.

The *Clear Cache* attribute (7) resets the interactive report on Page 4. The eighth attribute resets pagination of the target page. The *Link Text* attribute (9) is set to Total Sales, which specifies the column to be displayed as a link. Note that column names are enclosed in # symbol when you specify them in *Link Text* attribute.

At run-time the link is formed like this (if the application's Friendly URL attribute is turned off):
```
f?p=145615:4:8824748217892::NO:RP,RIR,4:IRGTE_ORDER_DATE:01012018
```

The above link is generated using the following syntax:
```
f?p=&APP_ID.:Page:Sessionid::NO:RP,RIR,4:IRGTE_(itemname):itemvalue (stored in &P1_THIS_MONTH item)
```

The following table defines the parameters used in the URL:

| Argument | Explanation |
|---|---|
| &APP_ID. | The first argument in the URL is reserved for application ID (18132). The expression used here is called a substitution string that holds the application ID. Instead of hard-coding application IDs, Oracle APEX uses this substitution string to make an application more portable. Note that substitution strings are always preceded with an "&" and post-fixed with a period. |
| : | The colon special character is used in the APEX URL as an argument separator. Since the URL contains no REQUEST argument, the position of this argument is left empty—see the additional colon before the debug argument (NO). |
| 4 | This is the target page (Page 4 – Orders) we are calling in the URL. |
| Sessionid | The number (8824748217892) appearing in the URL is the session ID of our application and is used to create links between application pages by maintaining the same session state among them. Note that session ids are managed automatically by Oracle APEX. |
| NO | References the debug flag, which is used to display application processing details. The value NO says do not enter the debug mode. |
| RP,RIR,4 | Placed in the URL's ClearCache position, this argument resets pagination for the interactive report on Page 4. *RP* stands for *Reset Pagination* and *RIR* for *Reset Interactive Report*. Pagination provides the end user with information about the number of rows and the current position within the result set. You control how pagination displays by making selections from *Pagination Type* attribute in the Property Editor. The clear cache section can have RIR or CIR or RP to reset, clear, or reset the pagination of the primary default reports of all interactive report regions on the target page. |
| IRGTE_ORDER_DATE | This argument is used in the *itemNames* position. The IR (Interactive Report) string is used along with the *greater than and equal to* operator (GTE), followed by an item name (ORDER_DATE - an item on Page 4). This argument acts as a filter and is used in conjunction with the *itemValue* (&P1_THIS_MONTH. mentioned underneath) to only display current month's orders. In simple words it says: *The order date in the interactive report is greater than or equal to the item value.* |
| &P1_THIS_MONTH. | Used in the *itemValue* position, the value stored in this hidden item is forwarded to the target page. To create a filter on an interactive report in a link, use the string *IR<operator>_<target column alias>* in the *ItemNames* section of the URL and pass the filter value in the corresponding location in the *ItemValues* section of the URL. See section 2.7 in Chapter 2 for further details on Oracle APEX f?p syntax. Other operators you can use to filter an interactive report include:<br><br>EQ = Equals (the default operator) / LTE = Less than or equal to<br>NEQ = Not Equals / GTE = Greater than or equal to<br>LT = Less than / LIKE = SQL LIKE operator<br>GT = Greater than / N = Null<br><br>To apply the filter, you must use correct date format mask in the SQL query for order_timestamp column. For example, if the Order Date column on Page 4 appears as 01-JAN-2017, then you must use 'DD/MON/YYYY' format mask. |

Select the **TOTAL_CUSTOMERS** column and set the *Type* attribute of this column to **Hidden Column**. By setting a column's *Type* property to *Hidden*, you make it invisible at run-time. Click the *Sales for This Month* region, and click the **Attributes** tab in the Properties pane on the right side. Switch its *Template* from *Standard* to **Badge List**, click the *Template Options* and set *Badge Size* to **128px**, *Layout* to **Span Horizontally**, and click **OK**. By setting these region properties, the derived one row summarized report will be presented as a badge list, spanned horizontally. Also set *Pagination Type* to **No Pagination (Show All Rows)**. Often only a certain number of rows of a report display on a page. To include additional rows, the application user needs to navigate to the next page of the report. Pagination provides the user with information about the number of rows and the current position within the result set. Pagination also defines the style of links or buttons used to navigate to the next or previous page.

Click **Save and Run Page** button to see this region with two badges on it displaying current month's sales and number of orders placed. The first badge acts as a link and leads you to Page 4 to display details of the summarized data. Since Page 4 will be created in Chapter 7, once again you will get *Page Not Found* message if you click this badge.

## 4.3.3 Sales by Product

This region is intended to show sale figures for individual products using a pie chart. You see those figures when you move the mouse pointer over the pie slices. Create another region as mentioned in the previous exercises, and set the following properties.

If you are creating a multi-series chart, then you can use legend (9) to identify each series on the chart. Using the legend properties you can specify whether to display it, and if so, where it should be placed on the chart. You will use these properties in Chapter 8.

| | Property | Value |
|---|---|---|
| 1 | Title | Sales by Product |
| 2 | Type | Chart |
| | Location | Local Database |
| | Type | SQL Query |
| 3 | SQL Query | SELECT   p.product_name\|\|' [\$'\|\|p.list_price\|\|']' product,<br>              SUM(oi.quantity * oi.unit_price) sales<br>FROM   demo_order_items oi, demo_product_info p<br>WHERE   oi.product_id = p.product_id<br>GROUP BY p.product_id, p.product_name, p.list_price<br>ORDER BY p.product_name desc |
| 4 | Start New Row | Off |
| 5 | Column | 9 |
| 6 | Column Span | 4 |
| 7 | Body Height *(under Template Options)* | 240px |
| | Click the **Attributes** tab in the Property Editor pane and set the following properties: | |
| 8 | Type | Pie |
| 9 | Show *(under Legend)* | Off |
| | Click the **New** sub-node under *Series* and set the following properties: | |
| 10 | Location *(under Source)* | Region Source |
| 11 | Label | PRODUCT |
| 12 | Value | SALES |
| 13 | Show *(under Label)* | On *(Specifies whether the label(s) should be rendered on the chart.)* |

## 4.3.4 Sales by Category

This region will present sale figures for each product category. Note that there are three categories in the products table: Men, Women, and Accessories. Each product in the DEMO_PRODUCT_INFO table belongs to one of these categories. This time, we will add a region using the drag and drop feature provided in Oracle APEX. Following the figure illustrated below, drag the **Chart** icon from the *Regions* gallery and drop it just under the *Top Orders by Date* region. A chart region will appear with relevant properties. After placing the chart region at its proper location, set the properties presented in the table provided on the next page.

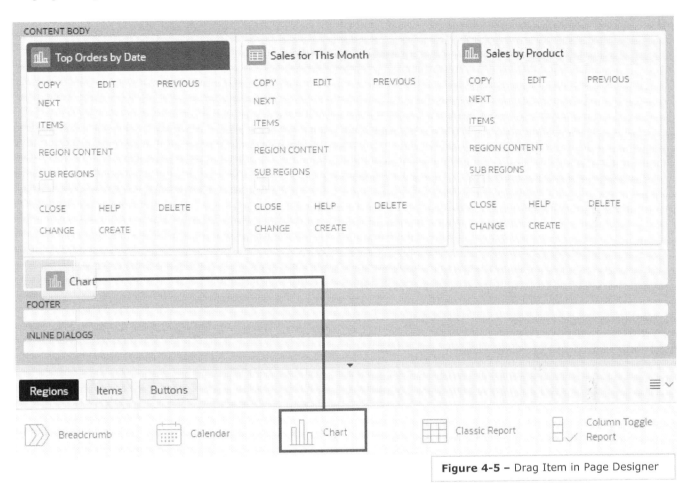

**Figure 4-5 – Drag Item in Page Designer**

Here are the modified region properties. Note that I changed the default chart color (13) using the Color Picker tool.

| | Property | Value |
|---|---|---|
| 1 | Title | Sales by Category |
| 2 | Type | Chart *(this time it is set by default)* |
| | Location | Local Database |
| | Type | SQL Query |
| 3 | SQL Query | SELECT    p.category Category, sum(o.order_total) Sales<br>FROM    demo_orders o, demo_order_items oi,<br>           demo_product_info p<br>WHERE   o.order_id = oi.order_id AND<br>          oi.product_id = p.product_id<br>GROUP BY category<br>ORDER BY 2 desc |
| 4 | Start New Row | On |
| 5 | Column | 1 |
| 6 | Column Span | 4 |
| 7 | Body Height *(under Template Options)* | 240px |
| | **Click the Attributes tab in the Property Editor pane and set the following properties:** | |
| 8 | Type | Bar |
| 9 | Show *(under Legend)* | Off |
| | **Click the New sub-node under Series and set the following properties:** | |
| 10 | Location *(under Source)* | Region Source |
| 11 | Label | CATEGORY |
| 12 | Value | SALES |
| 13 | Color *(under Appearance)* | #18A0C2 |

## 4.3.5 Top Customers Region

This region will display top six customers with highest orders and will present the information in text format. Create a new region by dragging the **Classic Report** icon ⊞ from the gallery and dropping it under the *Sales by Category* region. The source of a *Classic Report* is a SQL query. Each time the page is rendered, Oracle APEX evaluates the query and displays the result within the region. Once you specify row and column properties using the following table, the region will appear next to the *Sales by Category* region.

| | Property | Value |
|---|---|---|
| 1 | Title | Top Customers |
| 2 | Type | Classic Report *(should be already set)* |
| | Location | Local Database |
| | Type | SQL Query |
| 3 | SQL Query | SELECT b.cust_last_name \|\| ', ' \|\| b.cust_first_name<br>        \|\| ' - '\|\| count(a.order_id) \|\|' Order(s)' customer_name,<br>        SUM(a.ORDER_TOTAL) order_total,  b.customer_id **id**<br>FROM   demo_orders a, DEMO_CUSTOMERS b<br>WHERE a.customer_id = b.customer_id<br>GROUP BY b.customer_id, b.cust_last_name \|\| ', '  \|\|<br>         b.cust_first_name<br>ORDER BY NVL(SUM(a.ORDER_TOTAL),0) DESC |
| 4 | Start New Row | Off |
| 5 | Column | 5 |
| 6 | Column Span | 4 |
| 7 | Body Height *(under Template Options)* | 240px |

On the *Rendering* tab, expand the **Columns** node under the *Top Customers* region, and click the **CUSTOMER_NAME** column. Set the following properties to transform this column into a link. The *#ID#* substitution string references the third column in the above SELECT query. Just like you use substitution strings to reference a page item, the standard procedure in Oracle APEX to refer to a column value is to enclose it between the # symbols.

| | Property | Value |
|---|---|---|
| 8 | Type | Link |
| **Click No Link Defined** under *Target* and set the following properties: | | |
| 9 | Type | Page in this application |
| 10 | Page | 7 |
| 11 | Name | P7_CUSTOMER_ID |
| 12 | Value | #ID# |
| 13 | Clear Cache | 7 |

In this table, we specified properties about a link we want to create. The purpose of setting these properties is to place hyperlinks on customer name column to provide drill-down capability. We specified the CUSTOMER_NAME column in the *Link Text* attribute. When you run this page, each customer's name appears as a hyperlink, clicking which calls customer's profile page (Page 7). We set *Page* attribute to 7, which is the page we want to navigate to. We also forwarded the customer's ID (#ID#) to Page 7. The value P7_CUSTOMER_ID refers to an item on Page 7 that will be populated with the value held in #ID#. It is forwarded to Page 7 from the Home page to display profile of the selected customer.

Click the **ORDER_TOTAL** column and set *Format Mask* to **$5,234.10**. Select the **ID** column and set the *Type* property (under *Identification*) to **Hidden Column** to hide this column at run-time.

Click the **Attributes** tab and set the following properties for this region:

| Property | Value |
|---|---|
| Pagination Type | No Pagination *(Show All Rows)* |
| Maximum Row to Process *(under Performance)* | 6 |
| Type *(under Heading)* | None |

Pagination is suppressed since we want to see only six records in the region. We also set *Heading Type* to *None* to suppress column headings.

Click **Save and Run Page** button to test the progress.

## 4.3.6 Top Products Region

This region is similar to the *Top Customers* region and displays six top selling products. Due to similarity between the two regions, you will create this region by copying the *Top Customers* region. Right-click the *Top Customers* region, and select **Duplicate** from the context menu. A copy of the source region will be appended just under it. Set the following attributes for the new region.

| | Property | Value |
|---|---|---|
| 1 | Title | Top Products |
| 2 | Type | Classic Report |
| | Location | Local Database |
| | Type | SQL Query |
| 3 | SQL Query | SELECT  p.product_name\|\|' - '\|\|SUM(oi.quantity)\|\|' x' <br> \|\|to_char(p.list_price,'L999G99')\|\|'' product, <br> SUM(oi.quantity * oi.unit_price) sales, <br> p.product_id <br> FROM   demo_order_items oi,   demo_product_info p <br> WHERE oi.product_id = p.product_id <br> GROUP BY p.Product_id, p.product_name, p.list_price <br> ORDER BY 2 desc |
| 4 | Start New Row | Off |
| 5 | Column | 9 |
| 6 | Column Span | 4 |
| 7 | Body Height *(under Template Options)* | 240px |

Expand the *Columns* node and click the **PRODUCT** column to set the following properties:

| | Property | Value |
|---|---|---|
| 8 | Type | Link |
| Click **No Link Defined** under *Target* and set the following properties: | | |
| 9 | Type | Page in this application |
| 10 | Page | 6 |
| 11 | Name | P6_PRODUCT_ID |
| 12 | Value | #PRODUCT_ID# |
| 13 | Clear Cache | 6 |

Click the **SALES** column and set its *Format Mask* to **$5,234.10**. Select the **PRODUCT_ID** column and set its *Type* property to **Hidden Column**.

Click the **Attributes** tab to set the following properties:

| Property | Value |
|---|---|
| Pagination Type | No Pagination (Show All Rows) |
| Maximum Row  to Process *(under Performance)* | 6 |
| Type *(under Heading)* | None |

Click the **Save and Run Page** button to see how all the six regions appear on the Home page.

## 4.4 Create Buttons

After creating all the regions, your next task is to create buttons on top of each region. These buttons provide drill-down functionality and take user to relevant pages to dig further details for the provided summarized information. Some of these regions will have a pair of buttons (add and view) to create a new record and to browse further details of the provided information. For instance, if you click the *Add Order* button in the *Top Order by Date* region, you will be redirected to Page 11 to add a new order.

### 4.4.1 View Orders Button

This button is used to view a list of all customer orders. To create this button, right-click the **Top Orders by Date** region and select **Create Button** from the context menu. This way, the button will be created in the selected region.

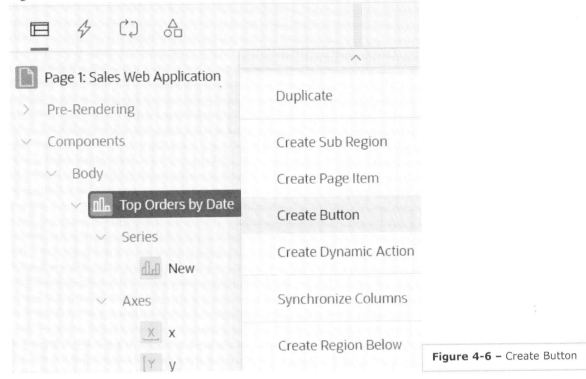

**Figure 4-6 –** Create Button

Set the following properties for the new button. Among these properties is the *Position* property, which provides you with over a dozen values. The best way to understand the other options is to try each one to see button placement on the page.

| Property | Value |
|---|---|
| Button Name | VIEW_ORDERS |
| Label | View Orders *(appears as a tooltip when you move over the button at run-time)* |
| Region | Top Orders by Date *(the region where the button will appear)* |
| Position | Edit *(try other options as well to observe different positions)* |
| Button Template | Icon *(the button will be displayed as an icon)* |
| Icon | fa-chevron-right *(the name of an icon from the APEX's repository)* |
| Action | Redirect to Page in this Application |
| Target | Type = Page in this application<br>Page = 4 |

## 4.4.2 Add Order Button

This one calls Order Wizard (to be created in Chapter 7) to place a new order. Right-click the **VIEW_ORDERS** button and select **Create Button Below**. A new button will be added just under the previous one. Set the following properties for this new button:

| Property | Value |
|---|---|
| Button Name | ADD_ORDER |
| Label | Enter New Order |
| Region | Top Orders by Date |
| Position | Edit |
| Button Template | Icon |
| Icon | fa-plus |
| Action | Redirect to Page in this Application |
| Target | Type = Page in this application<br>Page = 11<br>Clear Cache=11 |

## 4.4.3 View Orders For This Month Button

This button will drill-down into current month's order details. As illustrated in the following figure, drag an icon button from the *Buttons* gallery and drop it in the **EDIT** position under the *Sales for this Month* region. A new button will be added to this region. Select it and set the properties mentioned just after the illustration. The link properties set here are similar to those set earlier in section 4.3.2.

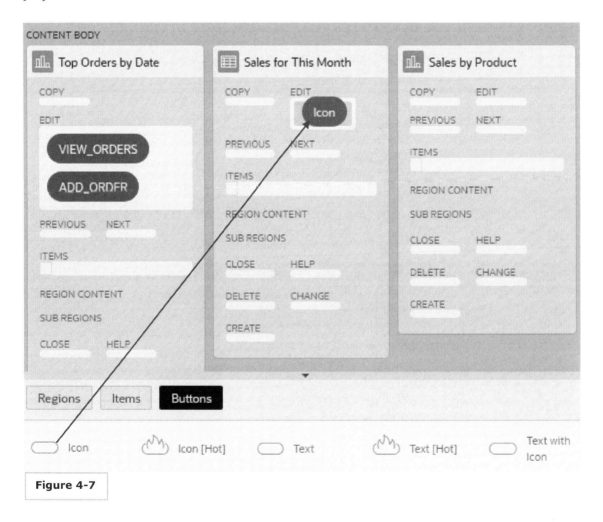

**Figure 4-7**

| Property | Value |
| --- | --- |
| Button Name | VIEW_MONTH_ORDERS |
| Label | View Orders for This Month |
| Region | Sales for This Month |
| Position | Edit *(already set)* |
| Button Template | Icon *(already set)* |
| Icon | fa-chevron-right |
| Action | Redirect to Page in this Application |
| Target | Type = Page in this Application<br>Page = 4<br>Name = IRGTE_ORDER_DATE<br>Value = &P1_THIS_MONTH.<br>Clear Cache = RIR,4 |

### 4.4.4 View Customers Button

You'll place two buttons in the *Top Customers* region. Create these buttons using either of the two methods applied above and set respective properties as mentioned below. The first button will be used to view a list of customers on Page 2 of the application.

| Property | Value |
| --- | --- |
| Button Name | VIEW_CUSTOMERS |
| Label | View Customers |
| Region | Top Customers |
| Position | Edit |
| Button Template | Icon |
| Icon | fa-chevron-right |
| Action | Redirect to Page in this Application |
| Target | Type = Page in this Application<br>Page = 2 |

### 4.4.5 Add Customer Button

This button is used to add a new customer record. When clicked, it will call Page 7 (Customers – to be created in the next chapter). The target page will appear on top of the Home page (as a modal dialog) carrying a blank form to enter new customer's credentials. Right-click the VIEW_CUSTOMERS button and select **Create Button Below** from the context menu. Set the following properties for the new button.

| Property | Value |
| --- | --- |
| Button Name | ADD_CUSTOMER |
| Label | Add Customer |
| Region | Top Customers |
| Position | Edit |
| Button Template | Icon |
| Icon | fa-plus |
| Action | Redirect to Page in this Application |
| Target | Type = Page in this application<br>Page = 7<br>Clear Cache = 7 |

## 4.4.6 View Products Button

Create the following two buttons in the *Top Products* region. The first one leads you to the main products page to display a list of all products.

| Property | Value |
|---|---|
| Button Name | VIEW_PRODUCTS |
| Label | View Products |
| Region | Top Products |
| Position | Edit |
| Button Template | Icon |
| Icon | fa-chevron-right |
| Action | Redirect to Page in this Application |
| Target | Type = Page in this Application<br>Page = 3 |

## 4.4.7 Add Product Button

This one calls Page 6 to add a new product.

| Property | Value |
|---|---|
| Button Name | ADD_PRODUCT |
| Label | Add Product |
| Region | Top Products |
| Position | Edit |
| Button Template | Icon |
| Icon | fa-plus |
| Action | Redirect to Page in this Application |
| Target | Type = Page in this Application<br>Page = 6<br>Clear Cache = 6 |

At this stage, all the seven buttons are placed at their proper locations with the expected functionalities and are ready for partial test. To remind you again, these buttons will be productive only after creating all relevant pages indicated in their respective *Target* properties.

## 4.5 Styling Page Elements

A cascading style sheet (CSS) provides a way to control the style of a web page without changing its structure. When used properly, a CSS separates visual properties such as color, margins, and fonts from the structure of the HTML document. Oracle APEX includes themes containing templates to reference their own CSS. The style rules defined in each CSS for a particular theme also determine the way reports and regions display. CSS can be added to APEX applications inline, as CSS file(s) or through ThemeRoller.

Depending on your requirements, you can add CSS to your application at the:

- Page Level
- Page Template Level
- Theme Style Level
- Theme Level
- User Interface Level

In this exercise, I'll demonstrate how to apply CSS at user interface level. Here you'll upload a custom CSS file carrying just one rule to style all six regions of the home page. The file named AppCss.css available in the source code contains the following rule, which creates a rounded border and places inset shadow around the regions. For more details on CSS, see Chapter 7 section 7.6.1.

.region {background:white;border-radius:10px 10px 10px 10px;box-shadow: inset 0px 0px 30px #dfdbdf}

Execute the following steps to apply CSS at user interface level:

1. Go to **Shared Components** page and click **Static Application Files** in the Files section.

2. Click the **Create File** button.

3. Click **Drag and Drop Files**, select **AppCss.css** file from the source code (Chapter 4 folder) and click the **Create** button. The css file will be added to the static application files listing. Copy the Reference entry (*#APP_FILES#AppCss.css*) appearing on this page to your clipboard by clicking the icon next to it. The APP_FILES substitution string is used to reference uploaded images, JavaScript, and cascading style sheets that are specific to a given application and are not shared over many applications. Recall that you used this substitution string earlier in chapter 3 to reference the application logo.

4. Next, add the CSS file to User Interface. In Shared Components' User Interface section, click **User Interface Attributes**.

5. On the *User Interface* tab, click the **Cascading Style Sheets** sub-tab and press **Ctrl+V** to append the reference text in the File URLs box under the existing URL.

**Figure 4-8**

6. Click **Apply Changes**.

7. Finally, you have to apply this CSS rule to your region. Here's how it is done. Open the home page (Page1) of your application and select the first region - *Top Orders by Date*. In the properties pane, scroll down to the *Appearance* section and enter **region** (a class defined in the AppCss.css file) in *CSS Classes* attribute. CSS allows you to specify your own selectors called "id" and "class". The id selector is used to specify a style for a single, unique element. It uses the id attribute of the HTML element, and is defined with a "#" identifier. The class selector, on the other hand, is used to specify a style for a group of elements. This means you can set a particular style for many HTML elements with the same class. It uses the HTML class attribute, and is defined with a "." identifier. Add the **region** class to the *CSS Classes* property of the remaining five regions.

## Test Your Work

Click the **Save and Run Page** button to see the Home page, which should now look similar to the one illustrated in Figure 4-1 at the beginning of this chapter.

## Summary

Congratulations! You've created your first professional looking page in Oracle APEX. In this chapter, you were provided with the flavor of declarative development where you added contents to a blank page using simple interactive procedures. You also learned how to modify properties to customize the look and feel of this page. This is the uniqueness and beauty of Oracle APEX that allows you to create pages rapidly without writing tons of code. The following list reminds you of Oracle APEX features you learned in this chapter:

- *Region* – You added six regions to the Home page to display different types of contents. You used different types of charts, badge list, and classic reports to populate these regions via simple SQL statements.

- *Grid Layout* – You learned how to arrange multiple regions on a page using Oracle APEX's 12 columns grid layout.

- *URL & Links* – Oracle APEX makes it fairly easy to link application pages together by setting a handful of properties. You also got an idea about how Oracle APEX formulates a URL and passes values to the target page using a handful of link properties.

- *Buttons* – A button can also be used to link application pages. You created a few buttons to access different application pages.

- *Apply Styles* – You learned how to add custom styles to page elements through user interface level.

In the next chapter, you will learn about Interactive Grid and how to create web forms to receive user input.

# 5

# MANAGING

# CUSTOMERS

## 5.1 About Customer Management

Whenever you create a sales application you add a mandatory customer management module to it. In this setup, you maintain profiles of customers including their ids, names, and addresses. This information is then used in other application segments – for example, customer orders and invoices. Every new customer is provided with a unique id, either manually or automatically, by a built-in process. In this book these ids will be generated automatically through a database object called a *Sequence*. Using the information from this module you can analyze a business from the perspective of customers. For example, you can evaluate how much business you have done with your customers either by location or by product, as you did in the previous chapter where you created the *Top Customers* region. In this chapter, you will create a setup to manage customers' profiles that will allow you to:

- Browse and search customer records
- Modify customers profiles
- Add record of a new customer to the database
- Remove a customer from the database

This module is based on the DEMO_CUSTOMERS table, which was created in chapter 2. In this chapter, you'll create two pages with the help of Oracle APEX wizard to view and edit customers' information. The first one (Page 2 Figure 5-1) is an interactive grid, which displays a list of all customers from the aforementioned database table using a SQL SELECT query. The second one (Page 7 Figure 5-6) is an input form to receive details of a new customer, modify the record of an existing customer, and delete one from the database. To keep data integrity, those customers who have some existing orders cannot be removed from the database – see chapter 2 section 2.10 step 11. Each customer's name appears as a link in the interactive grid. When you click the name of a customer, the form page appears with complete profile of the selected customer. Let's get our hands dirty with some practical work to learn more exciting declarative development features offered by Oracle APEX.

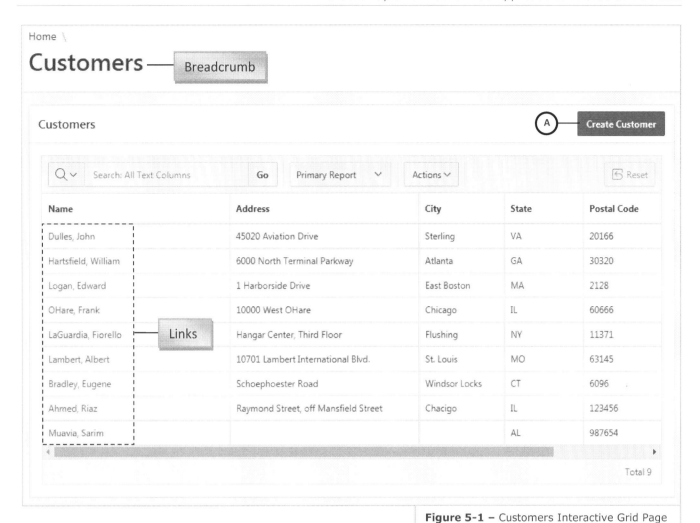

Figure 5-1 – Customers Interactive Grid Page

## 5.2 Create Pages to Manage Customers

The Home page of our application was created by the App Builder wizard at the time when the application was created. The rest of the pages in this application will be created manually with the help of wizards and copy utility. In this chapter, you will make use of Oracle APEX wizard to create pages for this setup by answering simple questions on different wizard screens. You can always move back to a previous wizard step by clicking the *Previous* button provided at the bottom of each screen. The following instructions step you through to create the two module pages via a built-in wizard.

1. In the main App Builder interface, click the Sales Web Application's **Edit** icon (A), and on the next page click the **Create Page** button (B). You'll use this button throughout this book to create new application pages.

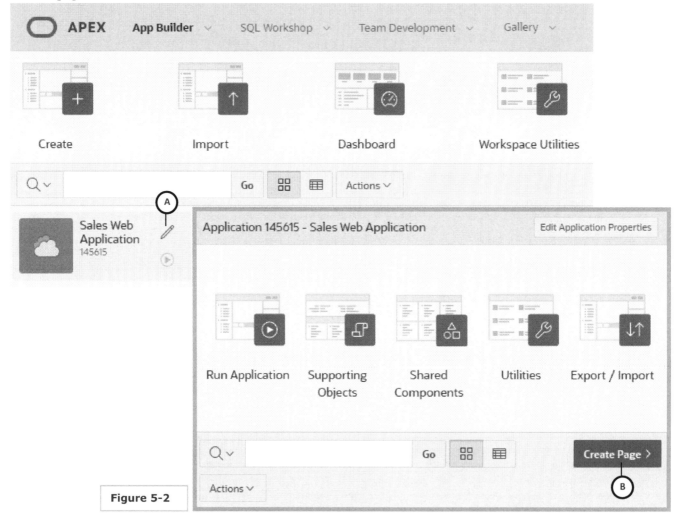

**Figure 5-2**

 If you want to delete an application page, open the page in Page Designer by clicking its name. Then, select *Delete* from the *Utilities* menu ⚒˅, which appear at the top-right.

2. On the first wizard screen, select the **Report** option. The initial wizard screen allows you to select a single option from a collection of multiple choices. We selected the *Report* option because the first page of this module will display a report of customers in an interactive grid.

110

3. On the next wizard screen, click **Interactive Grid**. This screen presents sub-categories of reports and requires a single selection the report will base on. The option you selected here means an interactive grid will act as a report to display all customers from the database.

**INTERACTIVE GRID**

Up to version 5.0 APEX used the Interactive Report feature to present data in a tabular form. Since version 5.1, you are provided with a new feature called an Interactive Grid, which is similar to the Interactive Report but allows you to manipulate data simply by clicking on a cell and editing its value. This functionality is the major difference between the two. The Interactive Grid includes every feature that the IR used to deliver. It introduces fixed headers, frozen columns, scroll pagination, multiple filters, sorting, aggregates, computations, and more. It is designed to support all item types and item type plug-ins. One more important thing about the Interactive Grid is that you can create mater-detail relationships to any number of levels deep and across. See section 5.6 in this chapter for further details.

4. On the next wizard screen, set the following properties for the interactive grid page and click **Next**.

| Property | Value |
|---|---|
| Page Number | 2 |
| Page Name | Customers |
| Page Mode | Normal |
| Breadcrumb | Breadcrumb |
| Parent Entry | Home (Page 1) |
| Entry Name | Customers |

In Application Express each page is identified with a unique number. The main page of this module (which will carry an interactive grid) will be recognized by number 2, whereas the form page (to be created next) will have number 7. Just like numbers, a page is provided with a unique *name* for visual recognition. You can recognize a page by its name in the App Builder interface.

The *Page Mode* property specifies how you want to see a page. It has two options: *Normal* and *Modal Dialog*. New pages created in Oracle APEX default to *Normal*. When you call a normal page, it simply replaces an existing page appearing in your browser. A *Modal Dialog* page, on the other hand, is a stand-alone page, which appears on top of its calling page and doesn't allow users to do anything else unless it is closed. A modal page can be displayed only on top of another page.

A breadcrumb shared component was created by the App Builder when you created this application earlier (see *Shared Components > Navigation > Breadcrumbs*). In this step, you selected the same breadcrumb component (fourth property value in the above table) and added an entry name (Customers) to it. Take a look at Figure 5-1 and see where the provided entry name appears in the breadcrumb region. A breadcrumb is a hierarchical list of links. It indicates where the user is within the application from a hierarchical perspective. Users can click a specific breadcrumb link to instantly switch back to any level. You use breadcrumbs as a second level of navigation at the top of each page. To create a hierarchy in this application, you selected the Home menu entry as the Parent Entry for this page.

5. On the *Navigation Menu* wizard screen, set *Navigation Preference* to **Identify an existing navigation menu entry for this page**, set *Existing Navigation Menu Entry* to **Setup**, and click **Next**. This step will make the *Setup* entry active in the main navigation menu (created in Chapter 3, section 3.2.1) when this page is accessed.

6.  On the *Report Source* screen, set the following properties.

| Property | Value |
|---|---|
| Editing Enabled | Off |
| Source Type | Table |
| Table/View Owner | *accept the displayed value that displays your Oracle schema* |
| Table/View Name | DEMO_CUSTOMERS (table) |

We disabled the most significant editing feature of the interactive grid because we will use a separate form to modify customers' records. You will see an example of editing records in an interactive grid later in this chapter.

In the *Source Type* attribute we specified to use a database table data to populate this interactive grid. Next, you selected the default value appearing in *Table/View Owner* attribute. This is usually the database schema to which you are connected. Once you select a schema, all tables within that schema are populated in the *Table/View Name* drop-down list from where you select a table – DEMO_CUSTOMERS in the current scenario whose data will be displayed in the interactive grid. Note that in the current scenario you can select only one table from the provided list.

If not visible, click the arrow icon next to the Column section to see the table columns. When you choose a table, all the columns from that table are selected (moved to the right pane in the Columns section). For this exercise, leave the following columns in the right pane and exclude others by moving them to the left pane using Ctrl+click and the left arrow ‹ icon. Here are the columns we want to *show* in the interactive grid.
**Cust_First_Name, Cust_Last_Name, Cust_Street_Address1, Cust_Street_Address2, Cust_City, Cust_State,** and **Cust_Postal_Code**

**Figure 5-3**

7. Click the **Create** button to finish the report page creation process.

The page is created and its structure is presented in the Page Designer. The only significant aspect of this page is the *Customers* Interactive Grid region under the *Rendering > Components > Body* node to your left. The wizard created this region with all the columns you specified in step 6 – see the *SQL Query* box in the Page Designer. All these columns appear under the *Columns* node.

The properties in the Interactive grid's *Attributes* tab control how an interactive grid works. For example, developers use these properties to determine if end-users can edit the underlying data, configure report pagination, create error messages, configure the toolbar and use download options, control if and how users can save an interactive grid, and add Icon and Detail Views to the toolbar. You will go through these properties later in this chapter. For now, walk around the Page Designer interface and observe page components and relevant properties.

Click the **Application 145615** breadcrumb at top-left to leave the Page Designer interface. Note that the ID of my application is 145615, so I will use it throughout this book to reference my application. In the next set of steps you will create a new page. This page will carry a form to add, modify, and delete customers and will be called from Page 2 – *Customers*. It will be created as a modal dialog. A modal dialog page is a stand-alone page, which appears on top of the calling page. An Oracle APEX page can be created as a dialog, which supports for all the functionality of a normal page, including computations, validations, processes, and branches.

1. Click the **Create Page** button. This time select the **Form** option 🖥 followed by another **Form** 🖩 option on the next wizard screen. The second option creates a form page based on a database table. After selecting the initial options, set the following properties on the next wizard screen.

   | Property | Value |
   |---|---|
   | Page Number | 7 |
   | Page Name | Customer Details |
   | Page Mode | Modal Dialog |
   | Breadcrumb | Breadcrumb |
   | Parent Entry | Customers (Page 2) |
   | Entry Name | Customer Details |

2. On the *Navigation Menu* screen, set *Navigation Preference* to **Identify an existing navigation menu entry for this page**, set *Existing Navigation Menu Entry* to **Setup**, and click **Next**.

3. On the *Source* screen, set the following properties and click **Next**.

   | Property | Value |
   |---|---|
   | Data Source | Local Database |
   | Source Type | Table |
   | Table/View Owner | *accept the displayed value* |
   | Table/View Name | DEMO_CUSTOMERS |

4. This time, select all columns from the DEMO_CUSTOMERS table to display all of them in the input form (Page 7) to populate the backend database table. For *Primary Key Type,* select the second option **Select Primary Key Column(s)**. Then, set the first *Primary Key Column* attribute to **CUSTOMER_ID**. Click the **Create** button to complete the form page creation process. In this step, you specified the primary key column. A primary key is a column or set of columns that uniquely identify a record in a table. Note that in the current scenario the primary key column for the customers table will be populated using DEMO_CUSTOMERS_SEQ Sequence object through BI_DEMO_CUSTOMERS trigger. The trigger fires when you insert a new customer. To browse this trigger, select SQL Workshop > Object Browser > Tables > click on DEMO_CUSTOMERS table and then click the SQL tab. A sequence is a database object that automatically generates primary key values for every new customer record. Forms perform insert, update, and delete operations on table rows in the database. The rows are identified using either a primary key defined on the table, or the ROWID pseudo column, which uniquely identifies a row in a table. Forms support up to two columns in the primary key. For tables using primary keys with more than two columns, the ROWID option should be used. For further details, see Chapter 2.

5.  Access the main App Builder interface by clicking the application ID breadcrumb to see the two new pages (*Customers* and *Customer Details*) with their respective page numbers. Click the **Customer Details** page (Page 7) to open its definitions in Page Designer. Expand the *Pre-Rendering* node and rename the process *Initialize form Customer Details* as **Initialize Customer Details**. Click the **Processing** tab and rename the process named *Process form Customer Details* to **Process Customer Data**.

 If you see a different process name, then there is nothing to worry about as it sometimes happens due to change in APEX version.

Oracle APEX is a low-code application development platform. The two pages you just created have everything you need to view and manipulate data. The *Customers* page (Page 2) contains an Interactive Grid in which you can view all customers' data. Click the *Customer Details* page (Page 7) to open it in Page Designer. On the *Rendering* tab, expand the *Pre-Rendering* node. Here, you will see an auto-generated process named *Initialize Customer Details* of *Form Initialization* type. This Process is responsible to initialize form region items. Initialization can either be fetching data from the region source, using the primary key value(s) or simple initialization of the form region items. The process fetches and displays data in page items when you select a customer by clicking the corresponding edit icon on the reports page and it initializes the page items when you create a new customer record. The *Customer Details* region is a *Form* type region, which connects to the local database and fetches data from DEMO_CUSTOMERS table into relevant page items listed under the Items node. The same page items are used to receive user input when a new customer record is created. In the *Buttons* section, you will see a bunch of auto-generated buttons (Cancel, Delete, Save, and Create). The *Database Action* properties of these buttons specify the function each button performs. When you click a button (for example, CREATE), the corresponding database action is submitted to a process named *Process Customer Data*, which resides under the *Processing* tab. This process is of *Automatic Row Processing (DML)* type and performs insert, update, or delete action on a form region – *Customer Details* region in the current scenario.

## 5.3 Modify Customers Page - Page 2

The main page of this module (Page 2) holds an interactive grid, which is generated by the wizard with some default data source values. In the following steps, you will learn how to change these values and produce a custom output using a SQL query.

### 5.3.1 Modify Region Properties

1. In the App Builder interface, click the **Customers** page (Page 2) to open it in the *Page Designer* for modification.

2. Click the **Customers** region ▦ Customers under the *Body* node. The standard method to modify properties of a page component is to click the corresponding node. This action refreshes the *Properties* section (located to your right) with the properties of the selected page component for alteration.

3. For *Type* (under the *Source* section), select **SQL Query** to see the default query generated for the interactive grid. Enter the following SQL statement in SQL Query text area, replacing the existing one. Here, the auto-generated SELECT SQL statement is replaced with a custom statement that uses the concatenation operator ‖ to join columns. The new statement joins last and first name of customers into a single column. The new concatenated column is recognized by *customer_name*. Similarly, the two address columns are combined to form a single address.

```
SELECT customer_id,
       cust_last_name || ', ' || cust_first_name customer_name,
       CUST_STREET_ADDRESS1 ||decode(CUST_STREET_ADDRESS2, null, null, ', ' ||
       CUST_STREET_ADDRESS2) customer_address,
       cust_city, cust_state, cust_postal_code
FROM demo_customers
```

| DECODE FUNCTION | |
|---|---|
| In the SELECT statement we used a DECODE function, which has the functionality of an IF-THEN-ELSE statement. It compares expression to each search value one by one. If expression is equal to a search, Oracle Database returns the corresponding result. If no match is found, Oracle returns default. If default is omitted, Oracle returns null. In this statement, the Decode function assesses if the returned value of the second street address is null, it stores null to the result; otherwise, concatenates the second address to the first address. The syntax and example of the Decode function provided in the right pane elaborates this concept further. | **Decode Syntax:**<br>decode( expression , search , result [, search , result]... [, default] )<br><br>**Example of Decode Function:**<br>SELECT customer_name,<br>DECODE(customer_id, 1, 'A', 2, 'B', 3, 'C', 'D') result<br>FROM customers;<br><br>The equivalent IF-THEN-ELSE statement for the previous Decode function would be:<br>IF customer_id = 1 THEN<br>  result := 'A';<br>ELSIF customer_id = 2 THEN<br>  result := 'B';<br>ELSIF customer_id = 3 THEN<br>  result := 'C';<br>ELSE<br>  result := 'D';<br>END IF; |

4. Expand the *Customers* region and then expand the *Columns* node. Click a column (for example, **CUSTOMER_NAME**) and change its heading (under the *Heading* section in the Properties pane) to **Name**. Change the headings of other columns as follows:
    **Address, City, State,** and **Postal Code**

5. In the Columns node, click the **CUSTOMER_ID** column, and change it *Type* property from *Number Field* to **Hidden**. This action will hide the column at runtime. Primary Key columns are added to database tables to enforce data integrity and are not displayed in applications. This is why such columns' *Type* property is set to hidden to make them invisible at runtime.

6. Run the page. Click the **Actions** menu (A). From the *Action* menu's list, select **Columns**. In the *Columns* window, make sure all the columns are selected – that is, they all have a checkmark (C) in the *Displayed* column. If you remove a checkmark from a column, it disappears from the interactive grid report. When you click a column in the left pane, the right pane (D) shows its name and width. You can input a numeric value to change the width of a column. Using the arrow icons (E), arrange the selected columns in the following order: **Name, Address, City, State,** and **Postal Code**

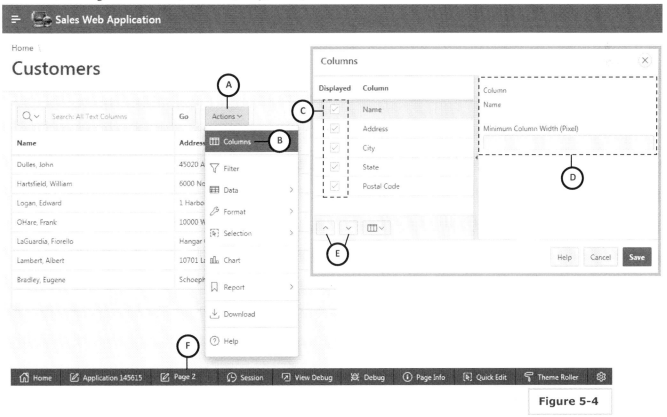

**Figure 5-4**

7. Click the **Save** button in the *Columns* window to apply the changes.

8. Click the **Actions** menu again, and select **Save** from the *Report* option. After you modify an interactive grid save it using this option, otherwise you'll lose the applied settings when you access it later.

9. Click **Page2** (F) in the Developer Toolbar at the bottom of your screen to access the Page Designer.

10. Click the **CUSTOMER_NAME** column to set the following properties. In these properties, you are transforming the customer name column into link that will lead to Page 7. When you click a customer's name in the interactive grid report at runtime, the ID of that customer is stored in a substitution string (&CUSTOMER_ID.) (G) and then it is forwarded to the corresponding page item (P7_CUSTOMER_ID) (H) on Page 7, which displays the profile of the selected customer using this ID. You created similar kind of link in Chapter 4 for a region named *Sales for this Month*. Scroll down to the *Link* section and click **No Link Defined** under *Target* to bring up the *Link Builder* dialog box. In the *Link Builder* dialog box, set the link properties as shown in the following figure. Use LOVs (I) in the *Set Items* section to select the item name and the value.

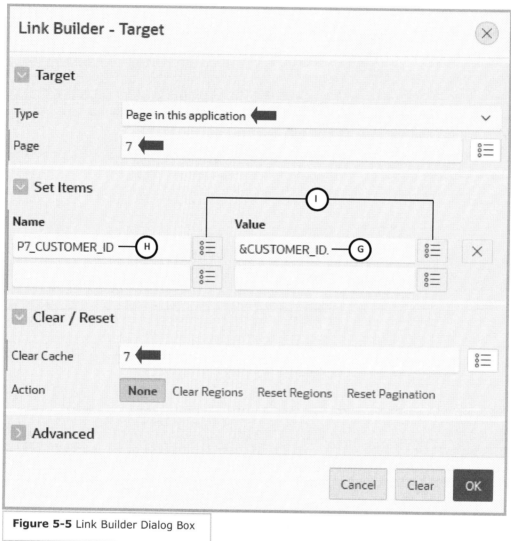

**Figure 5-5** Link Builder Dialog Box

11. After setting these properties, close the *Link Builder* dialog box using the **OK** button.

12. **Save and run** the page. The *Customer Name* column will now appear as a link. Click any customer name to see the details on Page 7, which pops up on top of Page 2.

## 5.3.2 Create Button

In the previous section, you created a link on the customer name column that helped you browse, modify, or delete an existing customer's record. To create a new customer, however, you need to create a button to call Page 7 with a blank form. Execute the following steps to create this button on Page 2 - Customers.

1. On the *Rendering* tab to your left, click the **Customers** interactive grid region and set its *Template* property to **Standard**. The selected template will place a title and a border for the interactive grid region. Right-click the Customers region and select **Create Button** from the context menu. A button named *New* will be added. Set the following properties for the new button.

| Property | Value |
|---|---|
| Name | CREATE |
| Label | Create Customer |
| Position | Copy |
| Hot | On |
| Action (*under Behavior*) | Redirect to Page in this Application |
| Target | Type = Page in this Application<br>Page = 7<br>Clear Cache =7 |

The *Label* of this button is set to *Create Customer* (A – Figure 5-1) and the button is placed in the *Copy* position. The *Position* property provides you with over a dozen values. The best way to understand the other options is to try each one to see its effect. The *Hot* attribute renders the button in a dark color. The remaining properties create a link to call Page 7. The *Clear Cache* property makes all the items on the target page (Page 7) blank.

2. Save and run Page 2, which should look similar to Figure 5-1.

3. Click the **Create Customer** button. This will call the *Customer Details* page (Page 7) on top of the calling page as a modal dialog.

## 5.4 Modify Customer Details Page - Page 7

With Page 7 being displayed in your browser, click **Edit Page 7** in the Developer Toolbar at the bottom of your screen to call this page in the Page Designer for modifications.

### 5.4.1 Modify Page Items Properties

Click each item under the *Items* node and apply the following properties. Just like region placement in a 12 columns grid layout, which you performed for the six Home page regions, the page items can also be placed accordingly using Oracle APEX's grid layout, as follows. The *Width* property sets items' width on the page. In the following table, some values for the *Value Required* property are set to *Yes*. If *Value Required* is set to *Yes* and the page item is visible, Oracle APEX automatically performs a NOT NULL validation when the page is submitted and you are asked to input a value for the field. If you set it to No, no validation is performed and a NULL value is accepted. This attribute works in conjunction with *Template = Required* to signify mandatory items visually.

| Page Item | Property and Value |
|---|---|
| P7_CUST_FIRST_NAME | Label=First Name<br>Sequence=20<br>Start New Row=On<br>Column=Automatic<br>Column Span=Automatic<br>Template=Required<br>Label Column Span=2    *(becomes visible in the **Layout** section only after setting the Template property)*<br>Width=50<br>Value Required=On |
| P7_CUST_LAST_NAME | Label=Last Name<br>Sequence=30<br>Start New Row=Off<br>Column=Automatic<br>New Column=On<br>Column Span=Automatic<br>Template=Required<br>Label Column Span=2<br>Width=50<br>Value Required=On |
| P7_CUST_STREET_ADDRESS1 | Label=Street Address<br>Sequence=40<br>Start New Row=On<br>Column=Automatic<br>Column Span=Automatic<br>Template=Optional<br>Label Column Span=2<br>Width=50<br>Value Required=Off |
| P7_CUST_STREET_ADDRESS2 | Label=Line 2<br>Sequence=50<br>Start New Row=Off<br>Column=Automatic<br>New Column=On<br>Column Span=Automatic<br>Template=Optional<br>Label Column Span=2<br>Width=50<br>Value Required=Off |

| Page Item | Property and Value |
|---|---|
| P7_CUST_CITY | Label=City<br>Sequence=60<br>Start New Row=On<br>Column=Automatic<br>Column Span=6<br>Template=Optional<br>Label Column Span=2<br>Width=50<br>Value Required=Off |
| P7_CUST_STATE | Label=State<br>Sequence=70<br>Start New Row=Off<br>Column=Automatic<br>New Column=On<br>Column Span=Automatic<br>Template=Required<br>Label Column Span=2<br>Width=make it null *(this item will be transformed into a select list)*<br>Value Required=On |
| P7_CUST_POSTAL_CODE | Label=Zip Code<br>Sequence=80<br>Start New Row=On<br>Column=Automatic<br>Column Span=6<br>Template=Required<br>Label Column Span=2<br>Width=8<br>Value Required=On |
| P7_CREDIT_LIMIT | Label=Credit Limit<br>Sequence=90<br>Start New Row=Off<br>Column=Automatic<br>New Column=On<br>Column Span=Automatic<br>Template=Required<br>Label Column Span=2<br>Width=8<br>Value Required=On |
| P7_PHONE_NUMBER1 | Label=Phone Number<br>Sequence=100<br>Start New Row=On<br>Column=Automatic<br>Column Span=Automatic<br>Template=Optional<br>Label Column Span=2<br>Width=12<br>Value Required=Off |
| P7_PHONE_NUMBER2 | Label=Alternate No.<br>Sequence=110<br>Start New Row=Off<br>Column=Automatic<br>New Column=On<br>Column Span=Automatic<br>Template=Optional<br>Label Column Span=2<br>Width=12<br>Value Required=Off |

| Page Item | Property and Value |
|---|---|
| P7_CUST_EMAIL | Label=Email<br>Sequence=120<br>Start New Row=On<br>Column=Automatic<br>Column Span=Automatic<br>Template=Required<br>Label Column Span=2<br>Width=50<br>Value Required=On |
| P7_URL | Type=Text Field<br>Label=URL<br>Sequence=130<br>Start New Row=Off<br>Column=Automatic<br>New Column=On<br>Column Span=Automatic<br>Template=Optional<br>Label Column Span=2<br>Width=50<br>Value Required=Off |
| P7_TAGS | Type=Textarea<br>Label=Tags<br>Sequence=140<br>Start New Row=On<br>Column=Automatic<br>Column Span=Automatic<br>Template=Optional<br>Label Column Span=2<br>Width=100<br>Value Required=Off |

Save your changes and call this page by clicking any customer's name on Page 2. It should come up with the profile of the selected customer, as illustrated in the following figure. Note that all the fields that were marked as *Required* are preceded with a red asterisk (*).

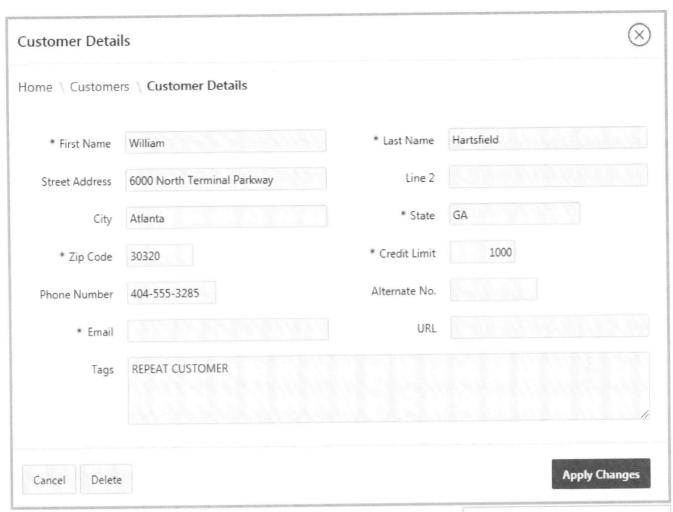

Figure 5-6 Customer Details Page

## 5.4.2 Change Item Type and Attach LOV

In the following set of steps, you'll work on the *State* column. First, you will alter its type from *Text Field* to a *Select List* and then you will attach a LOV to it. Oracle APEX allows you to change an item's type from its default state to another desirable type. For example, the P7_CUST_STATE item was generated as a text type by the wizard. Now, we want to change this item to a *Select List* to hold a predefined States list. To display this list, you'll attach the STATES LOV to this item. The LOV was created in Chapter 3 section 3.4.3 and will be tied to this field so that the user can save a valid State value for each customer.

1.  In the Page Designer interface, click the **P7_CUST_STATE** item.

2.  Change its *Type* property from *Text Field* to **Select List**.

3.  Set *Type* (under *List of Values*) to **Shared Components** and select **STATES** for *List of Values*. This step attaches the *States* LOV to the page item.

4.  **Turn off** *Display Extra Values* property. An item may have a session state value, which does not occur in its list of values definition. Select whether this list of values should display this extra session state value. If you choose not to display this extra session state value and there is no matching value in the list of values definition, the first value will be the selected value. For instance, while creating a new customer record you will see *-Choose a State-* as the first value in the list. This value is added to the list in the following steps.

5.  **Turn on** *Display Null Value* property, which is the default. The *Display Null Value* property makes it possible for a user to choose a null value instead of one of the list items. If you set this property to *Yes*, additional properties appear on the screen for you to specify the display value for this new entry. For example, - Choose State -.

6.  Enter - **Choose State** - in *Null Display Value*. This step, along with the previous one, generates a placeholder that appears on top of the LOV asking for a selection whenever you call this page to create a new customer record.

7.  Save your work.

## 5.4.3 Apply Input Mask to Items

Modify the two phone number items and set their *Value Placeholder* property (under *Appearance*) to **999-999-9999**. When a new customer record is added, this placeholder is shown in the two phone number items to receive input in the specified format. As you type in values, the placeholders will be replaced by the numbers entered.

## 5.4.4 Create Validation - Check Customer Credit Limit

Validations enable you to create logic controls to verify whether user input is valid. In this part, you'll create a validation to check customer's credit limit. The customer form contains a field named Credit Limit, which is used to assign a credit cap to each customer with a figure of $5,000. If you enter a value more than the assigned cap, you'll be prevented by presenting an appropriate message.

In the left pane of Page 7, click the *Processing* tab, right-click the *Validating* node, and select **Create Validation** from the context menu. This action will add a new validation.

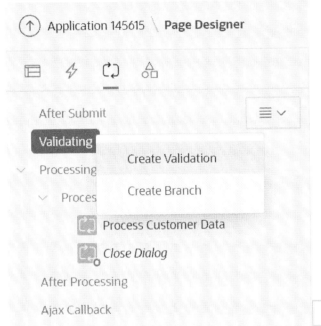

**NOTE:** If a validation passes the equality test, or evaluates to TRUE, then the validation error message does not display. Validation error messages display when the validation fails the equality test, or evaluates to FALSE, or a non-empty text string is returned.

**Figure 5-7 –** Create Validation

Set the following properties for this new validation. After providing a meaningful name to the validation, you set its *Type* to *PL/SQL Expression*. The selected type specifies an expression in valid PL/SQL syntax that evaluates to true or false. In the current scenario, if the value of the :P7_CREDIT_LIMIT page item is less than or equal to 5000, then the validation evaluates as true and the customer record is saved to the database. If the value of this item is more than 5000, then the validation evaluates as false and the message specified in the *Error Message* property is fired. Note that you use bind variables (the item name preceded with a colon) when you reference the value of a session state variable from within PL/SQL code.

| Property | Value |
|---|---|
| Name | Check Credit Limit |
| Type | PL/SQL Expression |
| PL/SQL Expression | :P7_CREDIT_LIMIT <= 5000 |
| Error Message | Customer's Credit Limit must be less than or equal to $5,000 |

## 5.4.5 Create Validation - Can't Delete Customer with Orders

This is the second validation to prevent the deletion of those customers who have placed orders. This check is performed to retain database integrity from the front-end. The validation is performed using a custom PL/SQL function, which returns either a true or false value. The return value is based on a SELECT query, which returns false if records exist for the selected customer. If the returned value is false, the error message is displayed and the record deletion process is aborted. The validation is associated to the DELETE button in the last attribute, which means that the validation will be performed only when the Delete button is pressed.

Once again, right-click the *Validating* node and select the **Create Validation** option to add a new validation under the previous one. Set the following properties for this new validation. You can control when and if a validation (or process) is performed by configuring *When Button Pressed* and *Condition Type* attributes of the validation. If you want a validation to execute only when the specified button is clicked, select a button from the list–see the last attribute in the following table. Setting a condition type involves selecting a condition from the list that must be met in order for a validation to be processed.

| Property | Value |
|---|---|
| Name | Can't Delete Customer with Orders |
| Type | PL/SQL Function Body (Returning Boolean) |
| PL/SQL Function Body (Returning Boolean) | begin<br>  for c1 in (select 'x' from demo_orders<br>       where customer_id = :P7_CUSTOMER_ID) loop<br>    RETURN FALSE;<br>  end loop;<br>    RETURN TRUE;<br>end; |
| Error Message | Can't delete customer with existing orders |
| When Button Pressed | DELETE |

Before running the customer module, let's take a look at the definitions of the *Customer Details* page – Page 7. If you see the definitions of this page, you'll observe some auto-generated buttons (Cancel, Delete, Save, and Create) with default functionalities. For example, when you fill in the form with a new customer's record and click the *Create* button, the record is added to the database table using a built-in process – discussed in a while.

Just like buttons, Oracle APEX performs many other tasks transparently without us having to write a single line of code. For instance, expand the *Pre-Rendering* node (under the root node - *Page 7: Customer Details*). Here, you will see a process of *Form Initialization* type created by the wizard. The purpose of this process is to fetch the record from the database using a specified key value, and put values of that record into relevant items on the page. For example, when you click a customer name in the Interactive Grid on Page 2, the ID of that customer is used by this process to fetch and display details of the selected customer on this page.

The wizard also created individual input items (under the *Customer Details* region) for each column in the table. The *Source Type* property of these columns is set to *Database Column* and *Database Column* property is set to the column name in the table. For example, the two properties set for the P7_CUST_FIRST_NAME page item tells the ARF process to set the item with the value retrieved from the CUST_FIRST_NAME table column.

Click the root node (*Page 7: Customer Details*) and scroll down to the *Function and Global Variable Declaration* section in the Property Editor, you'll see a global variable defined as *var htmldb_delete_message*. This variable was generated automatically along with a corresponding shortcut named DELETE_CONFIRM_MSG (in *Shared Components > Other Components > Shortcuts*) to control the record deletion process by presenting a confirmation dialog box before deleting a customer's record. Since this shortcut is created in Shared Components, other application pages will also utilize it to present the same confirmation.

Note that the *Delete* button was created by the wizard with a SQL DELETE database action. Similarly, INSERT and UPDATE database actions were set automatically for *Create* and *Save* buttons, respectively – see the *Database Action* attribute under *Behavior*. When clicked, these buttons perform the selected SQL operations to trigger the specified database action within the built-in *Automatic Row Processing (DML)* type process, also created automatically by the wizard on the *Processing* tab. This process is located under the *Processing > Processes* node and it is responsible to insert, update, or delete records into the backend database table. This process is used to process form items with a source of type Database Column. This process has three advantages. First, you are not required to provide any SQL coding. Second, Oracle APEX performs DML processing for you. Third, this process automatically performs lost update detection. Lost update detection ensures data integrity in applications where data can be accessed concurrently.

In addition, the wizard created a Dynamic Action (*Close Dialog*) to close this form when the *Cancel* button is clicked. These are some of the beauties of declarative development that not only generates basic functionalities of an application, but on the same time doesn't limit our abilities to manually enter specific and tailored code (demonstrated in subsequent chapters), both on the client and server sides to answer our specific needs.

**Test Your Work**

Save and run the application. Access this module by clicking the *Manage Customers* menu item (under *Setup*). You'll see Page 2 – *Customers*, as shown in Figure 5-1, carrying an interactive grid. The grid has a search bar comprising a magnifying glass, a text area, and a *Go* button. The bar allows you to search a string in the report appearing underneath. The magnifying glass is a drop down list. You can use this list to limit your search to a specific column. Type **albert** in the text area and click the **Go** button. You'll see a row displaying record of Albert Lambert. Click the remove filter icon ⊠ to reinstate the grid to its previous state. Alternatively, you can click the *Reset* button appearing on the top-right of the grid.

The *Actions* menu carries some more options that we'll explore in Chapter 7. Among other useful options, this menu has a couple of save options under *Report*. The first one (*Save*) is used when you customize the report by applying filters or moving columns. After modifying a report you must save it using this option, otherwise you'll lose the applied settings when you subsequently view the same report. Clicking the second option (*Save As*) presents a window with a *Type* drop-down list and a *Name* text box. Developers can save four types of reports: Primary, Alternative, Private, and Public. The initial interactive grid report rendered in your browser is called a *Primary* report. The default *Primary* report (you are looking at) is the initial report created by the application developer. It cannot be renamed or deleted. An *Alternative* report enables developers to create multiple report layouts. Only developers can save, rename, or delete an Alternative Report. An alternative report is based on the default primary report and is rendered in a different layout (see Section 7.3.3 in Chapter 7). A *Private* report is a report that can be viewed, saved, renamed, or deleted by the user who created it. In contrast, when you save a report as public, all users can view it. By default, end-users cannot save *Public* reports. To enable support for *Public* reports, developers edit the report attribute and enables users to save it as public report – see step 7 Section 7.3.1 in Chapter 7. After saving, all these reports display on the *Saved Reports* list on the toolbar. The Primary report is displayed under the heading, *Default*.

The *Create Customer* button calls the second page of this module (Page 7), where you enter profile of a new customer. As you can see, the customer name column appears as a link. If you want to modify a specific record, click the corresponding link. Again, the same form page comes up where all the fields are populated with relevant information from the database. Click the name of any customer to see the information, as presented in Figure 5-6. You are free to test your work. Try by adding, modifying, and deleting a new customer. Try to delete *Eugene Bradley's* record. You won't be able to do that because there are some orders placed by this customer and the validation you created in section 5.4.5 will prevent the deletion process. Also, check the credit limit validation by entering a value more than 5000 in the *Credit Limit* box.

You might encounter a primary key violation message while creating first customer record. This is because the Sequence object for this table is created with an initial value of 1. When you try to save the first customer record, 1 is assigned as its primary key, which already exists in the table. To cope with this situation, developers drop and re-create auto-generated sequence objects with a higher START WITH value. To keep things simple, I'd suggest beginners to click the Create button on the form page several times. After a few clicks the record will be save.

## 5.5 Add Dynamic Action

After adding a new customer record or editing an existing one, you might observe that the interactive grid on the Customers page doesn't reflect those changes. This is because the page doesn't get refreshed to show what you have added or amended. One way to see these modifications is to manually refresh your browser window, which in turn, retrieves fresh data from the database. But, a more professional approach would be to refresh the page automatically using a dynamic action. In this section, you will create a dynamic action to refresh the interactive grid region (Customers) when the modal dialog page (Page 7) is closed.

1. Open Page 2 (Customers) in Page Designer and click the **Dynamic Actions** tab ⚡ appearing in the left pane.

2. Right-click the **Dialog Closed** node and select **Create Dynamic Action** from the context menu.

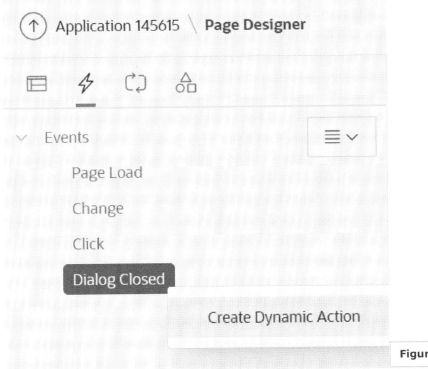

**Figure 5-8** – Create Dynamic Action

Set the following properties for this dynamic action.

| Property | Value |
|---|---|
| Name | Refresh Interactive Grid |
| Selection Type | Region |
| Region | Customers |

3. Click the *Refresh* sub-node and set *Region* to **Customers**. *Refresh* is an action, which executes when the condition evaluates to true – in other words, when the modal dialog page is closed. All is set! Save the page and run it. Now you will see immediate reflection of your modifications in the interactive grid.

## 5.6 Explore Interactive Grid

Interactive Grid is a page component, which is used to display data in row/column matrix. In appearance, it looks similar to an Interactive Report (used in the next chapter) and delivers all features of an Interactive Report, but it also allows you to manipulate data simply by clicking on a cell and editing its value, which is not available in Interactive Reports. In many ways this grid looks and acts like an Interactive Report. Here are some new features and differences:

- Rows are fixed height and columns have a specific width that can be adjusted by dragging the border between column headers (G) or with Ctrl+Left/Right keys when the column header has keyboard focus.

- Columns can be reordered with drag and drop (dragging the handle (E) at the start of a column heading) or with Shift+Left/Right keys when the column header has keyboard focus.

- Columns can be sorted using the buttons (F) in the column heading or by using Alt+Up/Down key combination. Use the Shift key to add additional sort columns.

- Columns can be frozen using the Freeze button (D) in the column heading pop-up menu. For example, to freeze the customers' name column (on Page 2), click the *Name* column heading. A pop-up menu will appear with four options: Hide (A), Control Break (B), Aggregate (C), and Freeze (D). Select *Freeze*. Drag the border between the *Name* and *Address* columns (F) toward right to expand the *Name* column.

- By default the toolbar and column headings stick to the top of the page and the footer sticks to the bottom when scrolling.

- By default pagination uses a "Load More" button.

- The grid is keyboard navigable with a focused cell and current selected row (single selection by default).

- The toolbar includes a Reset button by default, which restores all the report settings to their defaults.

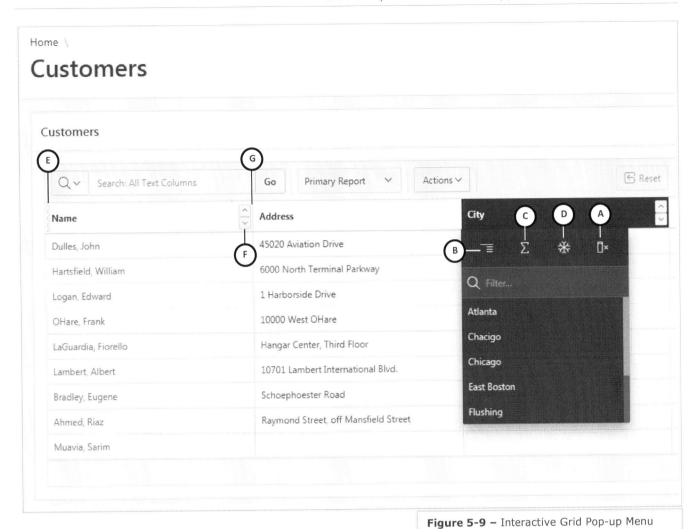

Home \

# Customers

Customers

Figure 5-9 – Interactive Grid Pop-up Menu

Let's put off the development process of our Sales Web Application till the next chapter and explore features of Interactive Grid. To get hands-on exposure, you need a couple of tables that come with a sample application. Execute the following steps to install the sample application to get the required tables.

1.  Click **Gallery** and then click on **Samples**.

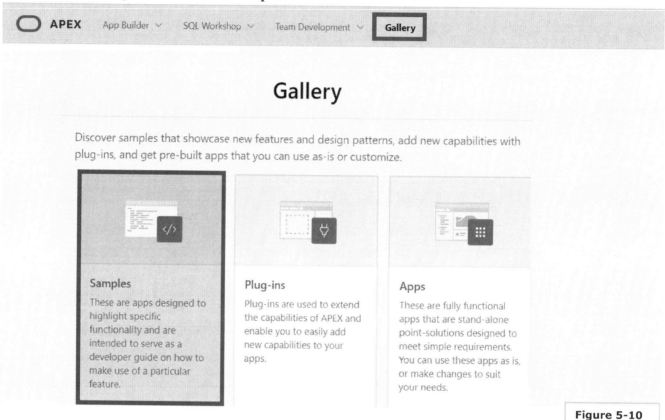

**Figure 5-10**

2.  Scroll down and click **Download App** button next to **Sample Interactive Grids** application. A file named *sample-interactive-grids.zip* will be downloaded to your computer.

3.  Click the **App Builder** main menu option.

4.  Click the **Import** icon.

5.  Click the **Drag and Drop** link. Select the **sample-interactive-grids.zip** file. Selecting the **Database Application, Page or Component Export** *File Type* option, click **Next**.

6.  Click **Next**, on *File Import Confirmation* screen.

7.  On the *Install* wizard screen, click the **Install Application** button.

8.  On the *Supporting Objects* screen, turn on the **Install Supporting Objects** and click **Next**. At this point application definition has been installed; however, the database objects, images, and seed data have not yet been created. When you turn this option on, these supporting objects are installed as well.

9.  On the *Confirmation* screen, click **Install** to complete the application installation process.

10. Click the **Object Browser** option in the **SQL Workshop** main menu and see the two required tables (EBA_DEMO_IG_EMP and EBA_DEMO_IG_PEOPLE) in the left pane under the *Tables* category.

# Column Groups

| Identity | | | | | Compensation | | Notes | | |
|---|---|---|---|---|---|---|---|---|---|
| Name | Job | Manager | Hire Date | Department No. | Salary | Commission | On Leave | Notes | Tags |
| KING | PRESIDENT | | 11/17/1981 | 10 | 5000 | | N | | |
| BLAKE | MANAGER | 7839 | 5/1/1981 | 30 | 2850 | | N | Lorem ipsum dolor si... | |
| CLARK | MANAGER | 7839 | 6/9/1981 | 10 | 2450 | | N | | |
| JONES | MANAGER | 7839 | 4/2/1981 | 20 | 2975 | | N | | |
| SCOTT | ANALYST | 7566 | 12/9/1982 | 20 | 3000 | | N | | |

**Figure 5-11** Column Grouping in Interactive Grid

Groups are used to associate columns together in the grid and Single Row View. Groups are added right-clicking the *Column Groups* node in the Rendering tree. Let's try this feature by executing the following steps:

1. Open Sales Web Application and create a new page by clicking the **Create Page** button. Select the **Report** option in the first wizard screen, followed by the **Interactive Grid** option on the next screen.

2. Enter **100** for *Page Number*, **Column Groups** for *Page Name*, set *Page Mode* to **Normal**, *Breadcrumb* to **Breadcrumb**, *Parent Entry* to **No Parent Entry**, *Entry Name* to **Column Groups**, and click **Next**.

3. Select the default *Navigation Preference* **Do not associate this page with a navigation menu entry**, because this page is not associated with our sales application. Click **Next**.

4. On the *Report Source* screen, keep the default **Off** value of *Editing Enabled*, set *Source Type* to **SQL Query**, and enter the following SQL Statement in *Enter a SQL SELECT Statement* text area.

   **SELECT empno, ename, job, mgr, hiredate, sal, comm, deptno, onleave, notes, flex4 as tags**
   **FROM EBA_DEMO_IG_EMP**

5. Click the **Create** button to complete the page creation process.

6. In the Page Designer, under the *Column Groups* region (in the *Rendering* tree), right-click the *Column Groups* node, and select **Create Column Group** (A) from the context menu. In the *Properties* pane, set the *Heading* attribute for this new group to **Identity**.

7. Repeat step 6 to create two more groups. Enter **Compensation** and **Notes** for their headings. The three column groups should look like (B).

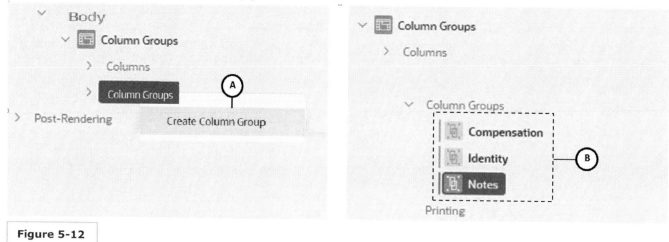

**Figure 5-12**

8. Under the *Columns Group* region, expand the *Columns* node. Click the **EMPNO** column and set its *Type* to **Hidden**.

9. Set the appropriate column headings, as shown in Figure 5-11.

10. Use the following table to associate each column with a group created in steps 6 & 7. To establish this association, click any column (ENAME, for example), scroll down to the *Layout* section, and set the *Group* property as follows:

| Column | Group Property |
|---:|---|
| ENAME | Identity |
| JOB | Identity |
| MGR | Identity |
| HIREDATE | Identity |
| SAL | Compensation |
| COMM | Compensation |
| DEPTNO | Identity |
| ONLEAVE | Notes |
| NOTES | Notes |
| TAGS | Notes |

11. Save your work and run the page. Column group headings can be used to reorder columns just like column headings. Play around with column reordering (using drag and drop – see E in Figure 5-9) to see how group headings are split and joined.

# Column Groups

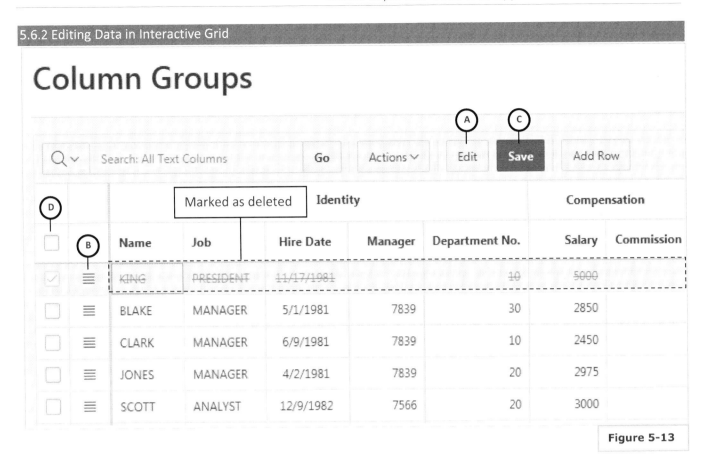

Figure 5-13

Interactive Grid allows you to manipulate data simply by clicking on a cell. When you add an Interactive Grid to a page, you specify (on *Report Source* wizard screen) whether it is editable–see step 4 in the previous section. If you initially turn this attribute off, you can always reverse it to make the Interactive Grid editable. Here are some points to know about editing:

- Normally the grid is in navigation mode where arrow keys move from cell to cell. To enter edit mode, press the *Edit* button (A). Alternatively, double-click a cell or press either the Enter key or F2 key in a cell.

- To exit edit mode, press the *Edit* button (A) again or press the Escape key in a cell.

- Use the Delete key on your keyboard to delete the selected rows. Use the Insert key to add a row.

- The second column (B) is a menu. It allows you to perform actions on the selected row such as Delete or Duplicate. Use the *Revert Changes* option from this menu to revert a record marked for deletion.

- Editing is also supported in Single Row View.

- All edits are stored locally until you press the *Save* button (C). If you try to leave the page while there are unsaved changes you will be notified.

- Any action that causes refreshing the data such as changing a filter or sorting will warn if there are unsaved changes. Pagination does not affect changes.

Execute the following steps to enable editing in the Interactive Grid you added to Page 100 in the previous section.

1. Click the **Column Groups** Interactive Grid region (A). In the Properties pane, click the **Attributes** tab (B). **Turn on** the *Enabled* attribute (C). Make sure all three data manipulation operations (D) are also enabled.

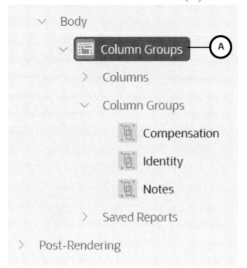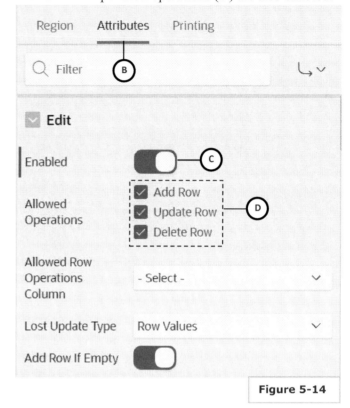

**Figure 5-14**

2. Scroll down to the *Toolbar* section to ensure that the *Show* property is turned on and the two toolbar buttons (*Reset* and *Save*) are also enabled. *Reset* removes any customizations, such as filters, column width, ordering, and so forth, and reloads the report definition from the server. *Save* will only save changes made to this interactive grid, without needing to save the whole page. The save button will be displayed only when the interactive grid is editable and the end user has the authorization to add, update, or delete records.

3. After making these changes, save and run the page. Notice that the row selector (D) and the Selection Actions menu (B) columns (in Figure 5-13) are added automatically. A process named *Save Interactive Grid Data* is also added to the *Processing* tab with an *Interactive Grid - Automatic Row Processing (DML)* type process to perform DML processing for you without writing any SQL code. This process is added by default when an Interactive Grid is made editable. Play around with the interactive grid by adding, modifying, and deleting rows.

 If you encounter the error `Interactive Grid 'Column Groups' doesn't have a primary key column defined which is required for editing or in a master detail relationship`, then click the **EMPNO** column in the Page Designer, and turn on the *Primary Key* property in the Source section. Save and run the page.

## 5.6.3 Changing Column Type

## Column Groups

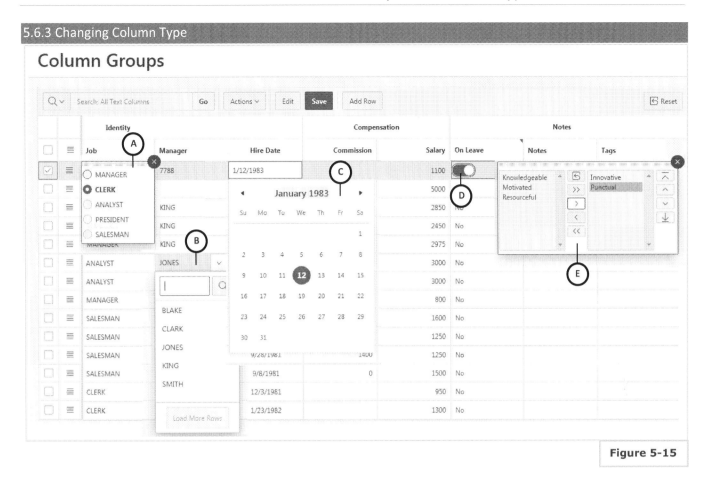

**Figure 5-15**

By default, the type of a column in an Interactive Grid is inherited from the base table. For example, the names of employees are displayed in a Text Field column type, while their salaries are shown in Number Field column type. In this exercise, you will change the default types of some columns to some other types, as follows:

    A.  The *Job* column will be presented as a *Radio Group* to select one from a list of distinct jobs

    B.  The value for the *Manager* column will be selected from a *pop-up LOV*

    C.  The *Hire Date* will use a *Date Picker* that opens on focus

    D.  Display *Yes*/No in *On Leave* column

    E.  The *Tags* column will use a *Shuttle* type to select multiple values

1.  With Page 100 being displayed in the Page Designer, expand the *Columns* node and click the *JOB* column. Set its *Type* attribute to **Radio Group**. When you select the radio group type, you are asked to associate a list of values to populate the item. For the *List of Values Type* attribute, select **SQL Query** and enter **SELECT DISTINCT job a, job b FROM EBA_DEMO_IG_EMP** in *SQL Query* box. Also **turn off** set *Display Extra Values* and *Display Null Values* properties – see section 5.4.2 for details. The SQL Query fetches distinct job IDs from the table and shows them in the *JOB* column using the radio group type.

2.  Next, click the *MGR* column and change its *Type* to **Popup LOV**. Then, select *SQL Query* for *List of Values Type* and enter the following statement in *SQL Query* box.
    **SELECT ENAME as d, EMPNO as r**
    **FROM EBA_DEMO_IG_EMP**
    **WHERE JOB = 'MANAGER' or JOB = 'PRESIDENT' order by 1**

3. Click the *HIREDATE* column and make sure that the *Type* attribute of this column is set to *Date Picker*.

4. Click the *ONLEAVE* column and set its *Type* to **Switch**. This will display either *On* or *Off* state for this column.

5. Finally, click the *TAGS* column. Change its *Type* from *Textarea* to **Shuttle**. Set *List of Values Type* to **Static Values** and enter static values (by clicking *Display1, Display2* text next to the Static Values property) as shown in the following screenshot. Recall that you created a Static LOV through Shared Components interface in Chapter 3 - Section 3.4.1. There you specified a pair of static *Display* and *Return* values. Here, you didn't use the *Return* value, because the *Return* value is optional. If a *Return* value is not included, the return value equals the display value. Click the **OK** button to close the Static Values screen.

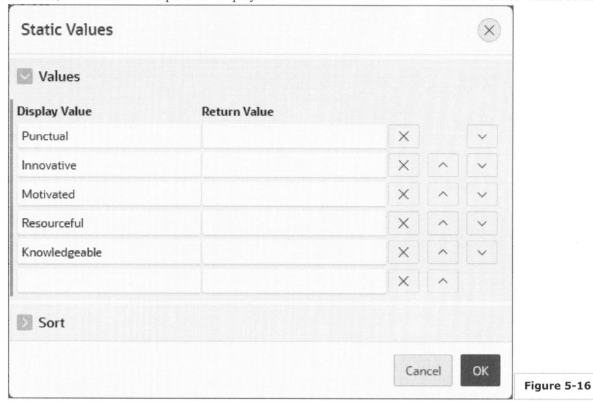

Figure 5-16

6. Save and run the page. Click different cells under the *JOB* column and press F2 to see values in a radio group (A). Similarly, press F2 in the *Manager* column. This will display a drop down list (B) in the selected cell carrying names of president and managers. Double click the column prior to the *Hire Date* column, and press the Tab key. The cursor's focus will move on to the *Hire Date* column and immediately the Date Picker window (C) will pop up. Keep pressing the Tab key to access the *On Leave* column, which will show a *Yes* and *No* switch (D). Access the *Tags* column, which should come up with a shuttle (E) carrying the five values defined in step 5. Using the arrow key in the shuttle, move all these values to the right pane and click the cross icon to close the shuttle. Click the **Save** button to write your changes to the database.

## 5.6.4 Protecting Rows in Interactive Grid

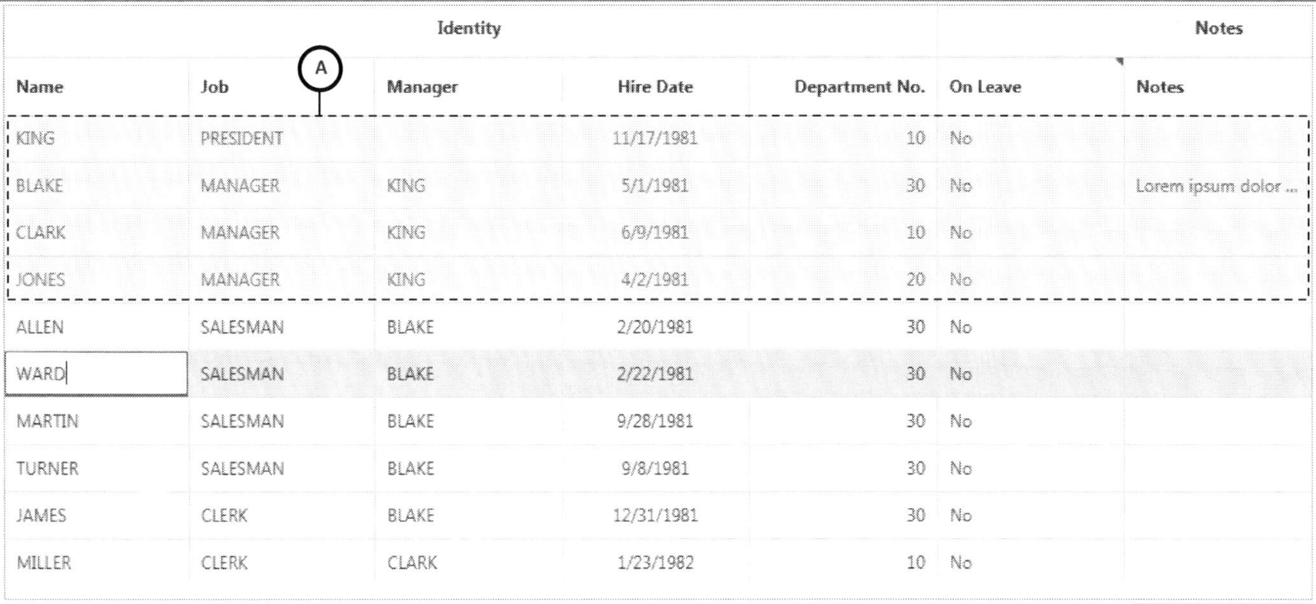

| | | Identity | | | | | Notes |
|---|---|---|---|---|---|---|---|
| Name | Job | Manager | Hire Date | Department No. | On Leave | Notes | |
| KING | PRESIDENT | | 11/17/1981 | 10 | No | | |
| BLAKE | MANAGER | KING | 5/1/1981 | 30 | No | Lorem ipsum dolor ... | |
| CLARK | MANAGER | KING | 6/9/1981 | 10 | No | | |
| JONES | MANAGER | KING | 4/2/1981 | 20 | No | | |
| ALLEN | SALESMAN | BLAKE | 2/20/1981 | 30 | No | | |
| WARD | SALESMAN | BLAKE | 2/22/1981 | 30 | No | | |
| MARTIN | SALESMAN | BLAKE | 9/28/1981 | 30 | No | | |
| TURNER | SALESMAN | BLAKE | 9/8/1981 | 30 | No | | |
| JAMES | CLERK | BLAKE | 12/31/1981 | 30 | No | | |
| MILLER | CLERK | CLARK | 1/23/1982 | 10 | No | | |

**Figure 5-17**

In this example, you will see how to protect rows in an Interactive Grid. For this purpose, you need to add a column named CTRL to implement a simple rule that Managers and Presidents cannot be edited or deleted. This column is then selected in the *Allowed Row Operations Column* property under the *Attributes* tab.

1. With Page 100 being displayed in the Page Designer, click the *Column Groups* region and amend the SELECT statement as follows (the amendment is shown in bold):

```
SELECT empno, ename, job, mgr, hiredate, sal, comm, deptno, onleave,
notes, flex4 as tags,
case when JOB = 'MANAGER' or JOB = 'PRESIDENT' then ' '
else 'UD' end as CTRL
FROM EBA_DEMO_IG_EMP
```

2. After amending the SQL query you will see the *CTRL* column under the *Columns* node. Click this column and set its *Type* to **Hidden**. Also **turn on** the *Query Only* property (under *Source*). For explanation, see Chapter 7 section 7.4.2.

3. Click the *Column Groups* interactive grid region and then click the **Attributes** tab in the Property pane. Select the **CTRL** column for *Allowed Row Operations Column* property in the *Edit* section.

4. Save the page and run it. Click the **Edit** button. Rows that cannot be edited or deleted are grayed out (A) in the edit mode.

## 5.6.5 Scroll Paging

Another exciting feature of Interactive Grids is scroll paging (also known as infinite scrolling or virtual paging). It is enabled by setting *Pagination* attribute to *Scroll*. After enabling this attribute, the region appears to carry the entire result set but rows are rendered on demand as you scroll. When you scroll down in the Interactive Grid, the model fetches data from the server as it is needed by the view. You can even drag the scroll bar handle all the way to the bottom and then scroll up. You need a database table with lots of records to assess this feature. In this exercise, you will use EBA_DEMO_IG_PEOPLE table, which carries over 4000 records.

1. Create a new page using the instructions mentioned earlier in Section 5.6.1. Set *Page Number* to **111**, set *Page Name* to **Scroll Paging**, and enter the following SELECT statement. Rest of the page properties will remain the same.

**SELECT name, country, rating FROM EBA_DEMO_IG_PEOPLE**

2. In the Page Designer, click the **Scroll Paging** region and then click the **Attributes** tab in the Properties pane. Set *Type* under the *Pagination* section to **Scroll** and **turn on** the *Show Total Row Count*.

3. Save and run the page and scroll down using your mouse wheel to test this amazing feature. You will see total number of records at the bottom of the Interactive Grid.

## 5.6.6 Master Detail. And Detail. And Detail.

Interactive Grid makes it effortless to create master-detail relationships and go any number of levels deep and across. You can create all types of master-detail-detail screens with ease. In this section, I'll demonstrate this feature.

1. From the *SQL Workshop* menu, select **SQL Scripts** and click the **Upload** button. In the *Upload Script* screen, click the **Choose File** button. In the *Open* dialog box, select **master_detail_detail.sql** file from Chapter 5 folder in the book's source code and click **Upload**. In the *SQL Scripts* interface click the **Run** button appearing in the last column. On the *Run Script* screen, click the **Run Now** button. The script will execute to create four tables (MD_continent, MD_country, MD_city, and MD_population) along with relevant data to demonstrate the master detail detail feature. You can view these tables from the *SQL Workshop > Object Browser* interface.

2. Create a new page by clicking the **Create Page** button in the App Builder interface. This time, select the first **Blank Page** option and click **Next**. Set *Page Number* to **112**, *Name* to **Master Detail Detail**, *Page Mode* to **Normal**, and click **Next**. On the *Navigation Menu* screen, select the first *Navigation Preference* to not associate this page with any sales app navigation menu entry. On the final wizard screen, click **Finish**.

3. In the Page Designer, right-click the *Components* node on the *Rendering* tab and select **Create Region**. Set the following properties for the new region. This region will display data from the *MD_continent* table.

| Property | Value |
|---|---|
| Title | Continents |
| Type *(under Identification)* | Interactive Grid |
| Type *(under Source)* | SQL Query |
| SQL Query | SELECT * FROM MD_continent |

After entering the SQL query, click anywhere outside the query box. Expand the *Columns* node under this region. Click the **CONTINENT_ID** column. Set its *Type* to **Hidden** and **turn on** the *Primary Key* property (under *Source*). You must define a primary key column for an interactive grid region, which is required to establish a master detail relationship.

4. Create another region under the *Continents* region by right-clicking the main *Components* node. This region will act as the detail for the *Continents* region. At run-time when you select a continent, this region will display a list of countries in the selected continent. Set the following properties for this new region.

| Property | Value |
|---|---|
| Title | Countries |
| Type *(under Identification)* | Interactive Grid |
| Type *(under Source)* | SQL Query |
| SQL Query | SELECT * FROM MD_country |

Expand the *Columns* node under the *Countries* region. Click the **COUNTRY_ID** column. Set its *Type* to **Hidden** and **turn on** the *Primary Key* property (under *Source*). You set the *Primary Key* property to *Yes,* because this region will act as a master for the *Cities* region created in the next step. Now, associate this detail region to its master (*Continents*). Click the *Countries* region and set the *Master Region* property (under *Master Detail*) to **Continents**. This should be set when this region is the detail region in a master-detail relationship with another region on the page. For the master-detail relationship to work correctly, you must also select the column(s) in the detail region, which are foreign keys to the master region, by setting the *Master Column* property. Click the **CONTINENT_ID** column (a foreign key) in the *Countries* region. Set its *Type* property to **Hidden** and *Master Column* (under *Master Detail*) to **CONTINENT_ID**, which references the same column in the master region.

5. Create another region and place it under the *Countries* region. This region will show a list of cities when you select a country from its master region. Set the following properties for this region:

| Property | Value |
|---|---|
| Title | Cities |
| Type (under Identification) | Interactive Grid |
| Type (under Source) | SQL Query |
| SQL Query | SELECT * FROM MD_city |
| Master Region | Countries |

Expand the *Columns* node under the *Cities* region. Click the **CITY_ID** column. Set its *Type* to **Hidden** and **turn on** the *Primary Key* property (under *Source*). Click the **COUNTRY_ID** column in this region. Set the *Type* of this column to **Hidden** and *Master Column* to **COUNTRY_ID** to point to the same column in the *Countries* region.

6. Create the last region to display population of a city.

| Property | Value |
|---|---|
| Title | Population |
| Type (under Identification) | Interactive Grid |
| Type (under Source) | SQL Query |
| SQL Query | SELECT * FROM MD_population |
| Master Region | Cities |

Expand the *Columns* node under the *Population* region. Click the **POPULATION_ID** column. Set its *Type* to **Hidden**. Since this is the last region, you do not need to specify this column as a primary key. However, you have to set a couple of properties for the CITY_ID column in this region to associate it with its master. Click the **CITY_ID** column, set its *Type* property to **Hidden** and *Master Column* to **CITY_ID**. That's it!

Save and run the page. Click the row representing Europe (A) in the first region. As you click this row, the second region will display countries in the Europe continent. Click Germany (B) in the second region. This will refresh the third region with a list of cities in Germany. Click the Berlin city (C) to see its population (D) in the fourth region.

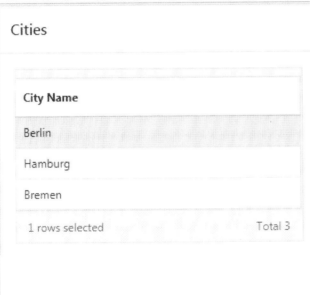

Figure 5-18

## Summary

Here is the summary of this chapter to see what we grasped in it. We learned the following techniques while performing various exercises in this chapter:

- Declaratively created report and form pages and linked them together
- Placed form input items using 12 columns grid layout
- Changed the default type of an item and used list of values
- Created validations to prevent customer record deletion with existing orders and to check customers' credit limits.
- Used a dynamic action to automatically refresh a page
- Used various features of the new Interactive Grid
- Learned how to change types of columns

- Got hands-on exposure to Master Detail Detail feature.

Let's get back to our sales application. The next chapter discusses how to manage products in a database application with some more useful techniques to explore the exciting world of Oracle APEX.

# 6

# SET UP PRODUCTS

# CATALOG

## 6.1 About Products Setup

Just like the Customers module, you'll create a Products setup to manage products information. This module will also have two pages: *Products* and *Product Details*. The main *Products* page (Page 3 – Figure 6-1) will have three different views: Icon, Report, and Details. Initially, the wizard will create the *Report View* version that you'll modify with a custom SQL statement. The remaining two views (*Detail* and *Icon*) are placed on the page by enabling respective properties found under the main Products region. Once you enable these views, their respective icons appear on the main Search bar. Using these icons you can switch among different views to browse products information. The *Product Details* page (Page 6) will be created to add, modify, and delete a product. To create these two pages you'll follow the same approach as you did in the previous chapter. Since most of the steps are similar to those already briefed in the Customers setup chapter, I'll elaborate the features new to this module.

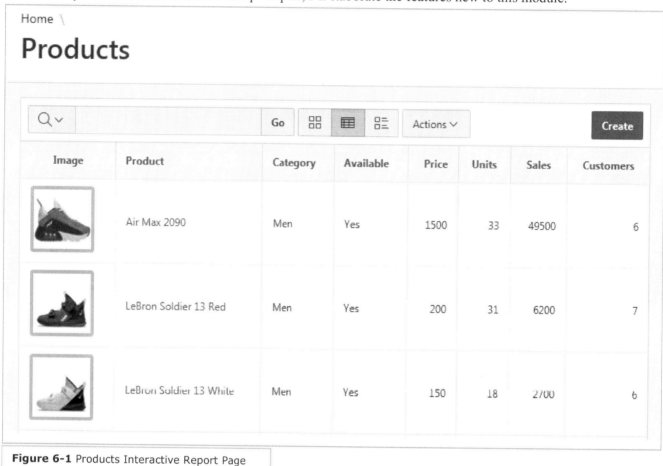

**Figure 6-1** Products Interactive Report Page

The new stuff added to this module includes image handling and styling. This module is based on the DEMO_PRODUCT_INFO table in the database. Among conventional columns exists the following four special columns to handle images in the database. Normally, specialized processing is required to handle images in a database. The Oracle APEX environment has eliminated the need to perform all that specialized processing with these additional columns. Your Oracle APEX application will use these columns to properly process images in the BLOB column.

**PRODUCT_IMAGE:** This column uses BLOB data type. A BLOB (Binary Large Object) is an Oracle data type that can hold up to 4 GB of data. BLOBs are handy for storing digitized information, such as images, audio, and video. You can also store your document files like PDF, MS Word, MS Excel, MS PowerPoint and CSV to name a few.

**MIMETYPE:** A Multipurpose Internet Mail Extension (MIME) type identifies the format of a file. The MIME type enables applications to read the file. Applications such as Internet browsers and e-mail applications use the MIME type to handle files of different types. For example, an e-mail application can use the MIME type to detect what type of file is in a file attached to an e-mail. Many systems use MIME types to identify the format of arbitrary files on the file system. MIME types are composed of a top-level media type followed by a subtype identifier, separated by a forward slash character (/). An example of a MIME type is *image/jpeg*. The media type in this example is image and the subtype identifier is jpeg. The top-level media type is a general categorization about the content of the file, while the subtype identifier specifically identifies the format of the file. The following list contains some file types and the corresponding MIME types that you can view via Object Browser in SQL Workshop after uploading such file types to the BLOB column in your table.

| File Type | MIMETYPE Metadata |
|---|---|
| JPEG | image/jpeg |
| PNG | image/png |
| PDF | application/pdf |
| WORD | application/vnd.openxmlformats-officedocument.wordprocessingml.document |
| EXCEL | application/vnd.openxmlformats-officedocument.spreadsheetml.sheet |
| POWERPOINT | application/vnd.openxmlformats-officedocument.presentationml.presentation |
| CSV | application/vnd.ms-excel |

**FILENAME:** A case-sensitive column name used to store the filename of the BLOB, such as bag.jpg or CV.pdf.

**IMAGE_LAST_UPDATE:** A case-sensitive column name used to store the last update date of the BLOB.

Besides image handling, you'll also learn the technique to incorporate style sheet in an Oracle APEX page. Web browsers refer to Cascading Style Sheets (CSS) to define the appearance and layout of text and other material.

## 6.2 Create Pages for Products Setup

The following set of steps use the same approach you followed in the previous chapter to create a report along with an input form. Note that this time you will be creating an interactive report to display a list of products instead of an interactive grid – see Chapter 2 Section 2.3.3 for further details on the interactive report.

1. Click the **Create Page** Create Page > button in the App Builder interface.

2. Click the **Form** option, followed by **Report with Form** option. These two selections will create a report page (Figure 6-1) to display all product records from the table (selected in step 5) and a form page (Figure 6-6) to add, modify, and delete products.

3. On the *Page Attributes* wizard screen, set the following properties and click **Next**. The form page (Page 6) is named *Product Details* and it will be linked to the report page (*Products* - Page 3).

| Property | Value |
|---|---|
| Report Type | Interactive Report |
| Report Page Number | 3 |
| Report Page Name | Products |
| Form Page Number | 6 |
| Form Page Name | Product Details |
| Form Page Mode | Modal Dialog |
| Breadcrumb | Breadcrumb |
| Parent Entry | Home (Page 1) |
| Entry Name | Products |

4. On the *Navigation Menu* screen, set *Navigation Preference* to **Identify an existing navigation menu entry for this page**, set *Existing Navigation Menu Entry* to **Setup**, and click **Next**. This step will highlight the *Setup* entry in the main navigation menu when you access the products setup.

5. On *Data Source* screen, select **Table** for *Source Type*, accept the default schema in *Table/View Owner*, and select **DEMO_PRODUCT_INFO (table)** for *Table/View Name*. The columns from the selected table to be shown in the interactive report will appear in the right pane. In the next section, you will add a custom SQL query for the report page. For now, accept all the table columns and click **Next**.

6. On the **Form Page** screen, add all columns (A) from the DEMO_PRODUCT_INFO table to Page 6, except MIMETYPE, FILENAME, and IMAGE_LAST_UPDATE (B). These three columns are used in the background to handle images of products. For *Primary Key Type*, choose **Select Primary Key Column(s)** (C). Set *Primary Key Column 1* attribute to **PRODUCT_ID (Number)** (D). PRODUCT_ID is a primary key column, which uniquely identifies a product and is populated behind the scene using a database sequence object (DEMO_PRODUCT_INFO_SEQ) via BI_DEMO_PRODUCT_INFO trigger when you add a new product – see the two objects by accessing Object Browser. Click the **Create** button to complete the wizard.

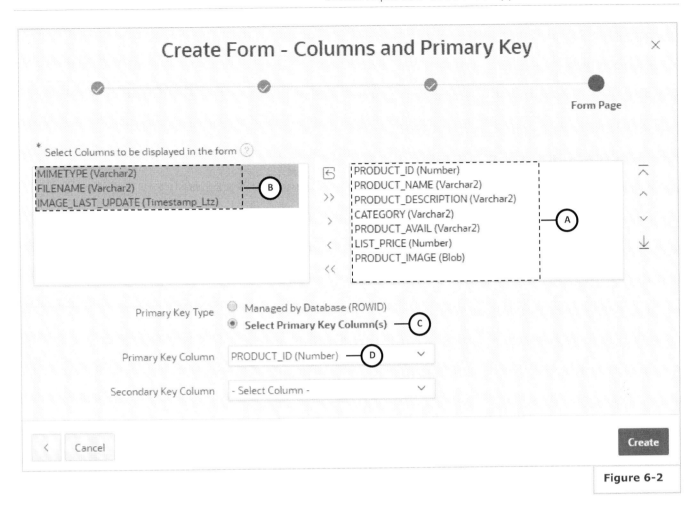

**Figure 6-2**

This time, the wizard creates two pages (3 and 6) as an initial structure for this module. In the upcoming exercises you will undergo some new techniques to transform these wizard-generated pages to give them a professional touch.

## 6.3 Modify Products Page - Page 3

Execute the instructions provided in the following sub-sections to first modify the Products (interactive report) page in Page Designer.

## 6.3.1 Modify Region Properties

Execute the following steps to modify the **Products** page (Page 3).

1.  Click the region named *Report 1* and set its *Title* to **Products**.

2.  In *SQL Query*, replace the existing SELECT statement with the following:

```
SELECT p.product_id,
       p.product_name,
       p.product_description,
       p.category,
       decode(p.product_avail, 'Y','Yes','N','No') product_avail,
       p.list_price,
       (select sum(quantity) from demo_order_items where product_id = p.product_id) units,
       (select sum(quantity * p.list_price) from demo_order_items where product_id = p.product_id) sales,
       (select count(o.customer_id) from demo_orders o, demo_order_items t
       where o.order_id = t.order_id and t.product_id = p.product_id group by p.product_id) customers,
       (select max(o.order_timestamp) od from demo_orders o, demo_order_items i where o.order_id =
       i.order_id and i.product_id = p.product_id) last_date_sold, p.product_id img,
       apex_util.prepare_url(p_url=>'f?p='||:app_id||':6:'||:app_session||
       ':::P6_PRODUCT_ID:'||p.product_id) icon_link,
       decode(nvl(dbms_lob.getlength(p.product_image),0),0,null,
       '<img alt="'||p.product_name||'" title="'||p.product_name||'" style="border: 4px solid #CCC;
       -moz-border-radius: 4px; -webkit-border-radius: 4px;"||
       'src="'||apex_util.get_blob_file_src('P6_PRODUCT_IMAGE',p.product_id)||'" height="75"
       width="75" />') detail_img,
       decode(nvl(dbms_lob.getlength(p.product_image),0),0,null,
       apex_util.get_blob_file_src('P6_PRODUCT_IMAGE',p.product_id)) detail_img_no_style
FROM demo_product_info p
```

The *icon_link* column in this query is formed using the PREPARE_URL function, which is a part of the APEX_UTIL package. It returns the f?p URL. The P_URL is a VARCHAR2 parameter passed on to this function. You will use this function throughout this book to form links. The link is formed to call the Product Details page – Page 6. The *detail_img* column holds images of products. The HTML <img> tag is used to display the images of products in conjunction with a built-in function named APEX_UTIL.GET_BLOB_FILE_SRC. This is an Oracle APEX function and it provides the ability to more specifically format the display of the image with height and width properties. The image is styled using CSS inline styling method. The *getlength* function of the *dbms_lob* package (*dbms_lob.getlength*) is used to estimate the size of a BLOB column in the table. The selection of the BLOB size is made to facilitate the inclusion of a download link in a report. If the length is 0, the BLOB is NULL and no download link is displayed.

3.  Expand the *Columns* node (under *Body | Products* region) and set meaningful column headings as follows:

    **Product, Description, Category, Available, Price, Units, Sales, Customers, Last Sold, Image, Icon Link, Image Detail,** and **Detail Image No Style**

4. Modify the following columns using the specified properties. These columns are marked as hidden to make them invisible at runtime. However, they will be visible to your application for handling images. These columns were also derived through the SQL SELECT statement defined in step 2. Note that you can use Ctrl+click or Shift+click keys combination to select multiple columns to change the *Type* properties at once. Each report column has the property *Escape special characters*. By default, this property is set to Yes. Selecting Yes for this property prevents Cross-Site Scripting (XSS) attacks and selecting *No* renders HTML tags stored in the page item or in the entries of a list of value.

| Column | Property | Value |
|---|---|---|
| PRODUCT_ID | Type | Hidden Column |
| IMG | Type | Hidden Column |
| ICON_LINK | Type | Hidden Column |
| DETAIL_IMG | Escape special characters *(under Security)* | Off *(otherwise image will not appear)* |
| DETAIL_IMG_NO_STYLE | Type | Hidden Column |

5. Click the **PRODUCT_NAME** column to transform it into a link. By selecting the Product Name column in the *Link Text* attribute you specify this report column to appear as a link. You created a similar kind of link in the previous chapter to call the Customer Details page. In Interactive Reports, you forward a value to the target page using special substitution strings (enclosed in # symbols) as compared to *&Item.* notation (for example, &CUSTOMER_ID.), which you use in the Interactive Grid – see Chapter 5 Section 5.3.1 Step 10.

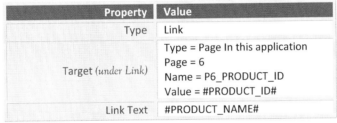

| Property | Value |
|---|---|
| Type | Link |
| Target *(under Link)* | Type = Page In this application<br>Page = 6<br>Name = P6_PRODUCT_ID<br>Value = #PRODUCT_ID# |
| Link Text | #PRODUCT_NAME# |

6. If you save and run the report page at this stage, you will see an EDIT column (represented with a pencil icon), which leads to the details page. Since we have already created a link (on the Product Name column), we will eliminate this column. Click the *Products* region, and then click the **Attributes** tab in the Properties pane. Set *Link Column* to **Exclude Link Column**.

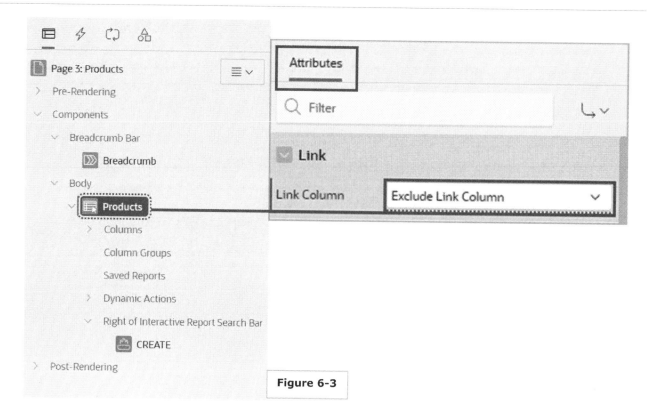

**Figure 6-3**

7. On the same *Attributes* tab, scroll down to **Icon View** section and set the following properties. By default, most interactive reports display as a report. You can optionally display columns as icons. When configured, an icon (*View Icons*) appears on the Search bar. To use this view, you must specify the columns to identify the icon, the label, and the target (that is, the link). As a best practice the *Type* attribute of these columns is set to hidden (as you did in step 4), because they are typically not useful for end users. The *Image Attributes* property will style height and width of images.

| Property | Value |
|---|---|
| Show | On |
| Columns Per Row | 5   (to display 5 images on a single row in View Icons interface) |
| Link Column | ICON_LINK |
| Image Source Column | DETAIL_IMG_NO_STYLE |
| Label Column | PRODUCT_NAME |
| Image Attributes | width="200" height="200" |

8. Just under the Icon View section, there is another section named Detail View. In the **Detail View** section, **turn on** the *Show* property. When configured, a *View Details* icon appears on the Search bar.

9.  In **Before Rows**, enter the following code. This attribute of the *Detail View* enables you to enter HTML code to be displayed before report rows. For example, you can use the <TABLE> element to put the database content in row/column format. Besides adding HTML code, styling information can also be incorporated using this attribute. The <style> tag is used to define style information for an HTML document. Inside the <style> element you specify how HTML elements should render in a browser. The code below uses custom CSS rules to override the default Oracle APEX Interactive Report (apexir) styles.

```
<style>
  table.apexir_WORKSHEET_CUSTOM {
    border: none !important;
    box-shadow: none;
    -moz-box-shadow: none;
    -webkit-box-shadow: none;}

  .apexir_WORKSHEET_DATA td {
    border-bottom: none !important;}

  table.reportDetail td {
    padding: 2px 4px !important;
    border: none !important;
    font: 11px/16px Arial, sans-serif;}

  table.reportDetail td.separator {
    background: #F0F0F0 !important;
    padding: 0 !important;
    height: 1px !important;
    padding: 0;
    line-height: 2px !important;
    overflow: hidden;}

  table.reportDetail td h1 {margin: 0 !important}

  table.reportDetail td img {
    margin-top: 8px;
    border: 4px solid #CCC;
    -moz-border-radius: 4px;
    -webkit-border-radius: 4px;}
</style>
<table class="reportDetail">
```

Remember that all APEX pages are HTML pages controlled by HTML properties and cascading style sheet (CSS) settings. When you create an interactive report, Oracle APEX renders it based on CSS classes associated with the current theme. Each APEX interactive report component has a CSS style definition that may be changed by applying standard CSS techniques to override the defaults. Such changes may be applied to a single interactive report, to a page template to effect changes across several interactive reports, or to all page templates of a theme to enforce a common look and feel for all reports in an application.

In the current step, you are changing the appearance of the report by overriding built-in styles for the table and subordinate elements.

10. In **For Each Row**, enter the following code. The code is applied to each record. In every <td> element you are referencing interactive report columns and labels with the help of a special substitution string (#) and are styling each record using inline CSS method. You used the substitution string to reference table column names and labels of page items as #PRODUCT_NAME# and #CATEGORY_LABEL#, respectively.

```
<tr>
  <td rowspan="5" valign="top"><img width="75" height="75" src="#DETAIL_IMG_NO_STYLE#"></td>
  <td colspan="6"><h1><a href="#ICON_LINK#"><strong>#PRODUCT_NAME#</strong></a></h1></td>
</tr>
<tr>
  <td><strong>#CATEGORY_LABEL#:</strong></td><td>#CATEGORY#</td>
  <td><strong>#PRODUCT_AVAIL_LABEL#:</strong></td><td>#PRODUCT_AVAIL#</td>
  <td><strong>#LAST_DATE_SOLD_LABEL#:</strong></td><td>#LAST_DATE_SOLD#</td>
</tr>
<tr>
  <td align="left"><strong>#PRODUCT_DESCRIPTION_LABEL#:</strong></td>
  <td colspan="5">#PRODUCT_DESCRIPTION#</td>
</tr>
<tr>
  <td style="padding-bottom: 0px;"><strong>#LIST_PRICE_LABEL#</strong></td>
  <td style="padding-bottom: 0px;"><strong>#UNITS_LABEL#</strong></td>
  <td style="padding-bottom: 0px;"><strong>#SALES_LABEL#</strong></td>
  <td style="padding-bottom: 0px;"><strong>#CUSTOMERS_LABEL#</strong></td>
</tr>
<tr>
  <td style="padding-top: 0px;">#LIST_PRICE#</td>
  <td style="padding-top: 0px;">#UNITS#</td>
  <td style="padding-top: 0px;">#SALES#</td>
  <td style="padding-top: 0px;">#CUSTOMERS#</td>
</tr>
<tr>
  <td colspan="7" class="separator"></td>
</tr>
```

11. In **After Rows**, enter </table> to complete the HTML code. In this attribute you enter the HTML to be displayed after report rows. It is the closing table tag </TABLE> to end the table.

12. Save and run the page from the **Manage Products** option in the *Setup* menu. Click the **View Reports** icon
. Note that the *Image Detail* column is blank at the moment, because we do not have any product image in the table. This is the column which will hold images of products. Click **Air Max 2090** link in the *Product* column to add the image of this product. On the Product Details page, click the **folder icon** representing the *Product Image* field at the bottom of the page. This will bring up the *Open* dialog box. Go to BookCode\Chapter6 folder and select **1_AirMax2090.png** file, and click **Open**. The image name will be displayed in the *Product Image* field. Click the **Apply Changes** button on the *Product Details* form to save the image. The image will appear on the interactive report page. Repeat this step to add images of the remaining products. Click the *View Icons* and *View Details* options on the interactive report toolbar and see the output, as illustrated in the following figure.

Figure 6-4

13. Click the **View Reports** icon. Click the **Actions** menu in the interactive report and select **Columns**. Make sure all columns (except Description and Last Sold) appear in *Display in Report section*. You can use the arrow icons to arrange columns in a desired order and click the **Apply** button. Only the columns you selected will appear in the interactive report.

14. Click the **Actions** menu again and select **Save Report** (under *Report*). From the *Save* drop-down list, select **As Default Report Settings**. Set *Default Report Type* to **Primary** and click **Apply**. After modifying an interactive report you must save it using this procedure, otherwise you'll lose the applied settings when you subsequently view this report. Developers can save two types of default interactive report: primary and alternative. Both reports display on the Report list on the Search bar. The primary default report (you just saved) cannot be renamed or deleted.

## 6.4 Modify Product Details Page - Page 6

The Page Designer toolbar carries a section called *Page Selector*. The Page Selector displays the current page. Click the down arrow (labeled *Page Finder*) to search for pages. Alternatively, enter a page number in the field and click *Go*. To navigate to the previous or next page, click *Navigate to Next Page* (up arrow) and *Navigate to Previous Page* (down arrow).

**Figure 6-5**

Using the Page Selector call **Page 6** in the Page Designer. Click the root node 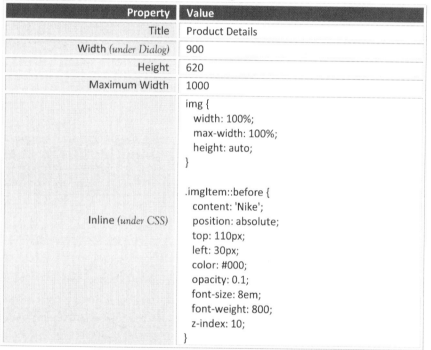 and set the following properties to adjust the dimension of the Product Details page. The *img* rule provided in the inline CSS property will make products' images responsive. The *::before* selector (used in the second rule) will insert the word *Nike* before images of products – see Figure 6-6.

| Property | Value |
|---|---|
| Title | Product Details |
| Width (*under Dialog*) | 900 |
| Height | 620 |
| Maximum Width | 1000 |
| Inline (*under CSS*) | img {<br>   width: 100%;<br>   max-width: 100%;<br>   height: auto;<br>}<br><br>.imgItem::before {<br>   content: 'Nike';<br>   position: absolute;<br>   top: 110px;<br>   left: 30px;<br>   color: #000;<br>   opacity: 0.1;<br>   font-size: 8em;<br>   font-weight: 800;<br>   z-index: 10;<br>} |

### 6.4.1 Making Page Item Mandatory

1. Make the product name item (**P6_PRODUCT_NAME**) mandatory using the following properties:

| Property | Value |
|---|---|
| Template (*under Appearance*) | Required |
| Value Required (*under Validation*) | On |

2. Also set the above two properties for **P6_CATEGORY, P6_PRODUCT_AVAIL,** and **P6_LIST_PRICE** page items. Click on P6_CATEGORY item, press and hold the Ctrl key on your keyboard, and then click the other two items to select them all. This way you can set properties for multiple items at once.

3. Set the Template property of P6_PRODUCT_DESCRIPTION and P6_PRODUCT_IMAGE page items to **Optional**.

## 6.4.2 Attach Categories LOV

We created a list of values (CATEGORIES) in Chapter 3 section 3.4.1. Here we're going to use that list to display predefined values of categories in a Select List. First, you will change the Category item from Text to a Select List, and then you'll define the list of values (LOV) to which the item will bound. Recall that you used this process in the Manage Customers module to display STATES LOV. In the Items node under the Product Details region, click the **P6_CATEGORY** item and amend the following properties in the Property Editor:

| Property | Value |
|---|---|
| Type (under Identification) | Select List |
| Type (under List of Values) | Shared Component |
| List of Values | CATEGORIES |
| Display Extra Values | Off |
| Display Null Value | Off |

## 6.4.3 Attach LOV to Product Available Column

Next, you will change the *Product Available* field to a Switch comprising two options: *On* and *Off*. Just like the previous steps, here as well, you're changing the item type from Text to Switch. At runtime, this item will show two options to specify whether the selected product is available or not. If you ignore this exercise and leave the item to its default type, users can enter whatever value they like, resulting in compromising application's integrity. This is a good example to restrict users to select valid values. Select the **P6_PRODUCT_AVAIL** item and set the following properties. Note that the last two properties in the table set Y (which stands for *On*) as the default value for this item.

| Property | Value |
|---|---|
| Type (under Identification) | Switch |
| Label | Product Available |
| Type (under Default) | Static |
| Static Value | Y |

## 6.4.4 Handling Image (Handle Image Exercise A)

Modify the following properties (in the *Settings* section) for the **P6_PRODUCT_IMAGE** item to map table columns. This mapping is necessary to display product images on the details form.

| Property | Value |
|---|---|
| MIME Type Column | MIMETYPE |
| Filename Column | FILENAME |
| BLOB Last Update Column | IMAGE_LAST_UPDATE |

In the *Settings* section, the *Storage Type* attribute is set to **BLOB column specified in item Source attribute** by default. The *Storage Type* attribute specifies where the uploaded file should be stored at. It has two values:

1. *BLOB column specified in item source attribute*. Stores the uploaded file in the table used by the "Automatic Row Processing (DML)" process and the column specified in the item source attribute. The column has to be of data type BLOB.

2. *Table APEX_APPLICATION_TEMP_FILE*. Stores the uploaded file in a table named APEX_APPLICATION_TEMP_FILE.

## 6.4.5 Create Region – Product Image (Handle Image Exercise B)

To show the images of selected products on Product Details page, we will create a *Static Content* sub-region. Note that this section will only create a blank region to hold an image. The image will be added to this region in a subsequent section. Right-click the *Components* node, and select **Create Region** from the context menu. Select the new region and modify the following properties. The *imgItem* CSS class references the rule you created in section 6.4 to place the word NIKE in the image. The region will be displayed only when there exists an image for a product and this evaluation is made using a condition based on a PL/SQL function.

| Property | Value |
| --- | --- |
| Title | Product Image |
| Type | Static Content |
| Sequence | 5 (*to place this region before the Product Details region*) |
| CSS Classes | imgItem |
| Type (*under Server-side Condition*) | Function Body |
| Language | PL/SQL |
| PL/SQL Function Body | (code below) |

```
1   DECLARE
2   BEGIN
3    if :P6_PRODUCT_ID is not null then
4     for c1 in (select nvl(dbms_lob.getlength(product_image),0) A
5            from demo_product_info
6            where product_id = :P6_PRODUCT_ID)
7     loop
8      if c1.A > 0 then
9       return true;
10     end if;
11    end loop;
12   end if;
13   return false;
14  END;
```

Click the **Product Details** region and **turn off** the *Start New Row* property to place this region beside the Product Image region you just added.

Page items are referenced in a PL/SQL block using bind variables in which a colon(:) is prefixed to the item name – :P6_PRODUCT_ID, for example.

### Code Explained

In Oracle APEX you make use of conditions to control the appearance of page components. The ability to dynamically show or hide a page component is referred to as *conditional rendering*. You define conditional rendering for regions, items, and buttons. These page components have a *Condition* section in the property editor, where you select a condition type from a list. In the current scenario, you set a condition based on a PL/SQL function, which returns a single Boolean value: True or False. If the code returns True, the region is displayed carrying the image of the selected product.

After selecting a condition type, you inform Oracle APEX to execute the defined PL/SQL code. The code first executes an IF condition (line 3) to check whether the product ID is not null by evaluating the value of the page item P6_PRODUCT_ID. If the value is null, the flow of the code is transferred to line 13, where a false value is returned and the function is terminated. If there exists a value for the product ID, then line 4 is executed, which creates a FOR loop to loop through all records in the DEMO_PRODUCT_INFO table to find the record (and consequently the image) of the selected product (line 4-11). On line 8, another IF condition is used to assess whether the image exists. If so, a true value is returned on line 9 and the function is terminated.

## 6.4.6 Create Item (Handle Image Exercise C)

In this section, you will create a new item named P6_IMAGE to display the product image in the *Product Image* region. Right-click the **Product Image** region and select **Create Page Item** from the context menu. Set the following properties for the new item. The *Display Image* item type displays an image stored in a database BLOB column, or based on an image URL. The *style* value in *Custom Attributes* sets a blue background for the image. We also specified the database image column and its type. By setting the *Rows Returned* condition and using a SQL query we ensured the existence of an image in the table.

| Property | Value |
|---|---|
| Name | P6_IMAGE |
| Type | Display Image |
| Label | *Clear the Label box to make it empty* |
| Region | Product Image |
| Template | Optional Floating |
| Custom Attributes | style="background: #006bdc;" |
| Form Region (under Source) | Product Details |
| Column | PRODUCT_IMAGE |
| Data Type | BLOB |
| Type (*under Server-side Condition*) | Rows Returned |
| SQL Query | SELECT mimetype from demo_product_info WHERE product_id = :P6_PRODUCT_ID AND mimetype like 'image%' |

## 6.4.7 Create Button to Remove Image (Handle Image Exercise D)

An image can be removed from the Product Details page and consequently from the underlying table by clicking this button. It is attached to a process (Delete Image) defined in the next section. Right-click the **Product Image** region and select **Create Button**. Set the following properties for the new button. The button will appear on top of the region. The Target value calls a confirmation box. This call is made using an Oracle APEX function (*apex.confirm*) by passing a message and the name of the Delete button. If you click Yes in the confirmation box, the process associated with the Delete button removes image references from the products table.

| Property | Value |
|---|---|
| Name | DELETE_IMAGE |
| Label | Remove Image |
| Region | Product Image |
| Position | Copy |
| Button Template | Icon |
| Hot | On |
| Icon | fa-cut |
| Action (*under Behavior*) | Redirect to URL |
| URL (*under Target*) | javascript:apex.confirm('Are you sure you want to delete this image? It will no longer be available for others to see if you continue.','DELETE_IMAGE'); |

## 6.5 Create a Process Under Processing to Delete Image (Handle Image Exercise E)

This is the process I mentioned in the previous section. It is associated with the Delete button to remove a product image. To remove an image stored in a database table, you are required to just replace the content of the relevant columns with a null. Click the **Processing** tab and then right-click the **Processing** node. From the context menu select **Create Process**. Set the following properties for the new process:

| Property | Value |
|---|---|
| Name | Delete Image |
| Type | PL/SQL Code |
| PL/SQL Code | UPDATE demo_product_info<br>    SET product_image=null,<br>        mimetype=null,<br>        filename=null,<br>        image_last_update=null<br>WHERE product_id = :P6_PRODUCT_ID; |
| Sequence | 15 *(to place it before the Close Dialog process)* |
| Success Message | Product image deleted |
| When Button Pressed | DELETE_IMAGE |

The Processing node contains two processes (Process form Product Details and Close Dialog) that were created by the page creation wizard. The first one is created to handle DML operations, while the second one closes Page 6 when you click Create, Save, or Delete button. The values of these buttons are mentioned in Server-side Condition of the process, which specifies that the dialog is to be closed only when any of the three buttons are clicked. Clicking the DELETE_IMAGE button won't close the page, because the name of this button is not in the Value list. Similarly, the Delete Image process will only be executed when the DELETE_IMAGE button is pressed.

## Test Your Work

Save your work and run the application. From the main navigation menu, select **Manage Products** from the *Setup* menu. On the main interactive report page (Figure 6-1), click the three report icons ▦ ▤ ▥ individually to see different views of products information. Clicking **View Icons** will present small icons of products. Each product is presented as a linked icon. If you click any icon, you'll be taken to the form page (Page 6 - Figure 6-6) where you'll see details of the selected product. Click the Report View icon. The Report View presents data in a table. Here, you can access the details page by clicking products' names. Click the Detail View icon. This View presents products information from a different perspective. You can access details of a product by clicking its name. This is the view that was styled in section 6.3.1 steps 8-11.

Click any product's name to call its details page (as illustrated in Figure 6-6). The form region (*Product Details*) was created by the wizard incorporating all relevant fields. The Product Image region was created in section 6.4.5. Also, note that the Remove Image button (you created in section 6.4.7) appears within this region.

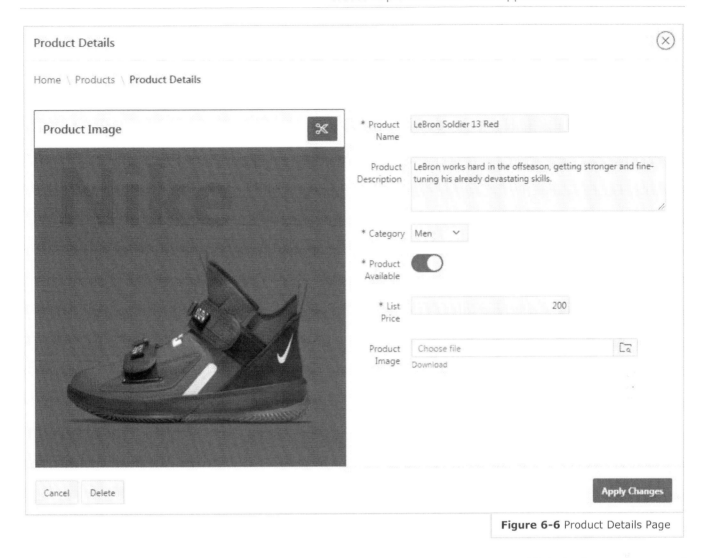

**Figure 6-6** Product Details Page

Create a new product record using the *Add Product* button on the Products report page. Click the *Browse* button and select any small image file to test image upload. You can use an existing product image by right-clicking the image and selecting *Save Image As* from the context menu. Or, use the *Download* link provided on the Product Details form page to get one for testing.

Once you have an image in place, fill in all the fields except List Price. Try to save this record by clicking the *Create* button. A message "*List price must have some value*" will appear informing you to provide some value for the List Price. Now, provide some alpha-numeric value like *abc123* for the List Price. Again, a message will come up reminding you to put a numeric value.

Finally, input a numeric value in the List Price field and save the record. You'll see the new product appears on the Products page among others with the image you uploaded. Edit this record and see the image. Change the category of this product, switch availability to the other option and apply changes. Call the product again and observe the changes you just made to it. Click the *Remove Image* button and see what happens. Click the *Delete* button followed by *OK* in the confirmation box. The product will vanish from the list.

You might encounter a primary key violation message (*ORA-00001: unique constraint (DEMO_PRODUCT_INFO_PK) violated*) while creating first product record. This is because the Sequence object for this table is created with an initial value of 1. When you try to save the first product record, 1 is assigned as the first primary key value, which already exists in the table. To cope with this situation, just click the Create button on the form page several times. After ten clicks the record will be save.

## 6.6 Uploading and Viewing PDF and Other Types of Files

As mentioned earlier in this chapter, you can store different types of files (up to 4 GB); such as images, audio, video, PDF, CSV, XLSX, DOC and more, in the BLOB column of your table. In this exercise, I'll demonstrate how to save and view a PDF. As far as the uploading is concerned, you are not required to perform any special steps to handle PDF or any other file type. You have already set the stage in the previous sections where you handled JPEG images. Here, you will just create two new pages that will be apart from your application.

1. Click the **Create Page** button in the App Builder interface.

2. Click the **Report** option.

3. Select **Interactive Report**.

4. On *Page Attributes* wizard screen, enter **303** for *Page Number* and **Products Catalog** for *Page Name*. Click **Next**.

5. On the *Navigation Menu* screen, set *Navigation Preference* to **Do not associate this page with a navigation menu entry** and click **Next**.

6. On *Report Source* screen, select **SQL Query** for Source Type and enter the following statement in the *Enter a SQL SELECT statement* area.

   ```
   SELECT p.product_id, p.product_name, dbms_lob.getlength(p.product_image) document
   FROM  demo_product_info p
   ```

7. Click the **Create** button to complete the page creation process.

## 6.6.1 Modify the BLOB Column

Execute the following steps to modify the BLOB column attributes.

1. In the Page Designer, expand the Columns node (under the Products Catalog interactive report region), click the **Document** column and set the following attributes for this column. In the *Download Text* property you set a string used for the download link. If nothing is provided, Download is used. The *Content Disposition* specifies how the browser handles the content when downloading. If a MIME type is provided and the file is a type that can be displayed, the file is displayed. If MIME type is not provided, or the file cannot be displayed inline, the user is prompted to download.

| Property | Value |
|---|---|
| Type | Download BLOB |
| Table Name (under BLOB Attributes) | DEMO_PRODUCT_INFO |
| BLOB Column | PRODUCT_IMAGE |
| Primary Key Column 1 | PRODUCT_ID |
| Mime Type Column | MIMETYPE |
| Filename Column | FILENAME |
| Last Updated Column | IMAGE_LAST_UPDATE |
| Download Text *(under Appearance)* | View/Download |
| Content Disposition | Inline |

## 6.6.2 Upload and View PDF

As just mentioned the product setup module created earlier in this chapter is ready to upload any type of file, so to save some precious time we are going to use that module to upload a PDF.

1. Run the application and select **Setup | Manage Products**.

2. Click the **Create** button on the main Products interactive report page.

3. Fill in the mandatory fields. Click the **Choose File** button, select **product_catalog.pdf** file, which is available in the source code, and click **Create**. The PDF will be uploaded to the DEMO_PRODUCT_INFO table. Take some time to verify the upload from *SQL Workshop | Object Browser*.

4. Switch back to Page Designer. With Page 303 appearing on your screen click the **Save and Run page** button. The Product Catalog page will appear displaying data from the corresponding table. Click the **View** link for the Product Catalog PDF document. The PDF will be opened in your browser or downloaded to your PC.

| Product Id | Product Name | Document |
|---|---|---|
| 1 | Air Max 2090 | View |
| 2 | LeBron Soldier 13 Red | View |
| 3 | LeBron Soldier 13 White | View |
| 4 | Air Max 720 | View |
| 5 | Air Max 270 | View |
| 6 | Air Jordan 6 | View |
| 7 | LeBron 17 BG | View |
| 8 | Air Max 270 Gradient | View |
| 9 | Air Max 180 Trainer | View |
| 10 | Jr Phantom Vision | View |
| 21 | Product Catalog | View |

1 - 11

ACCESSORIES    TOOLS

# ACCESSORIES

**DBRY-6**

Models
- DBRY100: Bulk 100 connectors
  (100 tubes loose in box, plus inner box with 100 wire nuts)
- DBRY2X25: 25 x 2-packs
  (2 tubes and 2 wire nuts in a plastic bag, x 25 units)

Features
- UL Listed for 600 Volts direct burial
- Improved red-and-yellow wire nut, eliminating the need for two different sizes
- A snap-lock feature that secures the wire nut in the bottom of the light blue waterproof tube
- 3 wire exit cutouts in the strain relief cap, to ease wire routing
- Meets Directive 2006/95/EC and IEC standards EN61984:2009, EN60998-1:2004, and EN60998-2-4:2005

**Waterproof Wire Connectors**
DBRY100, DBRY2X25

**HCV**

Models
- HC-50F-50F: ½" Female inlet x ½" Female outlet
- HC-50F-50M: ½" Female inlet x ½" Male outlet
- HC-75F-75M: ¾" Female inlet x ¾" Male outlet

Features
- Adjustment access through top of valve
- Adjusts to compensate for elevational changes up to 32": Maximum flexibility
- Variety of inlet and outlet options: Reduces need for additional fittings
- Meets schedule 80 specifications: Durable under high pressure

**HCV Check Valve**
Overall height: 3"

*Pressure loss charts for HCV products on page 180*

**Figure 6-7**

## Summary

In this chapter, you were equipped with some more skills that will assist you in developing your own applications. Most importantly, you knew the techniques to handle, store, and retrieve images to and from database tables. Play around with this module by tweaking the saved properties to see resulting effects on the two pages. This way, you will learn some new things not covered in this chapter. Of course, you can always restore the properties to their original values by referencing the exercises provided in the chapter. An important point to consider here is that a module of this caliber would have taken plenty of time and effort to develop using conventional tools. With Oracle APEX declarative development, you can create it in a couple of hours.

# 7

# TAKING ORDERS

## 7.1 About Sale Orders

This chapter will teach you how to create professional looking order forms. Orders from customers will be taken through a sequence of wizard steps. The first wizard step will allow you to select an existing customer or create a new one. In the second step, you will select ordered products. After placing the order, the last step will show summary of the placed order. Once an order is created, you can view, modify, or delete it through Order Details page using a link in orders main page. The list presented below displays the application pages you will create in this chapter:

| Page No. | Page Name | Purpose |
|----------|-----------|---------|
| 4 | Orders | The main page to display all existing orders |
| 29 | Order Details | Display a complete order with details for modification |
| 11 | Identify Customer (Wizard Step 1) | Select an existing customer or create a new one |
| 12 | Select Order Items  (Wizard Step 2) | Add products to an order |
| 14 | Order Summary (Wizard Step 3) | Show summary of the placed order |

You'll build this module sequentially in the sequence specified above. The first two pages (Page 4 and 29) will be created initially using a new wizard option: *Master Detail*. Both these pages are not part of the Order Wizard and will be utilized for order modification and deletion after recording an order. Page 4 is similar to the pages you created in Customer and Product modules and lists all placed orders, while Page 29 will be used to manipulate order details. For example, you can call an order in the usual way using the provided link in the master page. The called order will appear in the details page where you can:

- Add/Remove products to and from an order
- Delete the order itself

The purpose of each chapter in this book is to teach you some new features. Here as well, you'll get some new stuff. This chapter will walk you through to get detailed practical exposure to the techniques this module contains. After completing the two main pages, you will work on actual order wizard steps to create other pages of the module. Recall that in the previous chapter you modified the main interactive report (Page 3) to create a couple of views (Icon and Detail) and used the *Actions* menu to select and sort table columns. In this chapter, many other utilities provided under the Actions menu will be exposed. But first, let's create the two main pages using the conventional route.

1. Click the **Create Page** button in the App Builder.

2. On the first wizard screen, click the **Master Detail** option. A master detail page reflects a one-to-many relationship between two tables in a database. Typically, a master detail page displays a master row and multiple detail rows within a single HTML form. With this form, users can insert, update, and delete values from two tables or views. On the Master Detail page, the master record displays as a standard form and the detail records appear in an interactive grid region under the master section.

3. On the next wizard screen, select the **Drill Down** option, which opens input form in a separate page.

4. Fill in the next screen (*Page Attributes*) as illustrated below, and click **Next**.

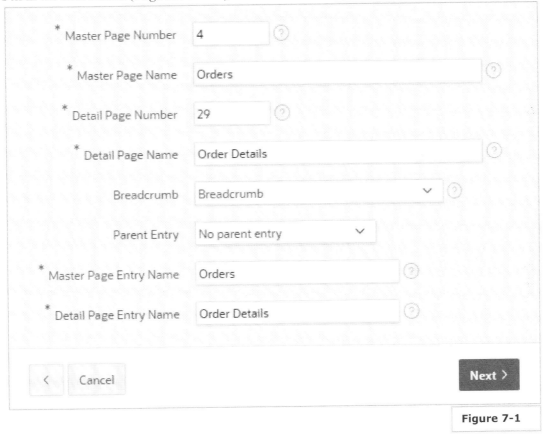

**Figure 7-1**

5. On the *Navigation Menu* screen, set *Navigation Preference* to **Identify an existing navigation menu entry for this page**, set *Existing Navigation Menu Entry* to **Orders**, and click **Next**.

6. Select the values in the *Master Source* screen (as shown in the following figure), and click **Next**. In this step, you select the parent table, which contains the master information for each order. You also specify the primary key column, which will be populated automatically behind the scene using a trigger named *BI_DEMO_ORDERS* via a sequence named *DEMO_ORDERS_SEQ*. You can view both these database objects from *SQL Workshop > Object Browser* interface. The ORDER_ID column selected in the *Form Navigation Order* list is the navigation order column used by the previous and next buttons on the *Order Details* page to navigate to a different master record.

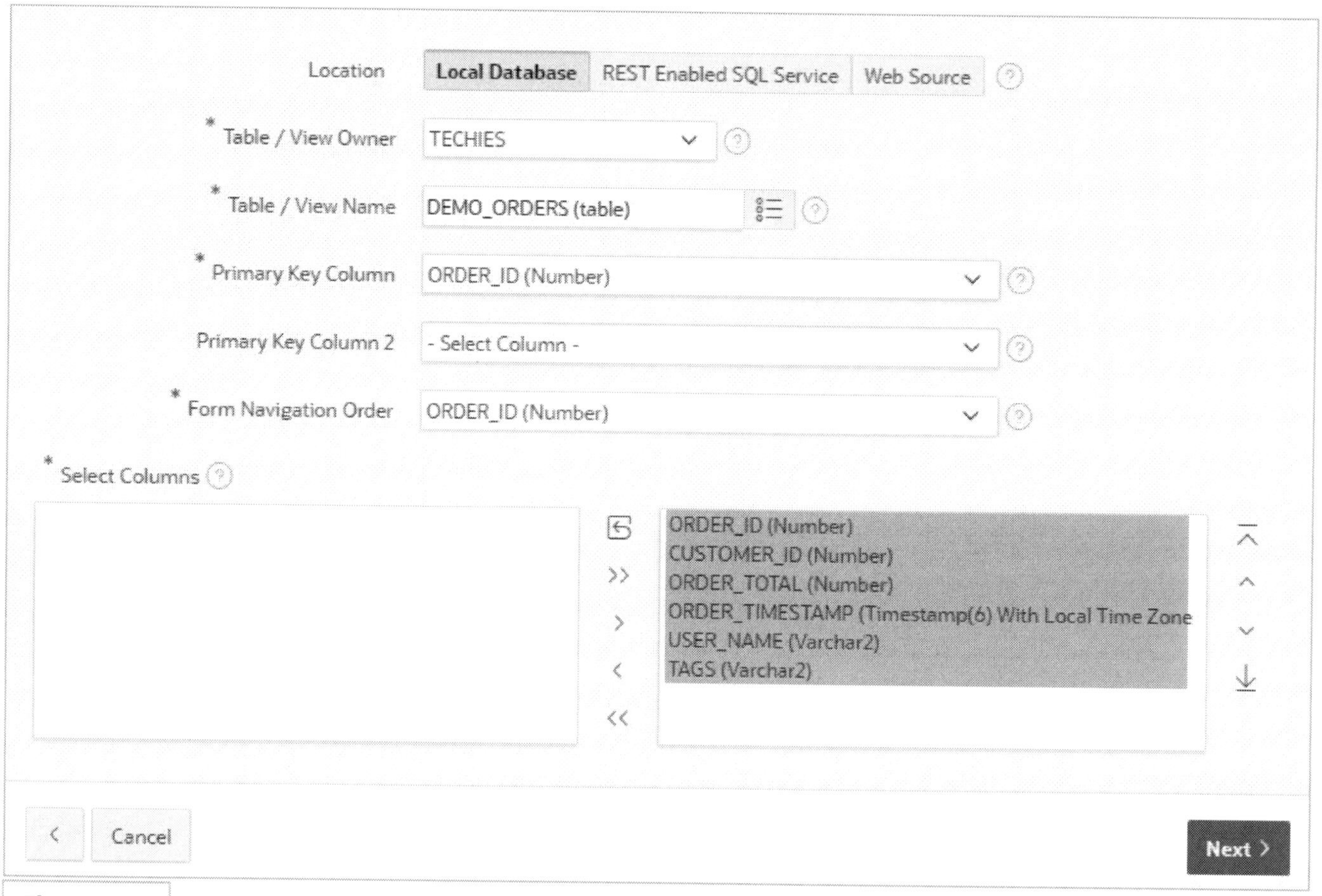

**Figure 7-2**

7. Set properties on the *Detail Source* screen as illustrated below and click **Create** to finish the wizard. On this screen, you specify the relational child table, which carries line item information for each order. The primary key column of this table will be populated automatically via a trigger named *BI_DEMO_ORDER_ITEMS*, which gets the next primary key values from a sequence named *DEMO_ORDER_ITEMS_SEQ*. In the *Master Detail Foreign Key* list you select the sole auto-generated foreign key, which creates a relationship between the master and detail tables.

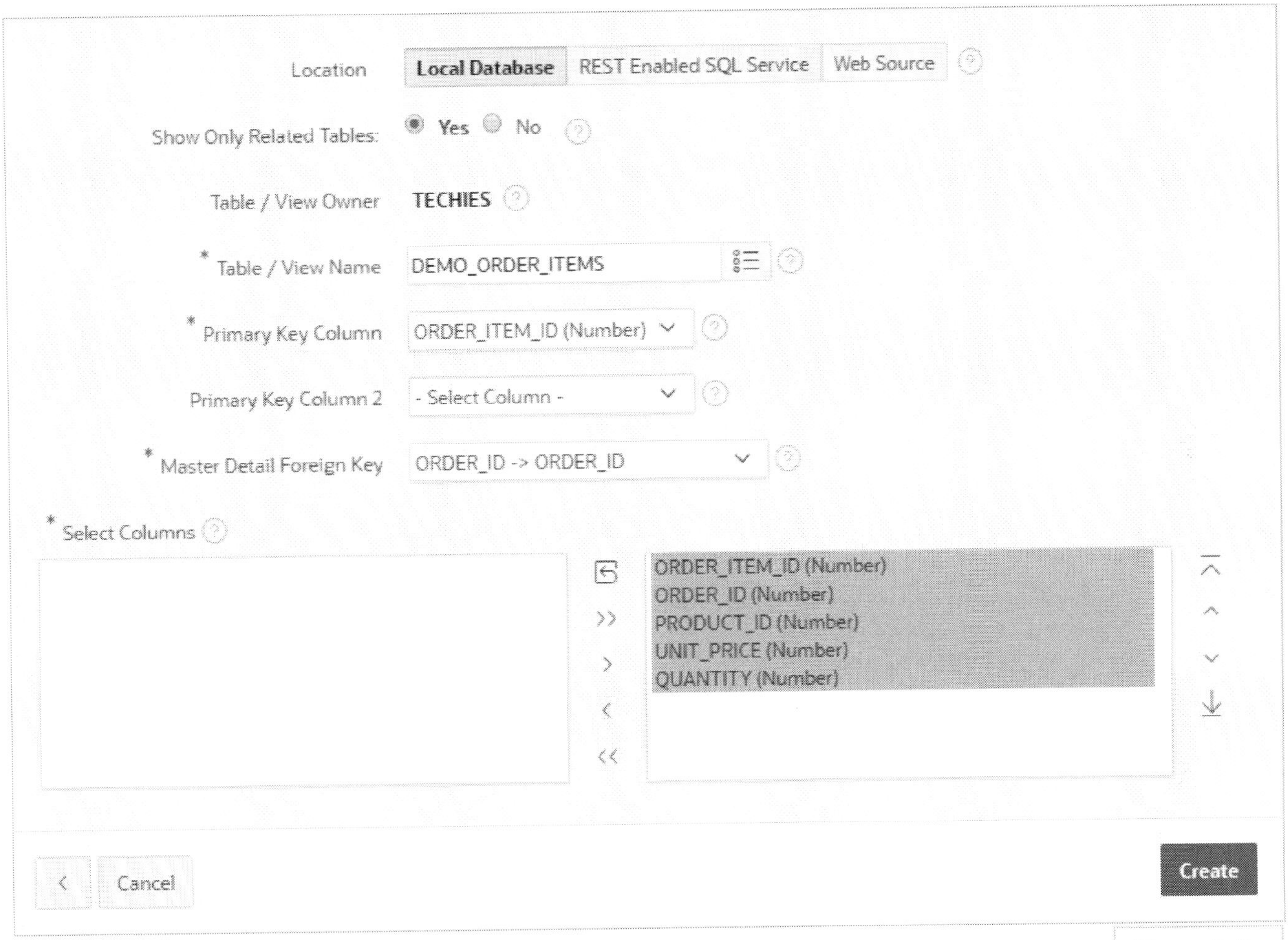

Figure 7-3

Before running these pages, let's see what the wizard has done for us. The master page (Page 4) is created with an Interactive Report to display a list of all order from the Orders Mater table. The details page (Page 29), on the other hand, has many things to reveal. The following table lists all those components created automatically for Page 29 by the wizard with complete functionalities to manage this module.

| Component: Pre-Rendering Process |
| --- |
| **Name:** Initialize form Form on DEMO_ORDERS |
| **Description:** Fetches master row from DEMO_ORDERS table. This process was briefed in Chapter 5 Section 5.4.5. If you see a different process name, then there is nothing to worry about as it sometimes happens due to change in APEX version. |

| Component: Region |
| --- |
| **Name:** Form on DEMO_ORDERS |
| **Description:** The page has two regions. The *Form on DEMO_ORDERS* region, which is a Static Content region, displays master information like customer ID, order date, and so on. The lower region shows product details along with quantity and price in an Interactive Grid. |

| Component: Buttons |
| --- |
| **Names:** GET_PREVIOUS_ORDER_ID and GET_NEXT_ORDER_ID |
| **Description:** These buttons are added to the master region to fetch previous and next orders, respectively. For example, when you click the Next button ❯, the page is submitted to get the next order record from the server by triggering the *Initialize form Form on DEMO_ORDERS* process using the value set for *Next Primary Key Item(s)* property in this process. The *Next Primary Key Item(s)* and *Previous Primary Key Item(s)* properties in this process are associated with respective hidden page items to fetch next and previous order ids. Based on the currently fetched order number, which is held in the page item P29_ORDER_ID, the process dynamically obtains the next and previous order numbers and stores them in two hidden page items: P29_ORDER_ID_NEXT and P29_ORDER_ID_PREV. The visibility of the *Next* and *Previous* buttons is controlled by a *Server-side Condition* (Item is NOT NULL), which says that these buttons will be visible only when their corresponding hidden items have some values. If you make any modification to an order on Page 29 and navigate to another order record using any of these buttons, the changes are saved to the two database tables. This is because the *Action* property of the two buttons is set to *Submit Page*. When the page is submitted, two processes (*Process form Form on DEMO_ORDERS* and *Order Details - Save Interactive Grid Data* defined later in this section) are executed to make the changes permanent. |

**Component:** Button

**Name:** Cancel

**Description:** The Cancel button closes Page 29 and takes you back to Page 4 without saving an order. For this, a redirect action is generated in the *Behavior* section with Page 4 set as the target.

**Component:** Button

**Name:** Delete

**Description:** The Delete button removes a complete order. When this button is clicked, a confirmation dialog pops up using its *Target* property, which is set to: *javascript:apex.confirm(htmldb_delete_message,'DELETE');* When you confirm the deletion, a *SQL DELETE action* (specified in *Database Action* property for this button) is executed within the built-in *Automatic Row Processing (DML)* processes–*Process form Form on DEMO_ORDERS* and *Order Details - Save Interactive Grid Data.*

**Component:** Button

**Name:** Save

**Description:** The Save button records updates to an existing order in the corresponding database table. This button is visible when you call an order for modification, in other words, P29_ORDER_ID is NOT NULL. The process behind this button is controlled by a *SQL UPDATE action* within the two built-in *Automatic Row Processing (DML)* processes.

**Component:** Button

**Name:** Create

**Description:** The Create button is used for new orders to handle the INSERT operation. This button is visible when you are creating a new order – that is, the page item P29_ORDER_ID is NULL. It uses the *SQL INSERT action* within the two built-in *Automatic Row Processing (DML)* processes.

**Component:** Region

**Name:** Order Details

**Description:** This is an Interactive Grid region, which is generated to view, add, modify, and delete line items using the parameters set in step 7. The information you provided in this interactive grid is saved to the DEMO_ORDER_ITEMS table through a process named *Order Details - Save Interactive Grid Data* – discussed next.

**Component:** Process

**Name:** Process form Form on DEMO_ORDERS

**Description:** This *Automatic Row Processing (DML)* type process is generated by the wizard to handle DML operations performed on the master row of an order, which gets into the DEMO_ORDERS table. It comes into action when you click Delete, Save, or Create buttons. The three buttons and their associated actions are depicted in the following figure.

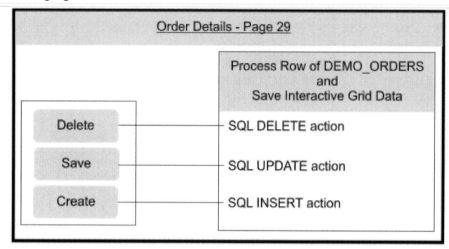

**Component:** Process

**Name:** Order Details – Save Interactive Grid Data

**Description:** The *Save Interactive Grid Data* process is responsible to handle DML operations on the details table (DEMO_ORDER_ITEMS). This process is associated with the details section (Interactive Grid) to insert, update, or delete Interactive Grid rows.

**Component:** Branches

**Name:** Go To Page 29, Go To Page 29, and Go To Page 4

When you submit a page, the Oracle APEX server receives a submit request and performs the processes and validations associated with that request. After this, it evaluates where to land in the application via these *branches*. By default, it selects the current page as the target page. For example, when you click the Next or Previous buttons on Page 29, you stay on the same page. If you want to land users to some other page, you can do this as well by creating branches. In the current scenario, you are moved back to Page 4 when you click any other button on Page 29. A branch has two important properties: *Behavior* and *Server-side Condition*. In the *Behavior* section you specify the page (or URL) to redirect to, and in *Condition* you specify when the branch is to be fired. Here, the first two branches are created to keep you on Page 29. These branches are associated with *Next* and *Previous* buttons–see *When Button Pressed* properties of these branches. The third one takes you back to Page 4 when you click any other button on this page – see the *Behavior* section that specifies the redirect.

**Run** this module from the *Orders* navigation menu entry. The first page (Page 4) you see is an interactive report. It is similar to the one you created in Chapter 6. It has a *Create* button, which is used to create a new order. Click the edit link (represented with a pencil icon) in front of any record to call the *Order Details* page (Page 29).

The *Order Details* page has two regions. The upper region, which is called the master region, displays information from the DEMO_ORDERS table, while the lower interactive grid region shows relevant line item information from the DEMO_ORDER_ITEMS table. Besides usual buttons, the master region has two navigational buttons at the top. These buttons help you move forward and backward to browse orders. The *Order Timestamp* field is supplemented with a *Date Picker* control. You can add more products to the details section by clicking the *Add Row* button.

From a professional viewpoint this page is not user friendly. If you try to add a new product, you have to enter its ID manually. Moreover, if you try to create a new order, you won't see the interactive grid. By default, this grid is visible only when you modify an existing order and it hides when you try to create a new order. This behavior is controlled by a server side condition (Item is NOT NULL) set for the Interactive Grid region (Order Details). With this condition set, the region is rendered only when the page item P29_ORDER_ID has some value. Choosing the – *Select* – placeholder for the *Server-side Condition Type* property removes this condition and makes the interactive grid visible every time you access Page 29. Even after this adjustment, you will face some constraint issues related to a backend table. To avoid all such problems, execute the instructions provided in subsequent sections to make the module user-friendly.

## 7.3 Modify Orders Page - Page 4

Execute the instructions provided in the following sub-sections to modify the Orders page.

## 7.3.1 Modify the Orders Interactive Report Region on Page 4

The Orders interactive report region on Page 4 fetches orders information from the DEMO_ORDERS table. Let's replace the existing auto-generated data fetching mechanism with a custom SQL query, which incorporates information of customers from the DEMO_CUSTOMERS table.

1. Open **Page 4** in the Page Designer, and click the **Orders** region. Modify the region using the values set in the following table:

| Property | Value |
|---|---|
| Location | Local Database |
| Type | SQL Query |
| SQL Query | SELECT lpad(to_char(o.order_id),4,'0000') order_number, o.order_id,<br>        to_char(o.order_timestamp,'Month YYYY') order_month,<br>        trunc(o.order_timestamp) order_date,<br>        o.user_name sales_rep, o.order_total,<br>        c.cust_last_name\|\|', '\|\|c.cust_first_name customer_name,<br>        (SELECT count(*)<br>         FROM demo_order_items oi<br>         WHERE oi.order_id = o.order_id and oi.quantity != 0) order_items,<br>        o.tags tags<br>FROM   demo_orders o,  demo_customers c<br>WHERE o.customer_id = c.customer_id |

2. Expand the *Columns* node under the *Orders* region and set the *Type* property for the ORDER_ID column to **Hidden Column**.

3. Set meaningful headings for all interactive report columns as follows.
   **Order #, Order Month, Order Date, Customer, Sales Rep, Order Items, Order Total,** and **Tags**

4. Edit the **ORDER_TOTAL** column and select the value **$5,234.10** for its *Format Mask* property.

5. Select the **Order Number** column (not Order ID) and turn it into a link using the following properties:

| Property | Value |
|---|---|
| Type | Link |
| Target *(in Link section)* | Type = Page in this application<br>Page = 29<br>Name = P29_ORDER_ID<br>Value = #ORDER_ID#<br>Clear Cache = 29 |
| Link Text | #ORDER_NUMBER# |

6. Click the **Attributes** tab of the *Orders* interactive report region. Select **Exclude Link Column** for *Link Column* property in the Property Editor. This action will exclude the default link column (denoted with a pencil icon) from the report as we have a custom link created in the previous step.

7. On the **Attributes** tab, scroll down to the *Actions Menu* section, and **turn on** the *Save Public Report* option, to include this option in the *Actions* menu at runtime. By enabling this option you can create a public report – see section 7.3.4.

8. Click the **Create** button and set the following properties for this button. New customer orders in this module will be recorded via some wizard steps, and Page 11 (to be created in a subsequent section) will be the first order wizard step.

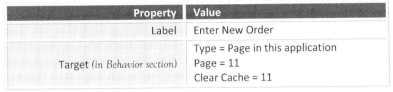

| Property | Value |
|---|---|
| Label | Enter New Order |
| Target *(in Behavior section)* | Type = Page in this application<br>Page = 11<br>Clear Cache = 11 |

9. Save your modifications.

## 7.3.2 Modify Interactive Report

Perform the following steps to change the look and feel of the default interactive report. After performing these steps, the interactive report will be saved as the *Default Primary Report*, which cannot be renamed or deleted. Note that these modifications are made using the *Actions* menu at runtime.

1. Click the **Save and Run Page** button to run Page 4.

2. Click the **Actions** menu (A), select the **Columns** option (B), arrange the report columns (C) as depicted in the following screen shot, and click **Apply**. This action will arrange the report columns in the specified order.

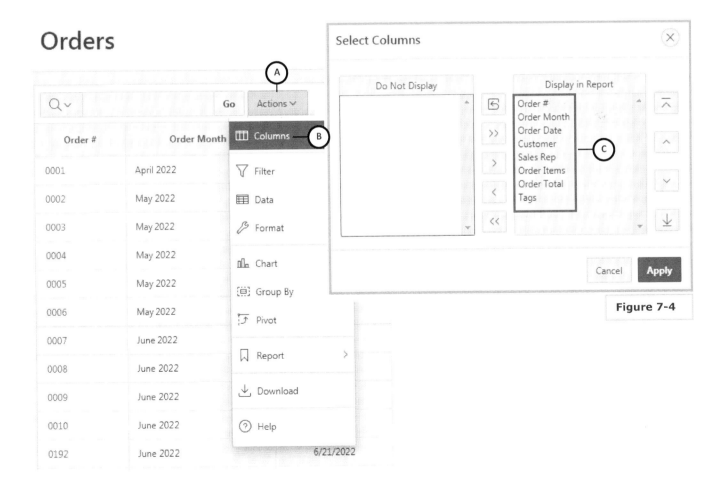

**Figure 7-4**

3. Click the Actions menu again, and select **Data** followed by the **Sort** option. In the *Sort* grid, select the **Order #** column in the first row, set the corresponding *Direction* to **Descending**, and click **Apply**. This action will display most current orders on top.

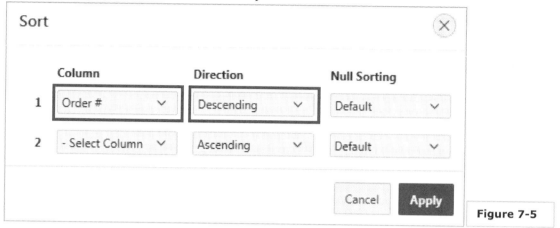

Figure 7-5

4. Click **Actions | Report | Save Report**. In the *Save Report* dialog box, select **As Default Report Settings** from the *Save* list, select **Primary** for *Default Report Type*, and click **Apply**.

Always save a report via the *Actions* menu whenever you make changes to it; otherwise, your modifications will not be reflected the next time you log in to the application. In Interactive Reports, you can apply a number of filters, highlights, and other customizations. Rather than having to re-enter these customizations each time you run the report, you tell Oracle APEX to remember them so that they are applied automatically on every next run. The application users can save multiple reports based on the default primary report, as discussed in the next couple of sections.

### 7.3.3 Create Alternative Report

Alternative report enables developers to create multiple report layouts. Only developers can save, rename, or delete an Alternative Report. This report (named Monthly Review) is based on the default primary report and will be rendered in a different layout using the *Control Break* utility on Order Month column. Execute the following steps on the primary interactive report on Page 4 to create three different views of the report.

### A. Report View

1. From the **Actions** menu, select **Save Report** (under *Report*). In the *Save Report* dialog box, select **As Default Report Settings** from the *Save* list. This time, select the **Alternative** option for *Default Report Type*, enter **Monthly Review** in the *Name* box, and click **Apply**. You will see a drop down list between the *Search* bar and the *Actions* menu carrying two reports: *Primary Report* and *Monthly Review*.

2. From the list, select the **Monthly Review** alternative report.

3. Click **Actions | Format | Control Break**. Under *Column*, select **Order Month** in the first row (A), set *Status* to **Enabled** (B), and click **Apply**. The *Control Break* feature enables grouping to be added to your report on one or more columns. The *Column* attribute defines which column to group on and the *Status* attribute determines whether the control break is active. When you click the *Apply* button, you will see the report results are grouped by the *Order Month* column and the *Control Break* column rule (C) is listed under the toolbar. A checkbox (D) is displayed next to the *Control Break* column and it is used to turn the control break rule on or off. The control break can be deleted from the report by clicking the small cross icon (E).

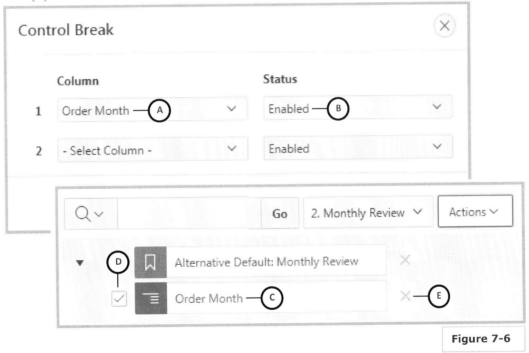

Figure 7-6

4. Click **Actions | Format | Highlight**. Type **Display Orders > $1000** (A) in the *Name* box, and set *Highlight Type* to **Cell** (B). Click the color picker (C), and select the green color for *Background Color*. Select the **red** color for *Text Color* (D). In the *Highlight Condition* section, set *Column* to **Order Total** (E), *Operator* to > greater than (F), *Expression* to **1000** (G), and click **Apply**. To distinguish important data from the rest, Oracle APEX provides you with conditional highlighting feature in interactive reports. The highlight feature in the Actions menu enables users to display data in different colors based on a condition. You can define multiple highlight conditions for a report. In this step, you're instructing to highlight the Order Total column in the report with green background and red text color where the value of this column is greater than 1000. Since you set the *Highlight Type* to *Cell*, the condition will apply only to the Order Total column. To modify an existing highlight rule, click its entry under the interactive report toolbar.

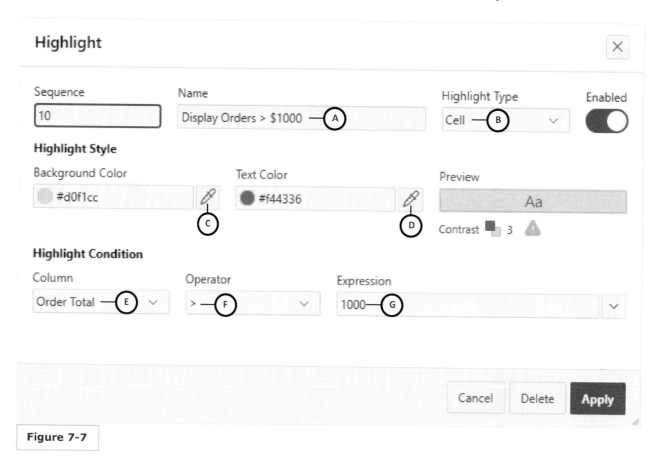

**Figure 7-7**

5. Click **Actions | Format | Highlight**. Type **Display Orders <= $999** in the *Name* field, set *Highlight Type* to **Row,** click **yellow** for *Background Color*, click **Red** for *Text Color*, in *Highlight Condition* set *Column* to **Order Total**, *Operator* to <= (less than or equal to), *Expression* to **999** and click **Apply**. This step is similar to the previous one with different parameters. In contrast to the previous action, where only a single cell was highlighted, this one highlights a complete row with yellow background and red text color and applies it to all rows in the report that have Order Total equaling $999 or less.

The resulting output should resemble the following figure.

**Order Month : June 2022**

| Order # | Order Date | Customer | Sales Rep | Order Items | Order Total | Tags |
|---|---|---|---|---|---|---|
| 0213 | 6/21/2022 | Lambert, Albert | DEMO | 1 | $500.00 | |
| 0212 | 6/21/2022 | Lambert, Albert | DEMO | 1 | $210.00 | |
| 0211 | 6/21/2022 | Bradley, Eugene | DEMO | 1 | $100.00 | |
| 0192 | 6/21/2022 | Bradley, Eugene | DEMO | 1 | $180.00 | |
| 0191 | 6/21/2022 | Dulles, John | DEMO | 1 | $800.00 | |
| 0010 | 6/20/2022 | Bradley, Eugene | DEMO | 3 | $870.00 | |
| 0009 | 6/17/2022 | Hartsfield, William | DEMO | 3 | $730.00 | |
| 0008 | 6/11/2022 | OHare, Frank | DEMO | 4 | $1,060.00 | |
| 0007 | 6/3/2022 | Logan, Edward | DEMO | 7 | $905.00 | |

**Order Month : May 2022**

| Order # | Order Date | Customer | Sales Rep | Order Items | Order Total | Tags |
|---|---|---|---|---|---|---|
| 0006 | 5/29/2022 | Logan, Edward | DEMO | 4 | $1,515.00 | |
| 0005 | 5/24/2022 | Lambert, Albert | DEMO | 5 | $950.00 | |
| 0004 | 5/14/2022 | LaGuardia, Fiorello | DEMO | 5 | $1,090.00 | |
| 0003 | 5/12/2022 | Hartsfield, William | DEMO | 5 | $1,640.00 | |
| 0002 | 5/1/2022 | Dulles, John | DEMO | 10 | $2,380.00 | LARGE ORDER |

1 - 17

**Figure 7-8** Monthly Order Review Report

179

## B.  Chart View

You can generate charts in Interactive Reports based on the results of a report. You can specify the type of chart together with the data in the report you want to chart. In the following exercise, you will create a horizontal bar chart to present monthly sales figures using the Order Month column for the chart labels and a sum of the Order Total column for the chart values.

1.   Click **Actions | Chart**.

2.   Select the first option (Bar) for the *Chart Type*.

3.   Select **Order Month** for *Label*.

4.   Enter **Month** in *Axis Title for Label*.

5.   Select **Order Total** for *Value*.

6.   Enter **Sales** in *Axis Title for Value*.

7.   Select **Sum** for *Function*.

8.   Set Orientation to **Horizontal**.

9.   Select **Label-Ascending** for *Sort*.

10.  Click **Apply**.

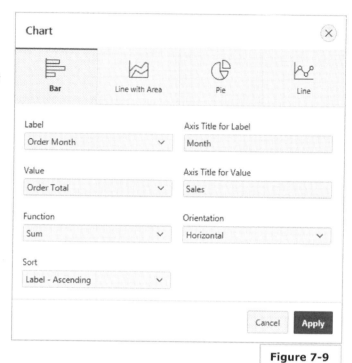

Figure 7-9

The chart should resemble the following figure. Note that the toolbar now has two icons: View Report and View Chart. If the chart doesn't appear, click the View Chart icon in the toolbar. Move your mouse over each bar to see total amount for the month.

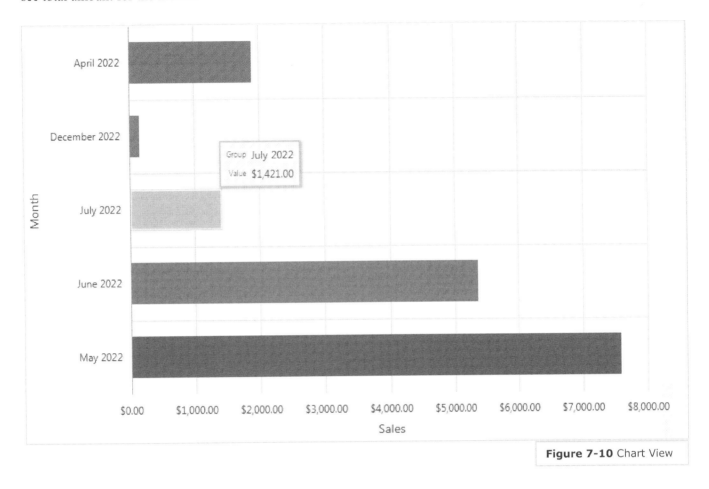

**Figure 7-10** Chart View

## C. Group By View

Group By enables users to group the result set by one or more columns and perform mathematical computations against the columns. Once users define the group by, a corresponding icon is placed in the toolbar, which they can use to switch among the three report views.

1. Click the **View Report** icon ▦ in the interactive report toolbar to switch back to the report view interface.

2. Click **Actions | Group By**.

3. Set the properties as show in the following figure and click **Apply**. Use the *Add Function* button to add the second function (Count). The first function calculates the monthly average of orders, while the second function counts the number of orders placed in each month.

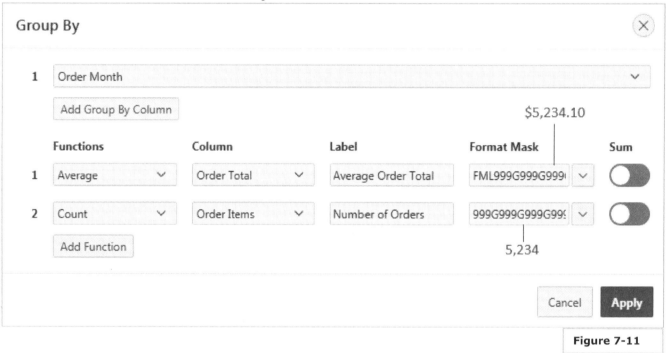

Figure 7-11

4. Click **Actions | Report | Save Report**. Select **As Default Report Setting** from the Save list. Select **Alternative** for the *Default Report Type*. The Name box should display **Monthly Review**. Click **Apply**.

The output of this view is illustrated in the following figure. Note that a third icon (*View Group By*) is also added to the toolbar.

| Order Month | Average Order Total | Number of Orders |
|---|---:|---:|
| July 2022 | $1,421.00 | 1 |
| April 2022 | $1,890.00 | 1 |
| December 2022 | $155.00 | 1 |
| May 2022 | $1,515.00 | 5 |
| June 2022 | $595.00 | 9 |
| | | 1 - 5 |

**Figure 7-12** Group By View

### 7.3.4 Create Public Report

This type of report can be saved, renamed, or deleted by end users who created it. Other users can view and save the layout as another report. Execute the following instructions to create the three views Report, Chart, and Group by of a public report. The Alternative report created in the previous section focused on orders, while this one is created from the perspective of customers.

### A. Report View

1. Select the default **1. Primary Report** from the *Reports* drop-down list in the toolbar.

2. From the **Actions** menu, select **Save Report** (under *Report*).

3. From the *Save* drop-down list select **As Named Report**. For report *Name*, enter **Customer Review**, put a check on **Public** and click the **Apply** button. A new report group (Public) will be added to the reports list in the toolbar, carrying a new report named *Customer Review*. Users can create multiple variations of a report and save them as named reports for either public or private viewing. When you click the Apply button, the report is displayed on your screen.

4. With the **Customer Review** report being displayed on your screen, click **Actions | Format | Control Break**. Select **Customer** in the first row under *Column*, set *Status* to **Enabled**, and click **Apply** to see the following output.

**Customer : Bradley, Eugene**

| Order # ↓≡ | Order Month | Order Date | Sales Rep | Order Items | Order Total | Tags |
|---|---|---|---|---|---|---|
| 0251 | December 2022 | 12/2/2022 | DEMO | 2 | $155.00 | |
| 0231 | July 2022 | 7/6/2022 | DEMO | 3 | $1,421.00 | |
| 0211 | June 2022 | 6/21/2022 | DEMO | 1 | $100.00 | |
| 0192 | June 2022 | 6/21/2022 | DEMO | 1 | $180.00 | |
| 0010 | June 2022 | 6/20/2022 | DEMO | 3 | $870.00 | |
| 0001 | April 2022 | 4/17/2022 | DEMO | 3 | $1,890.00 | |

**Customer : Dulles, John**

| Order # | Order Month | Order Date | Sales Rep | Order Items | Order Total | Tags |
|---|---|---|---|---|---|---|
| 0191 | June 2022 | 6/21/2022 | DEMO | 1 | $800.00 | |
| 0002 | May 2022 | 5/1/2022 | DEMO | 10 | $2,380.00 | LARGE ORDER |

Figure 7-13

## B. Chart View

1. Click **Actions | Chart**.

2. Set parameters for the chart as illustrated in the figure 7-14.

3. Click the **Apply** button. The output is illustrated in figure 7-15.

The chart uses the Average function (as compared to the Sum function used in the previous exercise). William Hartsfield has placed two orders amounting to $2,370. The average for this customer comes to $1,185 (2,370/2) and this is what you see when you move your mouse over the bar representing this customer.

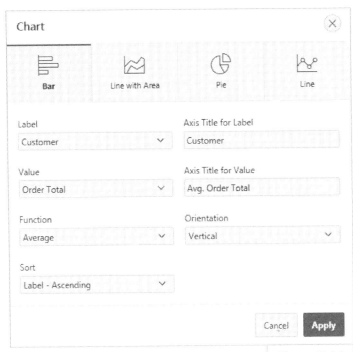

**Figure 7-14**

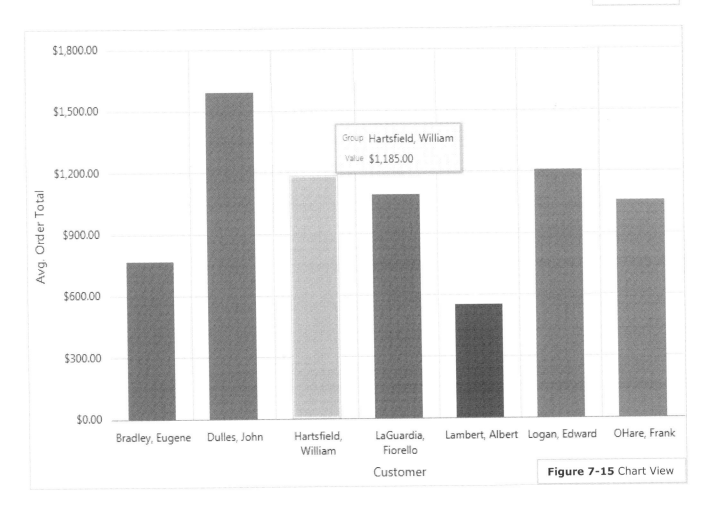

**Figure 7-15** Chart View

## C.    Group By View

1.    Click the **View Report** icon to switch back.

2.    Click **Actions | Group By**.

3.    Set parameters for this view as show in the following illustration. Turn on the Sum switch for all three functions to display grand totals.

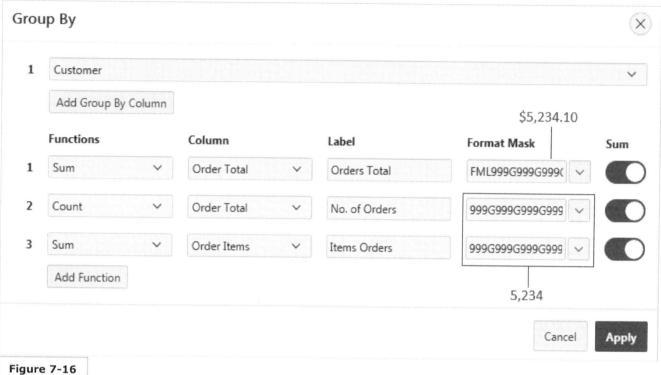

**Figure 7-16**

4.    Click **Apply**.

5.    Save your work using the **Actions** menu. Select **As Named Report** from the *Save* list. The *Name* box should be displaying **Customer Review**. Click **Apply**.

Select **Customer Review** from the report list in the toolbar, and click the **View Group By** icon. The following figure displays the output for the selections you just made. In this view, you applied Sum and Count functions to two columns: Order Total and Order Items. This view displays total amount of orders placed by each customer with number of orders and the total number of items ordered.

| Customer | Orders Total | No. of Orders | Items Orders |
|---|---|---|---|
| LaGuardia, Fiorello | $1,090.00 | 1 | 5 |
| Logan, Edward | $2,420.00 | 2 | 11 |
| Lambert, Albert | $1,660.00 | 3 | 7 |
| OHare, Frank | $1,060.00 | 1 | 4 |
| Bradley, Eugene | $4,616.00 | 6 | 13 |
| Hartsfield, William | $2,370.00 | 2 | 8 |
| Dulles, John | $3,180.00 | 2 | 11 |
| | **$16,396.00** | 17 | 59 |
| | | | 1 - 7 |

**Figure 7-17** Group By View

## D. Pivot View

The Pivot option is the Actions menu is used to create a cross tab view based on the data in the report. Let's see an instance of this option as well.

1. Click the **View Report** icon to switch back.

2. Click **Actions | Pivot**.

3. Set parameters as show in the following illustration. Don't forget to turn on the **Sum** switch to produce grand totals on the page.

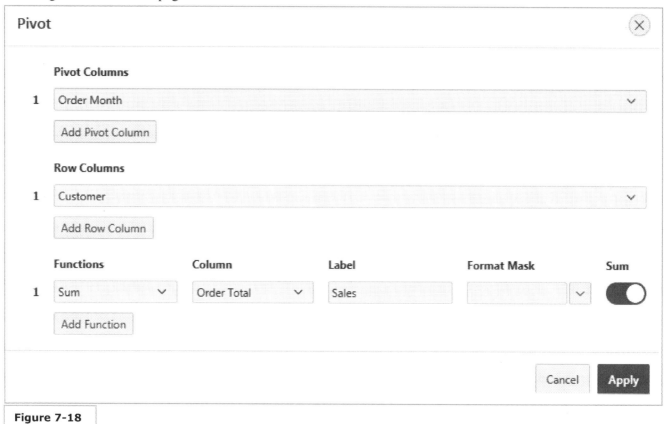

**Figure 7-18**

4. Click **Apply**.

5. Save your work using the **Actions** menu.

The following figure illustrates the output of these actions.

| Customer | April 2022 Sales | December 2022 Sales | July 2022 Sales | June 2022 Sales | May 2022 Sales |
|---|---|---|---|---|---|
| Dulles, John | | | | 800 | 2,380 |
| OHare, Frank | | | | 1,060 | |
| Bradley, Eugene | 1,890 | 155 | 1,421 | 1,150 | |
| Lambert, Albert | | | | 710 | 950 |
| LaGuardia, Fiorello | | | | | 1,090 |
| Hartsfield, William | | | | 730 | 1,640 |
| Logan, Edward | | | | 905 | 1,515 |
| | 1,890 | 155 | 1,421 | 5,355 | 7,575 |

1 - 7

**Figure 7-19** Pivot View

In the previous few sections you used some options from the *Actions* menu to customize the interactive report. However, the menu contains a few more, as listed below:

- **Filter** focuses the report by adding or modifying the WHERE clause on the query.

- **Rows Per Page** determines how many rows display in the current report.

- **Data** contains the following submenu:
    **Sort -** Changes the columns to sort on and determines whether to sort in ascending or descending order.
    **Compute -** Enables users to add computed columns to a report.

- **Flashback** enables you to view the data as it existed at a previous point in time by specifying number of minutes. To use this option, the Oracle database FLASHBACK feature must be turned on.

- **Reset** is used to reorganize the report back to the default report settings.

- **Help** provides descriptions of how to customize interactive reports.

- **Download** enables users to download a report. Available download formats depend upon your installation and report definition. To see these formats, click a region's *Attributes* tab and check the *Download* section in the Property Editor.

## 7.4 Modify Order Details Page - Page 29

Execute the instructions provided in the following sub-sections to modify the Order Details Page.

## 7.4.1 Modify Master Region Properties

Page 29 contains two regions. The master region (*Form on DEMO_ORDERS*) is of *Form* type and carries order header information, while the second region (*Order Details*) is an interactive grid, which contains line item details. Modify the master region using the following steps:

1. Open Page 29 in the Page Designer, click the root node (**Page 29: Order Details**) and set the *Page Mode* property to **Modal Dialog** to open it on top of Page 4. Set *Width, Height,* and *Maximum Width* properties to **900, 700,** and **1200**, respectively. Also, set *Dialog Template* (in the *Appearance* section) to **Wizard Modal Dialog**. Dialog templates are defined in the application theme. When a dialog page is created, the template is automatically set to *Theme Default*, which will render the page using the default page template defined in the current theme. The *Wizard Modal Dialog* provides a streamlined user interface suitable for input forms. When you switch to this template, the name of *Body* changes to *Wizard Body* and a new node named *Wizard Buttons* is added. We will use this node to place all our page buttons to make them visible all the time.

2. Click the **Form on DEMO_ORDERS** region and enter **Order #&P29_ORDER_ID.** (including the terminating period) for its *Title*. The expression consists of two parts. The first one (Order #) is a string concatenated to a page item (P29_ORDER_ID), which carries the order number. The string, when combined, would be presented as: *Order # 1*. Make sure that region's *Template* attribute (under *Appearance*) is set to **Standard** to show this title.

3. Create a new page item in the *Items* node under the master region and set the following properties. This item will present customer information on each order as display-only text. *Display Only* items are shown as non-enterable text item. Note that you may get an error message (ORA-20999) when you enter the SQL query specified in the table below. Save the page by clicking the Save button to get rid of this message.

| Property | Value |
|---|---|
| Name | P29_CUSTOMER_INFO |
| Type | Display Only |
| Label | Customer |
| Template | Optional |
| Type (*under Source*) | SQL Query (return single value) |
| SQL Query | SELECT cust_first_name \|\| ' ' \|\| cust_last_name \|\| ', ' \|\|<br>       cust_street_address1 \|\| decode(cust_street_address2, null, null, ' ' \|\|<br>       cust_street_address2) \|\| ', ' \|\| cust_city \|\| ', ' \|\| cust_state \|\| ' ' \|\| cust_postal_code<br>FROM  demo_customers<br>WHERE customer_id = :P29_CUSTOMER_ID |

 If you see an error message after providing the SQL query, ignore it and click the Save button to save the page. The error will vanish.

4. Using drag and drop arrange page items in the master region as illustrated in the following screenshot.

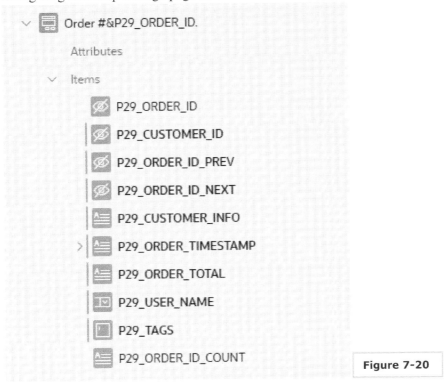

Figure 7-20

5. Edit the following items individually and set the corresponding properties shown under each item.

   a. **P29_ORDER_TIMESTAMP**

   | Property | Value |
   |---|---|
   | Type | Display Only |
   | Label | Order Date |
   | Template | Optional |
   | Format Mask | DD-MON-YYYY HH:MIPM |

   b. **P29_ORDER_TOTAL**

   | Property | Value |
   |---|---|
   | Type | Display Only |
   | Template | Optional |
   | Format Mask | $5,234.10 |

c. **P29_USER_NAME**

| Property | Value |
|---|---|
| Type | Select List |
| Label | Sales Rep |
| Template | Optional |
| Type *(List of Values)* | SQL Query |
| SQL Query | SELECT distinct user_name d, user_name r<br>FROM demo_orders<br>union<br>SELECT upper(:APP_USER) d, upper(:APP_USER) r<br>FROM dual<br>ORDER BY 1 |
| Display Extra Values | Off |
| Display Null Value | Off |
| Help Text | Use this list to change the Sales Rep associated with the order. |

In the *Help Text* attribute you specify help text for an item. The help text may be used to provide field level, context sensitive help. At run-time you will see a small help icon ⓘ in-front of this item. When you click this icon, a window pops up showing the help text.

d. **P29_TAGS**

| Property | Value |
|---|---|
| Template | Optional |

e. **P29_CUSTOMER_ID**

| Property | Value |
|---|---|
| Type | Hidden |
| Value Protected | Off |

f. **P29_ORDER_ID**

| Property | Value |
|---|---|
| Type | Hidden |
| Value Protected | Off |

6. In the *Region Buttons* node, set *Position* property to **Edit** for GET_PREVIOUS_ORDER_ID and GET_NEXT_ORDER_ID buttons to place them on top of the region.

## 7.4.2 Modify Details Region's Properties

After setting the master region, let's modify the details region to give it a desirable look.

1. Click the **Order Details** interactive grid region and set its Title to **Items for Order #&P29_ORDER_ID.** – including the terminating period.

2. Replace the auto-generated source attributes of the region with the followings:

| Property | Value |
|---|---|
| Location | Location Database |
| Type | SQL Query |
| SQL Query | SELECT  oi.order_item_id, oi.order_id, oi.product_id, oi.unit_price, oi.quantity, (oi.unit_price * oi.quantity) extended_price<br>FROM   DEMO_ORDER_ITEMS oi, DEMO_PRODUCT_INFO pi<br>WHERE oi.ORDER_ID = :P29_ORDER_ID and oi.product_id = pi.product_id (+) |

3. Save the page.

4. Under the *Columns* node, edit the following columns using the specified properties.

| Column | Property | Value |
|---|---|---|
| ORDER_ITEM_ID | Type | Hidden |
| | Value Protected | On |
| | Primary Key | On |
| ORDER_ID | Type | Hidden |
| | Value Protected | On |
| PRODUCT_ID | Type | Select List |
| | Heading | Product |
| | Alignment | Select the left icon |
| | Type *(LOV)* | Shared Components |
| | List of Values | Products With Price |
| | Display Null Value | Off |
| UNIT_PRICE | Alignment | Select the right icon |
| | Column Alignment | Select the right icon |
| | Format Mask | $5,234.10 |
| QUANTITY | Width *(under Appearance)* | 5 |
| | Type *(under Default)* | PL/SQL Expression |
| | PL/SQL Expression | 1 *(sets 1 as the default quantity)* |
| EXTENDED_PRICE | Type | Display Only |
| | Heading | Price |
| | Alignment | Select the right icon |
| | Column Alignment | Select the right icon |
| | Format Mask | $5,234.10 |
| | Query Only *(under Source)* | On |

After modifying an interactive grid query you must specify a primary column, which is required for editing and to specify master detail relationship. If not defined, you will encounter "Interactive Grid doesn't have a primary key column defined which is required for editing or in a master detail relationship" message. By setting the ORDER_ITEM_ID column as the primary key you eliminate this error.

The *Alignment* property sets the heading alignment, while the *Column Alignment* specifies the column display alignment. For product ID column, we changed two properties. First, we set its *Type* property to *Select List*. Secondly, we associated an LOV (*Products with Price*) to it. This LOV was created in Chapter 3 section 3.4.2 to display a list of products along with respective prices.

The *Query Only* property (under *Source* section) set for the *Extended Price* column specifies whether to exclude the column from DML operations. If set to *On*, Application Express will not utilize the column when executing the *Interactive Grid - Automatic Row Processing (DML)* process. In the current scenario, you excluded the *Extended Price* column, because it is not a physical table column and is calculated in the SELECT query stated above. If you keep the default value of this property for the *Extended Price* column, you will get "*Virtual column not allowed here*" error message when you try to save an existing order. All columns whose definitions include concatenations, inner selects, functions call, or a column in an updateable view that is based on an expression should be excluded. All columns that need to be included in any INSERT or UPDATE statements must have this option set to *Off*. Note that columns of type *Display Only* are also included in the *Automatic Row Processing* unless this option is turned on.

5. Using drag and drop arrange the five visible columns in the following order:
   PRODUCT_ID, UNIT_PRICE, QUANTITY, and EXTENDED_PRICE

6. Right-click the *Wizard Buttons* node and select **Create Region**. Set *Title* of the new region to **Buttons** and *Template* to **Buttons Container**. In the *Region Buttons* node, click the **Cancel** button, and set its *Region* property to **Buttons**. Set the same Buttons region for **Delete**, **Save**, and **Create** buttons, too. This action will place the four buttons under the Buttons region in the interactive grid.

7. On the *Processing* tab, make sure that the process "*Process form Form on DEMO_ORDERS*" is sitting before the *Order Details – Save Interactive Grid Data* process. If not, drag and place it before the *Order Details – Save Interactive Grid Data* process or set its *Sequence* property to a number lower than that of the *Save Interactive Grid Data* process. Note that this process must precede the *Save Interactive Grid Data* process; otherwise, you will get the error "*Current version of data in database has changed since user initiated update process*" when you try to manipulate data in the interactive grid.

8. Save the changes.

If you see a different process name, then there is nothing to worry about as it sometimes happens due to change in APEX version.

Run the application and click the *Orders* option in the main navigation menu. The page that comes up should look like Figure 7-21. Click any order number to call the *Order Details* page (Figure 7-22). Try to navigate forward and backward using the Next and Previous ⊲⊳ buttons. At the moment, you can only use these two pages to manipulate existing orders. In the next sections, you will create some more pages to enter new orders.

Call order number **0002** and click the **Add Row** button appearing in the Interactive Grid's toolbar. A new row will be added to the grid just under the first row with the Product column appearing as a list of values carrying all products with their respective prices. Select **Air Max 2090** (A) from this list, enter **1500** (B) in the *Unit Price* column, and put some value in the *Quantity* column (or accept the default quantity 1). Now, remove the checkmark appearing in the first column of the new record and put a check on the previous Air Max 2090 record (C). From the *Row Actions* menu (D), select **Delete Row** (E). The previous record will be marked as deleted (F). Click the **Apply Changes** button (G). Call the order again. The new record will be added to the table with the correct price of the product and the previous record will be removed.

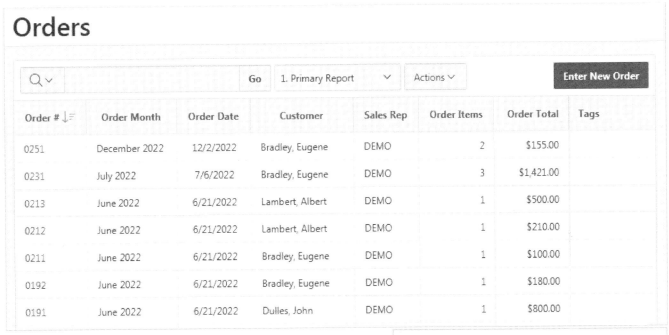

# Orders

| Q ⌄ | | | Go | 1. Primary Report ⌄ | Actions ⌄ | | Enter New Order |
|---|---|---|---|---|---|---|---|

| Order # ↓≡ | Order Month | Order Date | Customer | Sales Rep | Order Items | Order Total | Tags |
|---|---|---|---|---|---|---|---|
| 0251 | December 2022 | 12/2/2022 | Bradley, Eugene | DEMO | 2 | $155.00 | |
| 0231 | July 2022 | 7/6/2022 | Bradley, Eugene | DEMO | 3 | $1,421.00 | |
| 0213 | June 2022 | 6/21/2022 | Lambert, Albert | DEMO | 1 | $500.00 | |
| 0212 | June 2022 | 6/21/2022 | Lambert, Albert | DEMO | 1 | $210.00 | |
| 0211 | June 2022 | 6/21/2022 | Bradley, Eugene | DEMO | 1 | $100.00 | |
| 0192 | June 2022 | 6/21/2022 | Bradley, Eugene | DEMO | 1 | $180.00 | |
| 0191 | June 2022 | 6/21/2022 | Dulles, John | DEMO | 1 | $800.00 | |

**Figure 7-21** – Orders Interactive Report Page

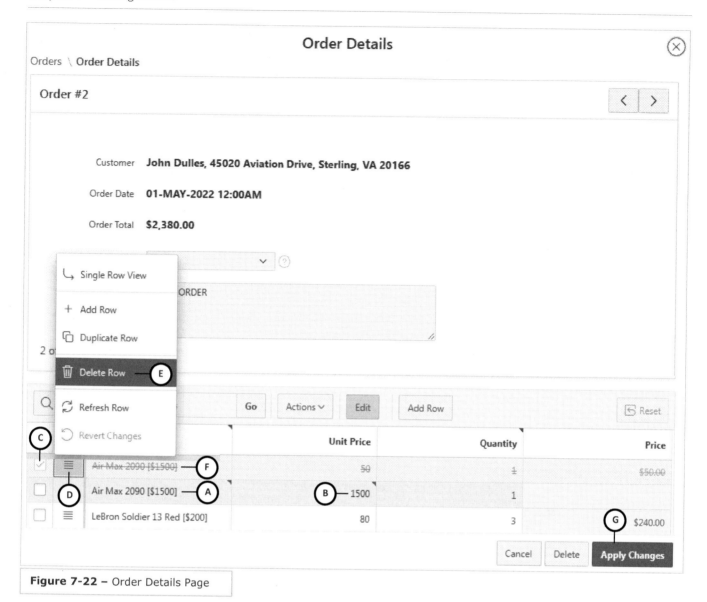

**Figure 7-22 –** Order Details Page

## 7.5 Create a Page to Enter a New Order - Page 11

As mentioned earlier, you will go through a series of steps to enter a new order. You identified and created these steps in *Order Wizard* list in Chapter 3 section 3.2.3. The top section (A) in Figure 7-23 reflects these steps. Each step will be associated to an application page. The rest of this chapter will guide you to create the three pages individually. In this exercise, you will create Page 11 - *Enter New Order*.

The order recording process initiates when you click the button *Enter New Order* on the *Orders* page (Page 4). The button calls Page 11, where you select a customer who placed the order. Besides selecting an existing customer, you can also create record of a new customer on this page. The Customer LOV button (B) calls a list of existing customers from which you can select one for the order. If you select the *New Customer* option (C), a region (*New Customer Details*) will be shown under the existing region. By default, this region is hidden and becomes visible when you click the *New Customer* option. This functionality is controlled by a dynamic action (*Hide / Show Customer*), which will also be created for this page.

In addition to various techniques taught in this part, you'll create this page from an existing page - *Customer Details* (Page 7) - to generate a new customer record. Here, you'll make a copy of that page and will tweak it for the current scenario. Let's see how it is done.

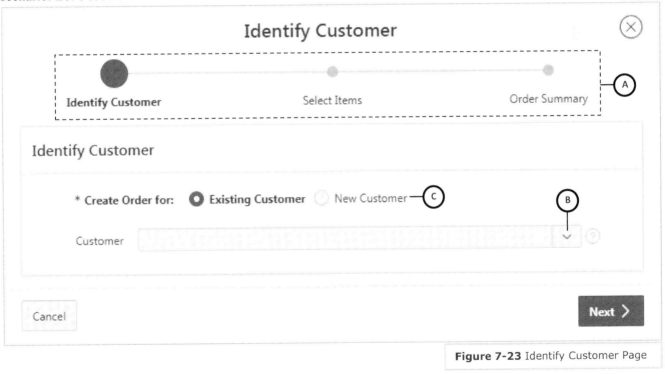

**Figure 7-23** Identify Customer Page

1. In the App Builder interface, click the **Customer Details - Page 7** to open its definitions in Page Designer.

2. Click the **Create** menu ⊞˅ at top-right in the toolbar and select **Page as copy**.

3. On the first wizard screen, select the option **Page in this application** for *Create a page as a copy of* and click **Next**.

4. Fill in the following values on *Page To Copy* screen and click **Next**.

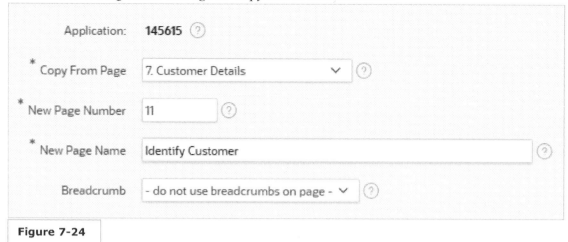

**Figure 7-24**

5. On the *Navigation Menu* screen select **Identify an existing navigation menu entry for this page**, select **Orders** for *Existing Navigation Menu*, and click **Next**.

6. Accept the names of existing page buttons and items on the *New Names* screen and click the **Copy** button to finish the wizard.

Look at the Page Designer. All the elements from Page 7 appear on the new page, especially the items section, which carries all input elements (with P11 prefix) to create a new customer record. This is the section we needed on our new page to spare some time.

## 7.5.1 Modify Page Properties

1. In Page 11, click the root node (**Page 11: Identify Customer**). In the Properties pane, set *Dialog Template* (under *Appearance*) to **Wizard Modal Dialog**. The template creates a region (*Wizard Progress Bar*) to hold the order progress list (A), as shown in Figure 7-23, and alters the name of the main region from *Content Body* to *Wizard Body*.

2. Set *Width* and *Height* properties to **700** and **500**, respectively.

3. Remove **htmldb_delete_message** variable from *Function and Global Variable Declaration* property. Save the page after removing the variable. This is an auto-generated variable associated with the customer record deletion process handled transparently by Oracle APEX. It is removed because the customer record deletion process is not required here.

4. Change *Maintain Session State* property (in *Source* section) of P11_CUST_FIRST_NAME, P11_CUST_LAST_NAME, P11_CUST_STREET_ADDRESS1, P11_CUST_STREET_ADDRESS2, P11_CUST_CITY, and P11_CUST_STATE,P11_CUST_POSTAL_CODE, P11_CREDIT_LIMIT, P11_PHONE_NUMBER1, P11_PHONE_NUMBER2, P11_CUST_EMAIL, P11_URL, and P11_TAGS page items to **Per Session (Disk)**. Switching to this value maintains the item value to access it across requests. See PL/SQL code line 22-30 in section 7.6.3 and *Place Order* process in section 7.6.8 later in this chapter where these items are referenced. If you keep the default *Per Request (Memory Only)* value for this property, none of the page item values can be referenced on other module pages and will not be inserted in the database table.

## 7.5.2 Create Region – Order Progress

Right-click the *Wizard Progress Bar* node (under *Components*) and select **Create Region**. Set the following properties for the new region. The *Order Wizard* list used here was created in Chapter 3 - section 3.2.3. The *Wizard Progress* value specified for the *List Template* property displays a progress train based on the list items and is well suited for wizards and multi-step flows.

| Property | Value |
|---|---|
| Title | Order Progress |
| Type | List |
| List | Order Wizard |
| Template | Blank with Attributes |
| List Template (*under Attributes tab*) | Wizard Progress |
| Label Display (*under Attributes | Template Options*) | All Steps (*displays labels of all wizard steps*) |

## 7.5.3 Create Region – Identify Customer

Right-click the *Wizard Body* node and select **Create Region**. Drag the new region and place it above the *Customer Details* region. Set the following properties for it. This region is created to act as a main container to hold a radio group item and a couple of sub-regions.

| Property | Value |
|---|---|
| Title | Identify Customer |
| Type | Static Content |
| Template | Standard |

## 7.5.4 Create Item

Right-click the new *Identify Customer* region and select **Create Page Item**. Set the following properties for the new item, which is a *Radio Group*. The list of values attached to this radio group item (*NEW OR EXISTING CUSTOMER*) was created in Chapter 3 - section 3.4.4 with two static values to create a new customer or select an existing one for a new order. The value set for the *Number of Columns* property displays these values in two separate columns. The first *Type* and *Static Value* properties (under *Source*) specify the source type the value of this item will based on when you access this page, whereas the second pair sets the EXISTING value as the default choice.

| Property | Value |
|---|---|
| Name | P11_CUSTOMER_OPTIONS |
| Type | Radio Group |
| Label | Create Order for: |
| Number of Columns | 2 |
| Template | Required |
| Label Column Span | 3 |
| Type (*under List of Values*) | Shared Component |
| List of Values | NEW OR EXISTING CUSTOMER |
| Display Null Value | Off |
| Type (*under Source*) | Static Value |
| Static Value (*under Source*) | EXISTING |
| Type (*under Default*) | Static |
| Static Value (*under Default*) | EXISTING |

## 7.5.5 Create a Sub Region – Existing Customer

Right-click the *Identify Customer* region and select **Create Sub Region**. This will add a sub region under the page item P11_CUSTOMER_OPTIONS. Set the following properties from the sub region.

| Property | Value |
|---|---|
| Title | Existing Customer |
| Type | Static Content |
| Template | Blank with Attributes |

## 7.5.6 Modify Item – P11_CUSTOMER_ID

In the *Items* section, click **P11_CUSTOMER_ID**. Set the *Name* property of this hidden item to **P11_CUSTOMER_ID_XYZ**. Set *Server-side Condition Type* to **Never** (last in the list). This item is renamed and suppressed from being rendered because a new item (of Popup LOV type) with the same name is created in the next section to display a list of customers, instead. By selecting the *Never* value for the *Server-side Condition Type* property, you permanently disable a page component. That is, the component is never rendered.

## 7.5.7 Add LOV

Right-click the *Existing Customer* sub-region and select **Create Page Item**. Set the following properties for this item. The *Type* value (under *Source*) is set to *Null*, because the IDs and names of customers are retreived using a SQL query and displayed in a Popup LOV.

| Property | Value |
|---|---|
| Name | P11_CUSTOMER_ID |
| Type | Popup LOV |
| Label | Customer |
| Template | Required |
| Width | 70 |
| Value Required | Off |
| Type (under *List of Values*) | SQL Query |
| SQL Query | SELECT cust_last_name \|\| ', ' \|\| cust_first_name d, customer_id r FROM demo_customers ORDER BY cust_last_name |
| Display Extra Values | Off |
| Display Null Value | Off |
| Type (under *Source*) | Null |
| Help Text | Choose a customer using the pop-up selector, or to create a new customer, select the New customer option. |

## 7.5.8 Modify Customer Details Region

Click the *Customer Details* region and set the following properties for this region. When you specify a parent region you make a region child of a parent region.

| Property | Value |
|---|---|
| Title | New Customer Details |
| Parent Region | Identify Customer |

## 7.5.9 Delete Validation, Processes, and Buttons

1. On the *Processing* tab, right-click the entry **Can't Delete Customer with Orders** under *Validations*, and select **Delete** from the context menu. Similarly, delete the process **Process Customer Data**.

2. Also, remove **Delete**, **Save**, and **Create** buttons from the *Buttons* region on the *Rendering* tab.

## 7.5.10 Delete Process

On the *Rendering* tab, expand the *Pre-Rendering | Before Header | Processes* node and delete the process named **Initialize Customer Details**. This is a default process created in the Customers module and is not required in the current scenario.

## 7.5.11 Create Button

Create a new button in the *Buttons* region and set the following properties for it. After identifying a customer, you click this button to advance to the second order wizard step. This button will appear under the *Cancel* button in the Page Designer. When this button is clicked, the *Action* property submits the page and a branch (created in section 7.5.18) takes control of the application flow and moves you on to the next wizard step.

| Property | Value |
|---|---|
| Button Name | NEXT |
| Label | Next |
| Position | Next |
| Button Template | Text with Icon |
| Hot | On |
| Icon | fa-chevron-right |
| Action | Submit Page *(default)* |

## 7.5.12 Create Process - Create or Truncate Order Collection

When developing web applications in Oracle APEX, you often need a mechanism to store an unknown number of items in a temporary location. The most common example of this is an online shopping cart where a user can add a large number of items. To cope with this situation in Oracle APEX, you use Collections to store variable information. Before using a collection, it is necessary to initialize it in the context of the current application session. After clicking the *Enter New Order* button, you're brought to this page (Page 11) and this is where your collection (named *ORDER*) is initialized using a PL/SQL process that fires *Before Header* when the user enters into the interface of Page 11. See sections 7.6.7 and 7.6.8 for relevant details on collections.

On the *Rendering* tab, expand the *Pre-Rendering* node. Right-click the *Before Header* node and select **Create Process**. Set the following properties for the new process.

| Property | Value |
|---|---|
| Name | Create or Truncate ORDER Collection |
| Type | PL/SQL Code |
| PL/SQL Code | apex_collection.create_or_truncate_collection (p_collection_name => 'ORDER'); |

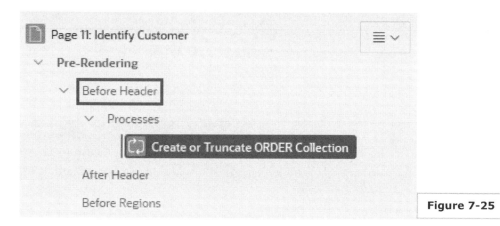

Figure 7-25

## 7.5.13 Create Dynamic Action (Hide / Show Customer)

Click the *Dynamic Actions* tab. Right-click the *Change* node and select **Create Dynamic Action**. Click the *New* node and set the following properties. The following settings inform Oracle APEX to fire the dynamic action when user changes (*Event*) the radio group item (*Selection Type*) P11_CUSTOMER_OPTIONS (*Item*) from *New Customer* to *Existing*.

| Property | Value |
|---|---|
| Name | Hide / Show Customer |
| Event | Change |
| Selection Type | Item(s) |
| Item(s) | P11_CUSTOMER_OPTIONS |
| Type (under Client-side Condition) | Item = value |
| Item (under Client-side Condition) | P11_CUSTOMER_OPTIONS |
| Value | EXISTING |

202

Click the **Show** node to set the following properties. The values for these properties are set to show the *Existing Customer* region when the EXISTING option is selected from the radio group. The *On* value set for the *Fire on Initialization* property specifies to fire the action when the page loads.

| Property | Value |
|---|---|
| Action | Show |
| Selection Type | Region |
| Region | ..Existing Customer |
| Fire When Event Result is | True |
| Fire on Initialization | On |

Right-click the *Show* node and select **Create Action**. Another Show node will be added just under the previous one. Set the following properties for it. This action is also assoicated with the previous two and is added to hide *New Customer Details* region when the EXISTING option is selected.

| Property | Value |
|---|---|
| Action | Hide |
| Selection Type | Region |
| Region | ..New Customer Details |
| Fire When Event Result is | True |
| Fire on Initialization | On |

Right-click the *Show* node again and select **Create Opposite Action**. This will add an opposite *Hide* action under the *False* node (with all properties set) to hide the *Existing Customer* region.

Right-click the *Hide* node under the *True* node and select **Create Opposite Action**. This will add a *Show* action under the *False* node to show the *New Customer Details* region.

If you run the page at this stage (by clicking the *Enter New Order* button on Page 4), you'll see the P11_CUSTOMER_ID item (in the *Existing Customer* region) is shown on the page. Now, select the *New Customer* option. The item P11_CUSTOMER_ID disappears from the page and the *New Customer Details* region becomes visible. Select the *Existing Customer* option again, the item becomes visible and the *New Customer Details* region hides.

## 7.5.14 Modify Validation – Check Credit Limit

On the Processing tab, click the **Check Credit Limit** validation. Set its *Sequence* to **100** and save the change to place this validation in a proper sequence after the following validations. Note that the *Sequence* property determines the order of evaluation.

## 7.5.15 Create Validation – Customer ID Not Null

Right-click the *Validations* node, and select **Create Validation**. Set the following properties for the new validation. You can control when a validation is performed by configuring its *Server-side Condition* property. Select a condition type from the list that must meet in order for a validation to process. In the current scenario, the condition (*item=value*) is formed like this: P11_CUSTOMER_OPTIONS = EXISTING. The validation fires when you select the *Existing Customer* option on the application page, and do not select a customer from the provided list. In case of an error at runtime, the *#LABEL#* substitution string specified in the *Error Message* property is replaced with the label of the associated item P11_CUSTOMER_ID – that is, *Customer*.

| Property | Value |
|---|---|
| Name | Customer ID Not Null |
| Sequence | 10 |
| Type (*Validation*) | Item is NOT NULL |
| Item | P11_CUSTOMER_ID |
| Error Message | Select a #LABEL# from the provided list. |
| Associated Item | P11_CUSTOMER_ID |
| Type (*Server-side Condition*) | Item = Value |
| Item | P11_CUSTOMER_OPTIONS |
| Value | EXISTING |

## 7.5.16 Create Validation – First Name Not Null

Create another validation. This validation will check whether the first name of a new customer is provided. It is fired only when the *New Customer* option is selected.

| Property | Value |
|---|---|
| Name | First Name is Not Null |
| Sequence | 20 |
| Type (*Validation*) | Item is NOT NULL |
| Item | P11_CUST_FIRST_NAME |
| Error Message | #LABEL# must have some value. |
| Associated Item | P11_CUST_FIRST_NAME |
| Type (*Server-side Condition*) | Item = Value |
| Item | P11_CUSTOMER_OPTIONS |
| Value | NEW |

Using the previous table, create NOT NULL validations for Last Name, State, Postal Code, and Credit Limit items.

## 7.5.17 Create Validation – Phone Number

Create the following validation to check input of proper phone numbers. *Regular Expressions* enable you to search for patterns in string data by using standardized syntax conventions rather than just straight character comparisons. The validation passes if the phone numbers matches the regular expression attribute and fails if the item value does not match the regular expression. The last three properties inform Oracle APEX to execute the validation only when a new customer is created.

| Property | Value |
|---|---|
| Name | Phone Number Format |
| Type (*Validation*) | Item matches Regular Expression |
| Item | P11_PHONE_NUMBER1 |
| Regular Expression | ^\(?[[:digit:]]{3}\)?[-. ][[:digit:]]{3}[-. ][[:digit:]]{4}$ |
| Error Message | Phone number format not recognized |
| Associated Item | P11_PHONE_NUMBER1 |
| Type (*Server-side Condition*) | Item = Value |
| Item | P11_CUSTOMER_OPTIONS |
| Value | NEW |

Create a similar validation for **P11_PHONE_NUMBER2** item.

Next, you have to **turn off** the *Value Required* attribute for P11_CUSTOMER_ID (in *Existing Customer* region), and P11_CUST_FIRST_NAME, P11_CUST_LAST_NAME, P11_CUST_STATE, P11_CUST_POSTAL_CODE, P11_CREDIT_LIMIT and P11_CUST_EMAIL (in *New Customer Details* region). The *Value Required* properties for these items were inherited from Page 7 where they were set to *On*, to mark them as mandatory. In the previous two sections, you used an alternate method to manually control the validation process for these items. If you don't reverse the *Value Required* status, then the application will throw NOT NULL errors for these items, even if you select an existing customer.

## 7.5.18 Create Branch

When the *Next* button is clicked, the defined button action (*Submit Page*) triggers after performing all validations. The submit page process executes instructions specified in this branch and moves the user to the next order wizard step. On the *Processing* tab, right-click the *After Processing* node and select **Create Branch**. Set the following properties for the new branch.

| Property | Value |
|---|---|
| Name | Go To Page 12 |
| Type (*under Behavior*) | Page or URL (Redirect) |
| Target | Type = Page in this Application<br>Page = 12<br>Clear Cache = 12 |
| When Button Pressed | NEXT |

## Test Your Work

From the main menu, select *Orders* and click the *Enter New Order* button. Your page should look like Figure 7-23. Select *Existing Customer* and click the LOV button ⌄ to call list of customers. Click the name of a customer from the list. The name of the selected customer appears in the *Customer* box. This is how an existing customer is selected for an order. Now, click the *New Customer* option, the Dynamic Action created in section 7.5.13 invokes and performs two actions. First, it hides the *Customer* box and the LOV. Second, it shows a form similar to the one you created in Chapter 5 to add a new customer record. Click the *Next* button without putting any value in the provided form. An inline message box will appear with six errors. This is the procedure you handled in the validation sections. After correcting all the form errors if you click *Next*, the message "*Sorry, this page isn't available*" pops up indicating that Page 12 doesn't exist. Your next task is to create Page 12 where you'll select products for an order.

## 7.6 Create Select Items Page - Pages 12

Having identified the customer, the second step in the order wizard is to add products to the order. In this exercise, you will create Page 12 of the application to select ordered items and input the required quantities.

1.  Click the **Create Page** button in the App Builder interface.

2.  This time, select the **Blank Page** option. This option is selected to create an application page from scratch. Using this option you can create and customize a page according to your own specific needs.

3.  Complete the first *Page Attributes* screen as show in the following figure and click **Next**.

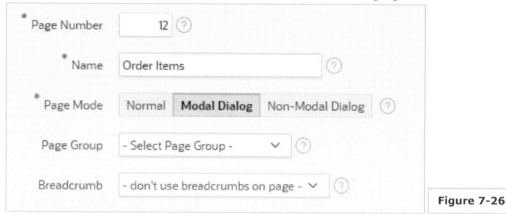

Figure 7-26

4.  On the *Navigation Menu* screen, set *Navigation Preference* to **Identify an existing navigation menu entry for this page**, *Existing Navigation Menu Entry* to **Orders**, and click **Next**.

5.  Click **Finish** to end the wizard.

## 7.6.1 Modify Page Properties

You styled the *Detail View* of an interactive report in the previous chapter to customize its look. Here as well, you will apply some styling rules to give the page a professional touch. Previously, you added rules to a single page element: HTML table. In the following exercise you'll apply rules to the whole page. Before getting your feet wet, go through the following topic to understand Cascading Style Sheets (CSS).

## Cascading Style Sheets

A cascading style sheet (CSS) provides a way to control the style of a web page without changing its structure. When used properly, a CSS separates visual properties such as color, margins, and fonts from the structure of the HTML document.

In this chapter, you will use CSS to style Page 12 (Select Items - Figure 7-27). On this page you will add class properties to PL/SQL code and will reference them in CSS in the HTML Head section. Before moving on to understand the actual functionality, let's first take a look at a simple example on how to use class attribute in an HTML document. The class attribute is mostly used to point to a class in a style sheet. The syntax is *<element class="classname">*.

```html
<html>
  <head>
    <style type="text/css">
      h1.header {color:blue;}
      p.styledpara {color:red;}
    </style>
  </head>
  <body>
    <h1 class="header">Class Referenced in CSS</h1>
    <p>A normal paragraph.</p>
    <p class="styledpara">Note that this is an important paragraph.</p>
  </body>
</html>
```

The body of this web page contains three sections:

- **<h1 class="header">Class Referenced in CSS</h1>** – The text *"Class Referenced in CSS"* is enclosed in h1 html tag. It is called level 1 heading and is the most important heading in a document. It is usually used to indicate the title of the document. The text is preceded by a class named "header".

- Considering the class syntax, *h1* is the *element* and *header* is the *classname*. This class is referenced in the style section using a CSS rule – *h1.header {color:blue;}* – to present the heading in blue color. A CSS rule has two main parts: a selector and one or more declarations. The selector is normally the HTML element you want to style. Each declaration consists of a property and a value. The property is the style attribute you want to change. Each property has a value. In the *h1.header {color:blue;}* rule, *h1* is the selector, *header* is the classname, and *{color:blue;}* is the declaration.

- **<p>A normal paragraph.</p>** – It is a plain paragraph without any style applied to it. HTML documents are divided into paragraphs and paragraphs are defined with the <p> tag. The <p> tag is called the start tag or opening tag, while </p> is called the end or closing tag.

- **<p class="styledpara">Note that this is an important paragraph.</p>** – It is a paragraph with a class named *"styledpara"*. In the style section, the selector *"p"* followed by the classname *"styledpara"* with the declaration*{color:red;}* is referencing this section to present the paragraph text in red color.

Now that you have understood how CSS is used in web pages, let's figure out how it is used in Oracle APEX.

1. Click the root node – **Page 12: Order Items**.

2. Set *Dialog Template* to **Wizard Modal Dialog**.

3. Set *Width* and *Height* to **500** and **600**, respectively.

4. Enter the following code for **inline** property under CSS section and save your work. You can find this code in *BookCode\Chapter7\7.6.1.txt* file. CSS rules entered in this box will be applied to all the referenced elements on the current page, as illustrated in Figure 7-27.

| Rule # | Rule | PL/SQL Ref. |
|---|---|---|
| | **A - CustomerInfo** | |
| 1 | div.CustomerInfo{margin: 10px 10px 0;} | 7-79 |
| 2 | div.CustomerInfo strong{font:bold 12px/16px Arial,sans-serif;display:block;width:120px;} | 11,22 |
| 3 | div.CustomerInfo p{display:block;margin:0; font: normal 12px/16px Arial, sans-serif;} | 12-19, 23-30 |
| | **B - Products** | |
| 4 | div.Products{clear:both;margin:16px 0 0;padding:0 8px 0 0;} | 36-42 |
| 5 | div.Products table{border:1px solid #CCC;border-bottom:none;} | 37,47 |
| 6 | div.Products table th{background-color:#DDD;color:#000;font:bold 12px/16px Arial,sans-serif;padding:4px 10px;text-align:right;border-bottom:1px solid #CCC;} | 37,47 |
| 7 | div.Products table td{border-bottom:1px solid #CCC;font:normal 12px/16px Arial,sans-serif; padding:4px 10px;text-align:right;} | 39 |
| 8 | div.Products table td a{color:#000;} | 39 |
| 9 | div.Products .left{text-align:left;} | 37,39,47 |
| | **C - CartItem** | |
| 10 | div.CartItem{padding:8px 8px 0 8px;font:normal 11px/14px Arial,sans-serif;} | 53-59 |
| 11 | div.CartItem a{color:#000;} | 54-55 |
| 12 | div.CartItem span{display:block;text-align:right;padding:8px 0 0;} | 56-57 |
| 13 | div.CartItem span.subtotal{font-weight:bold;} | 58 |
| | **D - CartTotal** | |
| 14 | div.CartTotal{margin-top:8px;padding:8px;border-top:1px dotted #AAA;} | 65-68 |
| 15 | div.CartTotal span{display:block;text-align:right;font:normal 11px/14px Arial,sans-serif;padding:0 0 4px 0;} | 66 |
| 16 | div.CartTotal p{padding:0;margin:0;font:normal 11px/14px Arial,sans-serif;position:relative;} | 66 |
| 17 | div.CartTotal p.CartTotal{font:bold 12px/14px Arial,sans-serif;padding:8px 0 0 0;} | 67 |
| 18 | div.CartTotal p.CartTotal span{font:bold 12px/14px Arial,sans-serif;padding:8px 0 0 0;} | 67 |
| 19 | div.CartTotal p span{padding:0;position:absolute;right:0;top:0;} | 66 |

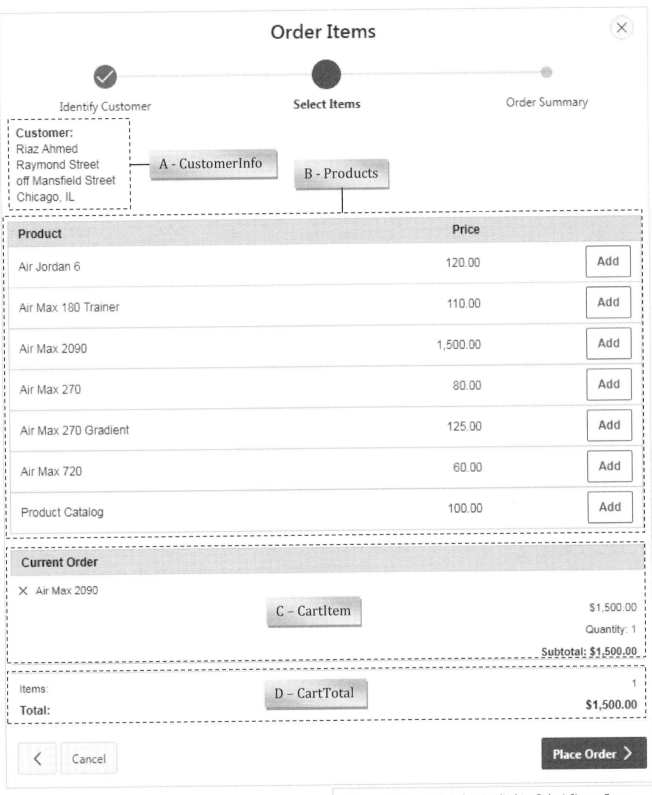

Figure 7-27 – CSS Rules Applied to Select Items Page

## 7.6.2 Create Region – Order Progress

Right-click the *Wizard Progress Bar* node and select **Create Region**. Set the following properties for the new region. A similar region was added previously to Page 11 to display the Order Progress bar.

| Property | Value |
|---|---|
| Title | Order Progress |
| Type | List |
| List | Order Wizard |
| Template | Blank with Attributes |
| List Template *(under Attributes tab)* | Wizard Progress |

## 7.6.3 Create Region – Select Items

The region being created in this section is based on a custom PL/SQL code. The code references CSS rules (defined in the previous section) to design the *Select Items* page, as illustrated in Figure 7-27.

### What is PL/SQL?

PL/SQL stands for Procedural Language/Structured Query Language. It is a programming language that uses detailed sequential instructions to process data. A PL/SQL program combines SQL command (such as Select and Update) with procedural commands for tasks, such as manipulating variable values, evaluating IF/THEN logic structure, and creating loop structures that repeat instructions multiple times until the condition satisfies the defined criteria. PL/SQL was expressly designed for this purpose.

The structure of a PL/SQL program block is:

```
Declare
   Variable declaration
Begin
   Program statements
Exception
   Error-handling statements
End;
```

PL/SQL program variables are declared in the program's declaration section. The beginning of the declaration section is marked with the reserved word DECLARE. You can declare multiple variables in the declaration section. The body of a PL/SQL block consists of program statements, which can be assigned statements, conditional statements, loop statements, and so on. The body lies between the BEGIN and EXCEPTION statements. The exception section contains program statements for error handling. Finally, PL/SQL programs end with the END; statement. Comments in PL/SQL code are added by prefixing them with double hyphens.

In a PL/SQL program block, the DECLARE and EXCEPTION sections are optional. If there are no variables to declare, you can omit the DECLARE section and start the program with the BEGIN command.

1. Right-click the *Order Progress* region and select **Create Sub Region** from the context menu.

2. Enter **Select Items** for its *Title* and set its *Type* to **PL/SQL Dynamic Content** to display the page content using PL/SQL code. PL/SQL Dynamic Content displays the HTML output from the PL/SQL code.

3. Add the code defined in the *PL/SQL Code* column (Table 7-1) in the *PL/SQL Code* property (in the *Source* section). You can find this code in *BookCode\Chapter7\7.6.3.txt* file. The first column (CSS Rule) in the following table references the rules defined in the previous section. These rules are applied to the injected HTML elements in the PL/SQL code. The second table column is populated with a serial number assigned to each PL/SQL code. These numbers are referenced in the explanation section underneath.

4. Do not set any option for the *Template* property (in other words, change it from the default *Standard* value to the **-Select-** placeholder).

| CSS Rule | Line No. | PL/SQL Code |
|---|---|---|
| | 1 | declare |
| | 2 | l_customer_id varchar2(30) := :P11_CUSTOMER_ID; |
| | 3 | begin |
| | 4 | -- |
| | 5 | -- **display customer information** |
| | 6 | -- |
| 1 | 7 | sys.htp.p('<div class="CustomerInfo">'); |
| | 8 | if :P11_CUSTOMER_OPTIONS = 'EXISTING' then |
| | 9 | for x in (select * from demo_customers where customer_id = l_customer_id) loop |
| | 10 | sys.htp.p('<div class="CustomerInfo">'); |
| 2 | 11 | sys.htp.p('<strong>Customer:</strong>'); |
| | 12 | sys.htp.p('<p>'); |
| | 13 | sys.htp.p(sys.htf.escape_sc(x.cust_first_name) \|\| ' ' \|\| sys.htf.escape_sc(x.cust_last_name) \|\| '<br>'); |
| | 14 | sys.htp.p(sys.htf.escape_sc(x.cust_street_address1) \|\| '<br>'); |
| | 15 | if x.cust_street_address2 is not null then |
| 3 | 16 | sys.htp.p(sys.htf.escape_sc(x.cust_street_address2) \|\| '<br>'); |
| | 17 | end if; |
| | 18 | sys.htp.p(sys.htf.escape_sc(x.cust_city) \|\| ', ' \|\| sys.htf.escape_sc(x.cust_state) \|\| ' ' \|\| sys.htf.escape_sc(x.cust_postal_code)); |
| | 19 | sys.htp.p('</p>'); |
| | 20 | end loop; |
| | 21 | else |
| 2 | 22 | sys.htp.p('<strong>Customer:</strong>'); |
| | 23 | sys.htp.p('<p>'); |
| | 24 | sys.htp.p(sys.htf.escape_sc(:P11_CUST_FIRST_NAME) \|\| ' ' \|\| sys.htf.escape_sc(:P11_CUST_LAST_NAME) \|\| '<br>'); |
| | 25 | sys.htp.p(sys.htf.escape_sc(:P11_CUST_STREET_ADDRESS1) \|\| '<br>'); |
| | 26 | if :P11_CUST_STREET_ADDRESS2 is not null then |
| 3 | 27 | sys.htp.p(sys.htf.escape_sc(:P11_CUST_STREET_ADDRESS2) \|\| '<br>'); |
| | 28 | end if; |
| | 29 | sys.htp.p(sys.htf.escape_sc(:P11_CUST_CITY) \|\| ', ' \|\| sys.htf.escape_sc(:P11_CUST_STATE) \|\| ' ' \|\| sys.htf.escape_sc(:P11_CUST_POSTAL_CODE)); |
| | 30 | sys.htp.p('</p>'); |
| | 31 | end if; |
| | 32 | sys.htp.p('<br></div>'); |

| CSS Rule | Line | PL/SQL Code |
|---|---|---|
| | 33 | -- |
| | 34 | **-- display products** |
| | 35 | -- |
| 4 | 36 | sys.htp.p('<div class="Products" >'); |
| 5 | 37 | sys.htp.p('<table width="100%" cellspacing="0" cellpadding="0" border="0"> |
| | | <thead> |
| 6,9 | | <tr><th class="left">Product</th><th>Price</th><th></th></tr> |
| | | </thead> |
| | | <tbody>'); |
| | 38 | for c1 in (select product_id, product_name, list_price, 'Add to Cart' add_to_order |
| | | from demo_product_info |
| | | where product_avail = 'Y' |
| | | order by product_name) loop |
| 7, 8, 9 | 39 | sys.htp.p('<tr><td class="left">' ||sys.htf.escape_sc(c1.product_name)||'</td> |
| | | <td>'||trim(to_char(c1.list_price,'999G999G990D00')) || '</td> |
| | | <td><a |
| | | href="'||apex_util.prepare_url('f?p=&APP_ID.:12:'||:app_session||':**ADD**:::P12_PRODUCT_ID:'|| c1.product_id)||'" class="t-Button t-Button--simple t-Button--hot"><span>Add<i |
| | | class="iR"></i></span></a></td> |
| | | </tr>'); |
| | 40 | end loop; |
| | 41 | sys.htp.p('</tbody></table>'); |
| | 42 | sys.htp.p('</div>'); |

| CSS Rule | Line | PL/SQL Code |
|---|---|---|
| | 43 | -- |
| | 44 | **-- display current order** |
| | 45 | -- |
| 4 | 46 | sys.htp.p('<div class="Products" >'); |
| 5 | 47 | sys.htp.p('<table width="100%" cellspacing="0" cellpadding="0" border="0"> |
| | | <thead> |
| 9 | | <tr><th class="left">Current Order</th></tr> |
| | | </thead> |
| | | </table> |
| 5 | | <table width="100%" cellspacing="0" cellpadding="0" border="0"> |
| | | <tbody>'); |
| | 48 | declare |
| | 49 | c number := 0; t number := 0; |
| | 50 | begin |
| | 51 | -- loop over cart values |
| | 52 | for c1 in (select c001 pid, c002 i, to_number(c003) p, count(c002) q, sum(c003) ep, |
| | | 'Remove' remove |
| | | from apex_collections |
| | | where collection_name = 'ORDER' |
| | | group by c001, c002, c003 |
| | | order by c002) |
| | | loop |
| 10 | 53 | sys.htp.p('<div class="CartItem"> |
| 11 | 54 | <a href="'|| |
| | | apex_util.prepare_url('f?p=&APP_ID.:12:&SESSION.:**REMOVE**:::P12_PRODUCT_ID:'||sys.h |
| | | tf.escape_sc(c1.pid))||'"><img src="#IMAGE_PREFIX#delete.gif" alt="Remove from cart" |
| | | title="Remove from cart" /></a>   |
| 11 | 55 | '||sys.htf.escape_sc(c1.i)||' |
| | 56 | <span>'||trim(to_char(c1.p,'$999G999G999D00'))||'</span> |
| | 57 | <span>Quantity: '||c1.q||'</span> |
| | 58 | <span class="subtotal">Subtotal: '||trim(to_char(c1.ep,'$999G999G999D00'))||'</span> |
| 12 | 59 | </div>'); |
| | 60 | c := c + 1; |
| 13 | 61 | t := t + c1.ep; |
| | 62 | end loop; |
| | 63 | sys.htp.p('</tbody></table>'); |

213

| CSS Rule | Line | PL/SQL Code |
|---|---|---|
| | 64 | if c > 0 then |
| 14,15 | 65 | sys.htp.p('<div class="CartTotal"> |
| 16,17 | 66 | <p>Items: <span>'||c||'</span></p> |
| 18,19 | 67 | <p class="CartTotal">Total: <span>'||trim(to_char(t,'$999G999G999D00'))||'</span></p> |
| | 68 | </div>'); |
| | 69 | else |
| | 70 | sys.htp.p('<div class="alertMessage info" style="margin-top: 8px;">'); |
| | 71 | sys.htp.p('<img src="#IMAGE_PREFIX#f_spacer.gif">'); |
| | 72 | sys.htp.p('<div class="innerMessage">'); |
| | 73 | sys.htp.p('<h3>Note</h3>'); |
| | 74 | sys.htp.p('<p>You have no items in your current order.</p>'); |
| | 75 | sys.htp.p('</div>'); |
| | 76 | sys.htp.p('</div>'); |
| | 77 | end if; |
| | 78 | end; |
| | 79 | sys.htp.p('</div>'); |
| | 80 | end; |

**Table 7-1** – PL/SQL Code

The ELSE block (lines 70-76) executes when the user tries to move on without selecting a product in the current order. The block uses a built-in class (*alertMessage info*) that carries an image (f_spacer.gif) followed by the message specified on lines 73-74.

In this PL/SQL code you merged some HTML elements to deliver the page in your browser. Before getting into the code details, let's first acquaint ourselves with some specific terms and objects used in the PL/SQL code.

### Using HTML in PL/SQL Code

Oracle APEX installs with your Oracle database and is comprised of data in tables and PL/SQL code. Whether you are running the Oracle APEX development environment or an application you built using Oracle APEX, the process is the same. Your browser sends a URL request, which is translated into an appropriate Oracle APEX PL/SQL call. After the database processes the PL/SQL, the results are relayed back to your browser as HTML. This cycle happens each time you either request or submit a page.

Specific HTML content not handled by Oracle APEX (forms, reports, and charts) are generated using the PL/SQL region type. You can use PL/SQL to have more control over dynamically generated HTML within a region, as you do here. Let's see how these two core technologies are used together.

## htp and htf Packages:

htp (hypertext procedures) and htf (hypertext functions) are part of PL/SQL Web Toolkit package to generate HTML tags. These packages translate PL/SQL into HTML understood by a web browser. For instance, the *htp.anchor* procedure generates the HTML anchor tag <a>. The following PL/SQL block generate a simple HTML document:

```
CREATE OR REPLACE PROCEDURE hello AS
BEGIN
    htp.htmlopen;              -- generates <HTML>
    htp.headopen;              -- generates <HEAD>
    htp.title('Hello');        -- generates <TITLE>Hello</TITLE>
    htp.headclose;             -- generates </HEAD>
    htp.bodyopen;              -- generates <BODY>
    htp.header(1, 'Hello');    -- generates <H1>Hello</H1>
    htp.bodyclose;             -- generates </BODY>
    htp.htmlclose;             -- generates </HTML>
END;
```

Oracle provided the htp.p tag to allow you to override any PL/SQL-HTML procedure or even a tag that did not exist. If a developer wishes to use a new HTML tag or simply is unaware of the PL/SQL analog to the html tag, s/he can use the htp.p procedure.

For every htp procedure that generates HTML tags, there is a corresponding htf function with identical parameters. The function versions do not directly generate output in your web page. Instead, they pass their output as return values to the statements that invoked them.

## htp.p / htp.print:

Generates the specified parameter as a string

## htp.p('<p>'):

Indicates that the text coming after the tag is to be formatted as a paragraph

## Customer::

Renders the text they surround in bold

## htf.escape_sc:

Escape_sc is a function, which replaces characters that have special meaning in HTML with their escape sequence.

converts occurrence of & to &amp
converts occurrence of " to &quot
converts occurrence of < to &lt
converts occurrence of > to &gt

To prevent XSS (Cross Site Scripting) attacks, you must call SYS.HTF.ESCAPE_SC to prevent embedded JavaScript code from being executed when you inject the string into an HTML page. The SYS prefix is used to signify Oracle's SYS schema. The HTP and HTF packages normally exist in the SYS schema and Oracle APEX relies on them.

## Cursor FOR LOOP Statement

The cursor FOR LOOP statement implicitly declares its loop index as a record variable of the row type that a specified cursor returns and then opens a cursor. With each iteration, the cursor FOR LOOP statement fetches a row from the result set into the record. When there are no more rows to fetch, the cursor FOR LOOP statement closes the cursor. The cursor also closes if a statement inside the loop transfers control outside the loop or raises an exception.

The cursor FOR LOOP statement lets you run a SELECT statement and then immediately loop through the rows of the result set. This statement can use either an implicit or explicit cursor.

If you use the SELECT statement only in the cursor FOR LOOP statement, then specify the SELECT statement inside the cursor FOR LOOP statement, as in Example A. This form of the cursor FOR LOOP statement uses an implicit cursor and is called an implicit cursor FOR LOOP statement. Because the implicit cursor is internal to the statement, you cannot reference it with the name SQL.

### Example A - Implicit Cursor FOR LOOP Statement

```
BEGIN
  FOR item IN (
    SELECT last_name, job_id
    FROM employees
    WHERE job_id LIKE '%CLERK%' AND manager_id > 120
    ORDER BY last_name
  )
  LOOP
    DBMS_OUTPUT.PUT_LINE ('Name = ' || item.last_name || ', Job = ' || item.job_id);
  END LOOP;
END;
/
```

**Output:**

Name = Atkinson, Job = ST_CLERK
Name = Bell, Job = SH_CLERK
Name = Bissot, Job = ST_CLERK
...
Name = Walsh, Job = SH_CLERK

If you use the SELECT statement multiple times in the same PL/SQL unit, define an explicit cursor for it and specify that cursor in the cursor FOR LOOP statement, as shown in Example B. This form of the cursor FOR LOOP statement is called an explicit cursor FOR LOOP statement. You can use the same explicit cursor elsewhere in the same PL/SQL unit.

**Example B - Explicit Cursor FOR LOOP Statement**

```
DECLARE
  CURSOR c1 IS
    SELECT last_name, job_id FROM employees
    WHERE job_id LIKE '%CLERK%' AND manager_id > 120
    ORDER BY last_name;
BEGIN
  FOR item IN c1
  LOOP
    DBMS_OUTPUT.PUT_LINE ('Name = ' || item.last_name || ', Job = ' || item.job_id);
  END LOOP;
END;
/
```

**Output:**
Name = Atkinson, Job = ST_CLERK
Name = Bell, Job = SH_CLERK
Name = Bissot, Job = ST_CLERK
...
Name = Walsh, Job = SH_CLERK

## TABLE 7-1 PL/SQL CODE EXPLAINED

**Display Customer Information (Lines 7-32)**
This procedure fetches information of the selected customer and presents it in a desirable format (as shown in Figure 7-27) using the CSS rules defined under the class *CustomerInfo*.

**Declare** (Line: 1)
This is the parent PL/SQL block. A nested block is also used under the *Display Current Order* section on line:48.

**l_customer_id varchar2(30) := :P11_CUSTOMER_ID; (Line: 2)**
Assigns customer ID, which is retrieved from the previous order wizard step (Page 11), to the variable *l_customer_id*. This variable is used in a SQL statement (on Line No. 9) to fetch details of the selected customer. In PL/SQL, the symbol := is called the assignment operator. The variable, which is being assigned the new value, is placed on the left side of the assignment operator and the value is placed on the right side of the operator.

:P11_CUSTOMER_ID is called a bind variable. Bind variables are substituion variables that are used in place of literals. You can use bind variables syntax anywhere in Oracle APEX where you are using SQL or PL/SQL to reference session state of a specified item. For example:

```
SELECT * FROM employees WHERE last_name like '%' || :P99_SEARCH_STRING || '%'
```

In this example, the search string is a page item. If the region type is defined as SQL Query, then you can reference the value using standard SQL bind variable syntax. Using bind variables ensures that parsed representations of SQL queries are reused by the database, optimizing memory usage by the server.

The use of bind variables is encouraged in Oracle APEX. Bind variables help you protect your Oracle APEX application from SQL injection attacks. Bind variables work in much the same way as passing data to a stored procedure. Bind variables automatically treat all input data as "flat" data and never mistake it for SQL code. Besides the prevention of SQL injection attacks, there are other performance-related benefits to its use.

You declare a page item as a bind variable by prefixing a colon character (:) like this:
:P11_CUSTOMER_OPTIONS.

When using bind variable syntax, remember the following rules:

- Bind variable names must correspond to an item name
- Bind variable names are not case-sensitive
- Bind variable names cannot be longer than 30 characters

Although page item and application item names can be up to 255 characters, if you intend to use an application item within SQL using bind variable syntax, the item name must be 30 characters or less.

**Begin** (Line: 3)
Read *What is PL/SQL* at the beginning of this section.
The code block from line number 7 to 32 creates the first section on the page (marked as A in Figure 7-27) using the <div> HTML element and styles it using Rule 1 and 2. The code between lines 9-20 is executed when the user selects an existing customer from the previous wizard step.

**sys.htp.p('<div class="CustomerInfo">'); (Line: 7)**
The <div> tag defines a division or a section in an HTML document. This is the opening tag, which references the *CustomerInfo* class in CSS rules to format the following elements. The ending tag is defined on Line 32.

**for x in (select * from demo_customers where customer_id = l_customer_id) loop** (Line: 9)
Initiates the FOR loop to locate and fetch record of the selected customer from the demo_customers table.

**sys.htp.p('<strong>Customer:</strong>'); (Line: 11)**
Displays the label "Customer:" in bold.

**sys.htp.p('<p>'); (Line: 12)**
The paragraph opening tag. It ends on Line 19.

**sys.htp.p(sys.htf.escape_sc(x.cust_first_name) || ' ' ||sys.htf.escape_sc(x.cust_last_name) || '<br>'); (Line: 13)**
Concatenates customer's first and last names using the concatenation characters (||). The <br> tag inserts a single line break.

**sys.htp.p(sys.htf.escape_sc(x.cust_street_address1) || '<br>'); (Line: 14)**
Show customer's first address on a new line.

**if x.cust_street_address2 is not null then** (Lines: 15-17)

  **sys.htp.p(sys.htf.escape_sc(x.cust_street_address2) || '<br>');**

**end if;**

It's a condition to check whether the customer's second address is not null. If it's not, print it on a new line.

**sys.htp.p(sys.htf.escape_sc(x.cust_city) || ', ' || sys.htf.escapte_sc(x.cust_state) || ' ' || sys.htf.escape_sc(x.cust_postal_code));** (Line: 18)

Displays city, state, and postal code data on the same row separating each other with a comma and a blank space.

**sys.htp.p('</p>');** (Line: 19)

The paragraph end tag.

**end loop;** (Line: 20)

The loop terminates here after fetching details of an existing customer from the database table.

**sys.htp.p('</div>');** (Line: 32)

The div tag terminates here. The output of this section is illustrated in Figure 7-27: A - CustomerInfo. The ELSE block (line 22-30) is executed when a new customer is added to the database from the order interface. In that situation, all values on the current page are fetched from the previous wizard step (Page 11).

## Display Products (Lines: 36-42)

Here you create a section on your web page to display all products along with their prices and include an option, which allows users to add products to their cart.

**sys.htp.p('<div class="Products" >');** (Line: 36)

Creates a division based on the Products class. HTML elements under this division are styled using rules 4-9.

**sys.htp.p('<table width="100%" cellspacing="0" cellpadding="0" border="0">** (Line: 37)

Here you are initiating to draw an HTML table. The <table> tag defines an HTML table. An HTML table consists of the <table> element and one or more <tr>, <th>, and <td> elements. The <tr> element defines a table row, the <th> element defines a table header, and the <td> element defines a table cell. The Width attribute specifies the width of the table. Setting 100% width instructs the browser to consume the full screen width to display the table element.

**<thead>** (Line: 37)

  **<tr><th class="left">Product</th><th>Price</th><th></th></tr>**

**</thead>**

The <thead> tag is used to group header content in an HTML table. The <thead> element is used in conjunction with the <tbody> and <tfoot> elements to specify each part of a table (header, body, footer). The <tr> tag creates a row for column heading. The three <th> tags specify the headings. The first two columns are labeled Product and Price, respectively. The third column heading is left blank. A specific declaration (class="left") is included that points toward the CSS rule (9) *div.Products .left{text-align:left;}* to align the title of the first column (Product) to the left. The second column (Price) is styled using a general rule (6).

**<tbody>'); (Line: 37)**

The <tbody> tag is used to group the body content in an HTML table. This section spans up to line 41 and is marked as B in Figure 7-27.

```
for c1 in (select product_id, product_name,  list_price, 'Add to Cart' add_to_order
from demo_product_info
where product_avail = 'Y'
order by product_name) loop  (Line: 38)
```

The FOR loop fetches Product ID, Product Name, and List Price columns from the products table. To display a button (Add) in the table, we appended a column aliased add_to_order and populated all rows with a constant value 'Add to Cart'. For further information on FOR LOOP, see the *Cursor FOR LOOP Statement* section earlier in this section.

```
sys.htp.p('<tr><td class="left">' ||sys.htf.escape_sc(c1.product_name)||'</td>
            <td>'||trim(to_char(c1.list_price,'999G999G990D00')) || '</td>
            <td><a href=" '||apex_util.prepare_url('f?p=&APP_ID.:12:'||:app_session||'
                 :ADD:::P12_PRODUCT_ID:'|| c1.product_id)||' "
                class="t-Button t-Button--simple t-Button--hot">
                <span>Add<i class="iR"></i></span></a>
        </td>
    </tr>'); (Line: 39)
```

This line displays product names with respective prices in two separate columns. The product column is styled using Rule 9, while the price column is styled using Rule 6. There is an *Add* button in the third column of the table, which is presented as a link using the HTML anchor tag <a> and is styled using a built-in class (t-Button). An anchor can be used in two ways:

1. To create a link to another document by using the href attribute.
2. To create a bookmark inside a document by using the name attribute.

It is usually referred to as a link or a hyperlink. The most important attribute of the <a> element is the *href* attribute, which specifies the URL of the page to which the link goes. When this button is clicked, the product it represents is moved to the Current Order section with the help of a process (*Add Product to the Order Collection*) defined in section 7.6.7.

The c1 prefix in front of column names, points to the FOR LOOP cursor. The TRIM function in the *trim(to_char(c1.list_price,'999G999G990D00'))* expression takes a character expression and returns that expression with leading and/or trailing pad characters removed. This expression initially formats the list price column to add thousand separators and decimal place. Next, it converts the numeric price value to text expression using the TO_CHAR function and finally applies the TRIM function. The TO_CHAR function converts a DATETIME, number, or NTEXT expression to a TEXT expression in a specified format. The table that follows lists the elements of a number format model with some examples.

| Element | Example | Description |
|---|---|---|
| 0 | 0999 | Returns leading zeros. |
|  | 9990 | Returns trailing zeros. |
| 9 | 9999 | Returns value with the specified number of digits with a leading space if positive or with a leading minus if negative. Leading zeros are blank, except for a zero value, which returns a zero for the integer part of the fixed-point number. |
| D | 99D99 | Returns in the specified position the decimal character, which is the current value of the NLS_NUMERIC_CHARACTER parameter. The default is a period (.). |
| G | 9G999 | Returns the group separator (which is usually comma) in the specified position. You can specify multiple group separators in a number format model. Use the following SQL statement to check the current value for decimal and group separator characters:<br>SELECT value FROM v$nls_parameters<br>WHERE parameter='NLS_NUMERIC_CHARACTERS'; |

The code,

```
<a href="'||apex_util.prepare_url('f?p=&APP_ID.:12:'||:app_session||':ADD:::P12_PRODUCT_ID:'|| c1.product_id)||'"
class="t-Button t-Button--simple t-Button--hot"> <span>Add<iclass="iR"></i></span></a>,
```

creates a link with an ADD request. The value of REQUEST is the name of the button the user clicks. For example, suppose you have a button with a name of CHANGE and a label *Apply Changes*. When a user clicks the button, the value of REQUEST is CHANGE. In section 7.6.7, you will create the following process named *Add Product to the order collection*.

```
for x in (select p.rowid, p.* from demo_product_info p where product_id=:P12_PRODUCT_ID)
loop
  select count(*)
  into l_count
  from wwv_flow_collections
  where collection_name = 'ORDER'
  and c001 =  x.product_id;
  if l_count >= 10 then
    exit;
  end if;
  apex_collection.add_member(p_collection_name => 'ORDER',
    p_c001 => x.product_id,
    p_c002 => x.product_name,
    p_c003 => x.list_price,
    p_c004 => 1,
    p_c010 => x.rowid);
end loop;
```

During the process creation, you'll select Request=Value in Condition Type and will enter ADD for Value. The ADD request in the <a> tag is referencing the same expression. When a user clicks the ADD button on the web page, the URL sends the ADD request to the process along with the selected product ID using a hidden item named P12_PRODUCT_ID to be created in section 7.6.4. In turn, the process adds the product to the Current Order section. The URL generated from this code looks something like this at runtime:

```
f?p=18132:12:13238397476902:ADD:::P12_PRODUCT_ID:10
```

**end loop;** (Line: 40)
End of FOR loop.

**sys.htp.p('</tbody></table>');** (Line: 41)
Table and body closing tags.

**sys.htp.p('</div>');** (Line: 42)
The closing div tag.

## Display Current Order (Lines: 46-79)

This section acts as a shopping cart. The products selected by a user are placed in this section.

**sys.htp.p('<div class="Products" >');** (Line: 46)
Defines the <div> tag and utilizes the Products class referenced in rules 4-9.

```
sys.htp.p('<table width="100%" cellspacing="0" cellpadding="0" border="0">
  <thead>
    <tr><th class="left">Current Order</th></tr>
  </thead>
</table>
```
(Line: 47)
Displays section heading as follows in the first row of a separate table.

**Current Order**

**Declare** (Line: 48)
This is a nested or child block. To nest a block means to embed one or more PL/SQL block inside another PL/SQL block to have better control over program's execution.

**c number := 0; t number := 0;** (Line: 49)
Declared two numeric counter variables and initialized them with zero. The variable c is used to evaluate whether any product is selected in the current order, while the variable t stores total value for the order.

**Begin** (Line: 50)

```
for c1 in (select c001 pid, c002 i, to_number(c003) p, count(c002) q, sum(c003) ep, 'Remove' remove
        from apex_collections
        where collection_name = 'ORDER'
        group by c001, c002, c003
        order by c001)
```

**loop** (Line: 52)

APEX Collection enables you to temporarily capture one or more non-scalar values. You can use collections to store rows and columns currently in session state so they can be accessed, manipulated, or processed during a user's specific session. You can think of a collection as a bucket in which you temporarily store and name rows of information.

Every collection contains a named list of data elements (or members), which can have up to 50 character properties (varchar2 (4000)), 5 number, 5 date, 1 XML type, 1 BLOB, and 1 CLOB attribute. You insert, update, and delete collection information using the PL/SQL API APEX_COLLECTION.

When you create a new collection, you must give it a name that cannot exceed 255 characters. Note that collection names are not case-sensitive and will be converted to uppercase. Once the collection is named, you can access the values (members of a collection) in the collection by running a SQL query against the database view APEX_COLLECTIONS.

The APEX_COLLECTIONS view has the following definition:

| | |
|---|---|
| COLLECTION_NAME | NOT NULL VARCHAR2(255) |
| SEQ_ID | NOT NULL NUMBER |
| C001 | VARCHAR2(4000) |
| C002 | VARCHAR2(4000) |
| C003 | VARCHAR2(4000) |
| C004 | VARCHAR2(4000) |
| C005 | VARCHAR2(4000) |
| ... | |
| C050 | VARCHAR2(4000) |
| N001 | NUMBER |
| N002 | NUMBER |
| N003 | NUMBER |
| N004 | NUMBER |
| N005 | NUMBER |
| CLOB001 | CLOB |
| BLOB001 | BLOB |
| XMLTYPE001 | XMLTYPE |
| MD5_ORIGINAL | VARCHAR2(4000) |

Use the APEX_COLLECTIONS view in an application just as you would use any other table or view in an application, for example:

```
SELECT c001, c002, c003, n001, clob001
FROM APEX_collections
WHERE collection_name = 'DEPARTMENTS'
```

The CREATE_OR_TRUNCATE_COLLECTION method creates a new collection if the named collection does not exist. If the named collection already exists, this method truncates it. Truncating a collection empties it, but leaves it in place.

In section 7.5.12, we created a process named *Create or Truncate Order Collection* under the page rendering section and used the following statement to create a collection named ORDER:

```
apex_collection.create_or_truncate_collection (p_collection_name => 'ORDER');
```

In the "For C1 in" loop, we're selecting records from the same ORDER collection. Columns from apex_collections in the SELECT statement correspond to:

| Column | Corresponds To |
|---|---|
| C001 – pid | Product ID (9) |
| C002 – i | Product Name (Men Shoes) |
| C003 – p | List Price (110) |
| C002 - q | Quantity (1) |
| C003 - ep | Extended Price (110) This value will increase with each Add button click to accumulate total cost of a product. |

**sys.htp.p('<div class="CartItem">** (Line: 53)
This line references another class (CartItem) to style the actual Current Order section.

```
<a
href=""||apex_util.prepare_url('f?p=&APP_ID.:12:&SESSION.:REMOVE:::P12_PRODUCT_ID:'||sys.htf.escape_sc(
c1.pid))||'"><img src="#IMAGE_PREFIX#delete.gif" alt="Remove from cart" title="Remove from cart" />
</a>   (Line: 54)
```

The <a> tag creates a link with a REMOVE request. This time, it uses product ID from the collection. In section 7.6.7 (B), there is a process named *Remove product from the Order Collection* (as shown below) where the request expression is set to REMOVE.

```
for x in
  (select seq_id, c001 from apex_collections
    where collection_name = 'ORDER' and c001 = :P12_PRODUCT_ID)
loop
apex_collection.delete_member(p_collection_name => 'ORDER', p_seq => x.seq_id);
end loop;
```

In HTML, images are defined with the <img> tag. The <img> tag has no closing tag. To display an image on a page, you need to use the src attribute. Src stands for "source". The value of the src attribute is the URL of the image you want to display.

Syntax for defining an image:
```
<img src="url" alt="some_text"/>
```

The URL points to the location where the image is stored. The value of IMAGE_PREFIX determines the virtual path the web server uses to point to the images directory distributed with Oracle APEX. We used "delete.gif" that is displayed in front of the product name. The required *alt* attribute specifies an alternate text for an image, if the image cannot be displayed.

When a user clicks the remove link [**X**] in the Current Order section, the URL sends a REMOVE request to the process along with the product ID. The DELETE_MEMBER procedure deletes a specified member from a given named collection using the *p_seq => x.seq_id* parameter, which is the sequence ID of the collection member to be deleted.

```
'||sys.htf.escape_sc(c1.i)||' (Line: 55)
```
Displays name of the selected product in the Current Order section.

```
<span>'||trim(to_char(c1.p,'$999G999G999D00'))||'</span> (Line: 56)
<span>Quantity: '||c1.q||'</span> (Line: 57)
<span class="subtotal">Subtotal: '||trim(to_char(c1.ep,'$999G999G999D00'))||'</span> (Line: 58)
```
The three lines display price, quantity, and sub-total of the selected product in the Current Order section, as shown below:

```
        $125.00
      Quantity: 10
Subtotal: $1,250.00
```

**</div>');** (Line: 59)

The ending div tag.

**c := c + 1;** (Line: 60)

This counter increments the value of c with 1 at the end of each loop. The variable c is used to calculate number of items selected in the current order.

**t := t + c1.ep;** (Line: 61)

Similar to the variable c, t is also incremented to sum up extended price **(c1.ep)** to calculate total order value.

```
if c > 0 then
    sys.htp.p('<div class="CartTotal">
    <p>Items: <span>'||c||'</span></p>
    <p class="CartTotal">Total: <span>'||trim(to_char(t,'$999G999G999D00'))||'</span></p>
    </div>');
else
    sys.htp.p('<div class="alertMessage info" style="margin-top: 8px;">');
    sys.htp.p('<img src="#IMAGE_PREFIX#f_spacer.gif">');
    sys.htp.p('<div class="innerMessage">');
    sys.htp.p('<h3>Note</h3>');
    sys.htp.p('<p>You have no items in your current order.</p>');
    sys.htp.p('</div>');
    sys.htp.p('</div>');
end if; (Line: 64-77)
```

The condition (IF c > 0) evaluates whether a product is selected in the current order. A value other than zero in this variable indicates addition of product(s). If the current order has some items added, the label *Total:* along with the value is displayed, which is stored in the variable t. If no items are selected, the message defined in the else block is shown using a couple of built-in classes.

## 7.6.4 Create Hidden Item

Create a hidden item in the *Select Items* region. When you click the Add button on Page 12 to add a product to an order, the ID of that product is stored in this hidden item using a URL specified in the PL/SQL code on line 39.

| Property | Value |
|---|---|
| Name | P12_PRODUCT_ID |
| Type | Hidden |

## 7.6.5 Create Region to hold Buttons

Right-click the *Wizard Buttons* node and select **Create Region**. Enter **Buttons** for the *Title* of this region and set its *Template* to **Buttons Container**. The region will hold three buttons: Cancel, Previous, and Next. These buttons are created in the next section.

## 7.6.6 Create Buttons

All the three buttons created in this section have one thing in common, the *Action* property, which is set to *Submit Page*. When you click any of these three buttons, the page is submitted and a corresponding branch (to be created in section 7.6.9) is fired to take you to the specified location. For example, if you click the *Cancel* button, the corresponding branch takes you back to the main Orders page (Page 4). Right-click the new *Buttons* region and select **Create Button**. Set the following properties for the new button:

| Property | Value |
|---|---|
| Button Name | CANCEL |
| Label | Cancel |
| Position | Close |
| Action | Submit Page |

Create another button under the *Cancel* button and set the following properties:

| Property | Value |
|---|---|
| Button Name | PREVIOUS |
| Label | Previous |
| Position | Previous |
| Button Template | Icon |
| Icon | fa-chevron-left |
| Action | Submit Page |

Create the final button under the *Previous* button and set the following properties:

| Property | Value |
|---|---|
| Button Name | NEXT |
| Label | Place Order |
| Position | Next |
| Button Template | Text with Icon |
| Hot | On |
| Icon | fa-chevron-right |
| Action | Submit Page |

## 7.6.7 Create Processes

The two processes created in this section handle the routine to either add a product to the *Current Order* section or remove one from it. The *add_member* function references the collection (*ORDER* created in section 7.5.12) to populate the collection with a new product. In Table 7-1, the link defined on line 39 in the PL/SQL code forwards an ADD request, which is entertained here after evaluating the request in step 4 below.

### A.  Add Product to the Order Collection

1.  On Page 12, expand the *Pre-Rendering* node (on the *Rendering* tab) and create a process under *Before Header* node.

2.  Enter **Add Product to the ORDER Collection** for the name of this new process and set its *Type* to **PL/SQL Code**.

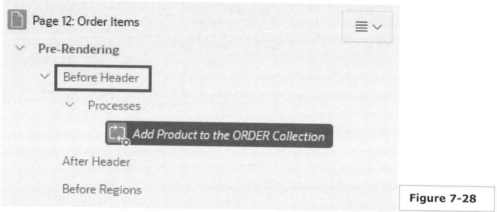

**Figure 7-28**

3.  Enter the following code in the *PL/SQL Code* box. Locate this code under *BookCode\Chapter7\7.6.7A.txt* file.

```
declare
  l_count number := 0;
begin
for x in (select p.rowid, p.* from demo_product_into p
          where product_id = :P12_PRODUCT_ID)
loop
  select count(*)
  into l_count
  from wwv_flow_collections
  where collection_name = 'ORDER'
  and c001 =  x.product_id;
  if l_count >= 10 then
    exit;
  end if;
  apex_collection.add_member(p_collection_name => 'ORDER',
    p_c001 => x.product_id,
    p_c002 => x.product_name,
    p_c003 => x.list_price,
    p_c004 => 1,
    p_c010 => x.rowid);
end loop;
end;
```

4.  In *Server-side Condition* section, set *Type* to **Request=Value**, and enter **ADD** in the *Value* property box.

**B.   Remove Product from the Order Collection**

The *delete_member* function is just opposite to the *add_member* function. It is called by a link (Table 7-1 line 54), which carries a *REMOVE* request. The request is evaluated by a condition set in Step 3 below. If the request matches, the selected product is deleted from the ORDER collection.

1.   **Create** another process under the previous one. *Name* it **Remove Product from the ORDER Collection** and set its *Type* to **PL/SQL Code**.

2.   Enter the following code in the *PL/SQL Code* property box. Get this code from *BookCode\Chapter7\7.6.7B.txt* file.

```
for x in
 (select seq_id, c001 from apex_collections
   where collection_name = 'ORDER' and c001 = :P12_PRODUCT_ID)
loop
  apex_collection.delete_member(p_collection_name => 'ORDER', p_seq => x.seq_id);
end loop;
```

3.   In *Server-side Condition* section, set *Type* to **Request=Value**, and enter **REMOVE** in the *Value* property box.

**7.6.8 Create Process – Place Order**

After selecting products for an order, you click the *Next* button. The process defined in this section is associated with this button. The PL/SQL code specified in this process adds new customer and order information in relevant database tables using a few SQL INSERT statements. After committing the DML statement, the process truncates the *ORDER* collection.

1.   On the *Processing* tab, create a new process under the *Processing* node.

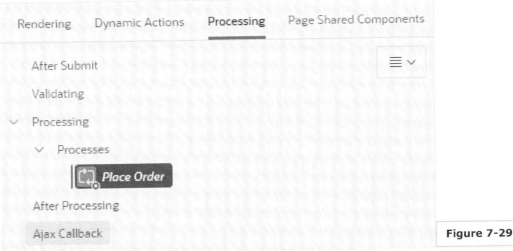

Figure 7-29

2. Enter **Place Order** for the name of this new process and set its *Type* to **PL/SQL Code**. Enter the following code in the *PL/SQL Code* box. Also, select **NEXT** for *When Button Pressed* property. The code is stored under *BookCode\Chapter7\7.6.8.txt* file.

```
declare
    l_order_id    number;
    l_customer_id varchar2(30) := :P11_CUSTOMER_ID;
begin
-- Create New Customer
    if :P11_CUSTOMER_OPTIONS = 'NEW' then
        insert into DEMO_CUSTOMERS (
            CUST_FIRST_NAME, CUST_LAST_NAME, CUST_STREET_ADDRESS1,
            CUST_STREET_ADDRESS2, CUST_CITY, CUST_STATE, CUST_POSTAL_CODE,
            CUST_EMAIL, PHONE_NUMBER1, PHONE_NUMBER2, URL, CREDIT_LIMIT, TAGS)
        values (
            :P11_CUST_FIRST_NAME, :P11_CUST_LAST_NAME, :P11_CUST_STREET_ADDRESS1,
            :P11_CUST_STREET_ADDRESS2, :P11_CUST_CITY, :P11_CUST_STATE,
            :P11_CUST_POSTAL_CODE, :P11_CUST_EMAIL, :P11_PHONE_NUMBER1,
            :P11_PHONE_NUMBER2, :P11_URL, :P11_CREDIT_LIMIT, :P11_TAGS)
        returning customer_id into l_customer_id;
        :P11_CUSTOMER_ID := l_customer_id;
    end if;
-- Insert a row into the Order Header table
-- The statement returning order_id into l_order_id stores the primary key value for
--   the order_id column (generated by the DEMO_ORD_SEQ sequence) into the local
--   variable l_order_id. This value is used in the INSERT statements to
--   populate the order_id column in DEMO_ORDER_ITEMS table.
    insert into demo_orders(customer_id, order_total, order_timestamp, user_name)
    values  (l_customer_id, null, systimestamp, upper(:APP_USER))
    returning order_id into l_order_id;
    commit;
-- Loop through the ORDER collection and insert rows into the Order Line Item table
    for x in (select c001, c003, sum(c004) c004 from apex_collections
            where collection_name = 'ORDER' group by c001, c003) loop
        insert into demo_order_items(order_item_id, order_id, product_id, unit_price, quantity)
        values (null, l_order_id, to_number(x.c001), to_number(x.c003),to_number(x.c004));
    end loop;
    commit;
-- Set the item P14_ORDER_ID to the order which was just placed
    :P14_ORDER_ID := l_order_id;
-- Truncate the collection after the order has been placed
    apex_collection.truncate_collection(p_collection_name => 'ORDER');
end;
```

## 7.6.9 Create Branches

Create the following three branches under the *After Processing* node on the *Processing* tab. The buttons referenced in these branches were created in section 7.6.6.

| Property | Value |
|---|---|
| Name | Go To Page 14 |
| Type (under Behavior) | Page or URL (Redirect) |
| Target | Type = Page in this Application<br>Page = 14 |
| When Button Pressed | NEXT |

| Property | Value |
|---|---|
| Name | Go To Page 4 |
| Type (under Behavior) | Page or URL (Redirect) |
| Target | Type = Page in this Application<br>Page = 4 |
| When Button Pressed | CANCEL |

| Property | Value |
|---|---|
| Name | Go To Page 11 |
| Type (under Behavior) | Page or URL (Redirect) |
| Target | Type = Page in this Application<br>Page = 11 |
| When Button Pressed | PREVIOUS |

## Test Your Work

Navigate to the Orders page using the main menu route and click the **Enter New Order** button. Select a customer using the *Existing Customer* option and click *Next*. Click the **Add** button next to *Air Jordan 6* shoes to add this product to the *Current Order* pane. Click the **Add** button again for this product and see increase in Quantity and Total. Add some more products and observe the change in the *Current Order* section. Click the cross sign ✕ to remove a product from the Current Order section. Click **Cancel** to return to Page 4 without saving the order.

## 7.7 Create Order Summary Page - Page 14

After adding products to the Order form, you click the *Place Order* button. The next page, *Order Summary*, comes up to show details of the placed order. In this section, you will create this page. It is the last step in the order creation wizard.

1. Create one more **Blank Page**.

2. Complete the first wizard step as show in the following figure and click **Next**.

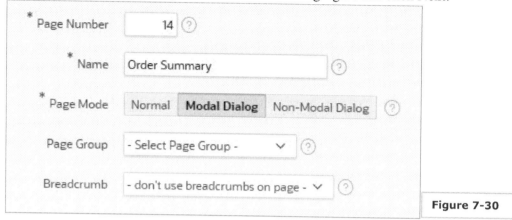

Figure 7-30

3. On the *Navigation Menu* screen, set *Navigation Preference* to **Identify an existing navigation menu entry for this page**, and set *Existing Navigation Menu Entry* to **Orders**. Click **Next**.

4. Click **Finish** to end the wizard.

5. Click the root node (**Page 14: Order Summary**) and set *Dialog Template* to **Wizard Modal Dialog**.

### 7.7.1 Create Region – Order Progress

Right-click the *Wizard Progress Bar* node and select **Create Region**. Set the following properties for the new region.

| Property | Value |
|---|---|
| Title | Order Progress |
| Type | List |
| List | Order Wizard |
| Template | Blank with Attributes |
| List Template *(under Attributes tab)* | Wizard Progress |

## 7.7.2 Create Region – Order Header

Right-click the *Wizard Body* node and select **Create Region**. Set the following properties for this region. Just like section 7.6.3, you define the region as *PL/SQL Dynamic Content*, which is based on PL/SQL that enables you to render any HTML or text.

| Property | Value |
|---|---|
| Title | Order Header |
| Type | PL/SQL Dynamic Content |
| PL/SQL Code | `begin`<br>`for x in (select c.cust_first_name, c.cust_last_name, cust_street_address1, cust_street_address2, cust_city,`<br>`cust_state, cust_postal_code from demo_customers c, demo_orders o`<br>`where c.customer_id = o.customer_id and o.order_id = :P14_ORDER_ID)`<br>`loop`<br>`  htp.p('<span style="font-size:16px;font-weight:bold;">ORDER #' ||`<br>`      sys.htf.escape_sc(:P14_ORDER_ID) || '</span><br>');`<br>`  htp.p(sys.htf.escape_sc(x.cust_first_name) || ' ' || sys.htf.escape_sc(x.cust_last_name) || '<br>');`<br>`  htp.p(sys.htf.escape_sc(x.cust_street_address1) || '<br>');`<br>`  if x.cust_street_address2 is not null then`<br>`    htp.p(sys.htf.escape_sc(x.cust_street_address2) || '<br>');`<br>`  end if;`<br>`  htp.p(sys.htf.escape_sc(x.cust_city) || ', ' || sys.htf.escape_sc(x.cust_state) || ' ' ||`<br>`      sys.htf.escape_sc(x.cust_postal_code) || '<br><br>');`<br>`end loop;`<br>`end;` |

## 7.7.3 Create Region – Order Lines

Add another region under the *Wizard Body* node and set the following properties for this region. After creating this region expand its *Columns* node and set suitable heading for each column. This region will carry line item information.

| Property | Value |
|---|---|
| Title | Order Lines |
| Type | Classic Report |
| Location | Local Database |
| Type | SQL Query |
| SQL Query | `SELECT p.product_name, oi.unit_price, oi.quantity, (oi.unit_price * oi.quantity) extended_price`<br>`FROM   demo_order_items oi, demo_product_info p`<br>`WHERE oi.product_id = p.product_id and oi.order_id = :P14_ORDER_ID` |

## 7.7.4 Create Item

Right-click the *Order Lines* region and select **Create Page Item**. Set the following properties for the new item. The value for this item was set in the PL/SQL code defined in section 7.6.8 and was utilized in the codes defined in section 7.7.2 and in section 7.7.3 to fetch order information.

| Property | Value |
|---|---|
| Name | P14_ORDER_ID |
| Type | Hidden |

## 7.7.5 Create Region – Buttons

Right-click the *Wizard Buttons* node and select **Create Region**. Enter **Buttons** for its *Name* and set its *Template* to **Buttons Container**. The region will hold the following button.

## 7.7.6 Create Button

Right-click the new *Buttons* region node and select **Create Button**. Set the following properties for the new button:

| Property | Value |
|---|---|
| Button Name | BACK |
| Label | Back To Orders |
| Position | Next |
| Hot | On |
| Action | Redirect to Page in this Application |
| Target | Type = Page in this application<br>Page = 4 |

## 7.7.7 Create Trigger

As the final step of this module, add the following trigger to your schema. The trigger will fire to write order total to the DEMO_ORDERS table when any order item is changed.

1.  From the main Oracle APEX menu, select **SQL Workshop | SQL Commands**.

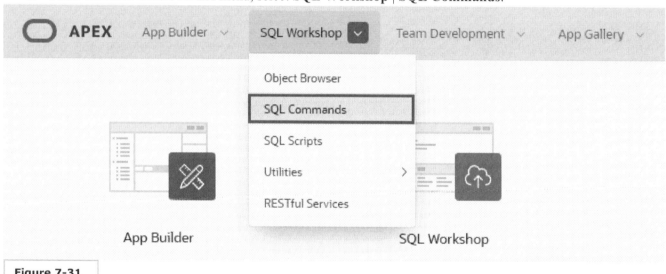

**Figure 7-31**

2. In the SQL Commands interface, enter the code for the new trigger named DEMO_ORDER_ITEMS_AIUD_TOTAL, as illustrated in the following figure, and hit the **Run** button. The trigger will be created and you will see a confirmation on the *Results* tab. The code for this trigger is available in *BookCode\Chapter7\7.7.7.txt* file.

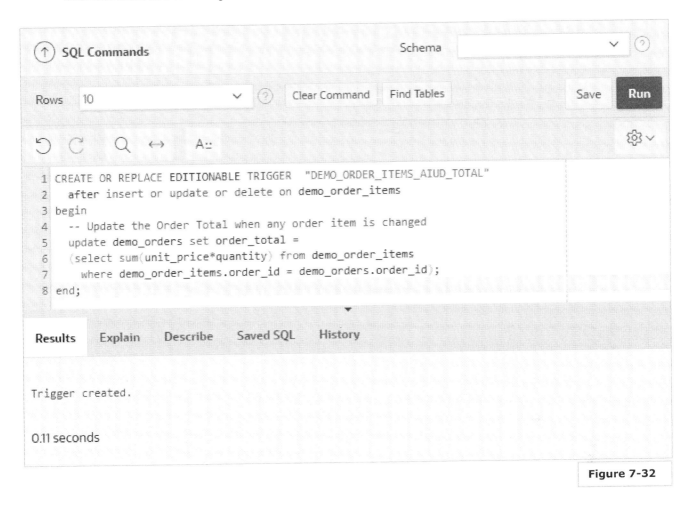

**Figure 7-32**

## Complete Testing

Congratulation! You have completed the most tiresome but interesting chapter of the book in which you learned numerous techniques. Now you are in a position to test the whole work you performed in this chapter.

1. Select **Orders** from the main navigation menu and then click the **Enter New Order** button.

2. Select **New Customer**.

3. **Fill in the New Customer form** using your own name, address, and so on. Click **Next** to proceed.

4. On the *Select Items* page **add some products** to the *Current Order* pane.

5. Click the **Place Order** button to see the *Order Summary* page, as illustrated in figure 7-33.

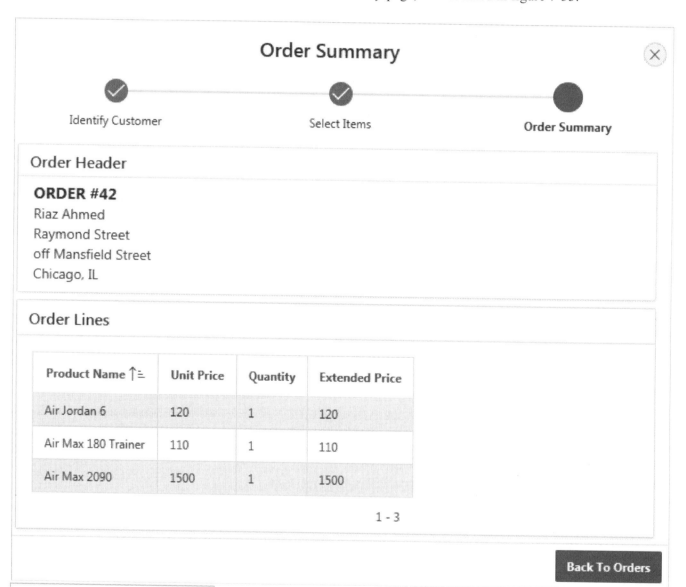

**Figure 7-33** Order Summary Page

You might encounter a primary key violation message (*ORA-00001: unique constraint (DEMO_ORDERS_PK) violated*) while creating first product record. This is because the Sequence object for this table is created with an initial value of 1. Keep clicking the Place Order button unless the record is saved.

6.  Click the **Back To Orders** button in the *Order Summary* page to return to the orders main page. The newly created order will appear in the orders list.

7.  Click the number of the new order to modify it in *Order Details* page (Page 29). Try to add or remove products on this page and save your modifications.

8.  Also, try the delete operation by deleting this new order.

## 7.8 Sending Email from Oracle APEX Application

You can enable users to send emails from your application by using *Send E-Mail* process and *Email Templates* with declarative substitutions. You can implement this process without writing a single line of code. Before sending email from an application, the Instance administrator must sign in to Oracle Application Express *Administration Services*, navigate to the *Instance Settings* page and configure Email attributes. Since we are using the online version of Oracle APEX, which is already configured to send emails, we don't need to execute this step. In this section we are going to send an order confirmation email to customers whose email addresses exist in the DEMO_CUSTOMERS table. The email will contain a link that customers can use to access their placed orders.

1. First, you need to create an email template. Go to **Shared Components**. Click **Email Templates** in *Other Components* section. The *Email Templates* page comes up where you can create email templates that you can use in your application to send emails.

2. Click **Create Email Template** button.

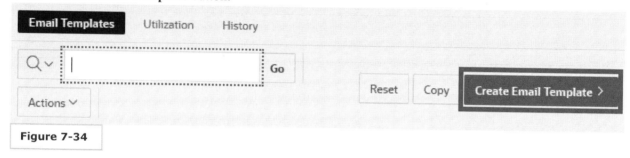

**Figure 7-34**

3. On the right side of *Template Details* page, click **Load Order Details** to use this sample email template.

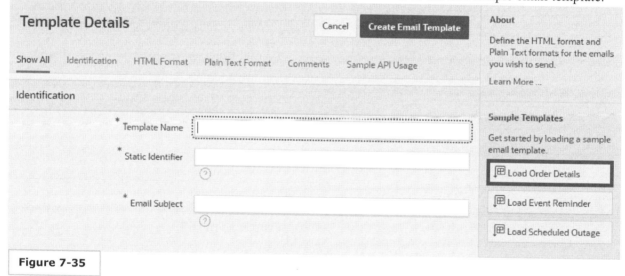

**Figure 7-35**

4. This action will load the sample template information with substitution strings including your application name, customer name, and order information that will be sent to customers. Tweak some properties of this template as follows. The anchor tag modified in the Body section takes customers to Page 30 of the application, where they can view their orders. The link specified in the Footer section lands them on the Home page of the application.

| Property | Value |
| --- | --- |
| Template Name | Send Email |
| Static Identifier | SEND_EMAIL |
| Email Subject | Order (#ORDER_NUMBER#) Confirmed! |
| Header | &lt;b style="font-size: 24px;"&gt;**Sales Web Application**&lt;/b&gt; |
| Body | *Change the anchor tag on the final line as follows to display customer's order on Page 30*<br>&lt;a href="https://apex.oracle.com/pls/apex/f?p=&APP_ID.:30:0::::P30_ORDER_ID: &P14_ORDER_ID."&gt; |
| Footer | *Change the anchor tag to link to your application*<br>&lt;a href="https://apex.oracle.com/pls/apex/f?p=&APP_ID."&gt; |

In the Body section of this template, you will see some strings enclosed in hash symbols (for example, #CUSTOMER_NAME#). These strings will be replaced with actual values in emails. When customers click the link in their emails, they are routed to Page 30. After providing their credentials on the sign in page, they will see details of their orders. This page is created next by making a copy of Page 29.

5. Click the **Create Email Template** button on the *Template Details* page.

6. Create Page 30 by making a copy of Page 29. Open Page 29 in Page Designer. From the *Create* menu, select **Page as Copy** – see section 7.5. Enter **30** for *New Page Number* and **Customer Order** for *New Page Name*. On the *Navigation Menu* screen, select **Identify an existing navigation menu entry for this page**, and select **Orders** for *Existing Navigation Menu Entry*. Click the **Copy** button on the final wizard screen. The customer order will be displayed in this new page when the link mentioned in the email template above is clicked. There is a couple of default securities setting on the new page (Page 30) that we need to change as well to allow access to the order.

7. Open **Page 30** in *Page Designer* and click the root node. Set *Page Mode* in the *Appearance* section to **Normal**. Scroll down to the *Security* section, and set *Page Access Protection* attribute to **Unrestricted**. This value is usually set for a page that is requested using a URL, with or without session state arguments, and having no checksum. If you don't set this value, you'll see the error *"No checksum was provided to show processing for a page that requires a checksum when one or more request, clear cache, or argument values are passed as parameters."*

8. Next, click **P30_ORDER_ID** page item located under *Body | Order #&P30_ORDER_ID.* region. Set *Session State Protection* under *Security* to **Unrestricted**. By setting this value the item's value can be set by passing the item in a URL or in a form and no checksum is required in the URL. If you don't set this value, you'll see the error *Attempt to save item P30_ORDER_ID in session state during show processing. Item protection level indicates: Item may be set when accompanied by a "session" checksum. No checksum was passed in or the checksum passed in would be suitable for an item with protection level "Item has no protection."*

7. Open **Page 14** (Order Summary) and create the following eight hidden items under the existing P14_ORDER_ID item. These items will fetch information of the current order from the database that will be used as substitutions in the e-mail template to replace #STRING_NAME#.

| Property | Value |
| --- | --- |
| Name | P14_CUSTOMER_NAME |
| Type | Hidden |
| Default Type | SQL Query |
| SQL Query | SELECT c.CUST_FIRST_NAME\|\|' '\|\|c.CUST_LAST_NAME FROM demo_customers c, demo_orders o WHERE c.customer_id=o.customer_id and o.order_id=:P14_ORDER_ID |

| Property | Value |
| --- | --- |
| Name | P14_CUST_EMAIL |
| Type | Hidden |
| Default Type | SQL Query |
| SQL Query | SELECT c.CUST_EMAIL FROM demo_customers c, demo_orders o WHERE c.customer_id=o.customer_id and o.order_id=:P14_ORDER_ID |

| Property | Value |
| --- | --- |
| Name | P14_ORDER_DATE |
| Type | Hidden |
| Default Type | SQL Query |
| SQL Query | SELECT o.order_timestamp FROM demo_orders o WHERE o.order_id=:P14_ORDER_ID |

| Property | Value |
| --- | --- |
| Name | P14_ORDER_TOTAL |
| Type | Hidden |
| Default Type | SQL Query |
| SQL Query | SELECT o.order_total FROM demo_orders o WHERE o.order_id=:P14_ORDER_ID |

| Property | Value |
| --- | --- |
| Name | P14_SHIP_TO |
| Type | Hidden |
| Default Type | SQL Query |
| SQL Query | SELECT c.cust_street_address1\|\|' '\|\|c. cust_street_address2 FROM demo_customers c, demo_orders o WHERE c.customer_id=o.customer_id and o.order_id=:P14_ORDER_ID |

| Property | Value |
| --- | --- |
| Name | P14_SHIPPING_ADDRESS_LINE_1 |
| Type | Hidden |
| Default Type | SQL Query |
| SQL Query | SELECT c.cust_street_address1 FROM demo_customers c, demo_orders o WHERE c.customer_id=o.customer_id and o.order_id=:P14_ORDER_ID |

| Property | Value |
|---|---|
| Name | P14_SHIPPING_ADDRESS_LINE_2 |
| Type | Hidden |
| Default Type | SQL Query |
| SQL Query | SELECT c.cust_street_address2<br>FROM   demo_customers c, demo_orders o<br>WHERE  c.customer_id=o.customer_id and o.order_id=:P14_ORDER_ID |

| Property | Value |
|---|---|
| Name | P14_ITEMS_ORDERED |
| Type | Hidden |
| Default Type | SQL Query |
| SQL Query | SELECT sum(oi.quantity) items_ordered<br>FROM   demo_customers c, demo_orders o, demo_order_items oi<br>WHERE  c.customer_id=o.customer_id and o.order_id=oi.order_id and<br>       o.order_id=:P14_ORDER_ID |

8. Modify the **Back** button on this page and set its *Action* property to **Submit Page**.

9. Switch to the *Processing* tab and add a process to send emails using the following attributes. The *Send E-mail* process type is used to send an email, and optionally one or more attachments, from the application. In the *From* property you enter the email address to display as the sender of the email. This email address must be a valid address. Otherwise, the message will not be sent. Here, we used substitution syntax *&APP_EMAIL.* which returns the Application Email defined at the application-level. In our case this will be *noreply@oracle.com*. The value for the *To* property is derived from the hidden page item P14_CUST_EMAIL. The *Send Email* template was created earlier in this exercise.

| Property | Value |
|---|---|
| Name | Send Email |
| Type | Send E-mail |
| From | &APP_EMAIL. |
| To | &P14_CUST_EMAIL. |
| Email Template | Send Email |
| Send Immediately | Turn On |
| Success Message | Order confirmation email sent to customer successfully! |
| Error Message | Something went wrong. Email could not be sent. |
| When Button Pressed | BACK |

Assign the following items and values to *Placeholder Values* property in the *Settings* section. These values, which are held in the hidden items, will replace the #STRING_NAME# in the email template.

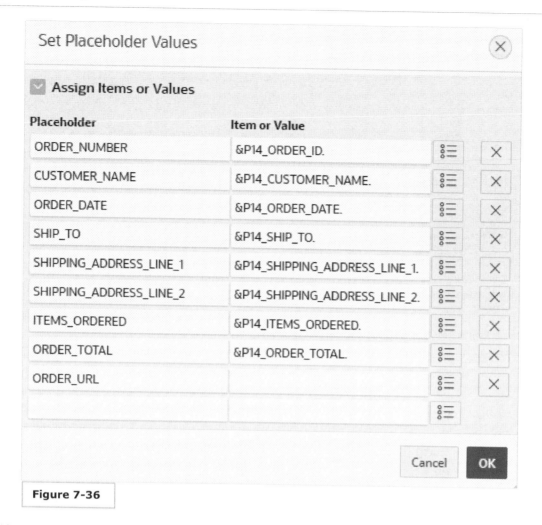

**Figure 7-36**

10. Create a branch under the *After Processing* node to move back to Page 4 after placing orders.

| Property | Value |
| --- | --- |
| Name | Go To Page 4 |
| Point | After Processing |
| Behavior Type | Page or URL (Redirect) |
| Target | Type: Page in this application<br>Page: 4 |

11. Modify a customer record using Manage Customer module, and add your email address for testing purpose.

All is set! Create a new order for this customer. When you click the *Back To Orders* button on the final wizard screen, you will see the message "Order confirmation email sent to customer successfully!" Log out from the application. After a while, you will receive an order confirmation email in your email account as shown in the following figure. Click the "Manage your order" link (A) to access the application login page. Immediately after providing your credentials, the copied order details page (Page 30) will appear on your screen displaying the order you just entered. The link labeled "Visit My Application and manage your email preferences" (B) will take you to the Home page after successful login.

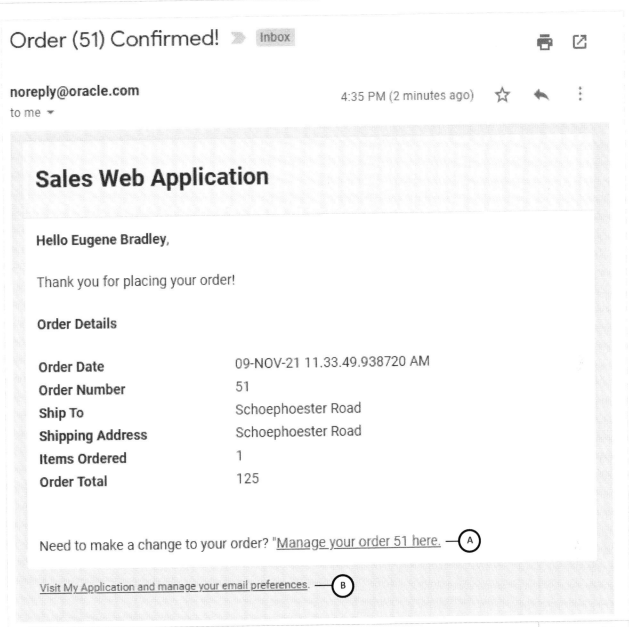

**Figure 7-37**

If you get *"Your session has expired. Please close this dialog and press your browser's reload button to obtain a new session."* message, then open Page 30, click its root node, and set *Page Mode* to **Normal**.

If you face any trouble, watch this video *https://www.youtube.com/watch?v=nQXTw6axAvI* which is related to this topic.

## 7.9 A More Simple Approach

I know as a beginner you might be confused with the stuff described in section 7.5 onward. I added this stuff purposely to present something that would be helpful to you in your future endeavors. However, in this section I'll demonstrate a simpler approach to add, modify, and delete orders using just one interface.

1. Execute all the steps mentioned in section 7.2 to create the two master and details pages. In step 4, set number of the *Master Page* to **404**, and number of the *Details Page* to **429**.

2. Open Page 404 and execute the instructions provided in section **7.3.1**. In step 5 of section 7.3.1, set *Page* and *Clear Cache* properties to **429** to point to the correct page number and set the *Name* property to **P429_ORDER_ID**. Skip the optional report sections (spanning from 7.3.2 to 7.3.4) at this stage to preserve some time.

3. Set the following attributes for the **CREATE** button. Note that previously this buttons was used to initiate the order wizard by calling Page 11. Here, we are calling Page 429 to directly enter a new order.

| Property | Value |
|---|---|
| Button Name | CREATE |
| Label | Enter New Order |
| Button Template | Text with Icon |
| Hot | On |
| Icon | fa-chevron-right |
| Action | Redirect to Page in this Application |
| Target | Type = Page in this Application<br>Page = 429<br>Clear Cache = 429 |

4. Save Page 404.

5. In the *Page Finder* box, enter **429** and press the **Enter** key to call **Page 429** in the Page Designer.

6. Click the root node (*Page 429: Order Details*) and set the *Page Mode* property to **Modal Dialog**. Set *Width, Height,* and *Maximum Width* properties to **900**, **800**, and **1200**, respectively. Also, set *Dialog Template* (in the *Appearance* section) to **Wizard Modal Dialog**.

7. Edit the following items individually and set the corresponding properties shown under each item. The customer ID item, which was displayed as *Display Only* item in the previous method, will now be rendered as a Select List carrying the names of all customers. The SQL query defined for the Select List automatically shows the correct customer name when you navigate from one order to another.

**P429_CUSTOMER_ID**

| Property | Value |
|---|---|
| Type | Select List |
| Label | Customer |
| Type (*List of Values*) | SQL Query |
| SQL Query | select cust_first_name ||' '|| cust_last_name d, customer_id r<br>from demo_customers |

**P429_USER_NAME**

| Property | Value |
|---|---|
| Type | Select List |
| Label | Sales Rep |
| Type *(List of Values)* | SQL Query |
| SQL Query | select distinct user_name d, user_name r<br>from demo_orders<br>union<br>select upper(:APP_USER) d, upper(:APP_USER) r<br>from dual<br>order by 1 |
| Display Extra Values | Off |
| Display Null Value | Off |
| Help Text | Use this list to change the Sales Rep associated with the order. |

8. In the *Region Buttons* node, set *Position* property to **Edit** for GET_PREVIOUS_ORDER_ID and GET_NEXT_ORDER_ID buttons to place them on top of the region.

9. Click the **Order Details** interactive grid region. Set its *Source Type* to **SQL Query**, and replace the default query with the one that follows:

```
SELECT oi.order_item_id, oi.order_id, oi.product_id, pi.product_name, oi.unit_price,
       oi.quantity, (oi.unit_price * oi.quantity) extended_price
FROM   DEMO_ORDER_ITEMS oi, DEMO_PRODUCT_INFO pi
WHERE oi.ORDER_ID = :P429_ORDER_ID and oi.product_id = pi.product_id (+)
```

10. In the *Order Details* interactive grid region, scroll down to *Server-side Condition* section, and choose – **Select** – placeholder for this property. When you try to create a new order using this page, you won't see the interactive grid. By default, this grid is visible only when you modify an existing order; it hides when you try to create a new order. This behavior is controlled by a server side condition (Item is NOT NULL) set for the Interactive Grid region. With this default condition, the region is rendered only when the page item P429_ORDER_ID has some value. Choosing the – *Select* – placeholder for the Server-side Condition Type property removes this condition and makes the interactive grid visible every time you access Page 429.

11. Under the *Columns* node, edit the following columns using the specified properties and values.

| Column | Property | Value |
|---|---|---|
| PRODUCT_ID | Type<br>Heading<br>Alignment<br>Type *(LOV)*<br>List of Values<br>Display Null Value | Select List<br>Product<br>left<br>Shared Components<br>Products With Price<br>Off |
| PRODUCT_NAME | Type | Hidden |
| QUANTITY | Width *(Appearance)*<br>Type *(Default)*<br>PL/SQL Expression | 5<br>PL/SQL Expression<br>1 *(sets 1 as the default quantity)* |
| EXTENDED_PRICE | Type<br>Heading<br>Alignment<br>Column Alignment<br>Format Mask<br>Query Only *(Source)* | Display Only<br>Price<br>right<br>right<br>$5,234.10<br>On |

12. Right-click the *Wizard Buttons* node and select **Create Region**. Set *Title* of the new region to **Buttons** and *Template* to **Buttons Container**. In *Regions Buttons* node, click the **Cancel** button and set its *Region* property (under *Layout*) to **Buttons**. Set this region for **Delete**, **Save**, and **Create** buttons, too. This action will place all the four buttons under the *Buttons* region.

13. Open Page 429 in the Page Designer. On the *Processing* tab make sure that the *Process form Form on DEMO_ORDERS* sits before the *Order Details - Save Interactive Grid Data* process.

14. Click the **Save Interactive Grid Data** process and switch its *Type* from *Interactive Grid - Automatic Row Processing (DML)* to **PL/SQL Code**. Enter the following code in the *PL/SQL Code* box. In this code, you specified SQL Insert, Update, and Delete statements to manually handle the three operations for the Interactive Grid data. The *:APEX$ROW_STATUS* is a built-in substitution string, which is used to refer to the row status in an Interactive Grid. This placeholder returns the status of *C* if created, *U* if updated, or *D* if deleted for the currently processed interactive grid row. Enter **"The DML operation performed successfully"** in the *Success Message* box. Similarly, enter **"Could not perform the DML operation"** in the *Error Message* box, and **save** your work.

```
begin
  case :APEX$ROW_STATUS
  when 'C' then
    insert into DEMO_ORDER_ITEMS
          (order_item_id, order_id, product_id, unit_price, quantity)
    values (null, :P429_ORDER_ID, :PRODUCT_ID, :UNIT_PRICE, :QUANTITY);
  when 'U' then
    update DEMO_ORDER_ITEMS
      set product_id  = :PRODUCT_ID,
        unit_price = :UNIT_PRICE,
        quantity = :QUANTITY
        where order_item_id = :ORDER_ITEM_ID and order_id = :ORDER_ID;
  when 'D' then
    delete DEMO_ORDER_ITEMS
    where order_item_id = :ORDER_ITEM_ID and order_id = :P429_ORDER_ID;
  end case;
end;
```

 All four input items in the Order Master section on Page 429 are rendered as floating elements (see Template property under Appearance section) in which the label is displayed inside of the input item, and it automatically shrinks once the input field has a value.

**Test Your Work**

Click the **Enter New Order** button (A) on Page 404. Select a customer (B) and pick an order date (C). Click the **Edit** button (D) in the *Order Details* region. With a product appearing in the first row (E) along with its default quantity (G), enter some value in the **Unit Price** column (F), and click the **Create** button (H). The order will be saved and you will see the success message. On the Order Master page, click the order number you just saved, and then click **Add Row** (I) to add some more products. Just select a product, enter some value in the *Quantity* column, and click **Save**. The modified order will be saved as well. Try to remove a product from this order using the **Delete Rows** option in the *Row Actions* menu. Finally, click the **Delete** button on the Order Details page to test order deletion. You're done!

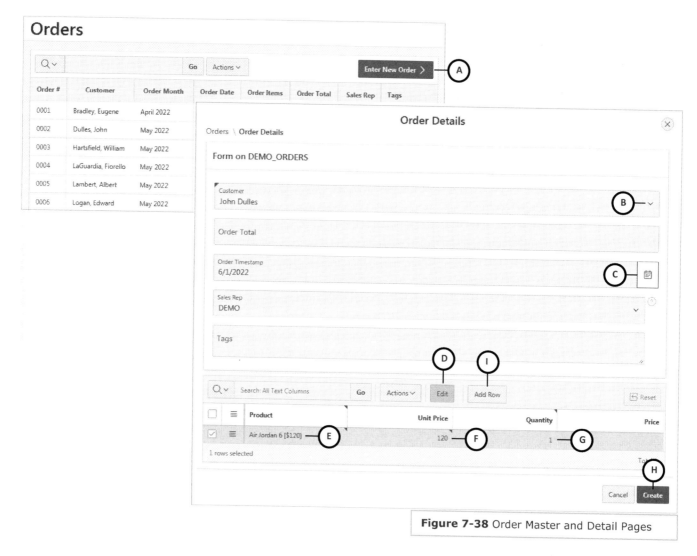

**Figure 7-38** Order Master and Detail Pages

## 7.10 Looping Through Interactive Grid

If you are an absolute beginner, I would recommend you to skip this section for the time being. Once you get a firm grip on APEX, revert to this section to learn some beyond stuff. In this section, you learn how to loop through each record in an interactive grid to perform some kind of validation. For example, here you will prevent addition of duplicate products in a single order. Of course, you can add a composite unique key constraint on the corresponding table to prevent duplication. But, there are some scenarios where this solution doesn't fit. For example, if you provide some free samples of a product in an invoice, you need to create two line item entries in your order screen for the same product – one with a price tag and another free. Execute the following steps to prevent product duplication in an order.

1. Open Page 429 in page designer. Click the *Form on DEMO_ORDERS* static content region (under *Wizard Body*) and set it Title to **Order Master**.

2. Click the *Order Details* interactive grid region and enter **ORDER** for its *Static ID* attribute (under *Advanced*). The ORDER static id will be used as the ID for the interactive grid region, which is useful in developing custom JavaScript behavior for the region, as you will see later in this exercise.

3. Right-click the *Items* node under the *Order Master* static content region (under *Wizard Body*) and select **Create Page Item**. Set the following attributes for this new item. It is a hidden item that will store 0 (as default) or 1 behind the scene. The value 1 in this item means that there are some duplicate products in the order. This evaluation will be done by a validation – *Check Duplicate Product*.

| Property | Value |
|---|---|
| Name | P429_PRODDUP |
| Type | Hidden |
| Value Protected | Off |
| Type *(under Source)* | Null |
| Type *(under Default)* | Static |
| Static Value | 0 |

4. Expand the **Columns** node (under the *Order Details* region), and set the following attributes for PRODUCT_NAME column:

| Property | Value |
|---|---|
| Type | Text Field |
| Heading | Product Name |

5. Switch to the *Dynamic Actions* tab. Right-click the main *Events* node and select **Create Dynamic Action**. Set the following attributes for this dynamic action. The dynamic action will execute a JavaScript code that will be fired before submitting the page. The JavaScript code is defined as a custom function – chkDUP() in step 7.

| Property | Value |
|---|---|
| Name | Check Duplicate Product |
| Event | Before Page Submit |
| Click the Show node (under True) to set the following attributes: | |
| Action | Execute JavaScript Code |
| Code | chkDUP() |

6. Create another dynamic action. This time right-click the *Change* node and select **Create Dynamic Action** from the context menu. Set the following attributes for this dynamic action, which is being created to fetch product name when a user selects a different product in the Order Details interactive grid.

| Property | Value |
|---|---|
| Name | Fetch Product Name |
| Event | Change |
| Selection Type | Column(s) |
| Region | Order Details |
| Column | PRODUCT_ID |
| Click the Show node (under True) to set the following attributes: | |
| Action | Execute PL/SQL Code |
| PL/SQL Code | select product_name into :PRODUCT_NAME from DEMO_PRODUCT_INFO where product_id = :PRODUCT_ID; |
| Items to submit | PRODUCT_ID |
| Items to Return | PRODUCT_NAME |

7. On the *Rendering* tab, click the root node - *Page 429: Order Details*. Scroll down to the *Function and Global Variable Declaration* section and append the following JavaScript function after the existing code:

```
function chkDUP() {
  var record;
  var prodDUP=0;
//Identify the particular interactive grid
  var ig$ = apex.region("ORDER").widget();
  var grid = ig$.interactiveGrid("getViews","grid");
//Fetch the model for the interactive grid
  var model = grid.model;
//Select all rows
  ig$.interactiveGrid("getViews").grid.view$.grid("selectAll");
//Fetch selected records
  var selectedRecords = grid.view$.grid("getSelectedRecords");

  for (idx1=0; idx1 < selectedRecords.length; idx1++) {
    record = model.gctRecord(selectedRecords[idx1][0]);
    prodcode1 = model.getValue(record,"PRODUCT_NAME");
    for (idx2=0; idx2 < selectedRecords.length; idx2++) {
      record = model.getRecord(selectedRecords[idx2][0]);
      prodcode2 = model.getValue(record,"PRODUCT_NAME");
      if (prodcode1 == prodcode2 && idx1 != idx2) {
        prodDUP=1;
        break;
      }
    }
    if (prodDUP == 1) {
      break;
    }
  }
  $s("P429_PRODDUP",prodDUP);
  if (prodDUP == 1) {
    alert("Duplication of product occurred - "+prodcode2);
  }
}
```

The function is called from the *Check Duplicate Product* dynamic action before the page is submitted. Initially the function identifies the Order Details interactive grid through its static ID. Then, after fetching the interactive grid's model, all rows in the interactive grid are selected. The function then initiates a FOR loop, which loops through every record in the interactive grid. In every loop, value from the Product Name column is stored (in prodcode1 variable) and then compared with another variable in an inner FOR loop. If a duplicate is found, the duplicate switch is turned on – prodDUP=1. If the switch is turned on, you see the client-side message specified in the alert function.

8. The JavaScript function in the previous step alerts you of duplicate products. After the alert, the page is submitted and the order is saved with duplication. A server-side validation must also be created to prevent this situation. On the *Processing* tab, right-click the **Validations** node and select **Create Validation**. Set the following attributes for the new validation, which evaluates the value of P429_PRODDUP hidden page item when either Save or Create buttons are clicked. If the value of this item is zero, the order is processed. If it is set as 1 by the chkDUP function, an error message is fired. Note that if a validation passes the equality test, or evaluates to TRUE, then the validation error message does not display. Validation error messages display when the validation fails the equality test, or evaluates to FALSE, or a non-empty text string is returned. Subsequent processes and branches are not executed if one or more validations fail evaluation.

| Property | Value |
|---|---|
| Name | Check Duplicate Products |
| Type *(under Validation)* | Item = Value |
| Item | P429_PRODDUP |
| Value | 0 |
| Error Message | Duplicated product found – cannot proceed further |
| Display Location | Inline in Notification |
| Server-side Condition section | |
| Type | Request is contained in Value |
| Value | SAVE,CREATE |

Save and run the module. Create a new order. Initially the Product column in the interactive grid defaults to Air Jordan 6. Select a different product to fire the dynamic action and fetch the product name in the Product Name column. Add another row and select the same product on the new row. Input unit price in both rows and click Create. First, you will get the client-side product duplication message from the JavaScript function followed by the error message defined in the validation, which is returned from the server.

## 7.11 Interactive Grid Native PDF Printing

Interactive Grid Downloads includes native PDF Printing which allows you to print PDF files directly from Interactive Grids. This feature produces a PDF file which retains Grid formatting such as highlighting, column grouping, and column breaks. Let's go through a simple demonstration to explore this feature.

1.  Open the Orders Interactive Report page (Page 4) in Page Designer.

2.  Right-click the **Orders** interactive report region, and select **Duplicate** from the context menu. A copy of this region will be created.

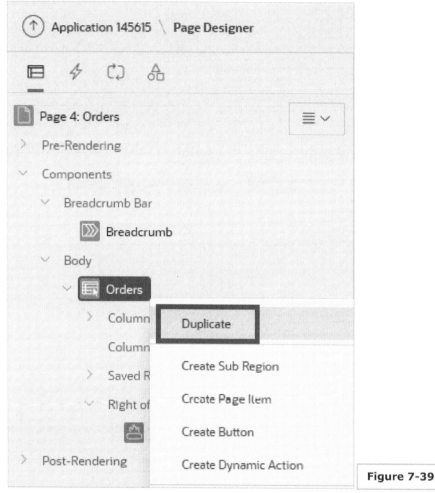

Figure 7-39

3.  Click the new **Orders** region, and change its *Type* property in the *Identification* section from *Interactive Report* to **Interactive Grid**.

4.  In the properties pane, click the **Attributes** tab of the new *Orders* region. Scroll down to *Download* section and ensure that **PDF** option (under *Download | Formats*) is checked. The checked download formats can be utilized by users to download the currently displayed columns in the interactive grid.

5.  Save and run the page. The page should now have two regions. Scroll down a bit to see the interactive grid region. From the interactive grid's **Actions** menu, select **Format | Control Break**.

6.  On the *Control Break* dialog, select **Order Month** from the *Column* list and click **Save**.

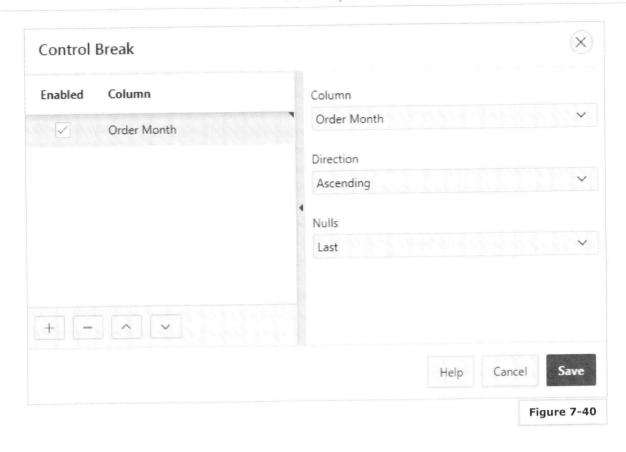

**Figure 7-40**

7. Next, select **Actions | Format | Highlight**. Set the following parameters in the *Highlight* dialog. Once you hit **Save** in the *Highlight* dialog, rows with 1000 or greater amount in the *Order Total* column will be highlighted.

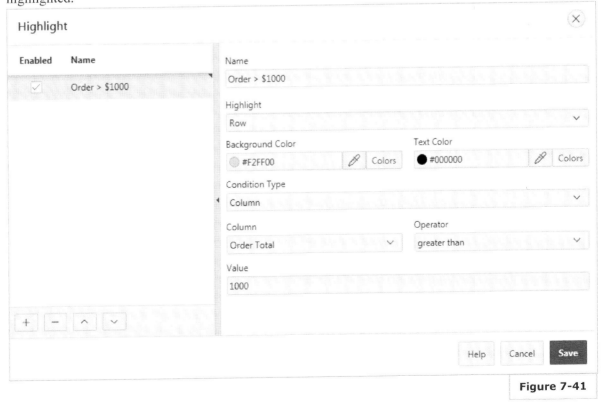

**Figure 7-41**

8.  Click the **Actions** menu again and select **Download**. In the *Download* dialog, select **PDF** and other options as illustrated in the following figure and click the **Download** button. The output of the interactive grid will be downloaded as a PDF to your device.

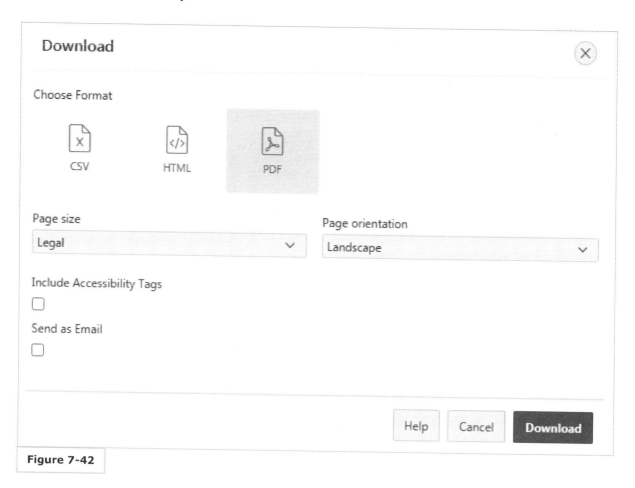

**Figure 7-42**

The following figure illustrates the downloaded PDF. As you can see both highlight and control break formatting is preserved in the PDF.

## Orders

| Order Number | Order Id | Order Total | Customer Name | Order Items |
|---|---|---|---|---|
| **Order Month : April 2022** | | | | |
| 0001 | 1 | 1890 | Bradley, Eugene | 3 |
| **Order Month : December 2022** | | | | |
| 0017 | 17 | 155 | Bradley, Eugene | 2 |
| **Order Month : July 2022** | | | | |
| 0016 | 16 | 1421 | Bradley, Eugene | 3 |
| **Order Month : June 2022** | | | | |
| 0009 | 9 | 730 | Hartsfield, William | 3 |
| 0015 | 15 | 500 | Lambert, Albert | 1 |
| 0014 | 14 | 210 | Lambert, Albert | 1 |
| 0013 | 13 | 100 | Bradley, Eugene | 1 |
| 0012 | 12 | 180 | Bradley, Eugene | 1 |
| 0007 | 7 | 905 | Logan, Edward | 7 |
| 0008 | 8 | 1060 | OHare, Frank | 4 |
| 0010 | 10 | 870 | Bradley, Eugene | 3 |
| 0011 | 11 | 800 | Dulles, John | 1 |
| **Order Month : May 2022** | | | | |
| 0002 | 2 | 2380 | Dulles, John | 10 |
| 0003 | 3 | 1640 | Hartsfield, William | 5 |
| 0006 | 6 | 1515 | Logan, Edward | 4 |
| 0005 | 5 | 950 | Lambert, Albert | 5 |
| 0004 | 4 | 1090 | LaGuardia, Fiorello | 5 |

**Figure 7-43**

## Summary

Here are the highlights of this chapter:

- *Master Detail* – You learned how to implement Master Detail page feature to handle data in two relational tables and went through the auto-generated page components added by the wizard to transparently manage the order processing module.

- *Interactive Report* – Created an interactive report and learned how to alter the report layout by applying highlighting, sorting, and using aggregate functions. You also applied Control Breaks to group related data and added Chart and Group By Views.

- *Primary, Public, and Alternative Interactive Report* – You created three variants of the interactive report and went through the concepts behind these variants.

- *Wizard Steps* – Learned how to create wizard-like interfaces to perform related tasks in a sequence.

- *Copy Page Utility* – The chapter provided a shortcut to utilize an existing page with all functionalities using a different number and for a different scenario.

- *Oracle APEX Collection* – You learned how to use collections to store and retrieve rows and columns information in session state.

- *Custom Processes and Dynamic Actions* – In addition to the auto-generated components and processes, you learned how to manually add your own processes and other components.

- *Using HTML in PL/SQL Code* – You used PL/SQL to have more control over dynamically generated HTML within a region.

- *Using CSS in Oracle APEX Pages* – You applied styling rules to give the page a more professional look.

- *Simple Approach* – Besides the advance techniques, you also learned how to create this module using a simple approach.

- *Looping through Interactive Grid* – In the final section of this chapter you learned how to loop through interactive grid records. You usually execute this procedure when you need to perform some sort of validation on the data in an interactive grid prior to storing it in your database.

# 8

# GRAPHICAL REPORTS

# & MOBILE

# INTEGRATION

## 8.1 About Graphical Reports

Presenting data in Oracle APEX, either graphically or in text format, is as easy as creating the input forms. You have had a taste of this feature when you designed the Home page of the application. In this chapter, you will take a step forward and will use some more chart types to create graphical reports. When creating reports for mobile devices, Oracle recommends some specific report types (mentioned in the following list) that provide an optimal user experience for small screens. Here's a list of reports you will create in this chapter.

| Report | Purpose | Page No. |
| --- | --- | --- |
| Customer Orders | Show total orders placed by each customer | 17 |
| Sales By Category and Product | Display sales by category and products | 16 |
| Sales by Category / Month | Total monthly sales for each category | 5 |
| Order Calendar | Show orders in a calendar view | 10 |
| Product Order Tree | Display sales data in a tree view | 19 |
| Gantt Chart | Displays the overall progress of an IT project | 20 |
| Box Plot Chart | Summarize large amounts of data | 21 |
| Pyramid Chart | Show data that is organized in some kind of hierarchical form | 22 |
| List View (Mobile) | Create a responsive report for mobile devices | 23 |
| Column Toggle Report (Mobile) | Lets you specify the most important columns to display on smaller screens | 24 |
| Reflow Report (Mobile) | It wraps each column or changes to displaying multiple lines on small screens | 25 |

## 8.2 Create Reports List Page

Prior to creating reports, you will create a page to list all the reports available in the application. The page carrying the reports list (as illustrated in the following figure) will appear when you click the *Reports* entry in the main navigation menu.

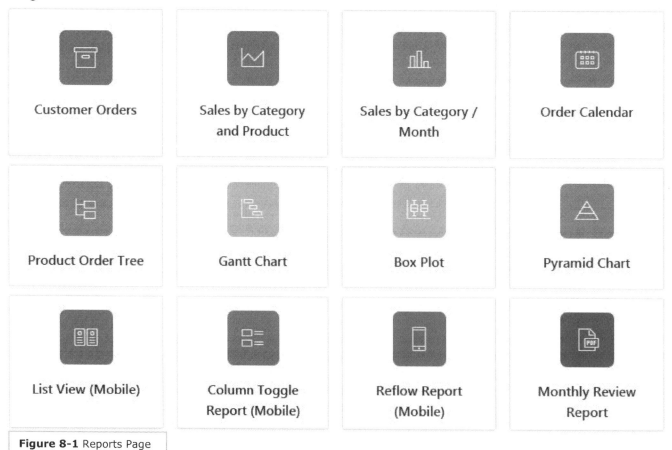

**Figure 8-1** Reports Page

1. Create a **Blank Page** and set the following properties for it:

| Property | Value |
|---|---|
| Page Number | 26 |
| Name | Reports |
| Page Mode | Normal |
| Breadcrumb | don't use breadcrumb on page |
| Navigation Preference | Identify an existing navigation menu entry for this page |
| Existing Navigation Menu Entry | Reports |

2. Right-click the *Body* node and select **Create Region**. Set the following properties for the new region. The region will display the *Reports List* you created in Chapter 3 section 3.2.2.

| Property | Value |
|---|---|
| Title | Reports |
| Type | List |
| List | Reports List |

3. Click the **Attributes** tab of the *Reports* region. Set *List Template* to **Cards** and the *Template Options* according to the following illustration. By choosing the *Cards* option, the images you set for the *Reports List* in Chapter 3 section 3.2.2 will be presented as cards – see Figure 8-1. *Template Options* allow for selecting a number of CSS customization settings to be applied directly against the component. Template options are defined as CSS classes in the associated templates. The best way to understand these attribute is to select, apply, and test the available options.

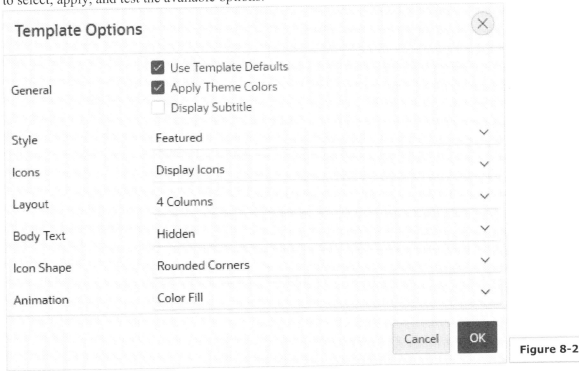

Figure 8-2

## 8.3 Customer Orders Report - Page 17

This graphical report is based on Oracle JET bar chart to display amount of orders by category placed by customers. Each bar in the chart has multiple slices representing amounts of different orders. When you move your mouse over these slices a tooltip (A) displays the corresponding amount. The chart will be created with drill-down functionality. That is, when you click a bar, you'll be taken to Page 7 where you will see profile of the selected customer. You will also make provision to change the chart's orientation (B) and will provide options to present it as either stacked or un-stacked (C).

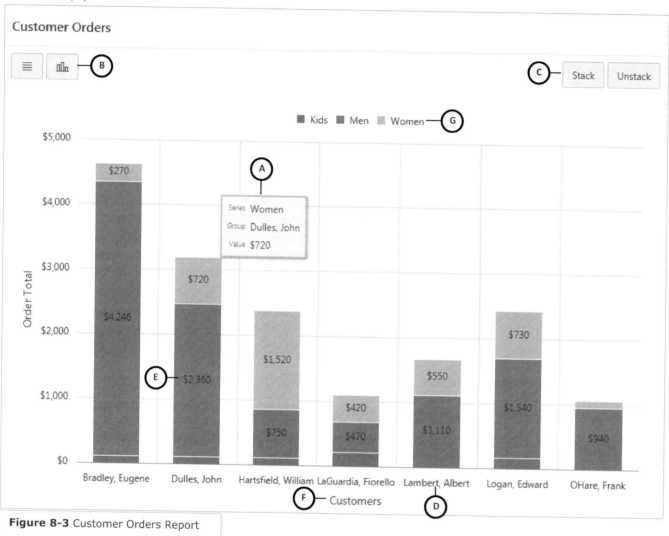

**Figure 8-3** Customer Orders Report

1. Create a **Blank Page** and set the following properties for it:

| Property | Value |
|---|---|
| Page Number | 17 |
| Name | Customer Orders |
| Page Mode | Normal |
| Breadcrumb | don't use breadcrumb on page |
| Navigation Preference | Identify an existing navigation menu entry for this page |
| Existing Navigation Menu Entry | Reports |

2. Right-click the *Body* node and select **Create Region**. Set the following properties for the new region. Immediately after switching the region's *Type*, a new node named *Series* along with a child node (*New*) is added under the region. Each product in this app is associated with one of the three categories: Men, Women, and Kids. The query below fetches summarized order figures by customers for each category.

| Property | Value |
|---|---|
| Title | Customer Orders |
| Type | Chart |
| Location | Local Database |
| Type | SQL Query |
| SQL Query | SELECT c.customer_id, c.cust_last_name\|\|', '\|\|c.cust_first_name Customer_Name,<br>    sum (decode(p.category,'Men',oi.quantity * oi.unit_price,0)) "Men",<br>    sum (decode(p.category,'Women',oi.quantity * oi.unit_price,0)) "Women",<br>    sum (decode(p.category,'Kids',oi.quantity * oi.unit_price,0)) "Kids"<br>FROM demo_customers c, demo_orders o, demo_order_items oi, demo_product_info p<br>WHERE c.customer_id = o.customer_id and o.order_id = oi.order_id and oi.product_id = p.product_id<br>GROUP BY c.customer_id, c.cust_last_name, c.cust_first_name<br>ORDER BY c.cust_last_name |

3. Click the **Attributes** tab of the *Customer Orders* chart region and set the following properties. The *Stack* property specifies whether the data items are stacked. We defined *Automatic* animation setting for the chart, which applies the Oracle JET's default animation settings. It specifies whether animation is shown when data is changed on the chart. A data change can occur if the chart gets automatically refreshed. In the current scenario, the animation takes place when you click one of the four buttons (B & C): Horizontal, Vertical, Stack, or Unstack. These buttons will be created in subsequent steps. The *Hide and Show Behavior* is performed when you click a legend item (G). For example, deselecting a legend item will hide its associated data series on the chart. With the value set to *Rescale* for this property, the chart rescales as you select or de-select a legend. This is useful for series with largely varying values.

| Property | Value |
|---|---|
| Type | Bar |
| Title | *Leave it blank* |
| Orientation | Vertical |
| Stack | On |
| Maximum Width | 800 |
| Height | 500 |
| On Data Change *(under Animation)* | Automatic |
| Show *(under Legend)* | On |
| Position *(under Legend)* | Top |
| Hide and Show Behavior *(under Legend)* | Rescale |

4. Click the **New** node (under *Series*) and set the following properties. Each series you create for your chart appears in a unique color to represent product category and displays sales figures for each category (using the *Value* property) that is derived from the SELECT statement specified in step 2. You set *Source Location* (on row 2) to *Region Source*, which specifies that the data of this series is to be extracted from the SQL query defined for the *Customer Orders* region (in step 2). In the *Label* attribute you select a column name that is used for defining the label(s) of the x-axis (D) on the chart, while the *Accessories* column selected for the *Value* property is used for defining the ordered value (E) on this chart. When you click a chart bar (representing *Accessories*), you're drilled down to Page 7 to browse customer details.

| Property | Value |
|---|---|
| Name | Kids |
| Location (*under Source*) | Region Source |
| Label (*under Column Mapping*) | CUSTOMER_NAME |
| Value | Kids |
| Type (*under Link*) | Redirect to Page in this Application |
| Target | Type = Page in this Application<br>Page = 7<br>Name = P7_CUSTOMER_ID<br>Value = &CUSTOMER_ID.<br>Clear Cache = 7 |
| Show (*under Label*) | On  (*to display sales figures*) |
| Position (*under Label*) | Center |

The above link will be active for the Kids category only.

5. Right-click the *Series* node and select **Create Series** from the context menu to add another series. Set the following properties for the new series. Use the same values as defined for the *Type* and *Target* properties in Step 4 to transform this series into a link to access Page 7.

| Property | Value |
|---|---|
| Name | Men |
| Location (*under Source*) | Region Source |
| Label (*under Column Mapping*) | CUSTOMER_NAME |
| Value | Men |
| Show (*under Label*) | On  (*to display sales figures*) |
| Position (*under Label*) | Center |

6. Create one more series and set the following properties. Create a link as you did in the previous two steps.

| Property | Value |
|---|---|
| Name | Women |
| Location (*under Source*) | Region Source |
| Label (*under Column Mapping*) | CUSTOMER_NAME |
| Value | Women |
| Show (*under Label*) | On  (*to display sales figures*) |
| Position (*under Label*) | Center |

7. Click the x-axis node (under *Axes*) and enter **Customers** for the *Title* attribute. The title will appear at the bottom of the chart (F).

8. Click the y-axis node and set the following properties. When you format a number as currency, the *Currency* property is required to be set to specify the currency that will be used when formatting the number. You enter a currency that is used when formatting the value on the chart. The value should be a ISO 4217 alphabetic currency code. If the format type is set to Currency, it is required that the *Currency* property also be specified. Visit http://www.xe.com/iso4217.php to see a list of standard currency codes.

| Property | Value |
|---|---|
| Title | Order Total |
| Format (*under Value*) | Currency |
| Decimal Places | 0 |
| Currency | USD |

9. In this step, you will add two buttons (B) to the *Customer Orders* region. When clicked, these buttons will change the chart's orientation using the default animation set in step 3. Right-click the *Customer Orders* region and select **Create Button** from the context menu. A new node named *Region Body* will be added with a button labeled *New*. Set the following properties for this button. The *Action* attribute set in the following table says that this button is associated with a dynamic action (step 10), which fires when the button is clicked.

| Property | Value |
|---|---|
| Button Name | Horizontal |
| Label | Horizontal |
| Position | Previous |
| Button Template | Icon |
| Icon | fa-bars |
| Action | Defined by Dynamic Action |

Right-click the *Region Body* node and select **Create Button** to add another button under the previous one. Set the following properties for the new button.

| Property | Value |
|---|---|
| Button Name | Vertical |
| Label | Vertical |
| Position | Previous |
| Button Template | Icon |
| Icon | fa-bar-chart |
| Action | Defined by Dynamic Action |

10. Now add two dynamic actions for the two buttons. Click the *Dynamic Actions* tab, right-click the *Click* node, and select **Create Dynamic Action**. Click the **New** node and set the following properties. This dynamic action is named *Horizontal Orientation* – you are free to give it any other name you deem suitable. The next three properties specify that this dynamic action should trigger when the *Horizontal* button is clicked.

| Property | Value |
| --- | --- |
| Name | Horizontal Orientation |
| Event | Click |
| Selection Type | Button |
| Button | Horizontal |

Click the **Show** node under the *True* node to set the following properties. When the *Horizontal* button is clicked, the JavaScript code (defined on row 2) is fired. In this code, *dualChart* is a static ID you will set in step 12 for the *Customer Orders* region. You control chart's orientation through the *ojChart* class, which has two options (*Horizontal* and *Vertical*), where Vertical is the default option. In this step, you inform the Oracle APEX engine to display the chart horizontally when the *Horizontal* button is clicked. Note that the chart orientation only applies to bar, line, area, combo, and funnel charts.

| Property | Value |
| --- | --- |
| Action | Execute JavaScript Code |
| Code | $("#dualChart_jet").ojChart({orientation: **'horizontal'**}); |
| Selection Type | Region |
| Region | Customer Orders |
| Event | Horizontal Orientation |
| Fire on Initialization | Off |

11. Right-click the *Click* node and select **Create Dynamic Action** to add one more for vertical orientation, as follows. Click the **New** node and set the following properties:

| Property | Value |
| --- | --- |
| Name | Vertical Orientation |
| Event | Click |
| Selection Type | Button |
| Button | Vertical |

Click the **Show** node under the *True* node and set the following properties:

| Property | Value |
| --- | --- |
| Action | Execute JavaScript Code |
| Code | $("#dualChart_jet").ojChart({orientation: **'vertical'**}); |
| Selection Type | Region |
| Region | Customer Orders |
| Event | Vertical Orientation |
| Fire on Initialization | Off |

12. If you run the pages at this stage, you will not see the orientation effect if you click any of the two buttons. This is because of the static ID (*dualChart*), which is mentioned in the JavaScript code to reference the *Customer Orders* region but has not been assigned to the region itself. Switch back to the *Rendering* tab, click the **Customer Orders** region, and in the *Advanced* section enter **dualChart** as the value for the *Static ID* property. Now the region can be recognized by this static ID.

13. Add two more buttons under the previous two buttons. These buttons will be used to render the series data as stacked or unstacked (C). Set the following properties for the two buttons:

| Property | Value (Button1) | Value (Button2) |
|---|---|---|
| Button Name | Stack | Unstack |
| Label | Stack | Unstack |
| Position | Next | Next |

14. Create two dynamic actions for the two buttons as follows. Set the **New** nodes' properties as defined in the first table below:

| Property | Value (New node) | Value (New node) |
|---|---|---|
| Name | Stack Chart | Unstack Chart |
| Event | Click | Click |
| Selection Type | Button | Button |
| Button | Stack | Unstack |

The *Stack Chart* dynamic event's **Show** node properties:

| Property | Value |
|---|---|
| Action | Execute JavaScript Code |
| Code | $("#dualChart_jet").ojChart({stack: 'on'}); |
| Selection Type | Region |
| Region | Customer Orders |
| Event | Stack Chart |
| Fire on Initialization | Off |

The *Unstack Chart* dynamic event's **Show** node properties:

| Property | Value |
|---|---|
| Action | Execute JavaScript Code |
| Code | $("#dualChart_jet").ojChart({stack: 'off'}); |
| Selection Type | Region |
| Region | Customer Orders |
| Event | Unstack Chart |
| Fire on Initialization | Off |

Save your work. Run the application and click *Reports* in the navigation menu. You will see the *Reports* page created in section 8.2. Click the first *Customer Orders* card to access Page 17. You will see a chart, as shown in Figure 8-3. Move your cursor over the chart bars and different portions within a particular bar. You will see a tooltip (A) showing order amount of the corresponding customer. Click the *Vertical* and *Horizontal* buttons (B) to change the chart's orientation. Similarly, click the *Stack* and *Unstack* buttons (C) to see respective animated effects.

## 8.4 Sales by Category and Products Report - Page 16

In this report, you'll present Category and Products sales data in two separate page regions using different charting options, as illustrated in the following figure.

### Sales by Category

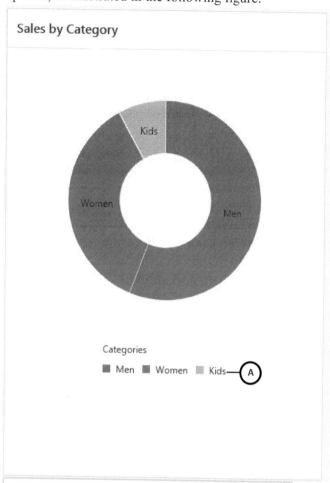

### Maximum & Minimum Sales by Product

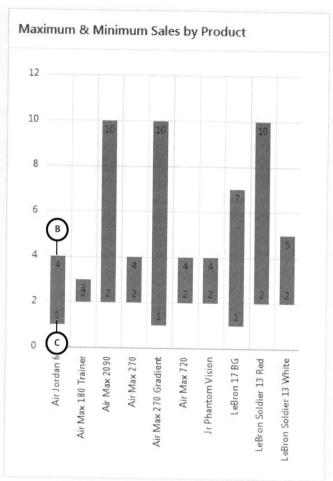

**Figure 8-4** Sales by Category and Products Report

1. Create a **Blank Page** and set the following properties for it:

| Property | Value |
|---|---|
| Page Number | 16 |
| Name | Sales by Category and Product |
| Page Mode | Normal |
| Breadcrumb | don't use breadcrumbs on page |
| Navigation Preference | Identify an existing navigation menu entry for this page |
| Existing Navigation Menu Entry | Reports |

2. In the Page Designer, right-click the *Body* node and select **Create Region**. Set the following properties for the new region.

| Property | Value |
|---|---|
| Title | Sales by Category |
| Type | Chart |

3. Click the **Attributes** tab of the *Sales by Category* region and set the following properties. Selecting *Yes* for *Dim on Hover* dims all data items when not currently hovered over and highlights only the current data item hovered over with respective order figures in US dollars. The *Hide and Show Behavior* is performed when you click a legend item (A). For example, deselecting a legend item will hide its associated data series on the chart. With the value set to *Rescale* for this property, the chart rescales as you select or de-select a legend. This is useful for series with largely varying values.

| Property | Value |
|---|---|
| Type | Donut |
| Height | 400 |
| Dim on Hover | On |
| Format | Currency |
| Decimal Places | 0 |
| Currency | USD |
| Show (*under Legend*) | On |
| Title (*under Legend*) | Categories |
| Hide and Show Behavior | Rescale |

4. Click the **New** node under *Series* and enter the following properties.

| Property | Value |
|---|---|
| Name | Donut Chart Series |
| Location | Local Database |
| Type | SQL Query |
| SQL Query | SELECT p.category label, sum(o.order_total) total_sales FROM demo_orders o, demo_order_items oi, demo_product_info p WHERE o.order_id = oi.order_id AND oi.product_id = p.product_id GROUP BY category order by 2 desc |
| Label (*under Column Mapping*) | LABEL |
| Value | TOTAL_SALES |
| Show (*under Label*) | On |

5. Right-click the *Body* node and select **Create Region** to add another region. This region will carry a *Range* chart to display maximum (B) and minimum (C) ordered quantities for each product. Set the following properties for the new region:

| Property | Value |
|---|---|
| Title | Maximum & Minimum Sales by Product |
| Type | Chart |
| Location | Local Database |
| Type | SQL Query |
| SQL Query | SELECT p.product_id, p.product_name, **min(oi.quantity), max(oi.quantity)** FROM demo_product_info p, demo_order_items oi WHERE p.product_id = oi.product_id GROUP BY p.product_id, p.product_name ORDER BY p.product_name asc |

267

6. Click the **Attributes** tab of the *Maximum & Minimum Sales by Product* region and set the following properties:

| Property | Value |
|---|---|
| Type | Range |
| Maximum Width | 500 |
| Height | 500 |

7. Click the **New** node under *Series* to set the following properties. The PRODUCT_NAME column will be used for defining the label(s) of the x-axis on the chart. Then, you specify *Low* and *High* column names to be used for defining the low and high values on this chart. In the last six properties you create a link to access Page 6 to browse details of the selected product.

| Property | Value |
|---|---|
| Name | Products |
| Location (under Source) | Region Source |
| Label (under Column Mapping) | PRODUCT_NAME |
| Low | MIN(OI.QUANTITY) |
| High | MAX(OI.QUANTITY) |
| Type (under Link) | Redirect to Page in this Application |
| Target | Type = Page in this application<br>Page = 6<br>Name = P6_PRODUCT_ID<br>Value = &PRODUCT_ID.<br>Clear Cache = 6 |
| Show (under Label) | On |

Save and access this page from *Sales by Category and Product* card on the *Reports* page. You will see the two charts, as illustrated in Figure 8-4. The page has two regions containing graphical data for category and product sales. Move the mouse cursor over each chart and see respective sales figures. Click the bar representing Jr Phantom Vision, the system will drill you down to Page 6 to show the details of this product.

## 8.5 Sales by Category / Month Report - Page 5

This chart is added to present category sales in different months. In this graphical report, you will make use of *Region Display Selector* (A) to display two different views of category sales data. *Region Display Selector* region enables you to include show and hide controls for each region on a page. This page will have two regions containing two different chart types. After adding the *Region Display Selector* and the two regions, you can switch the regions using the selector appearing on top of the page, as shown in the following figure. The page displays three tabs: *Show All*, *Sales by Category (Line)*, and *Sales by Month (Bar)*. If you click the *Show All* tab, the page displays all the regions. If you click any of the other two tabs, the page shows only the chosen region.

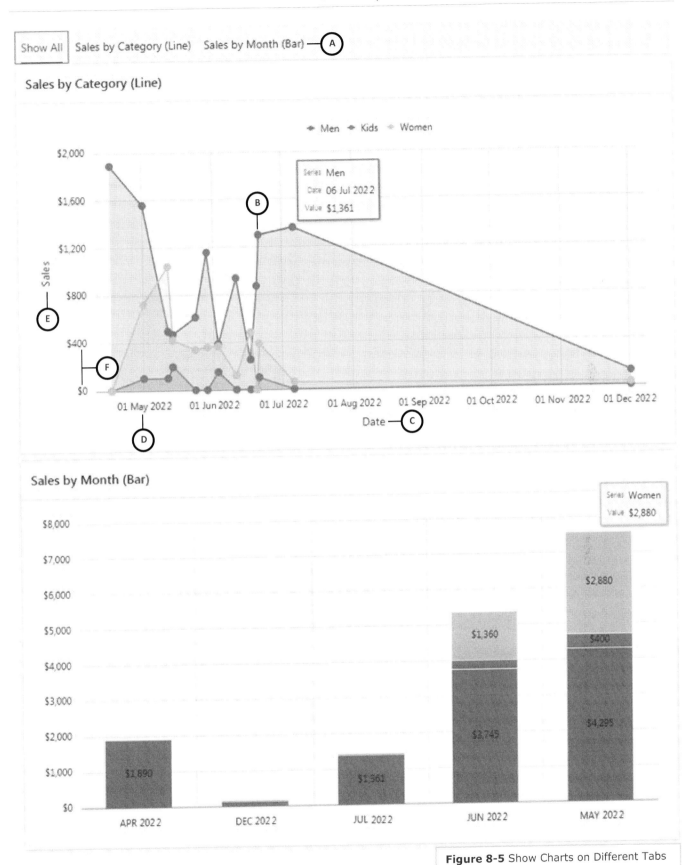

**Figure 8-5** Show Charts on Different Tabs

1. Create a **Blank Page** and set the following properties for it:

| Property | Value |
| --- | --- |
| Page Number | 5 |
| Name | Sales by Category Per Month |
| Page Mode | Normal |
| Breadcrumb | don't use breadcrumbs on page |
| Navigation Preference | Identify an existing navigation menu entry for this page |
| Existing Navigation Menu Entry | Reports |

2. Right-click the *Body* node and select **Create Region**. Set the following properties for this region. As mentioned earlier, this region will display other regions on the page as horizontal tabs (A). By removing the *Standard Template* (in the third property), the region looks as a part of existing regions.

| Property | Value |
| --- | --- |
| Title | Region Display Selector |
| Type | Region Display Selector |
| Template | -Select- *(that is, no template selected)* |

3. Create another region under *Body* and set the following properties. This region will hold a Line with Area chart.

| Property | Value |
| --- | --- |
| Title | Sales by Category (Line) |
| Type | Chart |

4. Click the **Attributes** tab of the *Sales by Category (Line)* chart region and set the following properties. The *Time Axis Type* property automatically renders the chart data in chronological order.

| Property | Value |
| --- | --- |
| Type | Line with Area |
| Height | 400 |
| Time Axis Type *(under Settings)* | Enabled |
| Show *(under Legend)* | On |
| Position *(under Legend)* | Top |
| Hide and Show Behavior | Rescale |

5. Click the **New** node under *Series* and set the following properties. The last two properties will show markers in shape of circles (B). The *Show* property (last in the table) specifies whether the label(s) should be rendered on the chart. By turning it off, the visibility of the sales figure is suppressed.

| Property | Value |
|---|---|
| Type (under Source) | SQL Query |
| SQL Query | SELECT     p.category **type**, trunc(o.order_timestamp) **when**,<br>           sum (oi.quantity * oi.unit_price) **sales**<br>FROM      demo_product_info p, demo_order_items oi, demo_orders o<br>WHERE    oi.product_id = p.product_id AND o.order_id = oi.order_id<br>GROUP BY p.category, trunc(o.order_timestamp),<br>           to_char(o.order_timestamp, 'YYYYMM')<br>ORDER BY  to_char(o.order_timestamp, 'YYYYMM') |
| Series Name | TYPE |
| Label | WHEN |
| Value | SALES |
| Show (under Marker) | Yes |
| Shape | Circle |
| Show (under Label) | Off |

6. Click the **x** node under Axes to set the following properties. In these properties, we set a title (C) and date format (D) for X-axis.

| Property | Value |
|---|---|
| Title | Date |
| Format (under Value) | Date - Medium |
| Pattern | dd MMM yyyy |

7. Set the following properties for y-axis. The *Sales* title (E) appears to the left of the chart. Sale values are displayed as currency in US dollars. In the *Step* property we enter the increment (F) between major tick marks.

| Property | Value |
|---|---|
| Title | Sales |
| Format (under Value) | Currency |
| Decimal Places | 0 |
| Currency | USD |
| Step | 400 |

8. Create another region under the *Body* node to hold a bar chart. Set the following properties for this new region:

| Property | Value |
|---|---|
| Title | Sales by Month (Bar) |
| Type | Chart |

9. Click the **Attributes** tab of the *Sales by Month chart* region and set the following properties. The *Show Group Name* specifies whether the group name should be displayed in the tooltip rendered on the chart. We turned it off to suppress the *order_timestamp* group mentioned in the SQL Query in step 10.

| Property | Value |
| --- | --- |
| Type | Bar |
| Stack | On |
| Height | 400 |
| Show Group Name *(under Tooltip)* | Off |

10. Click the **New** node under *Series* and set the following properties:

| Property | Value |
| --- | --- |
| Source Type | SQL Query |
| SQL Query | SELECT    p.category **type** , <br>           to_char(o.order_timestamp, 'MON RRRR') **month**, <br>           sum (oi.quantity * oi.unit_price) **sales** <br> FROM    demo_product_info p, demo_order_items oi, demo_orders o <br> WHERE   oi.product_id = p.product_id  AND o.order_id = oi.order_id <br> GROUP BY p.category, to_char(o.order_timestamp, 'MON RRRR'), <br>          to_char(o.order_timestamp, 'YYYYMM') <br> ORDER BY  to_char(o.order_timestamp, 'YYYYMM') |
| Series Name | TYPE |
| Label | MONTH |
| Value | SALES |
| Show *(under Label)* | On |

11. Set the following properties for y-axis:

| Property | Value |
| --- | --- |
| Format | Currency |
| Decimal Places | 0 |
| Currency | USD |

Save and then run this page from the *Reports* page. The output of this report should resemble Figure 8-5. The two charts display comparative sales figures for each category during a month. Click all the three options (individually) in the *Region Selector Toolbar* and observe the change.

## 8.6 Order Calendar Report - Page 10

In this report orders will be displayed in a calendar. Oracle APEX includes a built-in wizard for generating a calendar, which offers two options to view orders: *month* (C) and *list* (D). Using the two buttons provided at top left (A), you can switch between months. The *today* button (B) brings you back to the current date. The placed orders are displayed in respective date cells. Clicking an order in a cell (E) takes you to Page 29 to see its detail.

**Figure 8-6 –** Order Calendar Report

Execute the following steps to create a calendar report.

1.  Click the **Create Page** button to create a new page.

2.  One the first wizard screen, click the **Calendar** icon 📅.

3.  Fill in the next couple of pages according to the following table and click **Next**.

| Property | Value |
| --- | --- |
| Page Number | 10 |
| Name | Order Calendar |
| Page Mode | Normal |
| Breadcrumb | do not use breadcrumbs on page |
| Navigation Preference | Identify an existing navigation menu entry for this page |
| Existing Navigation Menu Entry | Reports |

4.  On the *Source* wizard screen, set *Data Source* to **Local Database**, and select the second option **SQL Query**. Put the following query in the *Enter Region Source* box and move on. In this query, order value is concatenated to each customer's name and is presented in $999,999,999,999.99 format. You can test this query in *SQL Commands* to see its output.

```
SELECT order_id,
       (SELECT cust_first_name||' '||cust_last_name
        FROM   demo_customers c
        WHERE  c.customer_id = o.customer_id ) ||' ['||
               to_char(order_total,'FML999G999G999G999G990D00')||']' customer,
       order_timestamp
FROM demo_orders o
```

5.  Set properties on the *Settings* screen as follows. The *Display Column* specifies the column to be displayed on the calendar, while the *Start Date Column* attribute specifies which column is to be used as the date to place an entry on the calendar. If you want to manage events through Calendar, then select the column that holds the start date for events displayed on this calendar in the *Start Date Column*. Next, select the column that holds the end date for events displayed on this calendar in the *End Date Column* attribute. If this attribute is specified, the calendar displays duration based events. The *Show Time* attribute specifies whether the time portion of the date should be displayed. The *Week* and *Day* views will be displayed on the calendar only when *Show Time* is set to *Yes*. If the start date or end date columns do not include time components, they will be shown as 12:00 am. Click **Create** to finish the wizard.

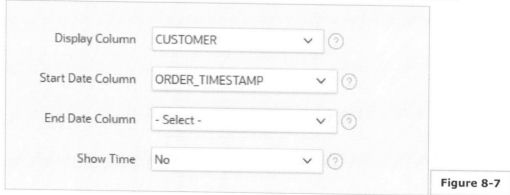

Figure 8-7

274

6. Click the **Attributes** tab of the *Order Calendar* region in the Page Designer. In the Properties pane, click the **View/Edit Link** attribute and set the following properties to create a link. The link will drill-down to the *Order Details* page (Page 29) to show the details when the user clicks an existing order.

| Property | Value |
|---|---|
| Target Type | Page in this application |
| Page | 29 |
| Name | P29_ORDER_ID |
| Value | &ORDER_ID. |
| Clear Cache | 29 |

7. Under the *Attributes* tab, click the **Create Link** property and set the following properties to create another link. This property is used to create a link to call Page 11 to enter a new order when the user clicks an empty calendar cell.

| Property | Value |
|---|---|
| Target Type | Page in this application |
| Page | 11 |

Save and run this page from the *Order Calendar* card on the *Reports* page – the page should look like Figure 8-6. If you don't see orders in the calendar, use the buttons available at top-left to switch back and forth – switch to May 2022. Click any name link in the calendar report to drill-down and browse order details. Click any blank date cell. This will start the Order Wizard to take new order entry. Note that a new order is created in the current date, irrespective of the month in view or the date cell you clicked.

## 8.7 Product Order Tree - Page 19

App Builder includes a built-in wizard for generating a tree. You can create a tree from a query that specifies a hierarchical relationship by identifying an ID and parent ID column in a table or view. The tree query utilizes a *START WITH .. CONNECT BY* clause to generate the hierarchy.

In this exercise you'll be guided to create a tree view of orders. The root node will show the three product categories you've been dealing with throughout this book. Level 1 node will be populated with individual categories and each category will have corresponding products at Level 2. The final node (Level 3) will hold names of all customers who placed some orders for the selected product along with quantity.

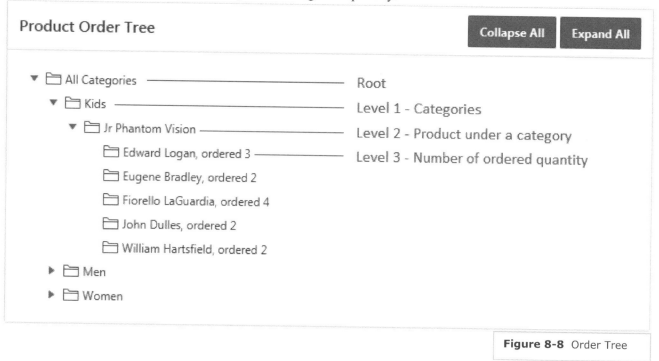

**Figure 8-8** Order Tree

Here are the steps to create the tree view.

1. Create a new page.

2. Select the **Tree** option on the first wizard screen.

3. Complete the next couple of screens using the following table and click **Next**.

| Property | Value |
|---|---|
| Page Number | 19 |
| Page Name | Product Order Tree |
| Page Mode | Normal |
| Region Template | Standard |
| Region Name | Product Order Tree |
| Breadcrumb | do not use breadcrumbs on page |
| Navigation Preference | Identify an existing navigation menu entry for this page |
| Existing Navigation Menu Entry | Reports |

4. On *Table/View Owner and Name* screen, select **DEMO_PRODUCT_INFO** for *Table Name*, and click **Next**.

5. Click **Next** to accept default entries on the *Query* screen, as illustrated below. A tree is based on a query and returns data that can be represented in a hierarchy. A *start with .. connect by* clause will be used to generate the hierarchy for your tree. On this screen you identify the columns you want to use as the ID, the Parent ID, and text that should appear on the nodes. The *Start With* column will be used to specify the root of the hierarchical query and its value can be based on an existing item, static value, or SQL query returning a single value.

Figure 8-9

6. Click **Next** again to skip the *Where Clause*.

7. In the final screen, put checks on **Collapse All** and **Expand All** to include these buttons on the page. Set *Tooltip* to **Static Assignment (value equals Tooltip Source attribute)** and enter **View Details** in *Tooltip Source*. The text "View Details" appears when you move over a tree node. Click **Next**.

8. Click **Create** to finish the wizard.

9. In the Page Designer, click the **Product Order Tree** node under *Body*.

10. Replace the existing **SQL Query** statement with the one shown below, which comprises links. After replacing the query save the page and run it from the *Reports* menu.

```
with data as
(
select 'R' as link_type,
        null as parent,
        'All Categories' as id,
        'All Categories' as name,
        null as sub_id
from demo_product_info
union
select distinct('C') as link_type, 'All Categories' as parent, category as id,
        category as name, null as sub_id
```

277

```
          from demo_product_info
          union
          select 'P' as link_type,
                category parent,
                to_char(product_id) id,
                product_name as name,
                product_id as sub_id
          from demo_product_info
          union
          select 'O' as link_type,
                to_char(product_id) as parent,
                null as id,
                (select c.cust_first_name || ' ' || c.cust_last_name
                 from demo_customers c, demo_orders o
                 where c.customer_id = o.customer_id and
                        o.order_id = oi.order_id ) || ', ordered '|| to_char(oi.quantity) as name,
              order_id as sub_id
          from demo_order_items oi
          )
        select case
              when connect_by_isleaf = 1 then 0
              when level = 1 then 1
              else -1
              end as status, level, name as title, null as icon, id as value, 'View' as tooltip,
            case
              when link_type = 'R'
               then apex_util.prepare_url('f?p='||:APP_ID||':3:'||:APP_SESSION||'::NO:RIR')
              when link_type = 'C'
               then apex_util.prepare_url('f?p='||:APP_ID||':3:'||:APP_SESSION||
                                   '::NO:CIR:IR_CATEGORY:' || name)
              when link_type = 'P'
               then apex_util.prepare_url('f?p='||:APP_ID||':6:'||:APP_SESSION||
                                   '::NO::P6_PRODUCT_ID:' || sub_id)
              when link_type = 'O'
               then apex_util.prepare_url('f?p='||:APP_ID||':29:'||:APP_SESSION||
                                   '::NO::P29_ORDER_ID:' || sub_id)
            else null
            end as link
        from data
        start with parent is null
        connect by prior id = parent
    order siblings by name
```

This custom query is used to form the tree using the following syntax:

```
SELECT status, level, name, icon, id, tooltip, link
FROM ...
WHERE ...
START WITH...
CONNECT BY PRIOR id = pid
ORDER SIBLINGS BY ...
```

| Line # | Tree Query Code |
|---|---|
| 1 | WITH data AS ( |
| 2 | select 'R' as link_type, null as parent, 'All Categories' as id, 'All Categories' as name, null as sub_id  from demo_product_info |
| 3 | UNION |
| 4 | select distinct('C') as link_type, 'All Categories' as parent, category as id, category as name, null as sub_id  from demo_product_info |
| 5 | UNION |
| 6 | select 'P' as link_type, category parent, to_char(product_id) id, product_name as name, product_id as sub_id from demo_product_info |
| 7 | UNION |
| 8 | select 'O' as link_type, to_char(product_id) as parent, null as id, (select c.cust_first_name || ' ' || c.cust_last_name from demo_customers c,  demo_orders o where c.customer_id = o.customer_id and o.order_id = oi.order_id ) || ', ordered '|| to_char(oi.quantity) as name, order_id as sub_id from demo_order_items oi ) |

The *WITH query_name AS* clause lets you assign a name to a subquery block. This statement creates the query name "data" with multiple SELECT statements containing UNION set operators. UNION is used to combine the result from multiple SELECT statements into a single result set.

| LINK_TYPE | PARENT | ID | NAME | SUB_ID | |
|---|---|---|---|---|---|
| R | - | All Categories | All Categories | - | Root Node - Query Line 2 |
| C | All Categories | Kids | Kids | - | |
| C | All Categories | Men | Men | - | Categories - Query Line 4 |
| C | All Categories | Women | Women | - | |
| P | Men | 1 | Air Max 2090 | 1 | |
| P | Men | 2 | LeBron Soldier 13 Red | 2 | |
| P | Men | 21 | Product Catalog | 21 | |
| P | Men | 3 | LeBron Soldier 13 White | 3 | Products - Query Line 6 |
| P | Men | 8 | Air Max 270 Gradient | 8 | |
| P | Men | 9 | Air Max 180 Trainer | 9 | |
| P | Women | 4 | Air Max 720 | 4 | |
| O | 1 | - | Albert Lambert, ordered 3 | 5 | |
| O | 1 | - | Edward Logan, ordered 2 | 7 | Orders - Query Line 8 |
| O | 1 | - | Eugene Bradley, ordered 10 | 1 | |
| O | 1 | - | Eugene Bradley, ordered 5 | 10 | |

Figure 8-10

| Line # | Tree Query Code |
|---|---|
| 1 | select case |
| 2 |     when connect_by_isleaf = 1 then 0 |
| 3 |     when level = 1 then 1 |
| 4 |     else -1 |
| 5 |     end as status, level, name as title, null as icon, id as value, 'View' as tooltip, |
| 6 |   case |
| 7 |    when link_type = 'R' |
| 8 |    then apex_util.prepare_url('f?p='\|\|:APP_ID\|\|':3:'\|\|:APP_SESSION\|\|'::NO:RIR') |
| 9 |    when link_type = 'C' |
| 10 |    then apex_util.prepare_url('f?p='\|\|:APP_ID\|\|':3:'\|\|:APP_SESSION\|\| '::NO:CIR:IR_CATEGORY:' \|\| name) |
| 11 |    when link_type = 'P' |
| 12 |    then apex_util.prepare_url('f?p='\|\|:APP_ID\|\|':6:'\|\|:APP_SESSION\|\|'::NO::P6_PRODUCT_ID:'\|\|sub_id) |
| 13 |    when link_type = 'O' |
| 14 |    then apex_util.prepare_url('f?p='\|\|:APP_ID\|\|':29:'\|\|:APP_SESSION\|\|'::NO::P29_ORDER_ID:' \|\| sub_id) |
| 15 |   else null |
| 16 |   end as link |
| 17 | from data |

The CASE statement within the SQL statement is used to evaluate the four link types (R=root, C=categories, P=products, and O=orders). It has the functionality of an IF-THEN-ELSE statement. Lines 8, 10, 12, and 14 make the node text a link. The R link type leads you to the main Products page (Page 3). The C link type also leads to Page 3, but applies a filter on category name. The P link type calls Product Details page (Page 6) to display details of the selected product. The final O link type displays details of the selected order on the Order Details page (Page 29).

The CONNECT_BY_ISLEAF pseudo column, in the first CASE statement, returns 1 if the current row is a leaf of the tree. Otherwise, it returns 0. This information indicates whether a given row can be further expanded to show more of the hierarchy.

If no condition is found to be true, then the CASE statement will return the null value defined in the ELSE clause on line 15.

Run all the reports you have created so far from the *Graphical Reports* submenu under the *Reports* menu. When you click the *Graphical Reports* option, a page (Page 26) comes up with a list of reports from where you can give them a test-run.

## 8.8 Gantt Chart

A Gantt chart allows you to effectively plan your complex projects. It enables you to plan all of your tasks in one place and helps you work out the minimum delivery time for your project and schedule when the right people are available to complete it. Gantt chart starts by listing all the tasks you need to complete to finish your project. You also need to specify the earliest date you can start each activity, how long you think each will take and whether any of them are dependent on the completion of other activities.

### 8.8.1 Data Workshop

To understand the functionality of this chart, you need to create a table and populate it with relevant data. For this purpose, you will use Oracle APEX's *Data Workshop* utility. The *Data Workshop* utility located under *SQL Workshop* enables you to load and unload text, DDL, and spreadsheet data to and from the database. You can load or unload XML files or delimited-field text files (such as comma-delimited (.csv) or tab-delimited files). You can also load data by copying and pasting from a spreadsheet. During loading and unloading process you can skip columns you do not need in your table. The utility allows you to load data into an existing table or create a new table from the loaded data. When loading into a new table, column names can be taken from the loaded data. Each time you load data from a file, file details are saved in a Text Data Load Repository. You can access these files from within the repository at any time.

Note that the wizards load and unload table data only, they do not load or unload other kinds of schema objects.

Execute the following steps to create a new table and load it with relevant data from a csv file.

1. Create a table named Project_Table using Project_Table.sql script provided in the book code. Open **SQL Workshop | SQL Commands** (A). Copy and then paste the CREATE TABLE statement from the script file (Project_Table.sql) into the command area (B), and then click the Run button (C), as shown in the following screen shot.

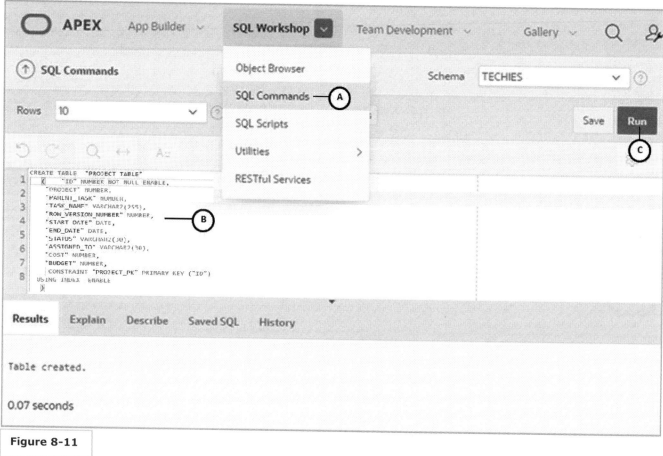

**Figure 8-11**

2. Click **SQL Workshop | Utilities | Data Workshop** to access the Data Load/Unload page.

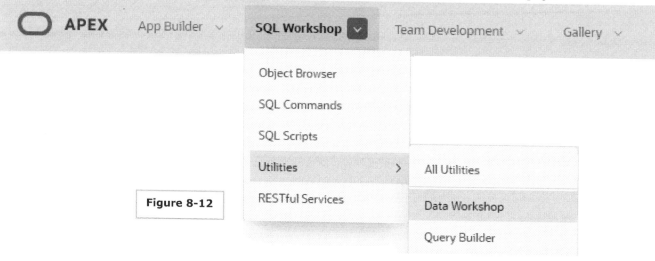

**Figure 8-12**

3. On the *Data Workshop* page, click the **Load Data** button.

4. On the *Load Data* page, select the **Upload a File** tab, and click the **Choose File** button. In the Open dialog box, select **Project_Table.csv** file from *BookCode\Chapter8* folder, and click **Open**.

5. On the next screen, click the **Existing Table** option (A), select the **PROJECT_TABLE** (B), and click the **Load Data** button (C). The database column names and columns in the data can be viewed in the *Preview* section.

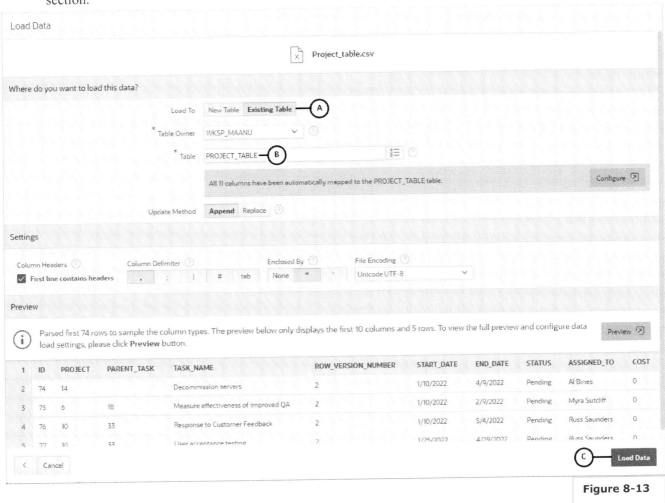

**Figure 8-13**

If everything goes well, the next screen appears with the message "*Data in table PROJECT_TABLE appended with 73 new rows!*". Click the View Table button at the bottom to complete the process.

## 8.8.2 Create Gantt Chart

Execute the following instructions to create a new page for the Gantt Chart:

1. Click **Create Page** in the main App Builder interface.

2. Click the **Chart** option.

3. On *Chart Type* screen, choose **Gantt**.

4. Fill in the next couple of screens as follows and then click **Next**.

| Property | Value |
|---|---|
| Page Number | 20 |
| Name | Gantt Chart |
| Page Mode | Normal |
| Breadcrumb | do not use breadcrumbs on page |
| Navigation Preference | Identify an existing navigation menu entry for this page |
| Existing Navigation Menu Entry | Reports |

5. On the *Source* screen, choose **SQL Query** for *Source Type*, and enter the following query in the SQL Query box. Click **Next** to proceed.

```
SELECT      task_name task_name,
            id task_id,
            start_date task_start_date,
            end_date task_end_date,
            decode(status,'Closed',1,'Open',0.6,'On-Hold',0.1,'Pending',0) status,
            (select min(start_date) -5 from project_table) gantt_start_date,
            (select max(end_date) from project_table)  gantt_end_date
FROM        project_table
ORDER BY id ASC
```

6. Fill in the Column Mapping screen as illustrated in the following figure:

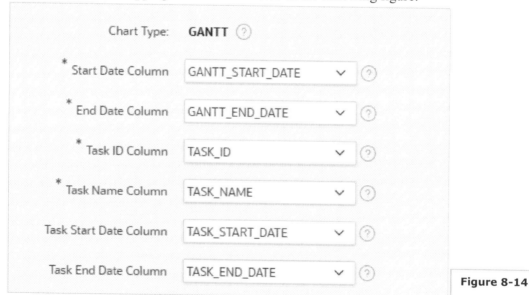

Figure 8-14

The following table provides details of the parameters:

| Start Date Column | Select the column name to be used for defining the start date of the Gantt chart. |
|---|---|
| End Date Column | Select the column name to be used for defining the end date of the Gantt chart. |
| Task ID | Select the column name to be used for defining the task ID on the Gantt chart. |
| Task Name | Select the column name to be used for defining the task name on the Gantt chart. |
| Task Start Date | Select the column name to be used for defining the task start date on the Gantt chart. |
| Task End Date | Select the column name to be used for defining the task end date on the Gantt chart. |

7. Click **Create** to complete the page creation process.

8. In Page Designer, click on **Series 1** and set *Progress* (under *Column Mapping*) to **Status**. The *Status* column defines the task progress on the Gantt chart.

9. Click **Save and Run** page button to test your work.

Press and hold the Ctrl key, and move the mouse wheel upward to enable the zoom buttons (A). Keep clicking the Zoom Out icon unless it is grayed out. The Gantt chart, as illustrated in the following screenshot, displays the overall progress of a project. Same-day tasks are shown in diamond shapes, completed tasks are represented in dark blue, while remaining tasks are displayed in light blue colors. Hovering the mouse pointer over a bar shows details of that particular task.

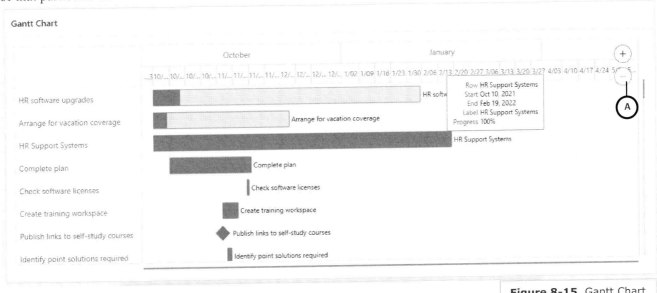

**Figure 8-15** Gantt Chart

## 8.9 Box Plot Chart

If you want to compare the annual sales figures of your products for the past 10 years, you would need a way to summarize all the data. A boxplot is an efficient chart type to summarize large amounts of data. A boxplot displays the range and distribution of data along a number line. The following illustration will help you further in reading this chart.

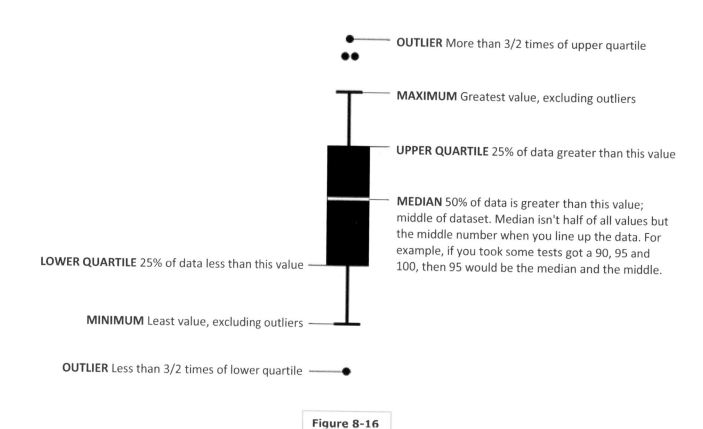

OUTLIER More than 3/2 times of upper quartile

MAXIMUM Greatest value, excluding outliers

UPPER QUARTILE 25% of data greater than this value

MEDIAN 50% of data is greater than this value; middle of dataset. Median isn't half of all values but the middle number when you line up the data. For example, if you took some tests got a 90, 95 and 100, then 95 would be the median and the middle.

LOWER QUARTILE 25% of data less than this value

MINIMUM Least value, excluding outliers

OUTLIER Less than 3/2 times of lower quartile

**Figure 8-16**

## 8.9.1 Data Workshop

Execute the following steps to create a table for this exercise and populate it with relevant data:

1. Access the Data Load/Unload page by clicking **SQL Workshop | Utilities | Data Workshop**.

2. Click the **Load Data** button on the Data Workshop page.

3. On the *Upload a File* tab, click the **Choose File** button and select **School_Stats.csv** file from the book code folder. Alternatively, drag and drop the file in the marked area.

4. On the *Load Data* page, select **New Table** for *Load To*, and enter **BoxPlot_Table** for *Table Name*. Click the **Load Data** button. After a while you will see "Table BOXPLOT_TABLE created with 15 rows!" message. Click the *View Table* button to browse the table.

 Note that when you create table and upload data in one go using this approach, the process automatically generates the primary key for the table.

## 8.9.2 Create Single Series Box Plot Chart

Create a new page to hold two Box Plot Charts. The first one, which is a single series chart, will be created using the wizard to show marks of school A only.

1. Click **Create Page** in the main Application Builder interface.

2. Select the **Chart** option.

3. On *Chart Type* screen, choose **Box Plot**.

4. Enter the following details for the new page and then click **Next**.

| Property | Value |
|---|---|
| Page Number | 21 |
| Name | Box Plot Chart |
| Page Mode | Normal |
| Breadcrumb | do not use breadcrumbs on page |
| Navigation Preference | Identify an existing navigation menu entry for this page |
| Existing Navigation Menu Entry | Reports |

5. On the *Source* screen, choose **SQL Query** for *Source Type*, and enter the following query in the SQL Query box. After entering the query, click **Next**.

   **Select course, schoola from boxplot_table**

6. On *Column Mapping* page, accept the **Vertical** Orientation, set *Label Column* to **COURSE**, *Value Column* to **SCHOOLA** and click **Create**.

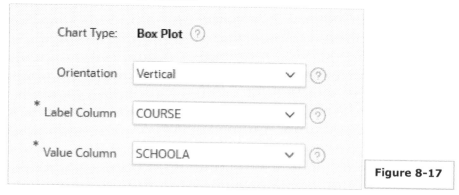

**Figure 8-17**

7. In Page Designer, click the *Box Plot Chart* region, set its *Title* to **Single Series Box Plot Chart** and change the default Series name from Series 1 to **School A**.

8. Save the page and run it from the Reports menu. Hover your mouse pointer over each box to see the values.

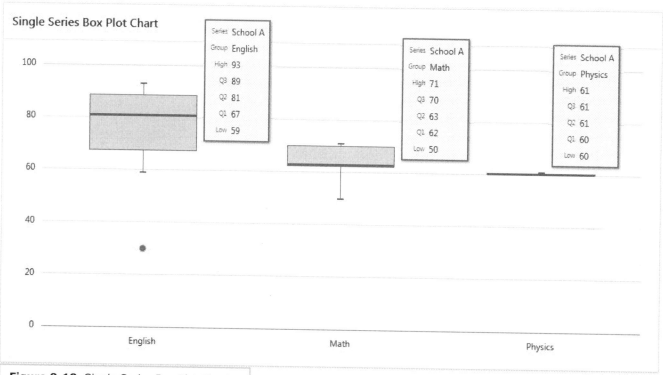

**Figure 8-18** Single Series Box Plot Chart

## 8.9.3 Create Multi-Series Box Plot Chart

This box plot chart will compare the marks of all three schools using multiple series.

1. In Page Designer, right click the *Components* node and select **Create Region**. Set the following parameters for the new region:

| Property | Value |
|---|---|
| Title | Multi-Series Box Plot Chart |
| Type | Chart |
| Location | Local Database |
| Type | SQL Query |
| SQL Query | select * from boxplot_table |
| Type (under Attributes) | Box Plot |
| Show (under Legend) | On |

2. Click on the **New** node under *Series*, and set the following attributes:

| Property | Value |
|---|---|
| Name | School A |
| Location (under Source) | Region Source |
| Label | COURSE |
| Value | SCHOOLA |

3. Right click the *Series* node and select **Create Series** to add another series. Set the following attributes for this series:

| Property | Value |
|---|---|
| Name | School B |
| Location (under Source) | Region Source |
| Label | COURSE |
| Value | SCHOOLB |

4. Create the final series for School C, as follows:

| Property | Value |
|---|---|
| Name | School C |
| Location (under Source) | Region Source |
| Label | COURSE |
| Value | SCHOOLC |

Save and run the page to see the multi-series Box Plot chart, as illustrated in the following figure.

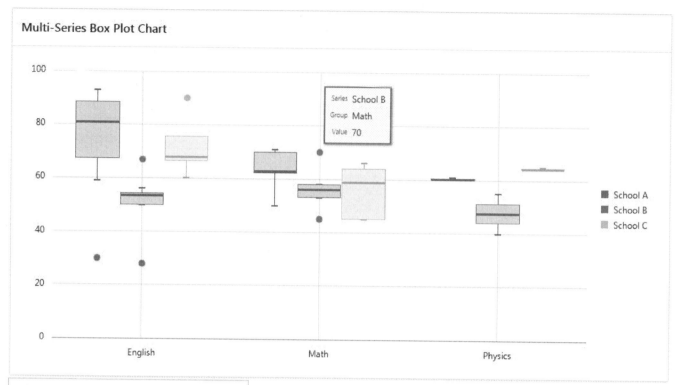

**Figure 8-19** Multi-Series Box Plot Chart

## 8.10 Pyramid Chart

A pyramid graph is a chart in the shape of a triangle or pyramid with lines dividing it into sections. A related topic or idea is placed in each section. Pyramid chart is best used for data that is organized in some kind of hierarchical form. Each section in a pyramid chart is a different width, which indicates a level of hierarchy among the topics. However, the width does not represent quantity. Pyramid charts use the row member order from bottom to top to form a pyramid chart.

1. Using the instructions provided in the previous section and the following illustration, create a new table named **Pyramid_Table** and upload data from **Products.csv** file provided with the source code. The table will be created with five records.

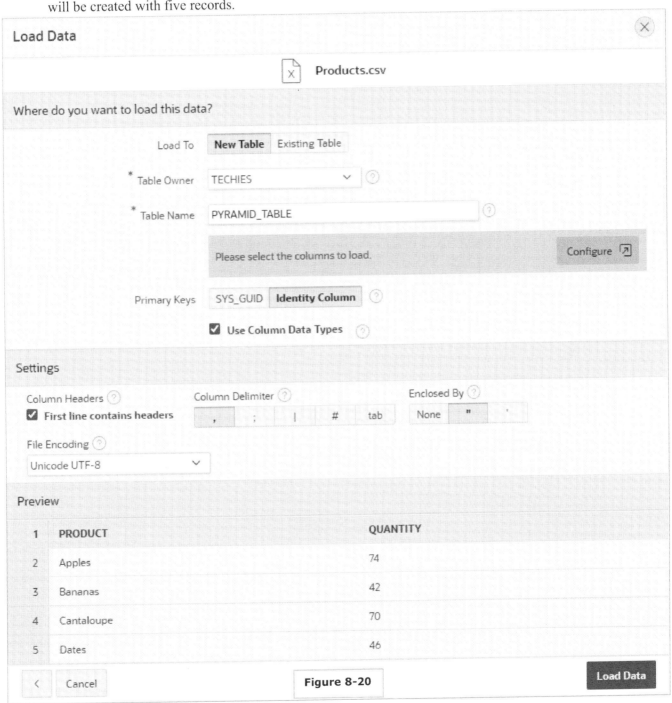

Figure 8-20

2.  Create a new page. On the first wizard screen, select the **Chart** option.

3.  Choose **Pyramid** for *Chart Type*.

4.  Set the following attributes for the new page:

| Property | Value |
| --- | --- |
| Page Number | 22 |
| Name | Pyramid Chart |
| Page Mode | Normal |
| Breadcrumb | do not use breadcrumbs on page |
| Navigation Preference | Identify an existing navigation menu entry for this page |
| Existing Navigation Menu Entry | Reports |

5.  On the *Source* screen, choose **SQL Query** for *Source Type*, and enter following query in the SQL Query box. After entering the query, click **Next**.

    **Select * From Pyramid_Table**

6.  Select the following columns in the *Column Mapping* screen and click the **Create** button.

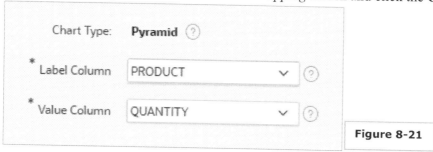

**Figure 8-21**

7.  In the Page Designer click the Pyramid Chart region and then click the *Attributes* tab to set the following attributes. In the *On Display* attribute you specify the type of animation used when initially displaying the chart, while the *On Data Change* specifies whether animation is shown when data is changed on the chart.

| Property | Value |
| --- | --- |
| Type | Pyramid |
| Maximum Width | 500 |
| Height | 400 |
| On Display (*under Animation*) | Alpha Fade |
| On Data Change | Automatic |
| Show (*under Legend*) | On |
| Hide and Show Behavior | Rescale |

Save and run the page. Turn a legend on or off to dynamically scale the chart. As mentioned earlier, in a pyramid chart row member order from bottom to top is used to form the chart. In this example, the first row member Apples becomes the lowest member of the pyramid; the next row Bananas becomes the next highest member, and so on. The bottom row member, Grapes, thus appears on top of the pyramid.

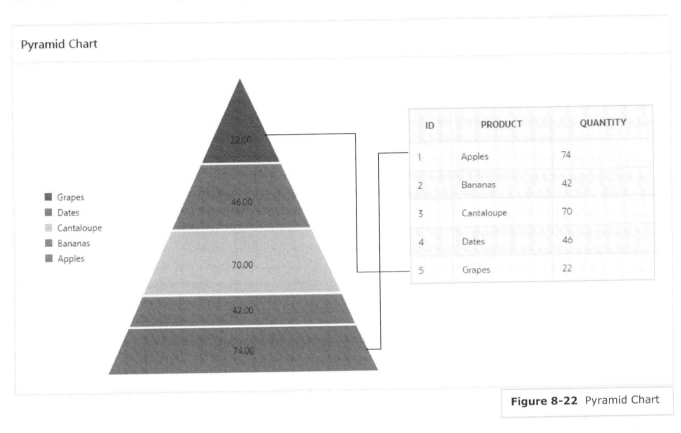

**Figure 8-22** Pyramid Chart

## 8.11 About Mobile Application Design

Mobile applications developed with Oracle APEX are browser-based applications that run inside the browser on the mobile device. Therefore, these applications must have a connection in order to communicate with the Oracle Database and cannot operate in a disconnected environment. Mobile devices that have HTML5 capabilities can utilize all of the capabilities that can be built into the applications, including HTML5 date-pickers, sub-types that display different keypads based on field definition, and so. Older devices will still render the application but they will offer less advanced features. The major advantage of developing browser-based applications is that you only need to develop them once for desktop and mobile devices. However, one major limitation is accessing on-device features such as contact lists. This limitation can be alleviated by integrating with solutions such as PhoneGap that support the creation of hybrid solutions, which use a native application wrapper to display the web applications. Solutions such as Phonegap provide various APIs to access many of the native phone features not currently available using HTML5 or JavaScript. To learn more, see: http://phonegap.com/

In previous APEX releases, developers selected the Mobile User Interface (which was based on jQuery Mobile) to optimize applications for mobile environments. Now, the Universal Theme - 42 is optimized to work equally well in either a mobile or desktop environment. Desktop UI now supports all mobile friendly components such as List View region, Column Toggle Report region, and Reflow Report.

jQuery Mobile and the jQuery Mobile User Interface used in previous releases have been desupported. If you have an existing mobile application that uses the jQuery Mobile User Interface, then you should migrate your existing application to the Universal Theme. To learn more about migrating existing applications to the Universal Theme, go to the Universal Theme application at https://apex.oracle.com/ut and select Migration Guide.

Universal Theme - 42 enables developers to build modern web applications without requiring extensive knowledge of HTML, CSS, or JavaScript. Responsive Design is the key of the Universal Theme. Responsive Design works just as well on small screen devices (such as smartphones and tablets) as it does on larger screen devices (including laptops and desktops). The UI components in Universal Theme work across varying screen resolutions while maintaining the same or similar functionality. In addition, Universal Theme takes full advantage of ultra-high screen resolutions by utilizing vector graphics where possible, and relying upon CSS3 features for UI styling.

## 8.11.1 Reports Optimized for Mobile Environments

Although the Universal Theme is optimized to work well on mobile devices, not all components are mobile friendly. For example, interactive reports and interactive grids do not work well in mobile environments. When creating reports for mobile devices, Oracle recommends the following report types that provide an optimal user experience for small screens.

- **List View**

  Features a responsive design to display data and provide easy navigation on Smartphones. It creates a page that contains the formatted result of a SQL query. You choose a table on which to build the List view and select a database column to be used for the List view entry.

- **Column Toggle Report**

  Creates a responsive report designed for mobile applications and Smartphones. By default, column toggle reports are created with all columns set to the same priority. However, the developer can edit the report column attributes and rank columns by importance. Columns with a lesser priority (larger number) are hidden at narrower screen widths. The report includes a Columns button which enables end users to select which columns they want to view.

- **Reflow Report**
  Creates a responsive report designed for mobile applications and Smartphones. When there is not enough space available to display the report horizontally, the report responds by collapsing the table columns into a vertical value pairs layout where each column displays on a separate row.

## List View

Execute the following steps to create a List View report that creates a responsive report for mobile applications. The report works by collapsing the table columns into a stacked presentation that looks like blocks of label and data pairs for each row. This switch occurs when there is not enough space available to display the report horizontally.

1. Create a new page by clicking the **Create Page** button.

2. Click the **Report** icon to move ahead.

3. On the subsequent wizard screen, select the **List View** option.

4. Type **23** for *Page Number* and **List View Report (Mobile)** for *Page Name*. Leave *Page Mode* to **Normal** and move on by clicking **Next**.

5. Set *Navigation Preference* to **Identify an existing navigation menu entry for this page**, select **Reports** for *Existing Navigation Menu Entry*, and click **Next**.

6. On the *Source* wizard screen, select **Local Database** for *Data Source*, select **SQL Query** as *Source Type*, and enter the following SQL statement in *Region Source*.
   ```
   SELECT    a.ROWID as "PK_ROWID", a.*
   FROM      "#OWNER#"."DEMO_PRODUCT_INFO" a
   ORDER BY a.product_name
   ```

7. Set properties on the *Settings* screen as illustrated in the following figure and click the **Create** button.

Features    ☐ Advanced Formatting ⑦

        ☑ **Show Image** ⬅

        ☐ Show List Divider

        ☐ Has Split Button

        ☑ **Enable Search** ⬅

        ☐ Is Nested List View

        ☑ **Inset List** ⬅

|  |  |
|---|---|
| Text Column | PRODUCT_NAME ⬅ ⑦ |
| Supplemental Information Column | - Select - ⑦ |
| Counter Column | - Select - ⑦ |
| Image Type | Image stored in BLOB ⑦ |
| Image BLOB Column | PRODUCT_IMAGE ⑦ |
| Image Primary Key Column 1 | PK_ROWID ⑦ |
| Image Primary Key Column 2 | - Select - ⑦ |
| Link Target | ⑦ |
| Search Type | Server: Like & Ignore Case ⬅ ⑦ |

**Figure 8-23**

When you click the option *Show Image*, some more relevant properties appear on your screen. The same behavior applies to the *Enable Search* option. The first option is checked because we need to display images of products, while the second option is checked to add search functionality. If lists are embedded in a page with other types of content, the *Inset List* option packages the list into a block that sits inside the content area with a bit of margin. The selected *Text Column*, PRODUCT_NAME, will appear next to the image at runtime. The *Image Type* attribute specifies what kind of image is displayed and where it is read from. The displayed image can be an icon with a size of 16x16 or a thumbnail with a size of 80x80. The source for the image can be a database BLOB column or a URL to a static file. After setting the *Image Type* attribute, you're required to provide the *Image BLOB Column*, which in our case is PRODUCT_IMAGE. The *Image Primary Key Column 1* attribute specifies the primary key or a unique database column that is used to lookup the image. The value for this attribute (PK_ROWID) is selected by the wizard. The *Search Type* attribute defines how a search will be performed. The selected option, *Server: Like & Ignore Case*, will use Oracle's LIKE operator (LIKE %UPPER([search value])%) to query the result.

8. After creating the page, click the **Attributes** tab of the *List View Report* region. Set *Search Column* to **PRODUCT_DESCRIPTION** and enter **Search by Product Description** in the *Search Box Place holder* property. The *Search Column* specifies an alternative database column used for the search. The text added to the *Search Box Placeholder* will appear in the search box at runtime to inform users what to put in the search box.

9. Right-click the *List View Report* region and select **Create Button**. Set the following properties for this button, which is being added to create a new product.

| Property | Value |
|---|---|
| Name | CREATE |
| Label | Create |
| Region | List View Report (Mobile) |
| Position | Copy |
| Hot | On |
| Action | Redirect to Page in this Application |
| Target | Type = Page in this application<br>Page = 6<br>Clear Cache = 6 |

Save the page and run it from the Reports option in the main menu. Enter **air max** in the search box and hit the Enter key. Four shoe products (Air Max 2090, Air Max 270, Air Max 270 Gradient, and Air Max 720) should appear. Enter **air max 270** in the search box. The page will be refreshed with two relevant records. Clear the search box to get the complete list of products.

Make this page more meaningful by performing the following steps. The *Advanced Formatting* option enables you to style your list even further. The mandatory option, *Text Formatting*, gives you the opportunity to show more in the list than just the product name. In this example, you wrap product name and description in a HTML <h3> heading element. You can add more stuff to the list with the help of *Supplemental Information*. The *Supplemental Information* appears on the right side of the list item to present product price.

1. Click the region's **Attributes** tab.

2. In the Property pane, put a check on **Advanced Formatting** to make the corresponding formatting properties visible.

3. In *Text Formatting*, type: **<h3>&PRODUCT_NAME.</h3><p>&PRODUCT_DESCRIPTION.</p>**

4. In *Supplemental Information*, type the following text including the terminating period: **Price:$&LIST_PRICE.**

5. Enter **<h1>&CATEGORY.</h1>** in the *List Divider Formatting* property to show the category of each product.

6. Save the changes and run the page to see an output similar to figure 8-24. Click the **Create** button to see the Product Details page (Page 6).

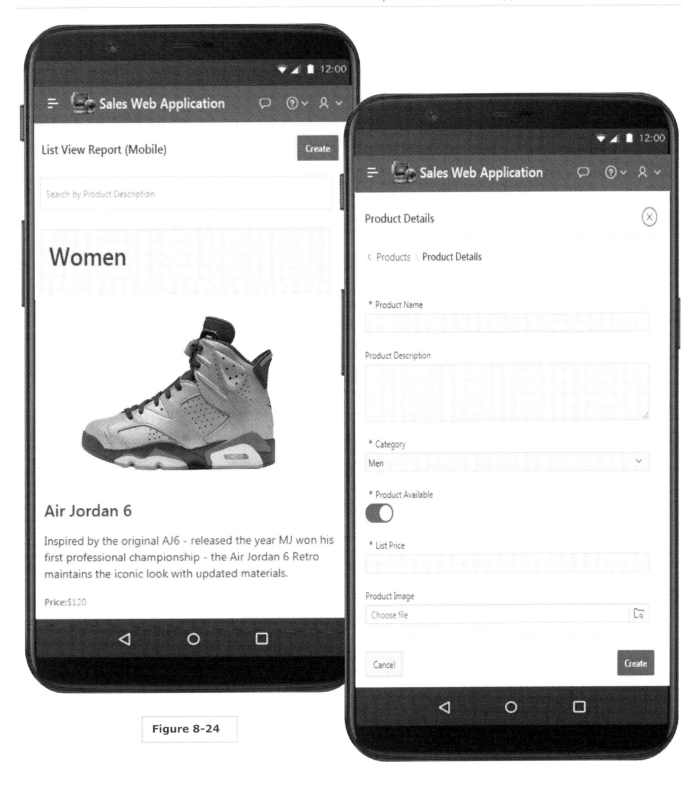

## Column Toggle Report

For desktop version you used the *Master Detail* option to simultaneously create *Orders* (Page 4) and *Order Details* (Page 29) pages. By setting a region to the *Column Toggle Report* type, you build reports that display all data on any mobile device. *Column Toggle* enables you to specify the most important columns and those that will be hidden as necessary on smaller screens.

1. Click the **Create Page** button. Select **Report** on the initial screen followed by the **Column Toggle Report** option.

2. Enter **24** for *Page Number* and **Column Toggle Report (Mobile)** for *Page Name*. Keeping the default *Page Mode* to **Normal**, click **Next**.

3. Set *Navigation Preference* to **Identify an existing navigation menu entry for this page**, select **Reports** for *Existing Navigation Menu Entry*, and click **Next** to proceed.

4. After selecting **SQL Query** as the *Source Type* for this page, enter the following SQL statement in *Region Source* and click the **Create** button.

```
select o.rowid,
       o.order_id,
       to_date(to_char(o.order_timestamp,'mm yyyy'), 'mm yyyy') order_month,
       o.order_timestamp order_date,
       o.user_name sales_rep,
       o.order_total,
       c.cust_last_name || ', ' || c.cust_first_name customer_name,
       (select count(*) from demo_order_items  oi
        where oi.order_id = o.order_id) order_items,
       o.tags tags
from  demo_orders o, demo_customers c
where o.customer_id = c.customer_id
order by order_timestamp desc
```

5. Right-click the *Column Toggle Report Mobile* region and select **Create Button**. The button will be used to create a new order. Set the following properties for this button:

| Property | Value |
|---|---|
| Name | CREATE |
| Label | Create |
| Region | Column Toggle Report (Mobile) |
| Position | Create |
| Hot | On |
| Action | Redirect to Page in this Application |
| Target | Type = Page in this application<br>Page = 11<br>Clear Cache = 11 |

6.  Save and run the page from the **Column Toggle Report (Mobile)** option on the Reports page. Initially, the page will display all the columns defined in the SQL query. Click the **Columns** button (A). In the ensuing columns list, remove checks from all columns, except **Order Id**, **Order Month**, and **Customer Name** to show these three columns in the main report, as illustrated in the following figure. Click the **Create** button to launch the *Order Wizard*.

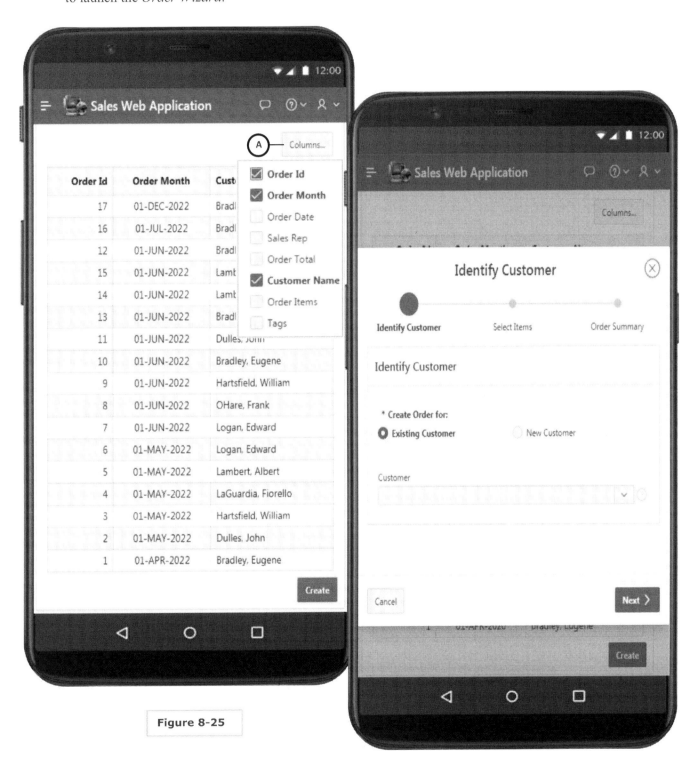

**Figure 8-25**

## Reflow Report

In this exercise, you will create a responsive report for mobile applications using the Reflow Report feature. Reflow Report wraps each column or changes to displaying multiple lines on very small screens. When there is not enough space available to display the report horizontally, the report works by collapsing the table columns into a stacked presentation that looks like blocks of label and data pairs for each row.

1.  As usual, click **Create Page**, and click the **Report** icon to move ahead.

2.  On the next screen, select the **Reflow Report** option.

3.  Type **25** for *Page Number* and **Reflow Report (Mobile)** for *Page Name*. Leave *Page Mode* to **Normal** and move on by clicking **Next**.

4.  Set *Navigation Preference* to **Identify an existing navigation menu entry for this page** and select **Reports** for *Existing Navigation Menu Entry*. Click **Next**.

5.  For *Source Type*, select **SQL Query** and enter the following query in *Region Source*:
    ```
    select customer_id, cust_first_name||' '||cust_last_name customer_name,
    cust_street_address1, cust_city, cust_state, cust_postal_code, cust_email,
    phone_number1, url, credit_limit, tags
    from DEMO_CUSTOMERS
    ```

6.  Click **Create** to finish the wizard.

7.  In the Page Designer, expand the **Columns** node and set suitable headings for all the columns.

8.  Click the **CUSTOMER_ID** column and turn off its *Show* property. This specifies to hide the column at run time. Even if hidden, columns can always be referenced using substitution syntax (&COLUMN_NAME.).

9.  Click the **CUSTOMER_NAME** column to set the following properties. The values set for these properties will transform the customer name column into a link. When clicked, it calls a form page where you can browse and manipulate customer information. For *Link Text*, click the adjacent Quick Pick button and select CUSTOMER_NAME from the list. The selected value will be displayed as a substitution variable.

| Property | Value |
|---|---|
| Type | Link |
| Target Type | Type = Page in this application<br>Page = 7<br>Name = P7_CUSTOMER_ID<br>Value = &CUSTOMER_ID.<br>Clear Cache = 7 |
| Link Text | &CUSTOMER_NAME. |

10. Click the **CREDIT_LIMIT** column and set its *Alignment* and *Column Alignment* properties to **left**. These two settings will left-align the column's heading and its value.

11. Save the page and run it from the **Reflow Report (Mobile)** option on the Reports page. The report should look like figure 8-26. Click any customer's name to see the details of that customer.

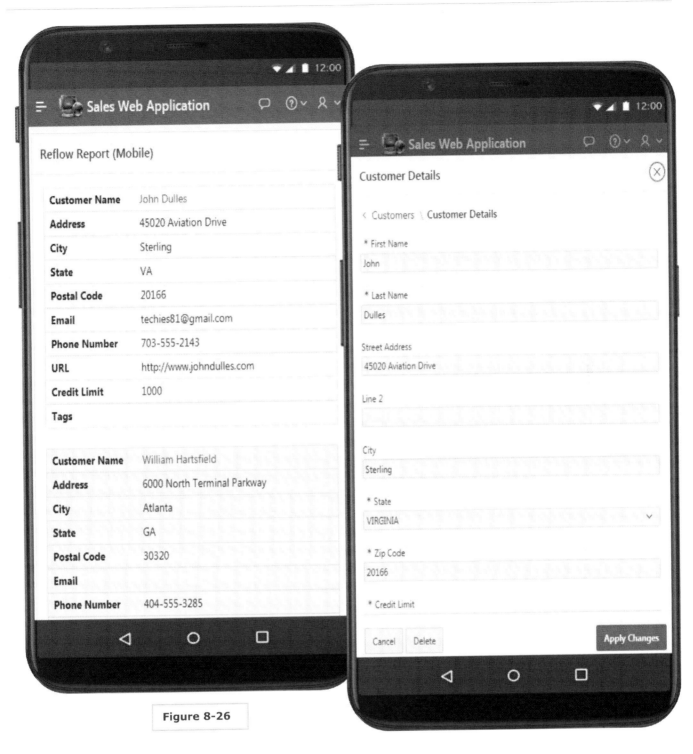

**Figure 8-26**

## Summary

Report is the most significant component of any application. It allows digging information from the data mine for making decisions. The chapter not only demonstrated the power of Oracle APEX to graphically present the information, but also exhibited how to drill-down to a deeper level to obtain detailed information using different types of charts, calendar, and tree. The chapter highlighted some mandatory properties related to charts and other features. There are many more and explaining each one of them is beyond the scope of this book. The best way to understand these properties is to make the Help tab active and experiment by changing the properties in various ways. The chapter also demonstrated how to create reports for small screen devices. The next chapter continues with this topic and reveals how to produce advance PDF reports in Oracle APEX.

# 9

# PRODUCE ADVANCE REPORTS

## 9.1 About Advanced Reporting

You have seen the use of interactive reporting feature in Oracle APEX to create professional looking onscreen reports. Interactive reports also have the ability to export reports to PDF, RTF, Microsoft Excel, and Comma Separated Values (CSV) formats. However, it is not possible to define a custom report layout in interactive reports. If you download PDF version of these reports to print a hard copy, what you get is a generic report in simple row-column format without any control breaks and conditional formatting. For serious printing, you have to define an external reporting server to present data in desired format. This chapter will teach you how to utilize Oracle BI Publisher to enjoy high level formatting.

Oracle APEX provides the following three printing options:

**Oracle REST Data Services** - Select this option if you are using the Oracle REST Data Services (formerly called Application Express Listener) release 2.0 or later. It enables you to use the basic printing functionality, which includes creating report queries and printing report regions using the default templates provided in Application Express and using your own customized XSL-FO templates. The Oracle REST Data Services option does not require an external print server; instead the report data and style sheet are downloaded to the listener, rendered into PDF format by the listener, and then sent to the client. The PDF documents in this setup are not returned back into the database, thus the print APIs are not supported when using the Oracle REST Data Services-based configuration.

**External (Apache FOP)** - Select this option if you are using Apache FOP on an external J2EE server. This one enables you to use the basic printing functionality, which includes creating report queries and printing report regions using the default templates provided in Application Express and using your own customized XSL-FO templates.

**Oracle BI Publisher** - This option requires a valid license of Oracle BI Publisher. With this option, you can take report query results and convert them from XML to RTF format using Oracle BI Publisher. Select this option to upload your own customized RTF or XSL-FO templates for printing reports within Application Express. You have to configure Oracle BI Publisher as your print server. Besides standard configuration, Oracle BI Publisher has Word Template Plug-in to create RTF based report layouts, which provides greater control over every aspect of your report and allows you to add complex control breaks, logos, charts, and pagination control. The following list contains some reports that can be created using this advance option:

- Tax and Government Forms
- Invoices
- Ledgers
- Financial Statements
- Bill of Lading, using tables and barcode fonts
- Operational Reports with re-grouping, conditional highlighting, summary calculations, and running totals
- Management Reports having Chart with summary functions and table with detail records
- Check Print, using conditional formatting and MICR fonts
- Dunning Letters

To print these professional reports, you have to pay for a valid Oracle BI Publisher license that is worth the price considering the following advantages:

- *Multiple Output Formats*: In addition to PDF, the other supported output formats include DOC, XLS, and HTML.
- *Included in Export/Import*: Being part of the application, RTF based layout are exported and imported along with the application.
- *Robust Report Layout*: Add complex breaks, pagination control, logos, header-footer, charts, and print data on pre-printed forms.
- *Report Scheduling*: This unique feature enables you to set up a schedule and deliver the report to the desired destinations including e-mail, fax, and so on.

To explore the features provided by this robust reporting server, you can download and install the limited license version to use the program only for the development purpose. Once again, this book protects you from all the hassle of downloading, installing and configuring BI Publisher Server in your environment, because in the online development environment you can enjoy this utility for free. The following list presents the steps you will perform to produce advance reports for Oracle APEX.

**Steps to Produce Advance Reports**
- Install BI Publisher Desktop
- Create report query in Oracle APEX
- Create report layout in Microsoft Word (I created my templates in Word 2003)
- Upload report layout to Oracle APEX
- Add links to run the report

### 9.2 Download and Install BI Publisher Desktop

In this chapter, you will take hard copies of reports in Portable Document Format (PDF). You will use Microsoft Word to create templates for these reports. For this purpose, you need Oracle BI Publisher Desktop to prepare the report templates. During BI Publisher Desktop installation, you might be asked to install Java Runtime Edition (JRE) and Dot Net Framework–in my scenario I executed `jre-6u11-windows-i586-p-s.exe` and `NetFx20SP1_x86.exe` files.

BI Publisher Desktop is a client-side tool to aid in the building and testing of layout templates. This consists of a plug-in to Microsoft Word for building RTF templates. You can download this small piece of software from:
`https://www.oracle.com/middleware/technologies/bi-publisher/downloads.html`

After the download, install the software on your PC using the .exe file. Once the installation completes, you'll see the BI Publisher plug-in as a menu item in Microsoft Word. In newer versions it is placed under the main Add-Ins menu.

Figure 9-1

## 9.3 Create Monthly Order Review Report

In Chapter 7 section 7.3.3, you created an onscreen alternative report named *Monthly Review* to view details of monthly orders. In the following exercise, you will create a PDF version of that report.

### 9.3.1 Create Report Query

You can print a report by defining a report query in Shared Component. A report query is a SQL statement that identifies the data to be extracted. You can associate a report query with a report layout and download it as a formatted document. If no report layout is selected, a generic layout is used. To make these reports available to end users, you integrate these reports with an application. For example, you can associate a report query with a button, list item, branch, or other navigational component that enables you to use URLs as targets. Selecting that item then initiates the printing process.

1. Go to **Shared Components** interface.

2. Click **Report Queries** in the *Reports* section.

3. Click the **Create** button to create a new report query.

4. Type **Monthly_Review** in the *Report Query Name* field, set *Output Format* to **PDF**, set *View File As* to **Attachment**, and then click **Next**. Enter the report query name as is or else you will encounter `Error occurred while painting error page: ORA-01403: no data found ORA-22275: invalid LOB locator specified` when you print this report. Using the *Attachment* value of the *View File As* attribute, you instruct the browser to download the file to your PC. The Inline value of this attribute display the report query document inside the browser window.

5. Enter the following statement in *SQL Query* text area and click **Next**:

```
SELECT o.order_id,
        to_char(o.order_timestamp,'Month yyyy') order_month,
        o.order_timestamp order_date,
        c.cust_last_name || ', ' || c.cust_first_name customer_name,
        c.cust_state,
        o.user_name sales_rep,
        (select count(*) from demo_order_items  oi
         where oi.order_id = o.order_id) order_items,
        o.order_total
  FROM  demo_orders o, demo_customers c
 WHERE o.customer_id = c.customer_id
```

6. Select **XML Data** for *Data Source for Report Layout*, to export your report definition as an XML file. The XML file contains column definitions and the data (fetched using the SELECT statement) to populate the report. Click the **Download** button. A file named **monthly_review.xml** will be saved to your disk. Double-click this file to see its contents.

7. Back in Oracle APEX, click the **Create Report Query** button.

8. On the *Confirm* screen, click the **Create** button to complete the wizard.

## 9.3.2 Create Report Template in Microsoft Word

The later versions of Microsoft Word produced errors while designing and testing report templates, so I created my templates in Microsoft Word 2003. If you fall into a situation like this, skip to section 9.3.8 and use the template provided in the book code.

1.  In **Microsoft Word**, click **Oracle BI Publisher** (or *BI Publisher*) in the main menu to make its ribbon visible.

2.  From the *Data* ribbon, select **Load XML Data** (or *Sample XML*) to load a data file. Select the **monthly_review.xml** file created in the previous section. The message *Data Loaded Successfully* will be is displayed.

3.  Select **Table Wizard** from the *Insert* ribbon. Select **Table** for *Report Format* and click **Next**.

4.  Click **Next** to accept **DOCUMENT/ROWSET/ROW** for *Data Set*.

5.  Add all fields to the report by moving them to the right pane using the double arrow button and click **Next**.

6.  Select **Order Month** in the first drop down list under *Group By* and click **Next**. This will group the report on the *Order Month* column.

7.  Select **Order Date** in the first *Sort By* list and select **Order ID** in the first *Then By* list to sort the report first on the *Order Date* column and then on the *Order ID* column. Click **Next**.

8.  On the label form screen, enter **State** for *Cust State* to give this column a meaningful name. Click **Finish** to complete the process. An output similar to Figure 9-2 will be displayed.

group ROW by ORDER_MONTH

**ORDER_MONTH**

| Order Id | Order Date | Customer Name | State | Sales Rep | Order Items | Order Total |
|---|---|---|---|---|---|---|
| F ORDER_I D | ORDER_DA TE | CUSTOMER_NA ME | CUST_STA TE | SALES_R EP | ORDER_ITE MS | ORDER_TOT AL E |

end ROW by ORDER_MONTH

**Figure 9-2** Raw Report Template Created in Microsoft Word

9.  Press **Ctrl+S** (or click the **Save** icon) to save the template. Enter **Monthly_Review** in the *File name* box, select **Rich Text Format** for its type, and click **Save**.

10. In the *Preview* ribbon, click the **PDF** option. The output as show in Figure 9-3 will be displayed. Note that you can format and preview this report offline if you have some data in the XML file.

11. **Close the PDF** and switch back to Microsoft Word.

## May 2022

| Order Id | Order Date | Customer Name | State | Sales Rep | Order Items | Order Total |
|---|---|---|---|---|---|---|
| 2 | 01-MAY-22 | Dulles, John | VA | DEMO | 10 | 2380 |
| 3 | 12-MAY-22 | Hartsfield, William | GA | DEMO | 5 | 1640 |
| 4 | 14-MAY-22 | LaGuardia, Fiorello | NY | DEMO | 5 | 1090 |
| 5 | 24-MAY-22 | Lambert, Albert | MO | DEMO | 5 | 950 |

## June 2022

| Order Id | Order Date | Customer Name | State | Sales Rep | Order Items | Order Total |
|---|---|---|---|---|---|---|
| 7 | 03-JUN-22 | Logan, Edward | MA | DEMO | 7 | 905 |
| 8 | 11-JUN-22 | OHare, Frank | IL | DEMO | 4 | 1060 |
| 9 | 17-JUN-22 | Hartsfield, William | GA | DEMO | 3 | 730 |
| 10 | 20-JUN-22 | Bradley, Eugene | CT | DEMO | 3 | 870 |

**Figure 9-3** Raw Report Template Output

## 9.3.3 Format Report

1. Place the cursor before the **ORDER_MONTH** field and type **Order Month:** in front of it to act as a label. You can use Microsoft Word's standard tools to change font, color, and size of the text. Also, drag field's width to a desired size.

2. Click the **ORDER_TOTAL** field and right-align it. Double-click it to call its properties. Select **Number** for its *Type* and **#,##0.00** for *Format*. Click **OK**.

3. Insert a blank line above **group ROW by Order_Month** text to add a title for this report. Type **ABC CORPORATION** and press **Enter** to add another line. Type **Monthly Orders Review Report** on the new line. You can also add a logo, page number, and other options using Microsoft Word's standard tools.

## 9.3.4 Conditional Formatting

In these steps, you will change font and background color of orders for which the amount is less than or equal to 900, as you did in the onscreen report version in Chapter 7.

1. Select the **Order Total** field by clicking its name (not the heading) in the column.

2. Select **Conditional Format** from the *Insert* ribbon.

3. Perform the following steps on the *Properties* tab:
   a. Select the **ORDER_TOTAL** column for *Data* field.
   b. Select **Number** in the adjacent list.
   c. Put a check on **Apply to Entire Table Row** to apply the condition to the whole report.
   d. Select **Less than or equal to** in the *Data* field.
   e. Enter **900** in the box next to the *Data* field.
   f. Click the **Format button**.
   g. Put a check on the **Background Color** option.
   h. Click the **Select** button to choose different *Font* and *Background* colors.
   i. Click **OK**.

4. Preview your work and see the application of conditional formatting to all the rows with Order Total less than or equal to 900.

Use the same procedure and change font and background color for orders greater than 2000. Select *Greater than* for the condition and enter 2000 in the value. This time, do not check the *Apply to Entire Table Row* option to highlight specific cells only. After performing these steps, save your work and preview the report.

## 9.3.5 Summary Calculation

In this section you will add a summary to reveal average orders for the month.

1.  Place your cursor on the blank line before the text **end ROW by ORDER_MONTH**.

2.  Click the **Field** option in the *Insert* ribbon.

3.  In the *Field* dialog box, click the **Order Total** field, select **average** for *Calculation*, select **On Grouping**, and click the **Insert** button. A summary field, *average ORDER_TOTAL* will be added to the report. Close the dialog box.

4.  Type **Monthly Average:** before the field to act as field's label. Double-click the calculated field, set the *Type* property to **Number**, and the *Format* property to **#,##0.00**. Align the whole expression to the right under the *Order Total* field.

## 9.3.6 Add a Summary Chart

1.  Insert a blank row above **group ROW by ORDER_MONTH**.

2.  Select **Chart** from the *Insert* ribbon.

3.  From the *Data* tree, drag the **ORDER_TOTAL** field to the *Values* box, set *Aggregation* to **Sum**, drag **ORDER_MONTH** to *Labels*, put a check on **Group Data**, select **Bar Graph - Horizontal** for *Type*, and **April** in *Style*. The completed screen should look like Figure 9-4. Click **OK** to close the dialog box.

4.  Right-click the newly added chart in Microsoft Word and select **Insert Caption**. Type **Monthly Orders Review** in *Caption*.

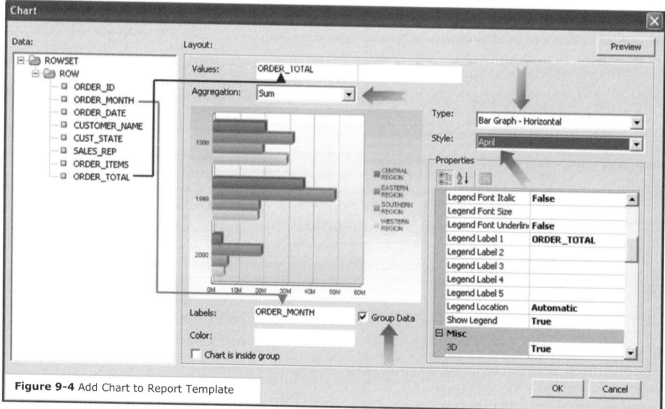

**Figure 9-4** Add Chart to Report Template

## 9.3.7 Add a Pivot Table

1. In Microsoft Word, click the line just after the text **end ROW by ORDER_MONTH**.

2. Select **Pivot Table** from the *Insert* ribbon.

3. Drag **CUST_STATE, CUSTOMER_NAME, ORDER_MONTH,** and **ORDER_TOTAL** fields to the layout section, as shown in Figure 9-5. Drag the CUST_STATE and CUSTOMER_NAME fields and drop them in the left layout pane one after the other. Click the **Preview** button to see the output within the dialog box. Click the **OK** button to dismiss the Pivot Table dialog box. Format the table using Microsoft Word's toolbar so that it matches the output shown in Figure 9-8. Browse the report in PDF. **Save the template** and close Microsoft Word.

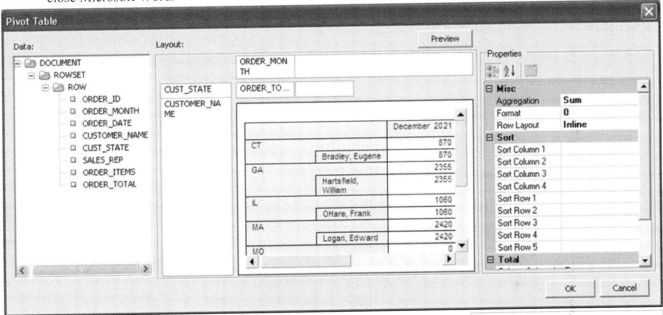

**Figure 9-5** Pivot Table Settings

## 9.3.8 Upload Report Template to Oracle APEX

Report Layouts are used in conjunction with report queries to render data in a printer-friendly format, such as PDF. A report layout has been designed using Oracle BI Publisher's plug-in for Microsoft Word and will now be uploaded to Oracle APEX as an RTF file type.

1. In the **Shared Components** interface, click **Report Layouts** under the *Reports* section.

2. Click the **Create** button.

3. Select the option **Named Columns (RTF)** and click **Next**. A named column report layout is a query-specific report layout designed to work with a defined list of columns in the query result set. This type of layout is used for custom-designed layouts when precise control of the positioning of page items and query columns is required. This layout is uploaded as an RTF file.

4. In *Layout Name* enter **monthly_review**, click the **Choose File** button, and select the Microsoft Word template file **Monthly_Review.rtf**, which was created in the previous section.

5. Click the **Create Layout** button.

6. Move back to **Shared Components**.

7. Click the **Report Queries** link under the *Reports* section.

8. Click the **Monthly_Review** icon.

9. In *Report Query Attributes* section, change *Report Layout* from *Use Generic Report Layout* to **monthly_review** to apply this layout to the report query.

10. Write down or copy the URL appearing in the *Print URL* box, which should be – *f?p=&APP_ID.:0:&SESSION.:PRINT_REPORT=Monthly_Review.* Report queries can be integrated with an application by using this URL as the target for buttons, navigation list entries, list items, or any other type of link. You will use this link in the next section to run the report.

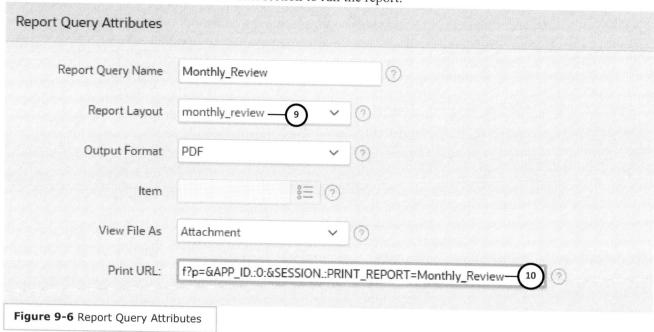

**Figure 9-6** Report Query Attributes

11. Click **Apply Changes**.

You have created the Report Layout in Oracle APEX by uploading a Microsoft Word template and linked it to your Report Query. In the next section, you will create a link to run this report.

## 9.3.9 Run the Report

In this section, you will configure *Monthly Review Report* menu entry in the main navigation menu to run this report.

1.  Switch back to the **Shared Components** interface.

2.  Click the **Lists** link under the *Navigation* section and then click **Navigation Menu**.

3.  Click the **Monthly Review Report** entry.

4.  Ensure that *Target Type* property is set to **Page in this Application** and *Page* property is set to **0**.

5.  Enter **PRINT_REPORT=Monthly_Review** in the *Request* box.

6.  Save your work by clicking the **Apply Changes** button.

7.  Run the application. Click **Monthly Review Report** under **Advance Reports** in the **Report** menu. The report will be downloaded to your PC. Open the report with Adobe Acrobat Reader, which should look something like Figure 9-7 and Figure 9-8. I formatted the layout using standard Microsoft Word tools, including header-footer, tables, page number, font, and so on.

Congratulations! You have successfully created a professional looking report that not only matches the onscreen report of Chapter 7, but also adds more value to it by incorporating a pivot table, to display the same data from a different perspective. Add a new order in the application and see its reflection in the report.

**Figure 9-7** Monthly Order Review Report

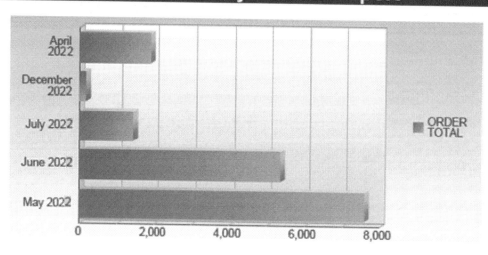

# ABC CORPORATION
35-A/3, ABC House, Raymond Street off Mansfield Street,
Chicago-IL, 6350, USA.

## Orders Monthly Review Report

Figure 1: Monthly Order Chart

### Order Month: April 2022

| Order# | Order Date | Customer | State | Sales Rep | Order Items | Order Total |
|---|---|---|---|---|---|---|
| 1 | 4/17/2022 | Bradley, Eugene | CT | DEMO | 3 | 1,890.00 |
| | | | | | | Average Order: 1,890.00 |

### Order Month: December 2022

| Order# | Order Date | Customer | State | Sales Rep | Order Items | Order Total |
|---|---|---|---|---|---|---|
| 17 | 12/2/2022 | Bradley, Eugene | CT | DEMO | 2 | 155.00 |
| | | | | | | Average Order: 155.00 |

### Order Month: July 2022

| Order# | Order Date | Customer | State | Sales Rep | Order Items | Order Total |
|---|---|---|---|---|---|---|
| 16 | 7/6/2022 | Bradley, Eugene | CT | DEMO | 3 | 1,421.00 |
| | | | | | | Average Order: 1,421.00 |

### Order Month: June 2022

| Order# | Order Date | Customer | State | Sales Rep | Order Items | Order Total |
|---|---|---|---|---|---|---|
| 10 | 6/20/2022 | Bradley, Eugene | CT | DEMO | 3 | 870.00 |
| 11 | 6/21/2022 | Dulles, John | VA | DEMO | 1 | 800.00 |
| 12 | 6/21/2022 | Bradley, Eugene | CT | DEMO | 1 | 180.00 |
| 13 | 6/21/2022 | Bradley, Eugene | CT | DEMO | 1 | 100.00 |
| 14 | 6/21/2022 | Lambert, Albert | MO | DEMO | 1 | 210.00 |
| 15 | 6/21/2022 | Lambert, Albert | MO | DEMO | 1 | 500.00 |
| 7 | 6/3/2022 | Logan, Edward | MA | DEMO | 7 | 905.00 |
| 8 | 6/11/2022 | OHare, Frank | IL | DEMO | 4 | 1,060.00 |
| 9 | 6/17/2022 | Hartsfield, William | GA | DEMO | 3 | 730.00 |
| | | | | | | Average Order: 595.00 |

**Figure 9-8** Pivot Table Report

# ABC CORPORATION

35-A/3, ABC House, Raymond Street off Mansfield Street,
Chicago-IL, 6350, USA.

## Order Month: May 2022

| Order# | Order Date | Customer | State | Sales Rep | Order Items | Order Total |
|---|---|---|---|---|---|---|
| 2 | 5/1/2022 | Dulles, John | VA | DEMO | 10 | 2,380.00 |
| 3 | 5/12/2022 | Hartsfield, William | GA | DEMO | 5 | 1,640.00 |
| 4 | 5/14/2022 | LaGuardia, Fiorello | NY | DEMO | 5 | 1,090.00 |
| 5 | 5/24/2022 | Lambert, Albert | MO | DEMO | 5 | 950.00 |
| 6 | 5/29/2022 | Logan, Edward | MA | DEMO | 4 | 1,515.00 |
| | | | | | | Average Order: 1,515.00 |

## Table 1: Revenue By States

| State | Customer | April 2022 | December 2022 | July 2022 | June 2022 | May 2022 | Total |
|---|---|---|---|---|---|---|---|
| CT | | 1,890.00 | 155.00 | 1,421.00 | 1,150.00 | 0.00 | 4,616.00 |
| | Bradley, Eugene | 1,890.00 | 155.00 | 1,421.00 | 1,150.00 | 0.00 | 4,616.00 |
| GA | | 0.00 | 0.00 | 0.00 | 730.00 | 1,640.00 | 2,370.00 |
| | Hartsfield, William | 0.00 | 0.00 | 0.00 | 730.00 | 1,640.00 | 2,370.00 |
| IL | | 0.00 | 0.00 | 0.00 | 1,060.00 | 0.00 | 1,060.00 |
| | OHare, Frank | 0.00 | 0.00 | 0.00 | 1,060.00 | 0.00 | 1,060.00 |
| MA | | 0.00 | 0.00 | 0.00 | 905.00 | 1,515.00 | 2,420.00 |
| | Logan, Edward | 0.00 | 0.00 | 0.00 | 905.00 | 1,515.00 | 2,420.00 |
| MO | | 0.00 | 0.00 | 0.00 | 710.00 | 950.00 | 1,660.00 |
| | Lambert, Albert | 0.00 | 0.00 | 0.00 | 710.00 | 950.00 | 1,660.00 |
| NY | | 0.00 | 0.00 | 0.00 | 0.00 | 1,090.00 | 1,090.00 |
| | LaGuardia, Fiorello | 0.00 | 0.00 | 0.00 | 0.00 | 1,090.00 | 1,090.00 |
| VA | | 0.00 | 0.00 | 0.00 | 800.00 | 2,380.00 | 3,180.00 |
| | Dulles, John | 0.00 | 0.00 | 0.00 | 800.00 | 2,380.00 | 3,180.00 |
| | TOTAL | 1,890.00 | 155.00 | 1,421.00 | 5,355.00 | 7,575.00 | 16,396.00 |

26/12/2021 6:32:19 AM

## 9.4 Create a Commercial Invoice

In this exercise, you will generate commercial invoices for the placed Orders. You will use the same techniques used in the previous section. This time, you will create a parameters form to print specific orders by passing parameter values to the underlying report query.

## 9.4.1 Create A List of Values

Create the following LOV from scratch in the Shared Components interface. You will utilize it in the next section to print only those orders entered by the user selected from this list.

| Property | Value |
|---|---|
| Name | Users |
| Type | Dynamic |
| Query | SELECT DISTINCT user_name d, user_name r FROM demo_orders |
| Return Column | R |
| Display Column | D |

## 9.4.2 Create Report Parameters Page

1. Create a **Blank Page** using the following parameters. The page will receive parameters to print specific invoices.

| Property | Value |
|---|---|
| Page Number | 50 |
| Name | Invoice Parameters |
| Page Mode | Normal |
| Breadcrumb | don't use breadcrumbs on page |
| Navigation Preference | Identify an existing navigation menu entry for this page |
| Existing Navigation Menu Entry | Reports |

2. Create a region under *Body*. Enter **Invoice Report** for the region's *Title*.

3. Add two *Page Items* under the *Invoice Report* region and set the following properties. Using these items you can print a single order or a range of orders.

After creating the first item, right-click its name in the *Rendering* tree, and select **Duplicate** from the context menu. This action will make a duplicate of the first item. Select the duplicate item, and set the values mentioned in the table's second column.

| Property | Value | Value |
|---|---|---|
| Name | P50_INVOICEFROM | P50_INVOICETO |
| Type | Text Field | Text Field |
| Label | From Invoice Number: | To Invoice Number: |
| Template | Required | Required |
| Value Required | On | On |
| Type (*Default*) | Static | Static |
| Static Value | 1 | 9999999999 |

4. Add a **Select List** under the two text field items and set the following properties. The select list will show the IDs of all users from which you can select one ID to print the orders entered by that particular user. The V('APP_USER') expression displays the ID of the logged-in user as a default value for this select list. For PL/SQL reference type, you use V('APP_USER') syntax of the built-in substitution string to assess the current user running the application.

| Property | Value |
|---|---|
| Name | P50_USER |
| Type | Select List |
| Label | Entered by: |
| Template | Optional |
| Type (*List of Values*) | Shared Components |
| List of Values | USERS |
| Type (*Default*) | PL/SQL Expression |
| PL/SQL Expression | V('APP_USER') |

5. Right-click the *Invoice Report* region and select **Create Button**. Set the following properties for the new button. When you click this button, the page is submitted and an associated branch (created in section 9.5) forwards a print request to the print server.

| Property | Value |
|---|---|
| Name | PRINT |
| Label | Print Invoice |
| Position | Edit |
| Hot | On |
| Action | Submit Page |

6. Save your work.

1.  Go to **Shared Components**.

2.  Click **Report Queries** under the *Reports* Section.

3.  Click the **Create** button to create a new report query.

4.  Type **Invoice** for *Report Query Name*, set *Output Format* to **PDF**, *View File As* to **Attachment**, and click **Next**.

5.  Enter the following statement in *SQL Query* text area and click **Next**. As you can see, the SQL query filters data using the three parameters passed to it from Page 50. You use bind variables (underlined in the WHERE clause) in SQL statements to reference parameter values.

```
     SELECT o.order_id, o.Order_timestamp, o.user_name,
            c.cust_first_name || ' ' || c.cust_last_name as customer,
            c.cust_street_address1, c.cust_street_address2, c.cust_city,
            c.cust_state, c.cust_postal_code, oi.ORDER_ITEM_ID,
            pi.PRODUCT_NAME, oi.UNIT_PRICE, oi.QUANTITY,
            oi.Unit_Price * oi.Quantity as Amount
      FROM  DEMO_ORDERS o, DEMO_ORDER_ITEMS oi,
            DEMO_PRODUCT_INFO pi, DEMO_CUSTOMERS c
     WHERE o.ORDER_id = oi.ORDER_id and pi.PRODUCT_ID = oi.PRODUCT_ID and
            o.customer_id = c.customer_id and
            o.ORDER_id BETWEEN :P50_INVOICEFROM and
            :P50_INVOICETO and o.user_name = :P50_USER
```

6.  Select **XML Data** for *Data Source for Report Layout* to export your report definition as an XML file. Click the **Download** button. A file named **invoice.xml** will be saved to your disk.

7.  Click the **Create Report Query** button followed by the **Create** button on the *Confirm* page. Unlike the previous XML file, this one doesn't contain any data due to the involvement of parameters. So, you cannot test the invoice report offline.

## 9.4.4 Create Invoice Template in Microsoft Word

Perform the following steps in Microsoft Word to create a template for the invoice report. For your convenience, I have provided both XML and RTF files with the book's code.

1. In Microsoft Word, select the **A4** size page and set the margins.

2. From the *Data* ribbon, select **Load XML Data | invoice.xml**, and then click **Open** to load the XML file you downloaded in the previous section.

3. From the *Insert* ribbon, choose **Table Wizard** to add a table. This table will be used to output order details. Set *Report Format* to **Table** and *Data Set* to **DOCUMENT/ROWSET/ROW**.

4. Move **Order Id, Product Name, Unit Price, Quantity,** and **Amount** columns to the right pane.

5. Select **Order Id** in *Group By* to group the report according to order numbers.

6. Do not select any field for *Sort By*.

7. Set **labels** (Product, Price, Quantity, and Amount) for the report columns.

8. Click **Finish**.

## 9.4.5 Template Formatting

Follow these steps to format the template:

1. Double-click the group field titled **group ROW by ORDER_ID**. On the *Properties* tab, set *Break* to **Page**. This will print each new invoice on a separate page.

2. From the **Insert** ribbon select **Field**. Select the **ORDER_ID** field and click the **Insert** button to add this field to the next row just after the group titled *group Row by ORDER_ID*. Similarly, add ORDER_TIMESTAMP, CUSTOMER, CUST_STREET_ADDRESS1, CUST_STREET_ADDRESS2, CUST_CITY, CUST_STATE, CUST_POSTAL_CODE, and USER_NAME on subsequent lines. I inserted a table to place these fields accordingly – see Figure 9-9.

3. Double-click the **AMOUNT** field. Set its *Type* to **Number** and *Format* to **#,##0.00**. Right-align the field using Microsoft Word's alignment option.

4. Add a **blank row** to the details table. Select **Field** from the *Insert* ribbon. In the *Field* dialog box, select **AMOUNT**. From **Calculation** list, select **sum**, put a **check** on 'On Grouping', and click **Insert**. Put a label **Total** and then format and align the field, as shown in the template. This step will add a new row (just after the last transaction) to display the sum of the *Amount* column.

5. Save the report to your hard drive as **invoice** and select **Rich Text Format (RTF)** as its *type*.

6. Close Microsoft Word.

## 9.4.6 Upload Template to Oracle APEX

1. Call the **Shared Components** interface and click **Report Layouts** under *Reports*.

2. Click the **Create** button.

3. Select the option **Named Columns (RTF)** and click **Next**.

4. In *Layout Name* enter **invoice**, click the **Choose File** button, select the template file **invoice.rtf**, and then click the **Create Layout** button.

5. Move back to **Shared Components**.

6. Under the *Reports* section, click the **Report Queries** link.

7. Click the **Invoice** icon.

8. In *Report Query Attributes* section, change *Report Layout* from *Use Generic Report Layout* to **invoice** to apply this layout.

9. Click **Apply Changes**.

## 9.5 Create Branch

Call Page 50 to create the following branch. This branch is being added to send a print request when the *Print Invoice* button is clicked. On the *Processing* tab, right-click the *After Submit* node, and select **Create Branch**. Set the following properties for the new branch. Note that the letter I in the word Invoice (in the *Request* attribute) should be in caps and the request value (PRINT_REPORT=Invoice) should not contain any leading or trailing space.

| Property | Value |
| --- | --- |
| Name | Run Invoice Report |
| Point | After Submit |
| Type *(Behavior)* | Page or URL (Redirect) |
| Target Type | Type = Page in this Application |
| Page | 0 |
| Request *(under Advance)* | PRINT_REPORT=Invoice |
| When Button Pressed | PRINT |

## Test Your Work

From the main navigation menu, select **Customer Invoice** under the *Advance Reports* menu. This will bring up the parameters form page (Page 50). For the time being, accept all the default values in the form, including the default user, and hit the *Print Invoice* button. Open the report with Adobe Acrobat Reader, which should resemble the one show in Figure 9-9. Also, try to get this report using different parameters to test your work.

**ABC CORPORATION**
35-A/3, ABC House,
Raymond Street Off
Mansfield Street, NJ 07901
Phone #(908) 316-5599
info@abccorp.com

**COMMERCIAL INVOICE**

**Customer:**
John Dulles
45020 Aviation Drive

Sterling
VA 20166

| Order Number | 2 |
|---|---|
| Order Date | 5/1/2022 |
| Sales Rep. | DEMO |

| Product Name | Unit Price | Quantity | Amount |
|---|---|---|---|
| Air Max 2090 | 50 | 3 | 150.00 |
| LeBron Soldier 13 Red | 80 | 3 | 240.00 |
| LeBron Soldier 13 White | 150 | 3 | 450.00 |
| Air Max 720 | 60 | 3 | 180.00 |
| Air Max 270 | 80 | 3 | 240.00 |
| Air Jordan 6 | 120 | 2 | 240.00 |
| LeBron 17 BG | 30 | 2 | 60.00 |
| Air Max 270 Gradient | 125 | 4 | 500.00 |
| Air Max 180 Trainer | 110 | 2 | 220.00 |
| Jr Phantom Vision | 50 | 2 | 100.00 |
| **TOTAL** | | | **2,380.00** |

Make all checks payable to ABC Corporation
THANK YOU FOR YOUR BUSINESS!

**NOTE:**
You may get the following error when you try to open the PDF: Acrobat could not open 'invoice.pdf' because it is either not a supported file type or because the file has been damaged (for example, it was sent as an email attachment and wasn't correctly decoded). This error message is displayed when there is no data for the given criteria. For example, the default user appearing in the Entered by list might not have created any order. So, change the user name and then hit the Print Invoice button. To cope with this problem, you can add a validation to check for the existence of data prior to calling the report. The error also emerges when Oracle APEX is not configured to use BI Publisher as its print server.

**Figure 9-9** Commercial Invoice

## Summary

The chapter revealed how to create advance reports and provided step-by-step instructions on how to generate pixel-perfect PDF reports in Oracle APEX using Oracle BI Publisher and MS Word. In my next-level book, *Oracle APEX Pro Hacks*, I've demonstrated how to create such reports in JasperReports.

# 10

# MANAGING USERS & APPLICATION ACCESS

## 10.1 Administer Applications in Oracle APEX

Oracle APEX has two types of administrators: Workspace administrators and Instance administrators. A workspace administrator, as the name suggests, is responsible to manage administrative activities of a workspace, such as manage user accounts, monitor workspace activities, and view log files. On the other hand, instance administrators manage the entire instance of Oracle APEX. In this book you will act as a workspace administrator because you are working in a hosted environment, where the role of instance administrator is not available and is performed by people on the Oracle APEX team.

Workspace administrators and developers can create user accounts for the purpose of logging in to the Oracle Application Express development environment and for end user authentication to applications developed within their workspaces. They can also control access to an application, individual pages, or page components via access control. Adding the Access Control feature to an application creates multiple pages and the following components:

- Adds an Access Control region to the Administration page
- Creates the access roles: Administrator, Contributor, and Reader
- Creates the authorization schemes: Administration Rights, Contribution Rights, and Reader Rights
- Creates the build option, Feature: Access Control
- Creates ACCESS_CONTROL_SCOPE Application Setting

Oracle APEX comes with three built-in privileges using which you can control access to an application or its components. These privileges are: administration, edit, and view. Each of these privileges correlates to an access role:

- Administration correlates to the Administrator role.
- Edit correlates to the Contributor role.
- View correlates to the Reader role.

When added to an application, the Access Control feature creates the following authorization schemes:

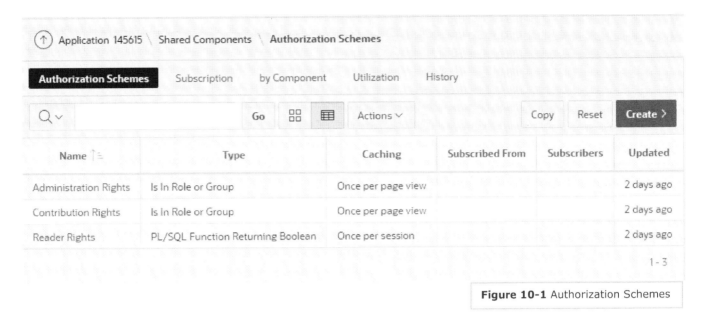

**Figure 10-1** Authorization Schemes

1. **Administration Rights** – This authorization scheme checks if the current user in the application is assigned ADMINISTRATOR role.

2. **Contribution Rights** – This authorization scheme checks if the current user in the application is assigned the ADMINISTRATOR role or the CONTRIBUTOR role.

3. **Reader Rights** – This authorization scheme returns TRUE if the access control is configured to allow any authenticated user access the application. If this behavior is not allowed, it checks if the current user in the application is assigned to any application role.

You can add the access control feature to your application at the time of creating the application (as you did in Chapter 2), or at a later stage using *Application Access Control* in Shared Components.

After creating an application, you create users and allow access to the application. This chapter will provide instructions whereby you will be able to control the access of your application using the built-in roles, privileges, and authorizations schemes just mentioned.

The following diagram depicts the security structure you will be implementing for your application. The left pane depicts a scenario for the user RIAZ, who has the Contributor role. When this user tries to access the Customers report page (Page 2), the Contribution Rights authorization scheme, which is associated with the Create button, is contacted. Since the user has the Contributor role and the Create button is associated with the Contribution Rights authorization scheme, the button appears on the page for this user. In other words, administrators and contributors can create new customers.

The second scenario (in the left pane), shows that the user AHMED has been granted the Reader role. When he tries to access the same Customers report page, the Create button is not displayed. This is because the button is associated with the Contribution Rights authorization scheme.

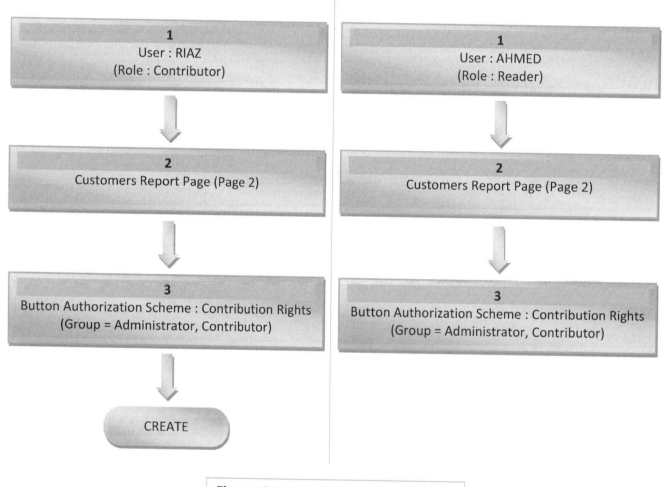

**Figure 10-2** Application Security Structure

## 10.2 Creating Users

Now that we are approaching the application deployed stage, lets first create a couple of users to test the application access control scenarios displayed on the previous page.

1. Click the **Administration** icon (A), and select **Manage Users and Groups** (B).

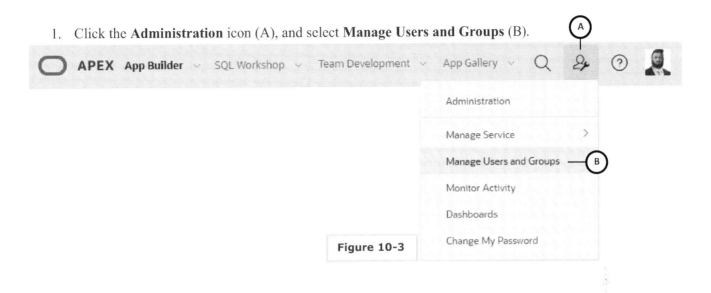

Figure 10-3

2. The Manage Users and Groups page will appear on your screen, displaying your existing workspace administrator user account (A). Click the **Create User** button (B) on this page.

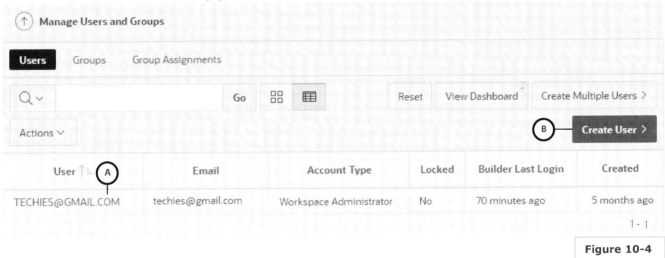

Figure 10-4

3. Set the following properties on the Create User page and click the **Create User** button.

| Property | Value |
|---|---|
| Username | RIAZ |
| Email Address | riaz@abc.com |
| Password | *Set a password for this user* |
| Confirm Password | *Confirm the above password* |
| Require Change of Password on First Use | Off |

Run the application and try to log into it using the above credentials – enter RIAZ for username. You will be denied with Access denied by Application security check message. This message is displayed because the user has not been granted access to the application. Execute the next steps to grant application access privilege to this user.

4.  On the error page, click the **OK** button to access the login page again. Enter your workspace administrator credentials to log in. Click the **Administration** option in the application menu, and then click the **Users** option in the *Access Control* pane to your right.

5.  On the *Manage User Access* page, click the **Add User** button. In the *Manage User Access* form, enter **RIAZ** for Username, and grant him the **Contributor** role, as shown in the following figure. Click the **Add User** button.

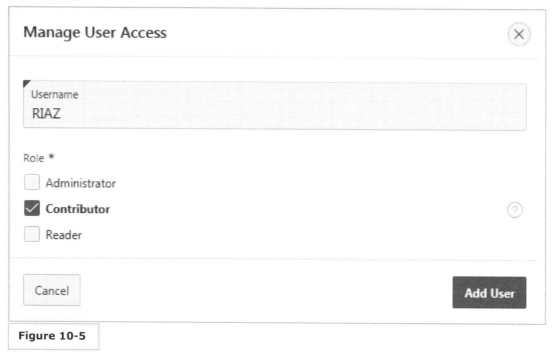

**Figure 10-5**

In my personal opinion, the Username field in the above form should be a select list, displaying the user we created in step 3, instead of the input text filed.

Log out and log back in using the new user's credentials. This time you will be granted access to the application. Note that the Administration menu will not be displayed for this user, because he is not an administrator.

6.  Add one more user (**AHMED**) using the instructions provided in the previous steps, and grant him the **Reader** role.

## 10.3 Implement Authorization

In the following set of steps you will implement the Contribution Rights authorization scheme to test access to page, page components, and application menu. We now have three users – you (workspace administrator), RIAZ (Contributor), and AHMED (Reader).

1. Open Page 2 (Customers) in Page Designer. On the *Rendering* tab to your left, click the **Create** button to select it. In the Properties pane, set *Authorization Scheme* (in the *Security* section) to **Contribution Rights**, and save the change. The button is now associated with the selected authorization scheme.

2. Run the application using RIAZ user's credentials. Select **Manage Customers** from the Setup menu. The Create button should be visible for this user, because he possesses the contributor role.

3. Log out and log back in using AHMED's credentials. Once again, select the **Manage Customers** option from the *Setup* menu. On this occasion, the Create button will not be rendered, because the user has the Reader role – that is, he cannot create new customers.

4. After testing page component access control, let's see how to restrict user from accessing an application page. Switch back to the designer interface. Click the root node - **Page 2: Customers**. In the Properties pane, scroll down to the *Security* section, and set *Authorization Scheme* to **Contribution Rights**. Save and run the page. This time the page itself will not be rendered and you will see a message "Insufficient privileges, user is not a Contributor" instead. Log in as RIAZ and observe that both page and the Create button are rendered for this user.

5. Finally, let's check out the application menu access. Go to Shared Components interface, and select **Navigation Menu** followed by the **Navigation Menu** option. Click the **Manage Customers** option. On the *List Entry* page, set *Authorization Scheme* to **Contribution Rights**, and click the **Apply Changes** button. Switch to the application tab in your browser, and refresh the Customers report page. The application menu should still be listing the *Manage Customers* entry for RIAZ. Sign out and log in as AHMED. There you go! The *Manage Customers* entry from the *Setup* menu has vanished. So, this step exhibited how you can prevent users from accessing menu entries.

## Summary

In this chapter you went through the built-in mechanism of Oracle APEX to administer your applications. You learned how to add application users and grant them built-in roles to control application access. In the final section, you assessed the access control mechanism by applying the built-in roles and authorization scheme to page, page components, and application menu. In my next-level book, *Oracle APEX Pro Hacks*, I've demonstrated how to create a robust custom security module for APEX applications.

# 11

# ENHANCE APPLICATIONS WITH NEW FEATURES

## 11.1 Faceted Search

A faceted search page, as illustrated in the following figure, features a faceted search region (A) and report (B). The faceted search region displays on the left side of the page and enables users to narrow down the search result by selecting facet values (C). A facet shows possible values together with the occurrence count (D) within the result set.

Narrowing the search result makes it easier for users to find the data they want. The right side of the results region is a classic report which displays in report or card view. Both the Create Application Wizard and Create Page Wizard support the creation of faceted search pages. After you change a facet, results, dependent facets and occurrence counts refresh immediately. Let's explore this exciting feature.

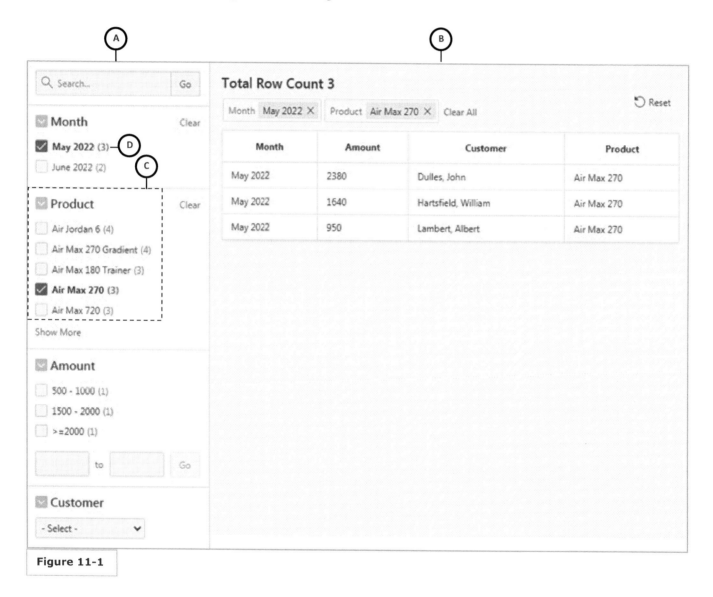

**Figure 11-1**

## 11.1.1 Create Faceted Search Page

Execute the following steps to create a faceted search page, as illustrated in Figure 11-1.

1. Click the **Create Page** button, and select **Report** for the new page type.

2. On the next wizard screen, select **Faceted Search**.

3. On *Page Attributes* screen, enter **400** for *Page Number*, **Faceted Search** for *Page Name*, and click **Next**.

4. On the *Navigation Menu* screen, select **Create a new navigation menu entry** for *Navigation Preference*. Enter **Faceted Search** for *New Navigation Menu Entry*. Select **Reports** for *Parent Navigation Menu Entry*. These selections will create a new menu entry named Faceted Search in the existing hierarchy under the main Reports menu. Click **Next** to move on. This is a direct method of creating menu entry.

5. On *Report Source* screen, select **Local Database** for *Data Source* and **SQL Query** for *Source Type*. Enter the following SQL statement in the provided box and click the **Create** button to complete the page creation process.

```
select to_char(o.order_timestamp,'Month YYYY') month,
       o.order_total amount,
       c.cust_last_name||', '||c.cust_first_name customer,
       p.product_name product
from  demo_orders o, demo_order_items oi, demo_customers c, demo_product_info p
where o.order_id = oi.order_id and
      p.product_id = oi.product_id and
      o.customer_id = c.customer_id
order by o.order_id
```

The page will be created comprising a classic report region, to show search results, and a region (*Search*) of the new Faceted Search type, which is going to hold the facets. The faceted search region (*Search*) will be linked to the Classic Report region, and each Facet will be linked to one of the Classic Report result columns. The Search facet (P400_SEARCH) allows the end user to perform some text based search on the result list. Only one search facet is supported for a faceted search region. The report columns to use for searching are configured in *Database Column(s)* property in the *Source* section within the attributes of the search facet.

6. Click Search facet (P400_SEARCH). Scroll down to the *Source* section, and ensure that the Database Column(s) property has the following columns: **MONTH,AMOUNT,CUSTOMER,PRODUCT**. As just mentioned, these columns (defined in the SQL query) will be used for searching.

7. Let's create some facets on the page. Right-click the **Facets** node (under the *Search* region), and select **Create Facet** from the context menu. Set the following properties for the new facet.

| Property | Value |
| --- | --- |
| Name | P400_MONTH |
| Type | Checkbox Group |
| Label | Month |
| Type *(under List of Values)* | Distinct Values |
| Database Column *(under Source)* | MONTH |
| Data Type | VARCHAR2 |

Facets can display as different UI types. Currently APEX provides the following facet types: Checkbox Group, Input Field, Radio Group, Select List, Range, and Search. Checkboxes allow you to pick multiple values to filter report results, whereas radio groups or select lists allow picking only one value. The Range option displays an item with a built-in list of values selector. The facet supports single or multiple selection, and manual entry. For single selection support, displays multiple values as radio group options, enabling the end user to select a single value. For multiple selection support, displays multiple values as check boxes, enabling the end user to select multiple values. For manual entry support, text fields will render below the facet, allowing the end user to manually enter the range of values they wish to use for filtering the Filtered region. By setting the *Distinct Values* for LOV type, the list of values will be based on an automatically generated query that selects the distinct column values. The source for this facet is set to the MONTH column and its type is set to VARCHAR2. Save and run the page to see an output similar to the following figure. The Month facet (A) will be displayed. Click the checkbox representing April 2020 (B). The report on the right side will be filtered to display orders for this month. Click the X icon (C) or the Clear link (D) or the Reset button (E) to remove the filter.

**Figure 11-2**

8. Create three more facets for product, amount, and customer columns using the following tables.
   **Facet 1:**

| Property | Value |
| --- | --- |
| Name | P400_PRODUCT |
| Type | Checkbox Group |
| Label | Product |
| Type *(under List of Values)* | Distinct Values |
| Database Column *(under Source)* | PRODUCT |
| Data Type | VARCHAR2 |

**Facet 2:**

| Property | Value |
|---|---|
| Name | P400_AMOUNT |
| Type | Range |
| Label | Amount |
| Select Multiple | On |
| Manual Entry | On |
| Type *(under List of Values)* | Static Values |
| Static Values | *See the following figure* |
| Database Column *(under Source)* | AMOUNT |
| Data Type | NUMBER |

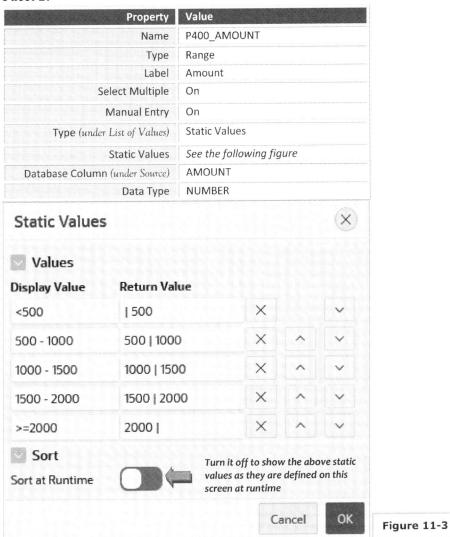

Figure 11-3

The Range Facet allows to filter the result list for values between a lower and upper boundary. A range facet consists of an LOV with predefined ranges to pick from, two text fields to manually enter the lower and upper boundary, or both. For the predefined ranges, the normal APEX LOV infrastructure is used: the LOV can thus be a static LOV, defined in Page Designer, or a dynamic one, using a SQL Query. In both cases, the LOV return value needs to use the pipe (|) character, to separate upper and lower values.

**Facet 3:**

| Property | Value |
|---|---|
| Name | P400_CUSTOMER |
| Type | Select List |
| Label | Customer |
| Type *(under List of Values)* | Distinct Values |
| Database Column *(under Source)* | CUSTOMER |
| Data Type | VARCHAR2 |

9. Save and run the page and play around with the four facets.

## Adding a Facet on a Column Containing Multiple Values

Faceted Search supports the ability to filter columns that store multiple values as one string separated by commas. The following example demonstrates how to create a Checkbox Group facet which filters a column containing features of three cars. You will have to create a new table based on the following data and a new page to explore this new Faceted Search feature.

| Brand | Features |
|-------|----------|
| Car 1 | Navigation, Satellite Radio, Keyless Ignition, Cruise Control, Sunroof |
| Car 2 | Bluetooth, Navigation, Satellite Radio, Keyless Ignition, Cruise Control, Sunroof |
| Car 3 | None |

The following are the facet attributes to filter the Features column in the above table:

| Property | Value |
|----------|-------|
| Name | Px_FEATURES *(here x represents the page number)* |
| Type | Checkbox Group |
| Label | Features |
| Type *(under List of Values)* | Distinct Values |
| Include Null Option | Turn on |
| Null Display Value | No Features *(to display Car3 record)* |
| Database Column *(under Source)* | FEATURES |
| Data Type | VARCHAR2 |
| Type *(under Multiple Values)* | Delimited List |
| Separator | ,   *Identifies the character which separates values from each other, such as a comma* |
| Filter Combination | OR (Union)   *Specifies how to combine individual values when filtering* |

When you run this kind of faceted search page, you will see a nicely spread out individual features list along with counts and no comma separated values. If you select the *Bluetooth* feature, you will see that the report gets filtered with Car2 record due to the OR (Union) *Filter Combination* property value. If you apply another filter (for example, *Navigation*), the report gets filtered with either Bluetooth or Navigation as part of comma separated values and you will see records of Car1 and Car2. What if you want the result to be an intersection of individual values? For example, if you would like to display the car with both *Bluetooth* and *Navigation* features, then change the *Filter Combination* property value to *AND (Intersect)*. This change would display Car2 only, because this car has both features.

## 11.2 Theme Roller – Style Your Application

Theme Roller (A) displays in the runtime Developer Toolbar, as shown in the following screenshot. Using the Theme Roller utility, you can change the appearance of an application. It is a live CSS editor that enables developers to quickly change the colors, add rounded corners to regions and specify other properties of their applications without touching a line of code. Theme Roller can also be used to modify an existing theme's CSS file.

Theme Roller has various options. Some most important options (B) are listed in the following figure. These options are tagged in Figure 11-5. To style a specific page component, expand its group, select the component, and apply the style. For example, to apply a new color to your application, expand Global Colors (C), click the color swatch next to Primary Accent (D) and select a new color (E).

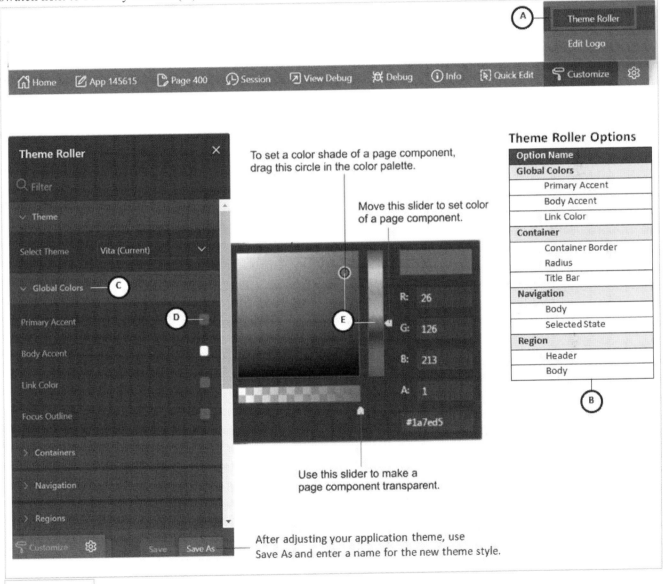

**Figure 11-4**

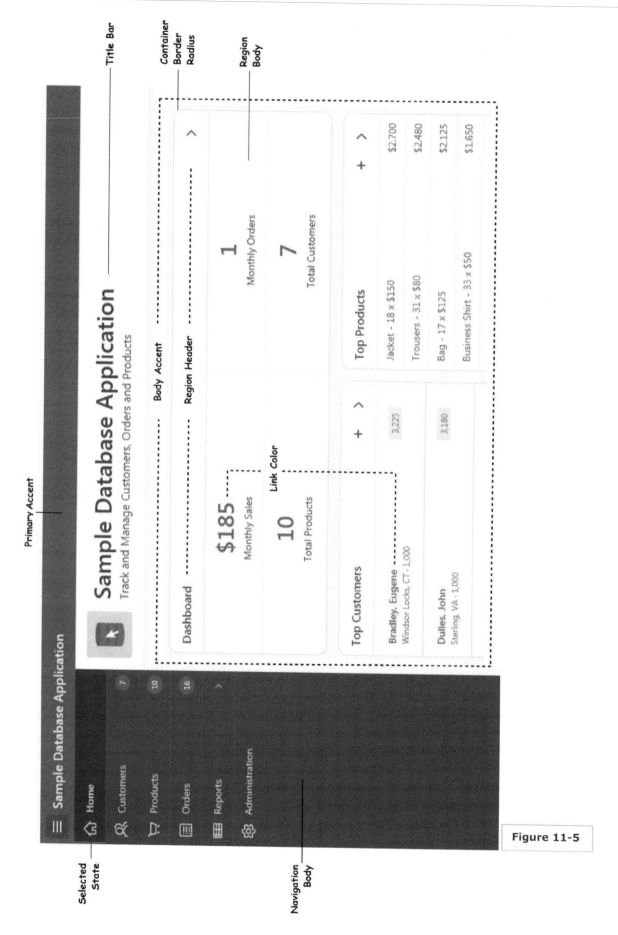

**Figure 11-5**

In the following set of steps I'll show you how to create a new style for your application using Theme Roller by changing header and body accent of a page. In addition, you'll also learn how to add border radius to form page items.

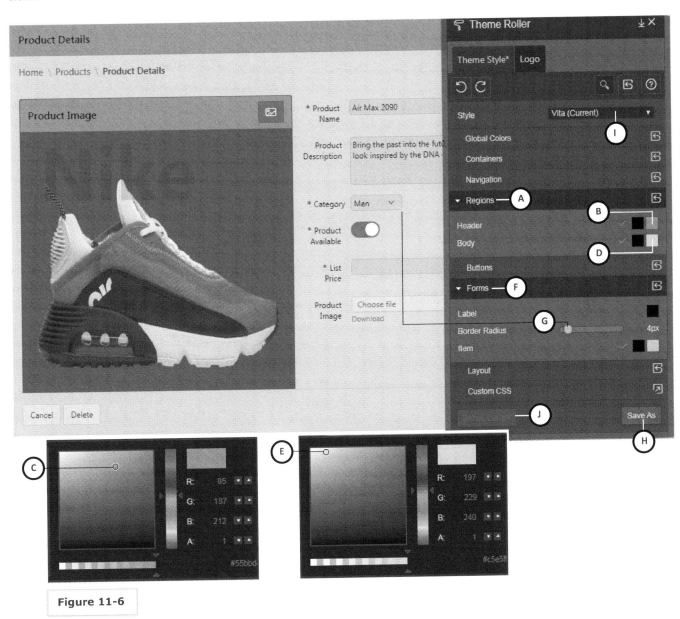

Figure 11-6

1.  Run the application, and select **Manage Products** from the *Setup* menu.

2.  On the *Products* page, click the name of a product to open its details page.

3.  In the *Developers Toolbar*, click **Customize** and then **Theme Roller**.

4.  In *Theme Roller*, expand **Regions** section (A), and click **Background** (B).

5.  Select a color from the color swatch (C). As you drag the small circle in the swatch, the change is immediately reflected on the application page.

6.  Next, click **Background** representing the *Body* component (D), and choose a light color (E) for the body.

7.  Click the **Forms** group (F), and drag the small circle (G) to the right side. This action will form a border radius around page items.

8.  Click the **Save As** button (H). In the *Save As* dialog, accept the default name or enter a name for the new style. Click **Save**. A message Theme style created successfully! will be displayed in a dialog box. Click **OK** to close this dialog. The name of this new style will appear in Theme Roller's Style list (I).

## 11.3 Styling Buttons

Button has been an important component of every application and is basically used to control the flow of applications. Buttons are created by right-clicking a region in which you want to place the button and selecting *Create Button* from the context menu. By placing buttons (such as Create, Delete, Cancel, Next, Previous, and more) on your web page, you can post or process the provided information or you can direct user to another page in the application or to another URL. You can also configure buttons to display conditionally or warn users of unsaved changes.

A button can:

o   Submit a page (for example to save changes)
o   Redirect to either a different page or a custom URL
o   Do nothing (for example if the button's behavior is defined in a Dynamic Action)

Universal Theme provides several options for adding buttons to your applications. This section introduces three button templates and the various template options you can avail to style your application buttons.

o   **Text Only**: This is Universal Theme's default button.
o   **Icon Only**: The icon only button is useful for easily recognized actions.
o   **Text With Icon**: This template enables you to display an icon next to your button label. You can easily position the icon to the right or left of the label using Template Options.

Figure 11-7

The following table contains samples of Text only buttons with relevant properties. Text only is the standard button in Universal Theme and its Button Template attribute is set to Text by default when you add a new button to your application page. To apply these samples, just set the attributes provided under Template Options.

| Text only Buttons | Attributes | Value |
|---|---|---|
| Small Button | Size | Small |
| Small Hot Button | Size | Small |
|  | Hot | On |
| Default Button | Size | Default |
| Default Hot Button | Size | Default |
|  | Hot | On |
| Large Button | Size | Large |
| Large Hot Button | Size | Large |
|  | Hot | On |

**Button with Stateful Colors:**

Stateful colors are used to convey additional meaning to a button. For example, you may choose to color a warning alert with a yellow tint. There are 6 stateful colors: normal, hot, primary, danger, warning, and success. You may customize these colors by modifying them in Buttons section within Theme Roller. In the following samples, I've used the Warning type. The other available options are Normal, Primary, Danger, and Success that render buttons in respective colors set within Theme Roller.

| | Attributes | Value |
|---|---|---|
| Default | Type | Warning |
|  | Style | Default |
| Simple | Type | Warning |
|  | Style | Simple |
| Link Button | Type | Warning |
|  | Style | Display as Link |

These symbolic buttons use **Icon** as Button Template. Other options available for the Type attribute are: Normal, Primary, Danger, and Success.

| Icon only Buttons | Attributes | Value |
|---|---|---|
| | Type | Warning |
| | Style | Default |
| | Icon | fa-warning |
| | Type | Warning |
| | Style | Simple |
| | Icon | fa-warning |
| | Type | Warning |
| | Style | Display as Link |
| | Icon | fa-warning |

This template enables you to display an icon next to your button label. You need to select **Text with Icon** for the Button Template.

| Text with Icon Buttons | Attributes | Value |
|---|---|---|
| | Label | Default Warning |
| | Type | Warning |
| | Style | Default |
| | Icon | fa-warning |
| | Label | Simple Warning |
| | Type | Warning |
| | Style | Simple |
| | Icon | fa-warning |
| | Label | Link Warning |
| | Type | Warning |
| | Style | Display as Link |
| | Icon | fa-warning |

Execute the following steps to get some hands-on exposure.

1.  Open Page 2 (Customers) in Page Designer.

2.  Click the **CREATE** button, and modify the following properties of this button.

| Property | Value |
|---|---|
| Button Template | Text with Icon |
| Hot | Off |
| Icon | fa-arrow-circle-o-right |
| **Template Options** | |
| Type | Success |
| Style | Default |
| Icon Position | Right |
| Icon Hover Animation | Push |

3.  Save and run the page. The CREATE button should now be rendered in green color. Hover the mouse pointer over the button to see the push effect.

4.  Switch back to the designer interface. Open the Template Options dialog box, and change the *Type* property of the button to **Danger**. Also set *Style* to **Display as Link**. Save and run the page. This time the button will be rendered as a link in red color. Set other values for the *Type* property and see respective effects.

## 11.4 Manage Events via Calendar

In chapter 8 section 8.6 you created a calendar report to display customer orders in a calendar region. Let's take a step forward to explore the actual usage of this component – handling events. Oracle APEX allows you to add calendars to your application with monthly, weekly, daily, and list views. You can create a calendar based on a table or SQL query. During the creation process, you are prompted to select date and display columns. Once you specify the table on which the calendar is based, you can create drill-down links to information stored in specific columns and enable drag and drop capability.

Using the Calendar component you can:

- Display calendar events on multiple views (Month, Week, Day, or List).
- Render duration (as shown in Figure 11-8) and non-duration based events.
- Render events from external sources using web service calls or Google Calendar feeds.
- Modify the start and end dates by dragging and dropping events on different dates. Drag and drop is only supported for local data sources, that is, database objects in the referenced database schema and not on external data sources such as a Google calendar.
- Edit or add new events on calendar using forms by clicking either on events or empty calendar cell.
- Use different CSS classes, developer can choose different styles for different types of events.
- Share events using multiple formats (iCal, CSV, XML).
- Enable tooltip to make it easier for users to have a quick look at details of each event.

To use the calendar, you need to prepare a SQL query with the following columns:

**Start Date** – the start date for events displayed on a calendar. It can include the starting time.

**End Date** – the column which holds the end date for events displayed on a calendar. If this attribute is specified, then the calendar displays duration based events.

**Display** – Holds the text displayed for events on a calendar.

**CSS Class** – the CSS class name to style the events displayed on a calendar. This column is optional.

**Primary Key** – primary key for the event. The column becomes necessary if you want to enable drag and drop feature.

**Supplemental Information** – additional information which is displayed in the List View and Tooltip. Use &COLUMN. syntax to show column values in HTML. Show Tooltip must be set to Yes in order for this supplemental information to be displayed in the Month, Week and Day views.

**Manage Events**

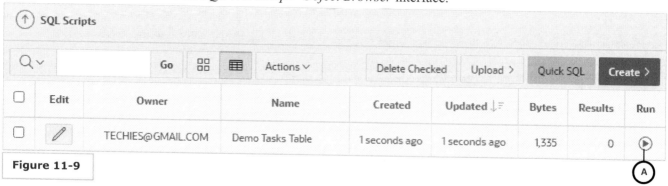

| | | | | March 2022 | | | | month | week | day | list |

*(Calendar header showing navigation controls ◀ ▶ today, March 2022 title, and view options: month week day list)*

**Figure 11-8**

Execute the following set of steps to explore some more features of the Calendar component.

1. From the *SQL Workshop* menu, select **SQL Scripts** and click the **Upload** button. In the *Upload Script* screen, click the **Choose File** button. In the *Open* dialog box, select **DEMO_TASKS.txt** file from Chapter 11 folder in the book's source code. For *Script Name*, enter **Demo Tasks Table** and click the **Upload** button. In the *SQL Scripts* interface click the **Run** button (A). On the *Run Script* screen, click the **Run Now** button. Six statements in the script will be successfully processed to create the table with 5 rows. You can view these tables from the *SQL Workshop > Object Browser* interface.

**↑ SQL Scripts**

| | Edit | Owner | Name | Created | Updated ↓⁼ | Bytes | Results | Run |
|---|---|---|---|---|---|---|---|---|
| ☐ | 🖉 | TECHIES@GMAIL.COM | Demo Tasks Table | 1 seconds ago | 1 seconds ago | 1,335 | 0 | ▶ |

*(Toolbar: Q▾ [search] Go  ⊞  Actions ▾  Delete Checked  Upload >  Quick SQL  Create >)*

**Figure 11-9**

(A)

2. Create a new page. Select **Calendar** option on the first wizard screen.

3. On *Page Attributes* screen, enter **401** for *Page Number*, **Manage Events** for *Page Name*, and click **Next**.

4. On the *Navigation Menu* screen, select **Create a new navigation menu entry** for *Navigation Preference*. Enter **Manage Events** for *New Navigation Menu Entry*. Select **Setup** for *Parent Navigation Menu Entry*. Click **Next** to move on.

5. On *Source* screen, select **Local Database** for *Data Source* and **SQL Query** for *Source Type*. Enter the following SQL statement in the provided box. Verify the SQL statement by clicking the **Validate** icon (A). If the statement is correct, you get *Validation successful* message (B). Click **Next** to proceed.

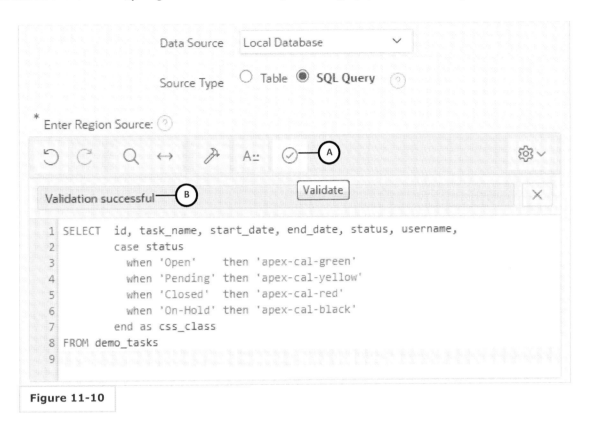

**Figure 11-10**

**SELECT  id, task_name, start_date, end_date, status, username,**
  **case status**
   **when 'Open' then 'apex-cal-green'**
   **when 'Pending' then 'apex-cal-yellow'**
   **when 'Closed'  then 'apex-cal-red'**
   **when 'On-Hold' then 'apex-cal-black'**
  **end as css_class**
 **FROM demo_tasks**

6. On the final *Settings* wizard screen, ensure that the **TASK_NAME** column is set as *Display Column*, **START_DATE** column as *Start Date Column*, and **END_DATE** as *End Date Column*. Selecting the END_DATE column will display the duration of events, as shown in Figure 11-8. If you want to also display the time portion of the date, then select **Yes** for *Show Time*. The Week and Day views will only be displayed when Show Time is set to Yes. If the start date or end date columns do not include time components, they will be shown as 12:00 am. Click the **Create** button.

7. After creating the page, click the **Attributes** tab (in the *Properties* pane) of the *Manage Events* region, and enter **Assigned to &USERNAME.** for *Supplemental Information* to display the name of the user the task is assigned to.

8. For *CSS Class* attribute, select the **CSS_CLASS** column (defined in the SQL query) to style the events using different colors, as shown in Figure 11-8.

9. Execute this step if you want to create a new task from within the calendar. The step assumes that you have already created a form where you create a new task. Click the **Attributes** tab of the *Calendar* region, and then click **No Link Defined** under *Create Link*. In the Link Builder dialog box, you have to provide the number of the target page to be called when the user clicks an empty cell, or outside of an existing calendar entry. Enter that number in both **Page** and **Clear Cache** attributes.

10. Execute this step if you want to access an existing task. Click the **No Link Defined** text for *View / Edit Link* attribute, and enter a target page to be called when the user clicks an existing entry. You also need to set task ID for the target page, as shown in the following screenshot.

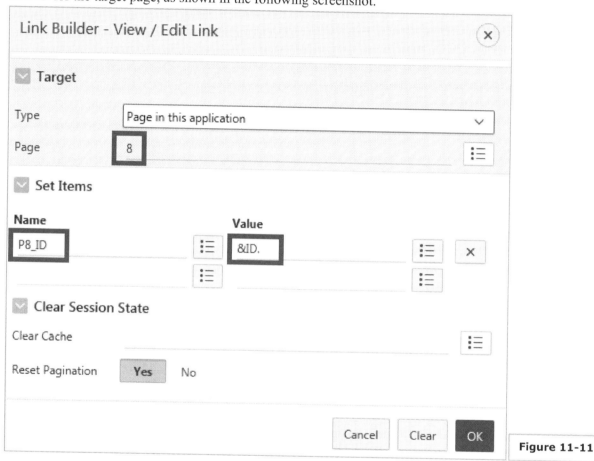

Figure 11-11

Let's test the last important segment of the calendar component - Drag and Drop.

11. Click the Calendar's **Attributes** tab and select **ID** for *Primary Key Colum*. This is the column which holds the primary key value for our calendar events. If the table has a multi-part primary key, then select ROWID. The value of this column is returned in the APEX$PK_VALUE substitution variable, which is utilized in the Drag and Drop Code attribute to identify the record to be updated.

12. When you select a primary key, a new attribute named *Drag and Drop* is added under *Calendar Views and Navigation* attribute. Turn **on** this attribute, and enter the following PL/SQL code for *Drag and Drop PL/SQL Code* attribute. The APEX$NEW_START_DATE substitution returns the revised start date, APEX$NEW_END_DATE returns the revised end date for duration based events, and APEX$PK_VALUE returns the value of the column specified in the Primary Key Column.

```
begin
  update demo_tasks
    set start_date = to_date(:APEX$NEW_START_DATE, 'YYYYMMDDHH24MISS'),
        end_date = to_date(:APEX$NEW_END_DATE, 'YYYYMMDDHH24MISS')
    where id = :APEX$PK_VALUE;
end;
```

Save and run the page, which should appear as shown in Figure 11-8. Drag and drop a task to some other date and observe the change in the DEMO_TASKS table via Object Browser.

## 11.5 Smart Filters

The Smart Filters is a new search component that provides end-users with numerous filters to narrow search results at run-time. Developers can use this component to provide users with a simplified search experience using custom filters that eliminates clutter and provides a single control to instantly find the information they are looking for. A smart filters page features a Search region which enables users to narrow down the search result and a report region such as classic report or cards report. Both the Create Application Wizard and Create Page Wizard support the creation of a smart filters page. Alternatively, you can add a smart filters region to an existing report in Page Designer.

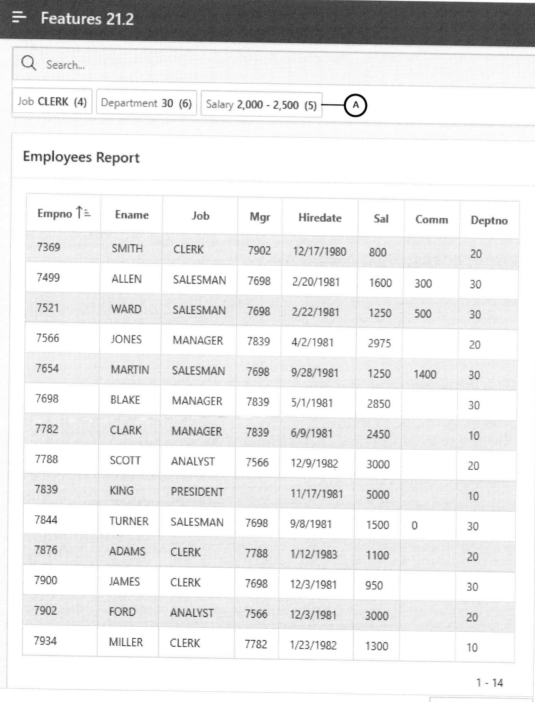

Figure 11-12a

In addition to the search bar, the Smart Filters region also contains Suggestion Chips (A) below the search bar. Filters are evaluated against your data and displayed below the search bar as chips, suggesting the top search filters most appropriate for your data set. Looking at these chips you can tell right away which is the top most data. For example, in the current scenario, the first chip labeled Job is displaying CLERK as the top most job, because this job has more number of records than others. Similarly, Department number 30 appears in the second chip as it has six employees that are more than any other department. The Salary chip reveals that five employees are earning between 2,000 and 2,500 which is the highest earning batch. If you click this number range, you will see the details of those five employees.

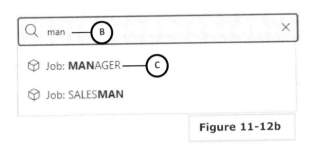

Smart Filters features a powerful new search bar that provides built-in auto-complete (B) for your filters. Search suggestions (C) are at the heart of Smart Filters. These suggestions are based on the filters you have defined and are displayed as you type.

**Figure 11-12b**

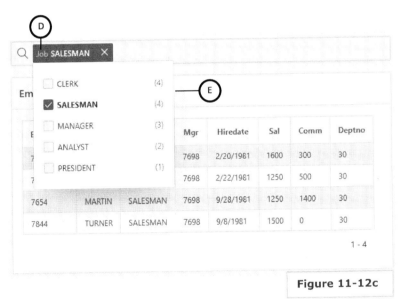

If you click on the chip label (D) you'll see a list of other values for that filter (E). You can make multiple selections in this list. When you make selections through this list, the data in the corresponding report is updated immediately.

**Figure 11-12c**

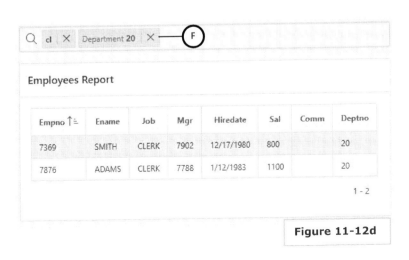

The Smart Filters feature also expands its search in multiple columns. What this means is that when you type something in the search bar, the Smart Filter searches for this value in all the columns. For example, if you type CL in the search box and hit enter, you will see records of CLERK job and an employee named CLARK. Now enter 20 in the search bar, and select the suggested filter – *Department: 20*. The report will be filtered further to display only relevant records. Clear all the filters using the cross icon (F) to reinstate the report to its actual state.

**Figure 11-12d**

As mentioned earlier, you can use both the Create Application Wizard and Create Page Wizard to create smart filters page. In this exercise, you will learn how to manually add a smart filters region to an existing application. Here are the steps:

1. Install the **EMP/DEPT** tables using the Sample Dataset.

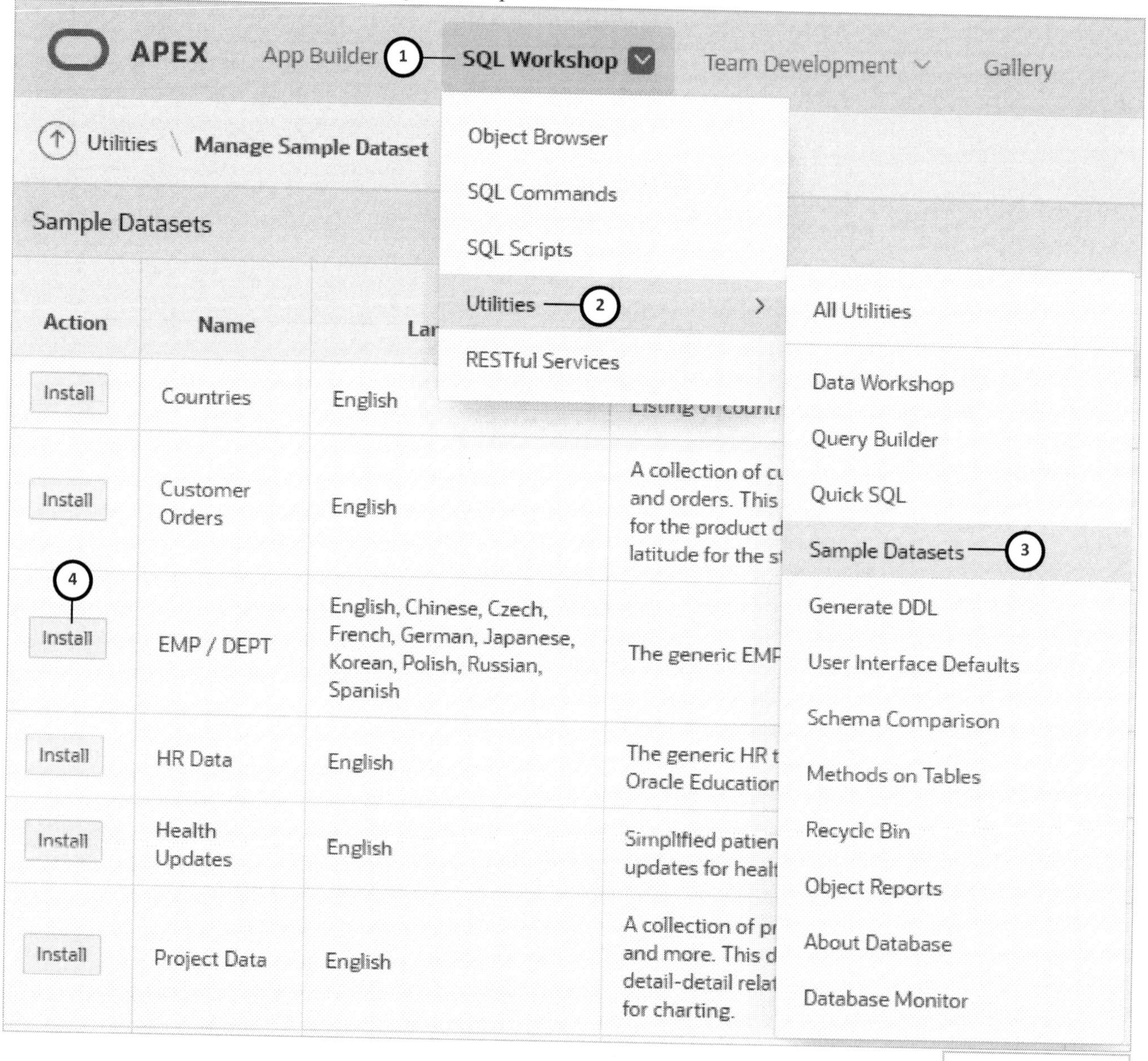

Figure 11-12e

2. Create a new **blank page**.

3. Add a simple **Classic report** region to the new page, set its *Title* to **Employees Report**, and populate it with records from the **EMP** table.

4. Add another region and place it above the classic report region. This region will hold the Smart Filters. Enter a *Title* for this region (for example, Smart Filters) and set its *Type* property to **Smart Filters**. Set *Filtered Region* attribute to the classic **Employees Report** region to associate the classic report region with the Smart Filters region.

5. Right-click the Filters node and select *Create Filter* from the context menu. Set the *Name* of this filter to **Px_JOB** where x represents the page number. Set *Type* property to **Checkbox Group**. The Checkbox Group type displays multiple values as check boxes, enabling the end user to select multiple values. A list of values is required for items displayed as check boxes.

6. For *List of Values Type*, select **Distinct Values**. By selecting this option the list of values will be based on an automatically generated query that will select the distinct values from the EMP table's JOB column.

7. Make sure that the **JOB** column is selected for *Database Column* property in the Source section to fetch values from this table column.

8. Create another filter for Department Number column using the following attributes:

| Property | Value |
| --- | --- |
| Name | Px_DEPTNO |
| Type | Checkbox Group |
| Label | Department |
| List of Values Type | Distinct Values |
| Database Column | DEPTNO |
| Data Type | Number |

9. Create the last filter for salaries as follows:

| Property | Value | |
| --- | --- | --- |
| Name | Px_SAL | |
| Type | Range | |
| Label | Salary | |
| Select Multiple | On | |
| List of Values Type | Static Values | |
| Static Values | **Display Value** | **Return Value** |
| | <900 | |900 |
| | 900 - 1#G#300 | 900|1300 |
| | 1#G#300 - 2#G#000 | 1300|2000 |
| | 2#G#000 - 2#G#500 | 2000|2500 |
| | 2#G#000 - 2#G#500 | 2500| |
| Database Column | SAL | |
| Data Type | Number | |

10. Save and run the page. Watch this video https://www.youtube.com/watch?v=wc8yhWYedx8 that is created for this tutorial.

## 11.6 Progressive Web Application (PWA)

Using the Progressive Web Application feature you can make your new and existing APEX applications fast, responsive and installable to your home screen. These applications will look and feel much closer to native applications and live on phone or tablet home screen or on a desktop menu bar. In PWA all apex resources and application static files are cached into user's devices allowing the apex engine to fetch files much faster. You create a Progressive Web App by running the Create Application Wizard and enabling the Install Progressive Web App feature (see Chapter 2) or, you can enable this feature in an existing application, as follows.

1. Go to **Shared Components** and click **User Interface Attributes** in the *User Interface* section.

2. Click the **Definitions** tab, and turn on the **Enable Progressive Web App** option (A). Also enable the **Installable** option (B) that appears when you turn on the first option.

3. Click the **Apply Changes** button (C).

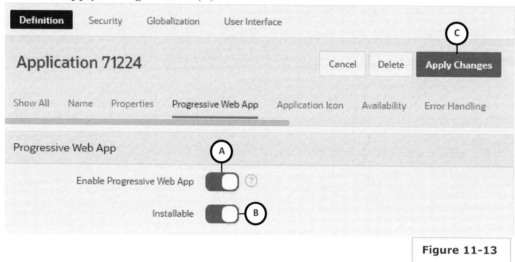

**Figure 11-13**

This interface also allows you to set the description of the application, screen orientation, application icon, or set the theme color for the PWA.

A Progressive Web App can be installed on devices. Once you enable this option, a new navigation bar entry labeled 'Install App' (D) is added to the selected application that allows users to install the APEX app on devices.

**Figure 11-14**

When you install the application using the *Install App* option, an icon (E) is added to the device home screen to feel like a native application. When you tap this icon on your home screen, you get access to a full screen experience without any browser's URL bar (F).

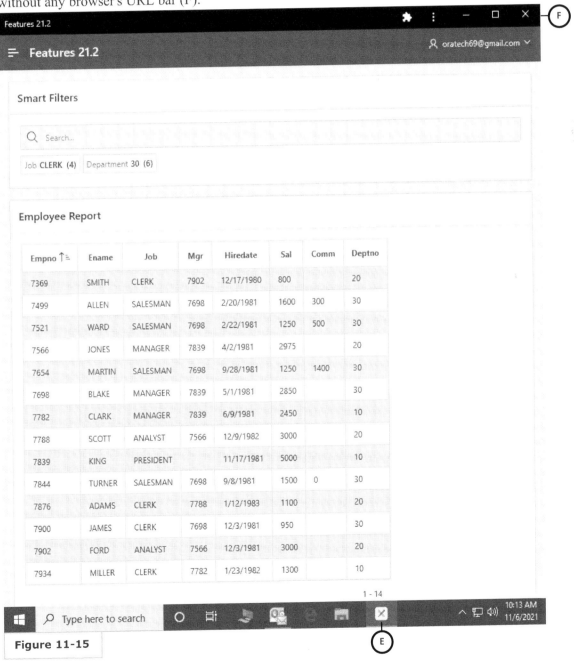

**Figure 11-15**

## 11.7 Integrating Maps in Your Applications

In this section you will learn how to integrate Maps in your Oracle APEX applications. Organizations today are realizing that the vast majority of their information assets have spatial components, for example, the location of customers, competitors, shipments, facilities, and so on. Most of the spatial data resides in their corporate databases and they need established solutions for providing spatial intelligence to databases. The new Map feature of Oracle APEX makes it easy to create and integrate maps in business applications to retrieve, analyze, and visualize spatial information.

Spatial data, also known as geospatial data, is a term used to describe any data related to or containing geographic information. A pair of latitude and longitude coordinates exists in this data, which defines a specific location on earth. Supported spatial geometry objects in Oracle APEX include Points, Lines, Polygons, Heat Map, and Extruded Polygons. In this section, you will learn how to create Points spatial geometry object. To learn about the other map objects, visit *https://www.youtube.com/c/TechMining69*.

The map in this exercise will be created using the Points object to visualize US population by cities. The pointers in the first layer in this map are marked in blue (A) and they display population of every city. The points marked in red (B) highlight those cities whose population is more than one million. The data for this map is fetched from a table named Population.

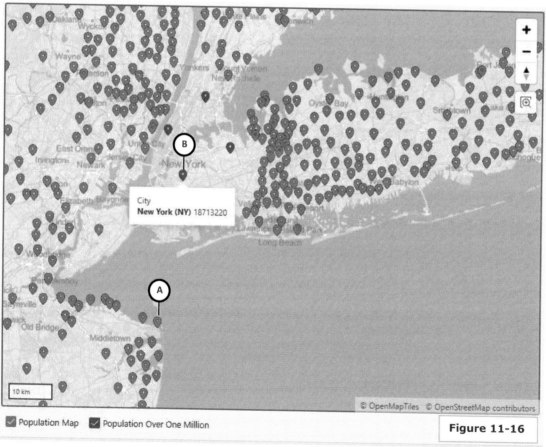

**Figure 11-16**

Now that we have seen how geographical data can be visualized using Oracle APEX Map, let's dive into the details and learn how to create it.

1. First of all you need to create the Population table using Population.csv file through the Data Workshop utility. See Chapter 2 on how to create table and load data. The csv file is available in Chapter 11 folder in the book code. The table contains population data by cities, states, and counties. Latitude (lat) and longitude (lng) columns in this table make up the grid system that helps us identify absolute, or exact, locations in the US map.

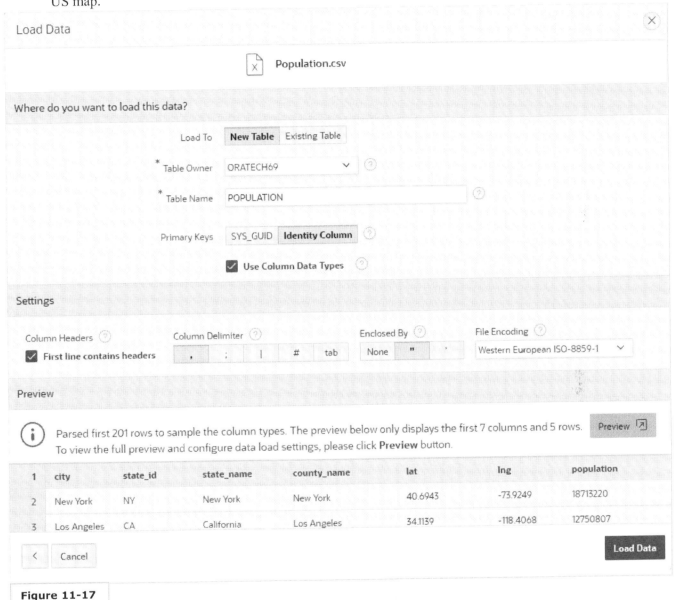

**Figure 11-17**

2. Create a map page to visualize data from the Population table. On the first Create Page wizard screen, select the **Map** option.

3. On the next screen, accept the page number and enter **Population Map** for the page name.

4. On the *Navigation Menu* screen, create a **new navigation menu entry**.

5.  On *Report Source* screen, select **Table** as *Source Type*, and select **POPULATION** for *Table/View Name*.

6.  Select options on the next screen as illustrated in the following figure. The *Points* option (A) is used to store the coordinate location of a customer site, a store location, a delivery address, and so on. Spatial objects (also known as geometries) to be displayed on the map can be sourced from a *Geometry Column* (B) or from *Two Numeric Columns* (C), containing longitude (D) and latitude (E) values. In this example, we are using the latter option because the Population table contains these two columns. We also picked the City column (F) whose value will be displayed as a tooltip when the mouse pointer is hovered over a spatial geometry on the map.

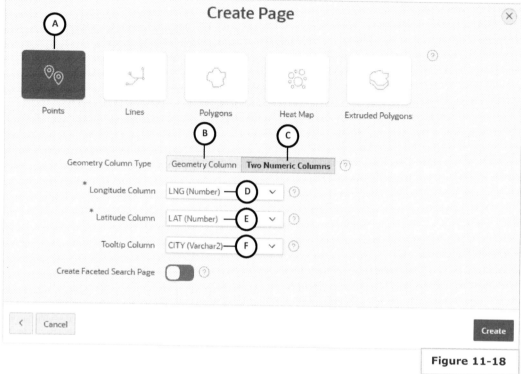

**Figure 11-18**

7.  After creating the page, click the *Population Map* under the *Layers* node in Page Designer and turn on **Advanced Formatting** option in the *Tooltip* section. Type the expression **City<br>&CITY. (&STATE_ID.) &POPULATION.** in the *HTML Expression* box to display city, state, and population information as tooltip.

8.  Save and run the page to see the effect of the HTML Expression. Now you can see the city name along with state id and population.

9. Right-click the *Layers* node and select **Create Layer** to create another layer. Set the following properties for the new layer. This layer will highlight the cities on the map whose population is more than one million.

| Property | Value |
| --- | --- |
| Name | Population Over One Million |
| Layer Type | Points |
| Table Name | POPULATION |
| Where Clause | Population > 1000000 |
| Geometry Column Data Type | Longitude/Latitude |
| Longitude Column | LNG |
| Latitude Column | LAT |
| Fill Color | Select Red color |
| Advanced Formatting | Turn on |
| HTML Expression | City<br>&CITY. (&STATE_ID.) &POPULATION. |

10. Save and run the page. The second layer you just created will display some cities, whose population is greater than one million, under the red markers as illustrated in the title figure provided at the top of this section.

## Display Map Item

With the Display Map item you can include a Map in your application that includes a pin dropped at the address of a location. It helps customers get directions. By adding a map in your application, it saves customers the steps of opening maps in another window and copying over the address. In this exercise you will add a Display Map item to show the location of Google Building 40 in a map, as illustrated in the following figure.

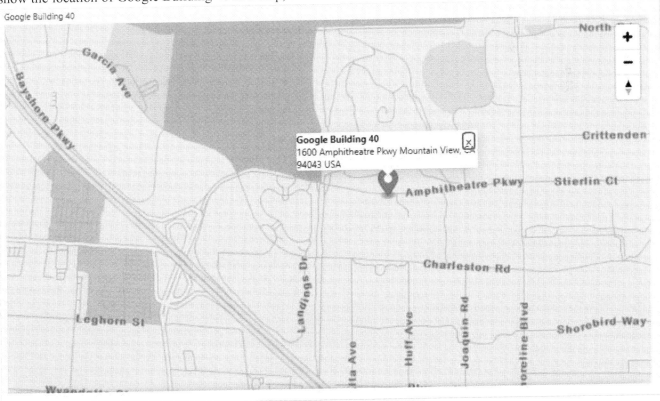

**Figure 11-19**

Here are the settings to integrate a map in your application using the Display Map item:

1.  Create a new page item and set the following properties:

| Property | Value |
| --- | --- |
| Name | Px_GOOGLEOFFICE |
| Type | Display Map |
| Label | Google Building 40 |
| Background | Oracle World Map |
| Tooltip | \Google Building 40\\<br><br>1600 Amphitheatre Pkwy<br>Mountain View, CA 94043<br>USA |
| Default Type | Static Value |
| Static Value | {"coordinates":[-122.083739,37.423021],"type" : "point"} |

Geocoding is the process of converting addresses (like "111 8th Avenue, New York, NY") into geographic coordinates (like longitude -122.083739 and latitude 37.423021), which you can use to place markers or position the map. Reverse geocoding is the process of converting geographic coordinates into a human-readable address. In this scenario we provided static coordinates in GeoJSON format to display the location.

## 11.8 Add Banners to Applications

You can also add a banner (A) just above the name and image of your application. In this section you will add a banner to the Global page so that it appears on every application page.

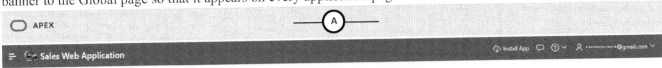

Execute the following steps to add the banner:

1. Open the **Global Page** of your application in Page Designer.

2. Right-click the *Components* node and select **Create Region** to create a new region.

3. Set the following attributes for the new region. The *banner.png* image (provided in the book source) acts as the application banner. The region is placed in the *Banner* position, as depicted in the above figure. By adding the banner content to the Global Page, it appears on every application page.

   | Property | Value |
   |---|---|
   | Title | Banner |
   | Type | Static Content |
   | HTML Code *(under Source)* | &lt;img src="#APP_FILES#banner.png"/&gt; |
   | Position | Banner |
   | Template | Blank with Attributes |

4. Save the Global page.

5. Next, go to *Shared Components* to upload the banner file. Click the **Static Application Files** link.

6. Click the **Create File** button.

7. Click **Drag and Drop Files** button and select **banner.png** file from the book source and click **Create**.

8. Run the application to see the banner.

## Summary

In this chapter you went through some miscellaneous but significant features of Oracle APEX to help improve your application development experience. You created a Faceted Search page that provides additional search capabilities and is useful to narrow down search results. You also learned the use of Theme Roller using which you can give a new look to your application. You were also guided on how to add styled buttons to your application. You saw another use of Calendar component that lets you manage events. In the final sections, you went through the new Smart Search, Progressive Web App, Maps, and Banner features provided in the latest version. Add all these features to make your applications more robust.

# 12

# DEPLOYING

# APEX APPLICATIONS

## 12.1 About Application Deployment

Oracle APEX application deployment consists of two steps. Export the desired components to a script file and import the script file into your production environment. Having completed the development phase, you definitely want to run your application in a production environment. For this, you have to decide where and how the application will run. The following section provides you some deployment options to choose from.

**No Deployment:** The development environment becomes the production environment and nothing is moved to another computer. In this option users are provided with just the URL to access the application.

**Application:** You will use this option if the target computer is already running a production Oracle database with all underlying objects. You only need to export the application and import it into the target database.

**Application and Table Structures:** In this deployment option you have to create two scripts, one for your application and another for the database table structures using the *Generate DDL* utility in *SQL Workshop*.

**Application and Database Objects with Data:** In this option you deploy your application along with all database objects and utilize oracle's data pump utility to export data from the development environment to the production environment.

**Individual Components:** With the development phase going on, you can supplement your deployment plan by exporting only selected components.

## 12.2 Export Application

For simplicity, we will deploy the application in the same workspace to understand the deployment concept. The same technique is applicable to the production environment. This section will demonstrate how to export an Oracle APEX application that you can import into a new or the same workspace.

1. Sign in to Oracle APEX and edit the **Sales Web Application**.

2. Click the **Export/Import** icon, as show in Figure 12-1.

3. On the ensuing page, click the **Export** icon.

4. In the *Choose Application* section, set *Application* to **Sales Web Application**, and click the **Export** button.

5. A file something like **f145615.sql** will be saved in the *Download* folder under *My Documents* or in another folder specified in your browser. Yours might be saved with a different name.

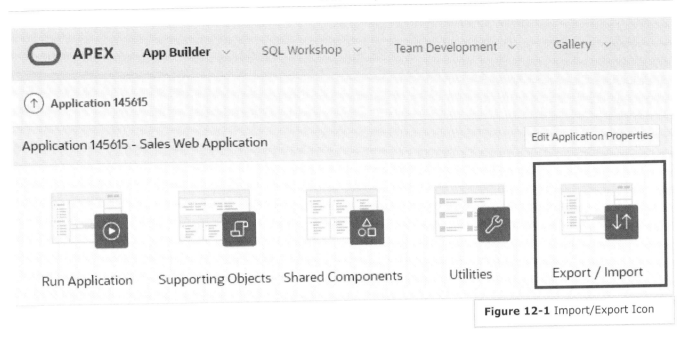

**Figure 12-1** Import/Export Icon

## 12.3 Export/Import Data

If you want to also export the data from your test environment into your production environment, then you have the option to utilize Oracle's export and import data pump utilities. Oracle Data Pump technology enables very high-speed movement of data and metadata from one database to another. It includes *expdp* and *impdp* utilities that enable the exporting and importing of data and metadata for a complete database or subsets of a database.

## 12.4 Import Application

In this exercise, you will import the exported application (f145615.sql) into the existing workspace you are connected to with a different ID.

1. Go to the App Builder interface and click the **Import** icon.

**Figure 12-2** Import/Export Icon

2. On the *Import* screen, click the **Choose File** button and select the exported file (f145615.sql). For *File Type*, select **Database Application, Page or Component Export** and click **Next**.

3. After a while a message *The export file has been imported successfully* will appear. The status bar at the bottom of your screen will show progress during the upload process. Click **Next** to move on.

4. On the *Install* screen, select the default value for *Parsing Schema*. Set *Build Status* to **Run and Build Application**, *Install As Application* to **Auto Assign New Application ID**, and click the **Install Application** button. After a short while, the application will be installed with a new ID for you to give it a test-run.

5. On the *Install* page, click the **Run Application** button. You will encounter an error saying "You are not authorized to view this application, either because you have not been granted access, or your account has been locked. Please contact the application administrator." Application users are not exported as part of your application. When you deploy your application you will need to manually manage your user to role assignments. Roles are exported as part of an application export and imported with application imports. Execute the following step to cope with this error.

6. On the *Install* page, click the **Edit Application** button. Go to **Shared Components**, and click **Application Access Control** in the *Security* section. Using the **Add User Role Assignment** button (A) add the three users as shown in the following figure.

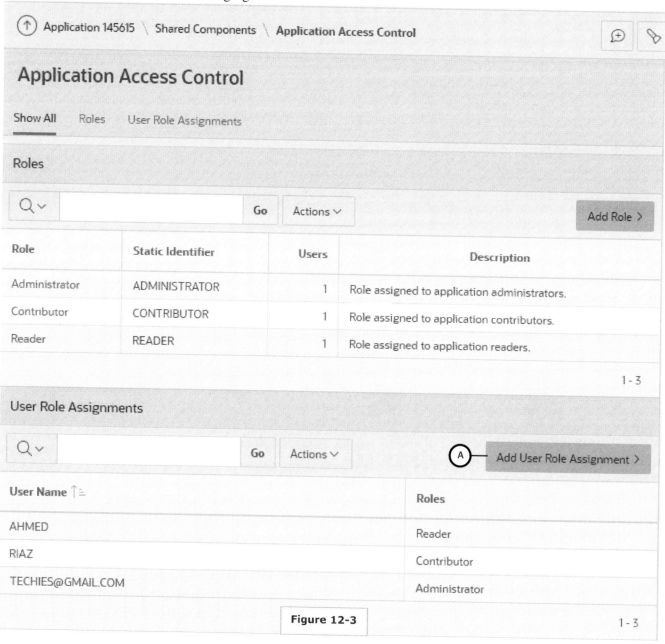

Figure 12-3

7. In Shared Components, click **Security Attributes**. Click the **Authorization** tab, and set *Authorization Scheme* to **No application authorization required** (A). Apply the change. Now you will be able to access the application.

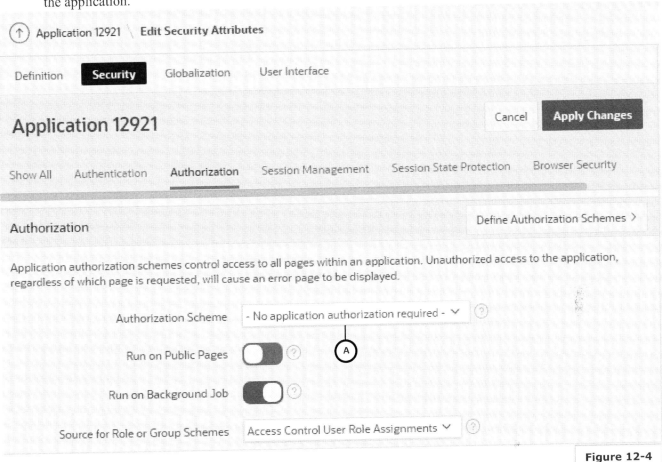

Figure 12-4

## 12.5 Prevent Application Modification and Remove Developers Toolbar

The Developers Toolbar is used to access the application source. In this exercise, we are going to prevent users from modifying the application by suppressing the toolbar.

1. Open the new application you just imported in the designer interface.

2. Click **Shared Components**.

3. Click the **Globalization Attributes** link (under *Globalization*).

4. Click the **Definition** tab.

5. Click the *Availability* tab, set *Build Status* to **Run Application Only**, and click **Apply Changes**.

6. Go to the App Builder interface and see that the new application doesn't have the Edit link. Click the **Run** button and provide your sign in credentials. Note that the Developer Toolbar has disappeared as well.

7. To make the application editable again, select **App Builder | Workspace Utilities | All Workspace Utilities** (A), as illustrated in the following figure. On the Workspace Utilities page, select **Build and App Status** (B) from the right sidebar. On *Build Status and Application Status* page, click the application ID in the first report column, change the *Build Status* to **Run and Build Application**, and apply the change.

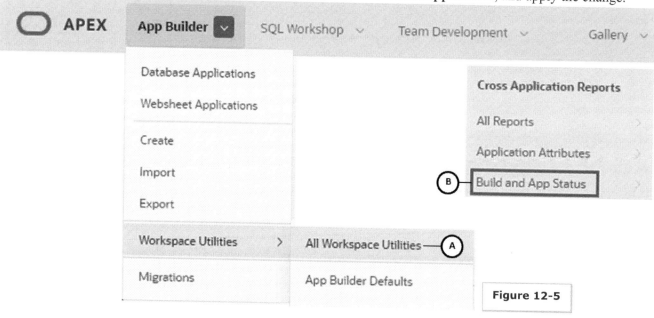

Figure 12-5

That's it. You have successfully deployed your application in the same workspace. You can apply the same procedure to deploy the application to another environment.

## 12.6 Data Packager

You can also easily migrate your applications from one instance to another and include data in tables using Data Packager in which you specify a table or a list of tables for which the data gets exported with an application. Here are the steps to use this utility:

1. Open your application and click the **Supporting Objects** option.

2. Click **Installation Scripts** link in the *Installation* section.

3. Click the **Create** button to create a new script.

4. Click the icon labeled **Create from Database Objects**.

> **NOTE**
>
> Since we have a BLOB column in the DEMO_PRODUCTS table, we cannot use this procedure to deploy this Sales Web Application, because as of this writing BLOB data type is not supported for export.

5. On the *Scripts Attributes* page, enter a name for the script - for example, **Tables.sql**. In *Object Type*, select **TABLE** and click **Next**.

6. Place a **check mark** in *Table Options* to include DDL statements related to tables. Move the tables you want for your application to the right pane, and click **Next**. The next screen will show the auto generated DDL statements that will create the selected tables. Click **Create** to complete this process.

7. If you have other objects like triggers or views, then you have to repeat steps 3 - 6 to create additional scripts for these objects. Suppose you have some views that you want to migrate with your application, then click the **Create** button again on the *Scripts* page.

8. Once again, click the icon labeled **Create from Database Objects**.

9. On the *Scripts Attributes* page, enter a name for the script – for example, **Views.sql**. In *Object Type*, select **VIEW** and click **Next**.

10. Move the required views to the right pane, click **Next** followed by clicking the **Create** button.

In the above steps we created scripts for supporting objects to package the application for installation in other environment. In order to move data as well with the application, you can use the Data Packager feature of Oracle APEX. Here are the steps to include your data:

11. Once again, click the **Create** button on the *Scripts* page.

12. On the *Create Script* page, click the **Data Package** option.

13. Enter a name for this script - for example, **Data.sql**. Move the required tables to the right pane and complete the wizard as usual.

Install data package script will be created and data package will be added to shared components. Now that you have the application as well as the underlying data packaged, you can export this application.

14. To export the application, open it and click the **Export/Import** icon.

15. Click **Export** on the next screen.

16. On the next screen, choose **Yes and Install on Import Automatically** for *Export Supporting Object Definitions*, and then click the **Export** button.

Now log into another workspace and import the exported application.

17. On the *App Builder* page, click **Import** and select the application that you just exported.

18. Navigate to *SQL Workshop | Object Browser* and review the application tables that are installed along with the underlying data.

## Conclusion

Oracle APEX has come a long way from its simple beginning. With the addition of new features in every release it provides so much possibilities and promises for today and for the days to come. I hope this book has provided you with a solid foundation of Oracle APEX and set a firm ground to develop robust application systems to fulfill the information requirements of your organization. The sky is the limit; you are limited by your imagination. Be creative, and put the power of Oracle APEX to your work. Good luck!

# Index

## Symbols

varchar2, 50, 211, 217, 223, 230
Video, 50, 147, 162
View Report, 181, 182, 186, 188
View/Edit Link, 275
Vita (theme style), 41

W

Web applications, 2, 3, 5, 18, 27, 28, 64, 202, 294
Web browser, 2, 18, 30, 215
Web input form, 7
Web Source, 89
When Button Pressed, 126, 160, 172, 205, 230, 231, 322
Wizard Body, 190, 198, 199, 233, 249
Wizard Buttons, 190

Wizard Modal Dialog, 190, 198, 208, 232, 244
Wizard Progress Bar, 198, 199
Workspace, 16, 20, 22, 23, 28, 43, 62, 69, 83, 86, 366, 367, 370
    request a free workspace, 22-23
Workspace (monitor activities), 326
Workspace administrators, 326
Workspace Files, 69
Workspace Utilities, 28

X

XML, 15, 223, 281, 306, 308, 309, 320, 321
XSL-FO Report, 69, 306
XSS (Cross Site Scripting), 81, 215

Made in the USA
Columbia, SC
26 March 2022

58195840R00213